A SHORT HISTORY

OF

REFORMATION

EUROPE

Dances over Fire and Water

Jonathan W. Zophy
University of Houston Clear Lake

PRENTICE HALL, UPPER SADDLE RIVER, NEW JERSEY 07458

Library of Congress Cataloging-in-Publication Data
Zophy, Jonathan W. (date)
 A short history of Reformation Europe : dances over fire and water
 / by Jonathan W. Zophy.
  p.   cm.
 Includes bibliographical references and index.
 ISBN 0–13–181561–X
  1. Europe—History—1492–1648. 2. Reformation—Europe.
 I. Title.
 D231.Z65 1997
 940.2'3—dc20   96–14363
                                                     CIP

This book was set in Palatino and Zapf Chancery by The Composing Room of Michigan, Inc.
It was printed and bound by Hamilton Printing Company.
The cover was printed by Phoenix Color Corp.

Acquisitions editor: Sally Constable
Editorial production/supervision: F. Hubert
Manufacturing buyer: Lynn Pearlman
Cover art: Albrecht Dürer, *Market Peasants*, Marburg /Art Resource

© 1997 by Prentice-Hall, Inc.
A Pearson Education Company
Upper Saddle River, NJ 07458

Printed in the United States of America
10 9 8 7 6 5 4 3 2

ISBN 0-13-181561-X

Prentice-Hall International (UK) Limited, London
Prentice-Hall of Australia Pty. Limited, Sydney
Prentice-Hall Canada Inc., Toronto
Prentice-Hall Hispanoamericana, S.A., Mexico
Prentice-Hall of India Private Limited, New Delhi
Prentice-Hall of Japan, Inc., Tokyo
Pearson Education Asia Pte. Ltd., Singapore
Editoria Prentice-Hall do Brasil, Ltda., Rio De Janeiro

CONTENTS

Preface   xi
Acknowledgments   xii

1   *Introduction*   1
Dances over Fire and Water?   2
General Chronology   3
Further Reading   4
Notes   6

2   *The Peoples of Europe*   7
The Peasantry   7
  A Culture of Poverty: Village Life   7
  The Continuities of Life for Men, Women,
  and Children   10
Town Dwellers   11
  Daily Life   12
  Urban Women   13
  Social Tensions   14
  The Rise of the Capitalists   14
  Jacob Fugger the Rich (1459–1525)   15
  Muslims   16
  Slaves from Africa and the Levant   18
  Jews   18
The Nobility   19
  Mercenary and Robber Nobles   19
  The Refinement of Manners   20
The Clergy   21
Further Reading   23
Notes   25

3   The States of Europe on the Eve of the Reformation   26

France under François I (r. 1515–1547)   26
England under Henry VIII (r. 1509–1547)   27
Spain   29
The Holy Roman Empire   30
The Netherlands   32
Scandinavia   32
Eastern Europe   33
Russia   33
Italy   34
Chronology   37
Further Reading   38
Notes   39

4   The Call for Reform   40

Late Medieval Critics of the Church   40
    The Western Schism (1378–1417)   41
    Marsilius of Padua (c. 1280–1342)   42
    John Wycliffe (c. 1320–1384)   43
    Jan Hus (c. 1372–1415)   45
The Failure of Reform Councils   47
Savonarola (1452–1498) versus Pope Alexander VI
(r. 1492–1503)   48
The Importance of Printing   51
The Challenge of the Humanists   52
    Lorenzo Valla (c. 1407–1457)   52
    Johann Geiler von Kaysersberg (1445–1510)   53
    A Reform Bishop: Guillaume Briçonnet
    (1470–1534)   53
    Desiderius Erasmus (c. 1467–1536)   54
    The Reuchlin Affair   56
Chronology   57
Further Reading   58
Notes   59

5   Martin Luther's Revolt   61

The Man with Seven Heads   61
    Martin Luther's Background   61
    The Indulgence Controversy   63
    The Rebel   65
    Choosing a New Caesar   66

Luther's Rebellion Intensifies   67
    Luther versus Charles V: The 1521 Diet
    of Worms   70
    Anticlericalism   72
    Luther at the Wartburg Castle, May 1521
    to March 1522   73
The Knights' Revolt of 1522 to 1524   74
    Franz von Sickingen (1481–1523)   74
Chronology   75
Further Reading   76
Notes   76

6

The Spread of Lutheranism   78

A New Pope and New Hope, 1522–1524   78
    The Diets of Nuremberg, 1522–1524   78
    The Spread of Lutheranism: The Case
    of Nuremberg   79
The German Peasants' War, 1524–1526   80
    The Outbreak of the Revolt, May 1524   81
    Thomas Müntzer (c. 1490–1525)   82
    The End of the 1524–1526 Peasants' War   83
    Martin Luther and the Peasants' War   84
Katherine von Bora (1499–1550)   84
The Emergence of Evangelical Politics   86
    The Diets of Speyer, 1526 and 1529   86
The Augsburg Confession of 1530   88
    Philip Melanchthon (1497–1560)   88
    The Formation of the Schmalkaldic League   89
Luther's Declining Years   90
    The Bigamy of Philip of Hesse   90
    Luther and the Jews   91
Lutheranism in Scandinavia   92
Chronology   93
Further Reading   94
Notes   95

7

Zwingli, Swiss Reform, and Anabaptism   97

Huldrych Zwingli (1484–1531)   97
    Early Years   97
    Not a Frivolous Musician: Zwingli in Zurich   98
    The Adoption of the Reform by Zurich   99
    The Marburg Colloquy   100
    Zwingli's Last Years   100

Heinrich Bullinger (1504–1575)   101
Big Names in the Reform of Basel   102
The Rise of Anabaptism   103
    Conrad Grebel (1498–1526)   103
    Michael Sattler (c. 1490–1527) and the Schleitheim
    Statement   104
    Balthasar Hubmaier (c. 1480–1528)   105
Charisma and Fanaticism at Münster   105
The Fall of "King" Jan   106
Menno Simons (1496–1561)   107
The Hutterites and the Community of Goods   108
Chronology   108
Further Reading   109
Notes   110

8   John Calvin and Calvinism   **111**
    Calvin's Early Years   111
    The Flight from Paris   112
Calvin's Theology   112
    The Call to Geneva   113
The Reform in Strasbourg   114
    Martin Bucer (1491–1551)   114
    Katherine Zell (c. 1497–1562)   115
Calvin's Return to Geneva   115
    The Michael Servetus Case   116
    The Threat of the Libertines   116
    Discipline in Calvin's Geneva   117
    Calvin and Women   118
    Calvin the Man   118
Theodore de Beza (1516–1605) and the Genevan
Academy   119
The Spread of Calvinism   120
    A Failed Calvinist Reformation
    in Brandenburg   120
    Calvinism Triumphant   123
Chronology   123
Further Reading   124
Notes   125

9   The Reformation in England to 1558   **126**
King Harry's Trouble with Women   126
    Cardinal Thomas Wolsey (1471–1530)   127

"Breaking Up Is Hard To Do": The Problem
of the Divorce   128
Replacements for Wolsey   128
Thomas Cromwell (1485–1540)   129
Exploiting Anticlericalism   130
The Legal Reformation   130
Unlucky in Love: Henry's Matrimonial
Difficulties   131
The Reformation under Edward VI (1537–1553)   133
The Tyndale Bible   134
The Fall of Edward Seymour   134
The Rise and Fall of John Dudley (c. 1502–1553)
and Lady Jane Grey (1537–1554)   134
The Reign of Mary I, Tudor, 1553–1558   135
Chronology   137
Further Reading   138
Notes   139

10   *A Tale of Two Queens: Elizabeth I of England
and Mary of Scotland*

140

The Young Queen Elizabeth   140
The Elizabethan Religious Settlement   141
Glorianna: The Successful Queen   142
Mary Stuart and the Reformation in Scotland   144
The Spread of Protestant Ideas   144
The Rise of John Knox, the "Thundering
Scot"   145
Mary, Queen of Scots   145
Mary's Life and Death in England
(1568–1587)   147
Chronology   148
Further Reading   149
Notes   150

11   *The Catholic Reformation*

151

Reform in Spain   151
Efforts at Reform in Italy   152
New Reform Orders: Capuchins, Theatines,
and Ursulines   153
Ignatius of Loyola (1491–1556) and the Society
of Jesus   154
The Founding of the Society of Jesus   155

The Organization of the Jesuits   156
The Jesuit Legacy   157
Teresa of Avila (1515–1582)   157
Pope Paul III and Reform   157
An Irenic Reformer: Gasparo Contarini
(1483–1542)   159
The Council of Trent, 1545–1563   160
The Conclusion of the Council of Trent
and Its Impact   161
Chronology   163
Further Reading   164
Notes   165

12 An Age of Religious Warfare, 1546–1660

The Empire Strikes Back: The Schmalkaldic War,
1546–1548   166
The Defection of Nuremberg and Brandenburg-
Ansbach   167
A Truce with the Ottomans   167
Imperial Initiatives   168
The Battle of Mühlberg, 1547   168
The Augsburg and Leipzig Interims   169
Splits in Lutheranism   169
The Religious Peace of Augsburg of 1555   170
The Religious Wars in France   171
The Reign of Henri II (r. 1547–1559)   171
The Power of Catherine de' Medici
(1519–1589)   172
The Saint Bartholomew's Day Massacre   172
The Reign of Henri III (r. 1574–1589)   173
Political Theorists   175
The War of the Three Henries, 1587–1589   175
Henri of Navarre as King of France,
1589–1610   176
Philip II's Crusades   177
The Character of the King   178
War against Islam   178
The Revolt of the Low Countries   179
The Spanish Armada of 1588   181
The Thirty Years' War, 1618–1648   183
Danish Intervention, 1623–1630   184
Swedish Intervention, 1630–1635   185
The Franco-Swedish Phase, 1635–1648,
and Aftermath   186

Chronology   187
Further Reading   188
Notes   190

13   *The Legacy*   191
Religious Life   191
    Theological Divisions and Social Discipline   191
    Marriage in Protestant Europe   193
    Margaret Fell (1614–1702) and Women
    as Preachers   194
    Roman Catholicism Revived   195
Witchcraft and Its Suppression   195
    Critics of the Witch Craze   197
The Rise of Western Science   197
    Astrology, Alchemy, and Magic   197
    Nicholas Copernicus (1473–1543)   198
    Brahe and Kepler   199
    Galileo Galilei (1564–1642)   200
    Medicine and Andreas Vesalius (1514–1564)   202
    The Scientific Method and Francis Bacon
    (1561–1626)   204
    Women Scientists   206
    René Descartes (1595–1650)   206
Political Changes   207
    The Constitutional Struggle in England,
    1642–1688   207
    The Rise of Absolutism   209
    French Style Absolutism   209
Chronology   210
Further Reading   211
Notes   214

Index   215

PREFACE

This book originated from the concerns of my students that my course in Reformation Europe needed a different textbook. They argued that the various texts I have been using over the past three decades are too detailed, too boring, and do not pay sufficient attention to the roles of women. Although I do not agree with them about some Reformation texts being either too lengthy or insufficiently stimulating, student suggestions did remind me how much of a gap there is between those of us who have studied a period intensely for a number of years and those who are learning about it in some cases almost for the first time. This text, like its predecessor on Renaissance Europe, is an effort to provide a bridge between the often different worlds of the professor and the student.

I seek to make the Reformation period more accessible to students, many of whom have not had much prior exposure to the subject. Deliberately adopting a conversational tone in my prose, I have attempted to write what might be called a student-friendly text by, for example, avoiding technical and foreign language terms as much as possible and attempting to introduce historical figures and concepts as they appear in the narrative. Since this is a brief history, it is more representative than comprehensive. This means, for example, that some ideas

and individuals are not discussed in great detail. This is somewhat compensated for by the greater coverage given to women as a group and some important individuals such as Katherine Zell or Teresa of Avila, who are not always found in traditional Reformation textbooks.

This textbook is organized around topics such as "The Call for Reform" (Chapter 4) or "Religious Warfare" (Chapter 12). However, topics are presented roughly in a chronological order throughout the book. Hence, the outbreak of Martin Luther's revolt appears in Chapter 5 of the book and the rise of science is discussed in the last chapter. Subtopics are presented in chronological order in each chapter. All but the second chapter on "The Peoples of Europe" feature a *Chronology* of important persons and events. My students have found these chronologies to be a helpful review aid in preparing for examinations. Even though I do not test them on their recall of specific dates, I want them to attain a relative sense of sequence—to know, for example, that Jan Hus lived before John Calvin or that Thomas More preceded Margaret Fell. It seems to me that to tell a good story it is usually a sensible notion to begin at the beginning and proceed to the end, even if life itself is a seamless web.

Each chapter also ends with a list of

suggestions for *Further Reading*. These are meant to recommend some of the best and most recent English-language scholarship on various topics covered in each chapter and in some cases throughout the book. Usually, I have selected books and collections of translated sources that I think serious students will enjoy reading, although I do not include novels or nonfiction works written by nonprofessional historians. In the interest of brevity, the lists have been kept relatively short, with only limited annotation. They are not at all comprehensive bibliographies. I do refer readers to some of the bibliographical literature such as William Maltby's *Reformation Europe: A Guide to Research*, John O'Malley's *Catholicism in Early Modern History: A Guide to Research*, Merry Wiesner's *Women in the Sixteenth Century: A Bibliography* or my own *Annotated Bibliography of the Holy Roman Empire*. Obviously, the scholarly monographs included have a wealth of citations in their notes and bibliographies.

Although I try to give some attention to the intellectual developments of the era, my emphasis for the most part has been on people of all ages and both genders. My experience is that the ideas of the period can best be learned by small group discussions of documents and texts. This brief text is meant to be used in conjunction with collections of documents such as David Englander, et al.'s *Culture and Belief in Europe 1450–1600*, Hans Hillerbrand's *The Protestant Reformation*, Lewis Spitz, Jr.'s *The Protestant Reformation* and John Olin's *The Catholic Reformation: Savonarola to Ignatius Loyola*. This text should also be supplemented by more specialized monographs. It is meant solely as a brief introduction to some of the major personalities, issues, events, and ideas of the age of Reformation. It is not a compendium or a grand *summa*. My hope is to capture your attention and interest and

stimulate you to make additional explorations of this rich and complex period in human history.

Acknowledgments

Since this book has grown out of more than twenty-five years of teaching college and university courses on Renaissance-Reformation Europe, I want to begin by thanking my students and colleagues at eight different institutions for their advice and their enthusiasm. They are: Carthage College, Lane College, Michigan State University, the Ohio State University, University of Houston Clear Lake, University of Maryland European Division, University of West Florida, and University of Wisconsin-Parkside. I have learned more from them than they have from me and have taken their specific suggestions for this book seriously. I particularly want to thank the students of History 3332 (fall of 1994) at the University of Houston Clear Lake. They graciously consented to serve as guinea pigs in using a draft of this text. Their comments and criticisms have been invaluable.

I also dared to assign the draft text to my graduate seminar in the fall of 1994 for their oral and written criticisms. They had great fun critiquing the work of their genial professor, but in the process helped make this a much more usable text. I was particularly pleased that they succeeded in using their imaginations to criticize the book as a text not for their own interests but for undergraduates. I want to mention the following students in particular for going beyond my assignment and providing detailed suggestions for the improvement of the text. Those stalwarts include: Mary Demeny, Diane De Vusser, Lisa Edwards, Gloria Flores, Deborah Goldman, Sue Grooms, Haydn Hutson, Piper Madland, Sandra Petrovich,

Rita Starostenko, and Sasha Tarrant. One of them, Karen Raines-Pate, deserves special mention for she had helped me with the text for the past two years as my research assistant. Her work on this project has been exemplary and invaluable. She is already a student-sensitive teacher as is her successor, Haydn Hutson.

As with my previous books, I received a great deal of help and inspiration from a variety of colleagues, friends, and family members. Several colleagues at the University of Houston Clear Lake went over all or parts of the early drafts, including Vivian Atwater, Marjo Avé Lallemant, Roger Bilstein, and Gretchen Mieszkowski. Lawrence Buck (Widener University), John Patrick Donnelly, S. J. (Marquette University), and William Wright (University of Tennessee-Chattanooga), experienced teachers of courses on Renaissance-Reformation Europe, all went painstakingly over drafts of the manuscript and made incredibly useful corrections and suggestions for further improvement. Colleagues at various meetings of the Sixteenth Century Studies Conference and the Society for Reformation Research have also offered various forms of aid and encouragement. My late mentors Harold Grimm and John Harrison taught me a great deal about the importance of textbooks as teaching tools. Such is the cooperative spirit of Renaissance and Reformation scholars and teachers. Readers for Prentice Hall also wrote perceptive comments in evaluating an earlier version of the manuscript: James R. Banker, North Carolina State University, Carl Christensen, University of Colorado at Boulder, Merry Wiesner-Hanks, University of Wisconsin at Milwaukee. Other scholarly debts are hinted at in the narrative, in the suggestions for *Further Readings*, and in the *Notes*.

At Prentice Hall, I owe special thanks to former executive editor Steven Dalphin for his wise counsel and support for this project. Carmine Batsford first persuaded me to approach Steve Dalphin about doing this book. Sally Constable, Serena Hoffman, Frank Hubert, Justin Belinsky, and many others at Prentice Hall have done an excellent job in putting this text together. Both Annette Weir and Eric de Bruyn of Art Resource in New York deserve special mention for their good taste and help in securing illustrations. The various art galleries listed with the illustrations throughout the text are also thanked for their help, as is the library staff of the University of Houston Clear Lake.

Finally, I must again thank the members of the Howard and Zophy families for their continued support and encouragement. My colleague-spouse, Dr. Angela Howard Zophy, who teaches Women and U.S. History in superb fashion at the University of Houston Clear Lake, continues to provide me with great inspiration and character-building lessons. I have dedicated a previous book to her so this book is in honor of two other wonderful teacher-scholars, Lawrence Buck of the Widener University and William Gunderson at Carthage College. They are two of the best friends and role models that anyone could ever know.

Jonathan W. Zophy

1

INTRODUCTION

The term *Reformation* has become a somewhat controversial historical fiction which was originally created in the nineteenth century to describe the movement for religious and societal changes that followed from the friar Martin Luther's attack against indulgences in 1517 and lasted well into the seventeenth century. Fifteenth- and sixteenth-century people had also used the term along with such words as *renovatio* (renewal) and *restauratio* (restoration) to express their concern for "a reformation and renewal of Christian life" and "a reformation of the spiritual and temporal estates."[1] The period historians call the Reformation involved substantial changes in theology, liturgy, and church government. It also had important social implications for the role of the clergy, church discipline, education, and social welfare. The era also witnessed the further development of the territorial state, a movement toward a world economy, and the beginnings of the Western scientific revolution.

Obviously, the Reformation as a historical period overlaps with the cultural movement known as the Renaissance, which began in Italy in the fourteenth century and spread to much of the rest of Europe by the end of the seventeenth. Many of the same individuals were involved in both movements. The celebrated humanist Erasmus of Rotterdam is an important example of this. His work was crucial both for the maturation of Renaissance humanism and Reformation theology. Similarly Albrecht Dürer was a leading Renaissance artist and an early supporter of the reform efforts of Martin Luther. Queen Elizabeth I of England, a central personality in the politics of the Reformation, also played an important role as a patron of such Renaissance dramatists as William Shakespeare. Renaissance technological breakthroughs such as the printing press were crucial for the spread of Reformation ideas.

The Reformation went through many phases and had many different focuses in church and state. One of the major reform movements began inside the Roman Catholic church with the important work of Pope Paul III, Ignatius of Loyola, and Teresa of Avila. That movement has often been called a Counter Reformation, but since the concern for renewal in the Catholic church predates the revolts sparked by Luther in Saxony and Huldrych Zwingli in Switzerland, the more inclusive term *Catholic Reformation* seems more appropriate. Certainly the sixteenth century was a problematic period for Catholicism, but it was also a time of fervent piety and revival. A great deal of good came out of some of the miseries of the age of Reformation, though it came at a very high

1

cost, given the resistance of humans to change and to the acceptance of diversity in religious and political thought.

Dances over Fire and Water?

The modern historian-novelist Sydney Alexander used the image of a "dance over fire and water" to evoke the Italian Renaissance and its almost superhuman artistic achievements.[2] While the term may be more appropriate to describe the incredible works of Leonardo da Vinci, Michelangelo, or Artemisia Gentileschi, it may also serve as a way to stimulate our imaginative response to the Reformation as well. After all, most Reformation intellectuals still thought the world was made up of earth, air, fire, and water—elements which could possibly be magically transformed by alchemy, a leading "science" of the day. Although most people still survived by tilling the earth, some of the privileged few "danced" in the airy world of theological speculation. If the Renaissance had its "superhumans" in art, the Reformation had its spiritual giants in Luther, John Calvin, Ignatius of Loyola, Teresa of Avila, and others.

Our image of fire and water also conjures up some of the horrific aspects of the period. The burning of religious minorities and dissenters in elaborate public rituals, called *autos de fé* (acts of faith) by the Holy Office of the Inquisition, sums up much of the worst of the period's collaboration of church and state. So does the torture and torching of those victims caught up in the agony of the witchcraft trials by both Catholics and Protestants in many places in Europe from about 1580 to 1640. Many Catholic and Protestant authorities also agreed on the need to use water to drown so-called Anabaptists, those who dared to believe that baptism should be used only for adults. Differences in religious opinion helped contribute to the wars of religion. Furthermore, the new gunpowder weapons increased the "firepower" available to the age's military.

According to the ancient Greek philosopher Heraclitus of Ephesus (c. 500 B.C.), fire and water were substances of change. Change or transition is one of the great themes of both the Renaissance and Reformation. The Renaissance brought new styles of art, literature, and music into being. The Reformation saw the religious unity of Latin *Christendom* (literally "the body of Christ," what contemporaries often called Europe) permanently shattered. In 1500 almost everyone in Europe thought of themselves as a part of the Roman Catholic church, with the exception of some Jews, Muslims, and Eastern Orthodox Christians. Only Spain had a large community of Muslims (about one-quarter of a million in 1500). By 1700 religious pluralism had become a grudgingly accepted fact of life in many parts of Europe. The era also witnessed stunning political transformations, intellectual ferment, and economic adjustments. Even the diet of some Europeans had begun to change because of new agricultural techniques and new food sources, some of which came from the New World of the Americas.

While there is no question that Renaissance and Reformation Europe was in flux, it should also be remembered that for most people the material circumstances of their lives of work changed very little. With the exception of thousands of religious refugees and victims of warfare, for the vast majority life continued as an often monotonous struggle to wrest a living from the soil. While gradual improvements in European agriculture over centuries did occur, most of Europe's peasants lived lives much like their ancestors. The same holds true for those who worked in the towns. Most crafts were still done in traditional ways. Servants

Pieter Brueghel the Elder, *Peasant Dance*. Kunsthistorisches Museum, Vienna, Austria. Foto Marburg/Art Resource.

still did the same chores in much the same manner, even if the mechanical clock they polished was of recent invention.

Social relations evolved at a glacial pace. Social distinctions between and within class groups continued and in some ways grew during this period. Although some merchants grew increasingly wealthy as part of the fluctuating economies of expanding capitalism, only a few were able to purchase titles and change their social status. *Patriarchy* (the rule of males) continued to prevail in families and states and in some ways was strengthened during the Reformation. While a few women such as Catherine de' Medici in France, Mary Tudor in England, and Mary Stuart in Scotland ruled, most women continued to be barred from political power. Women continued to have subordinate roles in the church even if a few women preachers appeared in the seventeenth century with the Society of Friends (Quakers). So while the Reformation can be considered an age of dances in the air over fire and water, it was also a time of the continuities of the earth.

General Chronology

1454	Johann Gutenberg uses newly invented moveable type to print a forty-two-line per page Bible.	1484	Birth of Huldrych Zwingli.
		1492	Spanish conquest of Islamic Granada; expulsions of Jews from Spain; birth of Marguerite of Navarre.
1483	Birth of Martin Luther.		

1494	King Charles VIII of France invades Italy; Rabelais born.	1545–1563	Council of Trent.
1495	Leonardo da Vinci begins *The Last Supper*.	1558–1603	Reign of Elizabeth I in England.
1497	Birth of Philip Melanchthon.	1567	Revolt of the Netherlands begins; birth of Monteverdi.
1512	Michelangelo completes the Sistine Chapel ceiling.	1571	Battle of Lepanto.
1513	Machiavelli writes *The Prince*.	1572	Massacre of St. Bartholomew's Day; death of John Knox.
1515	Birth of Saint Teresa of Avila; Erasmus's edition of the Greek New Testament and Thomas More's *Utopia* published.	1576	Death of Titian.
		1580–1640	Peak period for witchcraft trials.
1517	Martin Luther's "Ninety-five Theses against Indulgences."	1587	Death of Mary, queen of Scots.
1519	Charles V of Habsburg elected Holy Roman emperor; Cortés begins the conquest of Mexico.	1588	Defeat of the Spanish Armada.
		1589	Death of Catherine de' Medici.
1524–1526	Peasants' revolts in Germany and Austria; beginnings of Anabaptism.	1598	King Henri IV issues the Edict of Nantes.
		1602	William Shakespeare's *Hamlet*.
1526	Ottomans under Süleyman the Magnificent conquer much of Hungary.	1605	Cervantes publishes *Don Quixote*.
		1614–1702	Life of Margaret Fell (Fox).
1530	The Lutheran Augsburg Confession.	1616	Artemisia Gentileschi admitted to the Florentine Academy of Design; deaths of Shakespeare and Cervantes; Galileo ordered to cease and desist his new astronomy.
1531	Death of Zwingli; Parliament recognizes Henry VIII as "Supreme Head of the Church in England."		
1536	First edition of John Calvin's *Institutes of the Christian Religion*.	1618–1648	Thirty Years' War in Germany.
		1642–1649	Civil War in England.
		1647–1717	Life of Sibylla Merian.
1540	Pope Paul III authorizes the Society of Jesus (Jesuits) led by Ignatius of Loyola.	1685	Revocation of the Edict of Nantes.
1543	Publication of Copernicus's *On the Revolution of Celestial Spheres* and Vesalius's *On the Fabric of the Human Body*.	1688	Bloodless revolution brings William and Mary to the thrones of England and Scotland and marks the triumph of Parliament.

Further Reading

THE REFORMATION:
REFERENCE WORKS

Thomas Brady, Jr., Heiko Oberman, and James Tracy, eds., *Handbook of European History*

1400–1600: Late Middle Ages, Renaissance and Reformation, 2 vols. (1994 and 1995). Extremely important for its challenging essays by leading international authorities and helpful bibliographies.

G. R. Elton, ed., *New Cambridge Modern History*, 2nd ed., vol. 2, *The Reformation* (1990). A major resource.

Hans Hillerbrand, ed., *The Oxford Encyclopedia of the Reformation*, 4 vols. (1996). An outstanding collection of hundreds of short essays by capable scholars from around the world. Best coverage of women's topics of any reference work on subject to date. Useful bibliographies.

William Maltby, ed., *Reformation Europe: A Guide to Research II* (1992). A fine collection of bibliographical essays by important scholars.

John O'Malley, S. J., *Catholicism in Early Modern History: A Guide to Research* (1988). Well-done bibliographical essays by a talented group of academics.

Steven Ozment, ed., *Reformation Europe: A Guide to Research I* (1982). The first of an important series of bibliographical essays.

GENERAL SURVEYS

John Bossy, *Christianity in the West 1400–1700* (1987).

Euan Cameron, *The European Reformation* (1991). A fresh synthesis.

Owen Chadwick, *Pelican History of the Church*, vol. 3, *The Reformation* (1990).

A. G. Dickens, *Reformation and Society in Sixteenth-Century Europe* (1966).

———— and John Tonkin, *The Reformation in Historical Thought* (1985). A very important historiographical survey.

J. H. Elliot, *Europe Divided, 1559–1598* (1968).

G. R. Elton, *Reformation Europe, 1517–1559* (1963).

Timothy George, *The Theology of the Reformers* (1988).

Harold Grimm, *The Reformation Era*, 2nd ed. (1971).

Hans Hillerbrand, ed., *The Reformation: A Narrative History by Contemporary Observers* (1964).

————, *The World of the Reformation* (1973).

De Lamar Jensen, *Reformation Europe: Age of Reform and Revolution*, 2nd ed. (1992). An outstanding, comprehensive textbook which was the first to include some useful material on women.

Peter Klassen, *Europe in the Reformation* (1979).

H. G. Koenigsberger, George Mosse, and G. Q. Bowler, *Europe in the Sixteenth Century*, 2nd ed. (1989).

Carter Lindberg, *The European Reformations* (1996).

Alister McGrath, *Reformation Thought: An Introduction* (1993). Very readable.

M. A. Noll, *Confessions and Catechisms of the Reformation* (1991).

Heiko Oberman, *Masters of the Reformation: The Emergence of a New Intellectual Climate* (1981). Challenging.

Marvin O'Connell, *The Counter Reformation, 1559–1610* (1974).

Steven Ozment, *The Age of Reform, 1250–1550* (1980). Stresses intellectual developments and is quite readable.

Jaroslav Pelikan, *The Christian Tradition*, vol. 4, *Reformation of Church and Dogma* (1984).

Eugene Rice with Anthony Grafton, *The Foundations of Early Modern Europe, 1460–1559*, 2nd ed. (1994).

R. W. Scribner, *The German Reformation* (1986).

Lewis Spitz, Jr., *The Protestant Reformation, 1517–1559* (1985).

————, ed., *The Reformation: Basic Interpretations* (1972).

COLLECTIONS OF ESSAYS

Phillip Bebb and Sherrin Marshall, eds., *The Process of Change in Early Modern Europe* (1988). Lively essays by diverse authors dedicated to Miriam Usher Chrisman.

Peter Newman Brooks, ed., *Reformation Principle and Practice* (1980). Essays by multiple authors dedicated to A. G. Dickens.

Lawrence Buck and Jonathan Zophy, eds., *The Social History of the Reformation* (1972). Contributions by several authors in honor of Harold J. Grimm.

Richard De Molen, ed., *Leaders of the Reformation* (1984). Profiles by diverse authors of a range of personalities from Luther to Loyola.

Andrew Fix and Susan Karant-Nunn, eds., *Germania Illustrata: Essays on Early Modern German History* (1992). By various authors and dedicated to Gerald Strauss.

Jerome Friedman, ed., *Regnum, Religio et Ratio* (1987). Essays in honor of Robert Kingdon by various scholars.

B. A. Gerrish, ed., *Reformers in Profile: Advocates of Reform 1300–1600* (1967). Still valuable essays by a variety of scholars on figures ranging from Wyclif to Loyola.

Hans Guggisberg, Gottfried Krodel, and Hans Füglister, eds., *The Reformation in Germany and Europe: Interpretations and Issues* (1993). Mostly for advanced scholars.

R. Po-chia Hsia, ed., *The German People and the Reformation* (1988). Important essays by a variety of contributors.

Sherrin Marshall, ed., *Women in Reformation and Counter-Reformation Europe: Private and Public Worlds* (1987). Significant essays by the editor and others.

Heiko Oberman, *The Reformation: Roots and Ramifications* (1994). A challenging collection of some of his essays.

Andrew Pettegree, ed., *The Early Reformation in Europe* (1992). Wide-ranging essays by various contributors.

Kyle Sessions and Phillip Bebb, eds., *Pietas et Societas: New Trends in Reformation Social History* (1985). Diverse essays by several scholars.

Notes

1. Cited in Gerald Strauss, "Ideas of *Reformatio* and *Renovatio* from the Middle Ages to the Reformation," in Thomas Brady, Jr., Heiko Oberman, and James Tracy, eds., *Handbook of European History 1400–1600: Late Middle Ages, Renaissance and Reformation*, 2 vols. (Leiden: E. J. Brill, 1994 and 1995), vol. 2, p. 1.

2. Sidney Alexander, *Lions and Foxes: Men and Ideas of the Italian Renaissance* (Athens, Oh.: Ohio University Press, 1974), p. 142.

2

THE PEOPLES
OF EUROPE

The Peasantry

The Europe of the Renaissance and Reformation was much like Europe of the present
in languages and weather, but that is about
all. In sharp contrast to today's highly populated, polluted, and urbanized world, the
world of the fourteenth through seventeenth centuries was thinly populated and
mostly rural and agricultural. If only 1 to 2
percent of a modern, industrialized country's workforce is necessary to feed the rest,
nearly the opposite was true in the Renaissance. Crop yields were still minimal by
modern standards despite the wider use of
horse collars and oxen yokes, iron-tipped
plows, and a greater reliance on the three-
field system than had been the case in the
early Middle Ages. The three-field system
allowed a farmer to plant one field with
wheat in the fall and barley or rye in another in the spring, while letting one field
lie fallow each year. Even though this system improved the yield over the two-field
system, agricultural production was less
than abundant. The result was that every
able-bodied person in a Reformation-era
farm family, including women and children, had to work the land intensively. The
disabled and sometimes older children
looked after the toddlers left to play at
home.

A CULTURE OF POVERTY: VILLAGE LIFE

Most Europeans in the sixteenth century
lived in small farming villages of 500 to 700
inhabitants. These villages were usually
connected with generally self-sufficient
agricultural estates called *manors*. Typical
villages would be filled with windowless,
thatch-roofed huts with dirt floors. Usually
peasant huts had only two rooms plus an at-
tic and a barn or a cowshed. Privacy in our
sense was unheard of. Furthermore, lice and
vermin abounded, ventilation was poor,
and the smoke of the central fire of the
hearthstone mingled with the smells of humans and animals.

In addition to the peasant huts and
sheds, a village might have a miller to grind
grain, a tavern, a blacksmith shop, perhaps
a general store, a parish church, and maybe
the manor house of the principal landowner
of the region. Some agricultural communities were attached to monasteries and some
were located near the walls of a town. Other
manorial estates were remote and isolated.
The level of prosperity varied from year to
year and place to place. A village like Sennely in France outside of Orléans was constantly on the edge of poverty because it had
poor soil, although it never faced an all-out
famine. Other villages were not so lucky.

The peasants of Europe usually wore

Limbourg, *Month of March, Ploughing the Field.* Manuscript illumination from the *Trés Riches Heures du Duc de Berry.* Musée Condé, Chantilly, France. Giraudon/Art Resource.

simple, homespun clothes of sturdy fibers. Their underwear was usually made of wool with wool or linen outerwear. Many wore wooden shoes equivalent to modern clogs. Some well-off farmers had leather boots, whereas others went barefoot at times. Peasants tended to age rapidly and they were often bent over from frequent stooping in the fields. Some had yellowish skin, and others were deeply tanned in the summer from long hours in the sun. Almost every adult had poor teeth and fetid breath. Frequent bouts of ill health were a common occurrence for adults.

Coarse, dark bread was the staple of peasant diets throughout Europe, whether from grains of barley, rye, millet, wheat or some combination of several grains. Corn or maize did not come into Europe until after Christopher Columbus's voyages to the so-

called "New World" in the 1490s. Potatoes from Peru followed corn by two generations, first appearing in Spain in 1573 and then arriving in Italy by 1601. Even with the introduction of corn and potatoes, grains, whether baked as bread or mixed with water, remained the core of the European peasant diet.

When grain crops failed, starving peasants substituted acorns, tree bark, grass seeds, and even earth mixed with wheat flour. Fruit was usually too expensive for peasant households and green vegetables were rare. Dried beans, peas, and fish provided much needed protein and vitamins. Meat in any form was rare. King Henri IV, in the late sixteenth century, expressed the hope that every French rural family would be able to have "a chicken in its cooking pot every Sunday." Had this wish been fully realized in the Renaissance, it would have represented a considerable advance in the nutritional life of the French peasantry.

Such a dramatic change in the living standards of the peasantry did not occur during the Reformation, and their meager diets were reflected in the high levels of disease and malnutrition present throughout Europe and in the fact that some girls in northern Europe did not menstruate until the age of eighteen. Peasant girls in most of the rest of Europe typically had menarche between ages twelve and fourteen. Women in the northern parts of Europe married at about age twenty-three, usually to older husbands. An estimated one-third of all babies died in their first year. Couples averaged three to four children, with only about 45 percent reaching adulthood. Life spans were about half of what they are now and few peasant households had living grandparents.

In some senses, however, things were slowly improving for Europe's peasantry during the period. Pockets of relative prosperity expanded, especially in France and the Low Countries. Most European peasants were no longer "bound to the soil" as serfs. Serfdom did linger on in parts of eastern Europe and in Russia until well into the nineteenth century, but many western European peasants owned some land. Better-off peasants might possess their own horses for plowing and even their own wooden plows. A prosperous peasant family in France often had an estate worth about 2,000 livres. Those farmers just below them on the social scale who did not own horses and plows might be worth about 600 livres. They often rented most of their land and were in constant danger of falling into the status of hired hands. Hired hands often owned nothing other than a hut, a garden, and maybe a pig.

Considerable albeit slow progress was made between the sixteenth and eighteenth centuries in Europe by the introduction of the so-called "new husbandry." It involved a set of adjustments in agricultural practices that first made their appearances in the Low Countries in the late Middle Ages and then slowly spread to other parts of Europe. The basic elements of the new husbandry were all closely related: new crops, staff feeding of cattle, and the elimination of fallowing. The result was that farmers were able to maintain more and better-fed cattle, thereby increasing the supply of animal products. Healthier livestock produced more fertilizer, which helped to increase cereal yields. The new fodder crops, such as alfalfa, clover, and turnips, also turned out to be invaluable as alternating crops to cereals in better rotations.

Improvements also took place in the use of energy for farm work. Windmills were improved greatly in the course of the sixteenth century and their use spread like wildfire throughout Europe. The Dutch led the way not only in the improvement of the windmill, but in applying wind and water power to fulling (the pounding and stretching of cloth) and pumping. By applying the windmill to an Archimedean screw (invented by the clever Archimedes of Syracuse, c. 287–212 B.C.) or a series of buckets, they could not only keep seawater outside their protective dikes but even pump inland lakes. By 1500 the Netherlanders had already reclaimed or safeguarded over 285,000 acres of good farmland from the sea. Other parts of Europe followed their lead in draining swamps and marshes.

Regardless of their relative wealth or poverty, all peasants, including children, worked exceedingly hard for most of the year. Men worked the fields, gathered wood, and repaired equipment. Children assisted their parents in all farm activities as soon as they were able. Peasant women usually helped the men with the plowing, manure spreading, weeding, reaping, and threshing. Women were expected to do all the household chores as well as to gather kindling, haul well water, garden, tend animals, suckle infants, cook, sweep, and tend the fires. In addition to doing laundry for themselves and sometimes others, peasant women often sold cheese and butter, cared for children, and made the family's clothes. As a nineteenth-century Sicilian proverb put it, "If the father is dead, the family suffers. If the mother dies, the family cannot exist."[1]

THE CONTINUITIES OF LIFE
FOR MEN, WOMEN, AND CHILDREN

Other constants in the peasants' world besides hard work included death and taxes. Peasants who lived on manors had to pay fees to use the lord's grain mill or to breed livestock. They had to perform certain seasonal duties for the lord, such as road and fence repairs. A peasant son had to surrender his best animal to inherit his father's tenancy. Normally a family had to pay about a third of their harvests to landlords, priests, and tax collectors. When the harvest was bad, people starved to death and infants were abandoned in larger numbers than usual. Survival was not taken for granted by the peasantry in the culture of poverty that still existed for too many in Reformation Europe.

In parts of Europe such as the Mediterranean basin, northern England, Scotland, Ireland, and Scandinavia, agricultural production was not as tightly organized as in regions of richer soils, where the communal farming of the manors predominated. Regardless of regional differences, the lives of the rural working men, women, and children of Reformation Europe can be described as difficult and only slightly improved over

that of their medieval ancestors. That superstitions still persisted, such as belief in the magical powers of bull's blood, for example, is hardly surprising for people who sought help in a variety of ways.

Given the lives of drudgery that most peasants experienced, it is little wonder that church holidays, weddings, services, visits to market towns, and occasional fairs meant so much to them. These were among the few occasions when a peasant family did not have to labor from sunrise to sunset. Fairs allowed a peasant family to buy a few items, such as magical potions they could not make for themselves, and to dance, drink, and swap stories with friends. If peasant dancing was often frenetic, that is understandable, considering the hardships of their lives.

Even an occasional holiday, however, could not disguise the essential harshness of peasant life nor the contempt which they sometimes experienced from the more privileged estates. Crude jests about "dumb and illiterate" peasants abounded. To be a peasant was often to be looked down upon and taken for granted by those whom you fed and served. Sometimes the level of anger was so intense that peasants risked everything to rebel against their often absentee landlords. Major peasant revolts had broken out in Flanders between 1323 and 1328; in France in 1358; in 1381 in England; and in various places in Germany throughout the fifteenth century (called *Bundschuh* revolts for the clog-like shoes most peasants wore). Between 1524 to 1526 a major Peasants' War was fought in southern Germany and spread to Austria, as we shall discuss in more detail in Chapter 6. Since the peasantry was not generally trained in the use of arms and military leadership, all their revolts were brutally crushed by the authorities. These occasional, violent eruptions reflected the deep-seated desperation that often lay just below the surface calm of "those who work."

Town Dwellers

Although most Europeans lived in rural villages during the Reformation, the third estate of commoners also included those who lived in walled towns. As an old legal maxim confirmed: "Only a wall separates the burgher from the peasant." Even though the feudal nobility may have lumped town dwellers with the peasants, the wealthiest members of an early modern urban community considered themselves to be more closely allied with Europe's noble families. Indeed, sometimes leading citizens of a powerful and wealthy city might declare themselves to be noble, as did the wealthy merchant families of Venice in the fourteenth century. Other urban elites simply styled themselves patricians, thereby forging a link with the aristocrats of ancient Rome.

The so-called patricians of the towns of Europe seldom numbered more than 5 to 6 percent of a community's populace, although they often had more than their share of political power. Ranking below the patriciate were the smaller merchants, skilled artisans, shop owners, lawyers, and teachers. The size of the clerical populations varied, but even a town without a resident bishop, such as sixteenth-century Nuremberg, might have had as many as 10 percent of its population in the ranks of the clergy. Since the clerical estate made up roughly 2 to 4 percent of the European population as a whole, the figure for Nuremberg shows how the clergy would often cluster around the protective walls of towns. Towns that were seats of bishops would have large clerical populations, whereas remote rural parishes often had difficulty in keeping enough priests.

At least a third of a typical town's population were apprentices, journeymen, gardeners, servants, prostitutes, unskilled laborers, paupers, and peddlers. In times of economic difficulties, the ranks of a city's poor would swell. Nuremberg, for example, distributed free bread on a daily basis to 13,000 people in 1540 and 1541. Famine was always a possibility even inside a town with its grain storage warehouses, but usually cities seemed much more prosperous than the countryside. This can also be seen in the hordes of beggars who lined the roads leading to most urban centers. The upper echelon of urban society, in sharp contrast, ate the best the surrounding countryside could provide, including white bread made of the finest available grains, as well as fresh vegetables and meat on a regular basis.

Although Europe remained predominantly rural throughout the preindustrial age, towns had generally increased in size and wealth since the eleventh century. Even though urban populations may have fallen by as much as a third during the disasters associated with the widespread and lethal effects of the Black Death between 1347 and 1350, by the late fifteenth century trade and towns began to grow again. By 1500 modest increases had brought the European population up to 60 to 75 percent of what they had been before the mid-fourteenth century. Europe's population would continue to increase gradually over the course of the sixteenth century.

Most towns, however, numbered only a few thousand inhabitants. There were a few large communes such as Cologne in Germany and Marseilles in France, both of which had about 40,000 residents inside their walls in the beginning of the sixteenth century. Ghent in the Low Countries had around 50,000 inhabitants, as did London, Lyon, and Seville. Readers should be aware that all Reformation-era population figures are a matter of considerable debate. However, it appears that Florence, Milan, Rome, Venice, and Palermo in Sicily all had populations nearing 100,000, as did Lisbon in Portugal. Paris may have had almost 200,000 residents. Mighty Naples had perhaps as many as 230,000 people, thus rivaling Constantinople and the Aztec capital of Tenochtitlán in Mexico before its destruction in 1521 by Hernan Cortés and his allies.

All of these comparatively large cities had great ports or were near major land trade routes. Nuremberg, for example, was not a port city or on a navigable river, but it was located near twelve different trade routes in the heart of central Europe. Trade and financial centers such as Amsterdam, Antwerp, Lisbon, London, and Paris grew during the sixteenth and seventeenth centuries. There commercial life increased as the Atlantic Ocean and the North Sea gradually replaced the Mediterranean as the focal point of long-distance trade in the early modern world.

Most towns had surrounding clusters of peasant villages and sometimes smaller client towns as well. People liked the feeling of security that came from being near walled, fortified places. Some towns bristled with armaments and fortifications, such as wealthy Nuremberg with its several rings of walls, large trenches, eighty-four towers on the inner wall and forty on the outer wall, and protected gates. York in northern England had fortifications going back to the Norman conquest; Chester's walls and gates dated to Roman times, as did Trier's in Germany and Lyon's in France. Spanish towns such as Avila and Segovia bristled with barriers and defenses that had been used in the wars with the Muslims.

Inside even the largest of towns, people lived close together and their behavior was closely regulated by the community's leading male citizens. The majority of town dwellers lived in small, half-timbered cabins with some of the poor huddled in crude sheds clustered alongside town walls. Shopkeepers and their families and servants usually lived in a few rooms above their places of business. Only a few rich merchants and bankers such as the Medici of Florence or the Fuggers of Augsburg had imposing town houses and sometimes country homes as well. Goods were displayed for sale on the lower floor and sometimes sold on the streets and in the market square. Every town had its Weavers' Lane, its Butchers' Row, and its Fishmongers' Alley. The narrow streets were crowded with people, animals (scavenging pigs being a particular favorite), and various kinds of refuse, including human excrement often dumped from second-floor windows. The practice of burying the dead within town walls did nothing to lower the threshold of disease.

DAILY LIFE

Church and town hall bells awoke the burghers and punctuated their days. Bells were also used to warn the inhabitants of the danger of approaching enemies. During the day, towns were filled with activity. Goods were made, bought, and sold, as were the food products of the countryside. Inns and taverns were filled with travelers and locals. Religious processions, holy days, and civic festivals provided welcome distractions from the routine work activities. At sundown, gates were locked, vagrants were expelled, and curfews were enforced as darkness and quiet descended over the towns. City streets at night were places for honest citizens to avoid, even though crime was severely and publicly punished. Entrance gates to towns were often "decorated" with the severed, eyeless heads of executed criminals.

Despite the severity of punishment, Renaissance towns could often be dangerous places. The presence of unmarried journeymen away from the restraints of their hometowns posed a constant threat. Sexual assaults and drunken brawls were common. In sixteenth-century Venice, violence was ritualized to the point where several times each year, workers and artisans would gather on a Sunday or a holiday afternoon to battle with sticks and fists for the possession of a bridge. These prearranged, organized "wars" would be watched regularly by thousands of spectators. Violence, whether organized or not, was as much a part of urban life as barter in the marketplace or high-quality craft production in the workshops.

Maintaining law and order was the great preoccupation of most urban governments. Urban communities were usually governed by councils made up of the leading male merchants who were sometimes joined by prosperous guildsmen. Crafts were still organized in the form of economic associations, called *guilds*, which regulated production and employment standards, set prices, and provided benefits for the widows and orphans of their members. The guilds also served as social and religious brotherhoods and typically sponsored floats in carnival parades and religious processions. Therefore, they were something like labor unions, but with management functions and a firm commitment to religion as well.

URBAN WOMEN

Women were typically not allowed to be members of guilds and go through the training course of being apprentices, journeymen, and finally masters. Often wives and daughters of a master craftsman learned the skills of the trade, and sometimes widows were allowed to take over their deceased husband's shop for a limited period of time. This was done chiefly to avoid having to provide financial support for widows and their children out of collective guild funds. As was the case of farm families, everyone was expected to work. Guild widows had to pay guild fees, but had no voice in the running of the guilds. Although most urban women worked as housekeepers, others found additional employment primarily as shopkeepers, tavern maids, and servants. Legal restrictions made it difficult for women to own much property or to conduct business.

Because women were denied economic power, they also had little political power in most towns. They were not eligible for public office and not allowed to make public policy decisions. The laws that bound them were made exclusively by males. Inside families, men ruled supreme and were able to enforce their power by brute force if necessary. Wife beating was common, even though the church made efforts to limit it. While theorists such as the architect Leon Battista Alberti (c. 1404–1472) urged husbands to treat their wives with kindness, there was no question where ultimate power resided.

Renaissance governments mirrored family structure in being not only patriarchal, but also paternalistic. Tight social control was the supposedly divinely sanctioned order of the day and it was exerted by wealthy men over men of lower status, all women, and children. City fathers took responsibility for regulating not only all aspects of market life, but also the personal lives of their fellow citizens. For example, a typical town council spent time deliberating "how the extravagance of children in dressing during Holy Week might be prevented" or whether or not a woman "was too ardent in bed with her husband."[2] Nothing was considered beneath the notice of the paternalistic town rulers, whether they be bishops, dukes, or councils of merchants and guildsmen.

SOCIAL TENSIONS

Although animosities between men and women seldom erupted into public violence, many Renaissance towns experienced considerable tension between rich merchants, professionals, and the mostly illiterate masses who worked with their hands. The patriciate considered themselves to be "honorable men who earn their living in respectable business, not lowly manual work," as the lawyer Christoph Scheurl (1481–1542) put it.[3] Increasingly the business of government required more and more lawyers to transact. Towns kept lawyers on their payrolls as consultants and used men with legal training as bureaucrats despite the reputation of the legal profession for avarice, as Marinus van Reymerswaele's 1545 painting of a law office reveals. The artist was responding to a Dutch proverb: "If you go to a lawyer to get back your cow, you will have to bring the lawyer another to pay his fee." Despite the presence of those trained in the law and other public officials preoccupied with maintaining law and order, towns were filled with festering jealousies and social grievances that often threatened to erupt into public violence. While life in the urban centers was sometimes turbulent, it was seldom dull, even if there were those who hoped for fundamental changes.

THE RISE OF THE CAPITALISTS

The growth of towns in the late Middle Ages had accompanied the rise of capitalism. Capitalism involves private or corporate ownership of capital goods and investment

Marinus van Reymerswaele, *The Lawyer's Office* (1545). Courtesy of the New Orleans Museum of Art, Ella West Freeman Foundation Matching Fund.

decisions. Capitalists usually favor letting free markets determine prices, production, and distribution. During the Middle Ages, capitalists had struggled against the Old Testament injunction against "taking usury or increase" on loans. The highly influential theologian St. Thomas Aquinas (c. 1225–1274) and other leading church intellectuals agreed with Aristotle that "money is sterile" and that a good Christian should not take advantage of a neighbor in need.

Generally the Europeans lagged behind the Asians and Muslims as merchants and in technology and medicine during much of the medieval period. None of the European overland trade routes compared to the Asian "silk road" from Samarkand to Beijing in China. The Asians also had better ships and navigational instruments than the Europeans until the time of the Renaissance.

All of this began to change even before the fourteenth century. For example, the idea of usury became more and more acceptable as Christian bankers helped fund the Crusades and endowed chapels and hospitals at home and abroad. The medieval Crusades to the Holy Land (1096 to 1291) helped stimulate demand in Europe for luxury goods such as cottons, silks, muslin, dye-stuffs, medicines, perfumes, spices, and much else. Once Europeans had sampled ginger and nutmeg, they were never going to be content again with just plain, but still expensive, salt as their main spice.

Italian merchants from port cities such as Genoa and Venice had long been active in trading with Byzantine and Arab merchants. Several members of the thirteenth-century Polo merchant family of Venice had spent decades in the Asia of Kublai Khan, grandson of the Mongol conqueror Genghis Khan (c. 1160–1227). Marco Polo (c. 1254–1324) eventually wrote *Travels*, a widely read account of his time spent in the East. Some scholars now question its accuracy. Be

that as it may, by the thirteenth and fourteenth centuries, dozens of Italian cities were heavily involved in the growing trade in the Mediterranean.

That trade also included a lucrative traffic in human flesh as the thirteenth century witnessed a resurgence of the slave trade. Prisoners of war and children of desperate parents were sold in the markets of various towns such as bustling Genoa. Slaves came from Africa as well as the Balkans and the Black Sea regions. Africans, Asians, and Ottomans were especially valued as house servants and for tasks in the expanding cloth industries of Italy. This shameful traffic in human beings also fueled the growth of capitalism.

To facilitate expanding and increasingly long-distance trade, banking operations had to be expanded and modernized. Bills of exchange and other written instruments of credit, together with more stable currencies such as the gold florin of Florence and the ducat of rich Venice, all helped increase long-distance trade. Florence became the banking capital of Europe as eighty banking houses were located there by 1338. What the Italians mastered, other Europeans emulated. Great financial centers such as Antwerp, Amsterdam, London, and Paris emerged in the north of Europe.

JACOB FUGGER THE RICH (1459–1525)

In the Holy Roman Empire, the mighty banking empire of Jacob Fugger the Rich became the major bankroll behind Emperor Maximilian I. Fugger was a member of a prominent Augsburg banking family, his mother, Barbara (d. 1497) was one of the leading businesswomen of the period. Jacob had studied bookkeeping and business in Venice as a youth as families involved in international business typically sent their sons to work abroad. This allowed them to ex-

Portrait engraving of Jacob Fugger. Bibliotheque Nationale, Paris, France. Giraudon/Art Resource.

pand their horizons and learn foreign business techniques, customs, currencies, and languages. Business was not studied in schools, but learned on the job. In 1485 Jacob took charge of a Fugger branch bank in Innsbruck, Austria, and made several successful ventures into the growing mining industry in the Tyrolian Alps. By 1502, after extending the family's mining interests into Hungary and Silesia, he became the virtual head of the Fugger family business. The Habsburgs, whose loans Fugger shrewdly secured by a claim against the royal salt mines, were among his most notable customers.

Amazingly successful, Jacob the Rich's motto was "I shall gain while I am able." To do that, Fugger not only loaned money to powerful princes at a high rate of interest, but he also involved his firm in the new East

India spice trade opened up by the recent voyages of discovery. He also hired theologians such as Dr. Johann Eck of Ingolstadt to write defenses of usury. It was Jacob Fugger who loaned Albrecht of Brandenburg the 29,000 gulden necessary to secure the archbishopric of Mainz, which triggered Martin Luther's famous protests against the sale of indulgences. Fugger also secured Charles V's election as Holy Roman emperor in 1519 by loaning him 544,000 gulden in bribe money. Jacob the Rich also used some of his wealth to found the Fuggerei in Augsburg, the world's first housing project for poor and retired workers. Towns all over Europe could only dream of having families like the Fuggers in their midst. Capitalists with or without consciences were here to stay.

MUSLIMS

Added to the social mix of some sixteenth-century communities were a small number of religious and ethnic minorities. It should be remembered that the overwhelming majority of Europe's people at the beginning of the sixteenth century were Roman Catholics. A minority in the eastern parts of Europe were Orthodox Christians, who used either the Greek or the Slovonic rites. People thought of themselves not as Europeans, but as part of the body of Christ (Christendom). Diversity in religion was not tolerated in very many parts of Christian Europe. Muslims predominated only in southern Spain until the fall of their last major stronghold, Granada, in 1492 to the armies of Isabella of Castile (1451–1504), the pious warrior-queen. By 1500 Spain was still unique in Europe, with a sizeable Muslim population of about one-quarter of a million people.

After a period of initial toleration, Queen Isabella found herself under intense pressure to end religious pluralism. For many prominent Christians, those who kept other religious traditions were in danger of losing their immortal souls and infecting those around them. There was doubtless also a great deal of Christian jealousy about the sophisticated business and medical practices of a number of the Muslims. Therefore, the only allowed option for the thousands of Spanish Muslims was to convert to Christianity or leave the Iberian peninsula. Thousands converted, but even more surrendered their property and fled to various places in Europe, Africa, and the Middle East—often with dire consequences.

Although Islam was severely reduced in what became the Spanish kingdom, it grew apace on Europe's eastern flank after the Ottoman conquest of Constantinople, or Byzantium, in 1453. Sultan Mehmed II (r. 1451–1481) used cannons to breach the huge sea walls which protected the mighty city on the straits. Known to contemporaries for his intellectual curiosity, Mehmed then ad-

vanced to besiege Athens, which fell in 1456. His forces then moved on to conquer the rest of Greece and pushed on up the Balkans to take Serbia, Bosnia, Herzegovina, and Albania while spreading Islam in their wake.

After a period of consolidation and expansion to the east against the Persians, the Ottomans renewed their war of conquest against the Christian West under the leadership of the poetry-writing Sultan Süleyman I (r. 1520–1566), the Lawgiver. Süleyman's great armies took Belgrade in 1521, crushed the Hungarians in central Hungary in 1526, and threatened Vienna in 1529. Had well-fortified Vienna fallen, it is hard to imagine any force in Europe strong enough to resist the Ottomans. In fact, the Ottomans would have been an even greater threat had their feudal officers not found it necessary to return periodically to their home estates around Constantinople (now known as Istanbul). Such sudden departures by many

Gentile Bellini, *Sultan Mehmed II Fahti, "The Conqueror"* (c. 1479–1481). National Gallery, London, Great Britain. Erich Lessing/Art Resource.

members of the officer corps made sustaining lengthy sieges and campaigns difficult. Sultan Süleyman also worried about the effects of European winters on his beloved herds of cavalry horses. Nevertheless, his western campaigns permanently established Islam in the Balkans.

SLAVES FROM AFRICA AND THE LEVANT

In addition to Muslims, Europe's minority populations also included Africans of various religious and tribal backgrounds, who served primarily as domestic slaves in prosperous homes in Italy during the fifteenth century with the beginning of the Portuguese black slave trade in West Africa. Captured Africans as well as Tartars and Turks from the Levant were sold at the slave markets in Ancona, Genoa, Pisa, and Venice. It is difficult to determine how much cultural influence they exerted on their masters, but some cross-cultural stimulation was inevitable. Black faces fascinated a number of Renaissance artists, including Albrecht Dürer. Merchants from Africa had appeared in England by the 1550s. William Shakespeare's play *Othello* uses black-white relations and racial prejudice as powerful themes.

During the sixteenth century the supply of domestic slaves in Italy was sharply reduced by rising costs and the growing domination of the Ottomans, who fought to gain control of the slave markets. Slaves and prisoners continued to row galleys that plied the Mediterranean, although most rowers were free men. Domestic slavery did not develop in other parts of Europe in part because of the abundance of poorly paid workers, but became a major part of the growing slave trade to the "New World" of the Americas. There slave labor came to be in great demand.

Albrecht Dürer, *Head of a Black* (1508). Charcoal drawing. Graphisches Sammlung Albertina, Vienna, Austria. Foto Marburg/Art Resource.

JEWS

Europe also had a small Jewish population in the sixteenth century despite periodic waves of expulsions, forced conversions, and judicial murder. Although often placed under the protection of a ruling prince, Jews were prohibited from owning land in most parts of Europe and barred from many other occupations. They worked for the most part as butchers, bookbinders, domestic workers, notaries, scribes, itinerant peddlers, money lenders, pawnbrokers, and physicians. Given the many restrictions that Jews lived under, they played only a minor part in the economy.

At the end of the fifteenth century, Jews in Castile and Aragon were forced to convert to Christianity or to leave. Thousands converted, but continued to be treated with great suspicion and suffered waves of persecution as "New Christians." Others risked everything to migrate to Africa, the Middle East, and other parts of Europe, especially Italy. Many Jews and "New Christians" were the victims of the notorious Spanish Inquisition. Ritual public burnings of Jews in Spain continued until late in the seventeenth century, with a particularly elaborate *auto de fé* held in Madrid's "Theater of Blood" in 1680. Portugal in 1496 under King Joao also forced its Jewish population to convert to Christianity or to flee. By 1517 Jews had been almost completely driven out of Spain and southern Italy.

During the sixteenth century, Jews had made something of a comeback in other parts of Europe, although they still made up less than 1 percent of the Continent's population. Even the largest known Jewish communities outside Italy such as those in Prague and Vienna did not number more than 500 to 700 members. Most others were considerably smaller. Some large towns such as Nuremberg had no Jewish citizens in the sixteenth century. Nuremberg had been given permission to expel its Jews in 1498 by Emperor Maximilian I (r. 1493–1519). Some of those driven from Nuremberg moved only a few miles away to the smaller town of Fürth, but their synagogue on the city's market square was torn down and replaced with a church dedicated to the Virgin Mary. Maximilian's grandson and successor, Charles V (r. 1519–1555), inspired by the Renaissance humanists, took a more benevolent attitude toward the empire's Jews. He was also impressed by the eloquence of Rabbi Joseph of Rosheim from Alsace. Emperor Charles did allow a few persecutions in the Holy Roman Empire, but conditions for Jews gradually improved throughout much of the empire and in Europe as a whole during the later part of the sixteenth century despite the scorn and neglect of the predominantly Christian society.

The Nobility

Although some rich city folk claimed to be noble, they were generally looked down upon by the remnants of the old feudal nobility or, as contemporaries viewed it, "those who fight." For the most part, the "nobles of the sword," who made up the second estate, were in relative decline for much of the later part of the Renaissance. Their landed estates did not produce as much wealth as could be secured from international trade by merchants and bankers. Some nobles tried to expand their incomes by changing the forms of peasant obligations, substituting cash for customary services, for example. These so-called commutations helped to free up peasant living conditions to a degree, but they failed to make some of the lesser nobility feel more economically secure.

Innovations in warfare had made the nobility as the major source of military strength largely obsolete even as early as the fourteenth century. Longbows and gunpowder made knights in shining armor a thing of the past, except for the tournaments, which continued to flourish until King Henri II of France died after receiving a fragment of a shattered lance in the eye during a joust in 1559. The premature death of this chivalrous king had a chilling effect on the noble sport of tournament jousting, which began to fall out of fashion in respectable circles.

MERCENARY AND ROBBER NOBLES

To meet rising expenses, some nobles were reduced to the role of mercenaries—hired paladins at the beck and call of the highest bidder. While some such as Federigo da Montefeltro (1422–1482) of Urbino were honest, pious, and highly cultivated, others lapsed into thuggery or worse. Sigismondo Malatesta (c. 1417–1468), ruler of Rimini, was convicted of murder, rape, wife beating, sacrilege, perjury, incest, and adultery. Yet he was also an important patron of art and scholarship. Trained to kill from their early youth, it is not surprising that some nobles resorted to crime and robbery. Gangs of noble thugs and their armed retainers attacked merchant caravans moving from town to town.

One such robber knight was Götz von Berlichingen (c. 1480–1562). Götz was born to a German noble family and took service at the court of the margrave of Brandenburg-Ansbach. In 1504 he lost his right hand in combat in the War of the Bavarian Succession. Berlichingen hired a craftsperson to make him an iron hand, which he used to strike terror into the hearts of his enemies. Those enemies came to include the prosperous citizens of towns such as Bamberg, Mainz, and Nuremberg, whose merchant caravans he plundered for many years. In 1519 he fought as a mercenary for Duke Ulrich of Württemberg. Six years later, Berlichingen lowered himself socially by fighting for cash on the side of rebellious peasants, but deserted them in time to avoid being destroyed by their defeat in the summer of 1525.

Although placed under imperial ban as an outlaw on four occasions and jailed twice, Berlichingen fought for Emperor Charles V against the Ottomans in 1542 and against the French in 1544. Robber knights like Berlichingen often had family and friends in high places and were difficult to suppress. As much as princes might decry robber barony, they still needed skilled warriors to make up their officer corps.

THE REFINEMENT OF MANNERS

Those nobles of the higher strata who stayed out of trouble and had sufficient revenues saw their lifestyles improve in the course of the Renaissance. Castles became better heated and more luxuriously furnished and much better designed. Country estates came to be surrounded by lovely gardens, stocked fishponds, and ample facilities for leisure. During the sixteenth century, the nobility of Europe withdrew more and more from their contact with the lower orders. They stopped eating with their retainers in great halls and withdrew into separate dining rooms. Nobles in Lombardy stopped wrestling with their peasants and stopped killing bulls in public in Spain.

To further set themselves apart, nobles learned to talk and behave in a more formal and self-conscious style. Manners improved and became more refined as more was expected of the nobility than just skill in combat. Baldassare Castiglione's 1528 *Book of the Courtier* set new standards for noble behavior. To succeed at court, noblemen were expected by the humanist and former diplomat Castiglione (1478–1529) to be able to dance, play games, ride, recite and understand poetry, speak clearly, and give good advice. As for the noble women of the court, according to Castiglione:

> I wish this Lady to have knowledge of letters, of music, of painting, and know how to dance and how to be festive, adding a discrete modesty and the giving of a good impression of herself to those other things that are required of the Courtier.[4]

Noblewomen of all ranks were responsible for producing meals, supervising servants, and doing all sorts of needlework.

Although the nobility of early modern Europe may have been in a state of relative and gradual decline, overall it was a most privileged elite. Its male members especially had an enviable existence. After all, the nobility was still at the top of the social heap. Those at the top of the top were part of the extended family of the crowned heads of Europe. They held vast amounts of lands and had many privileges. Nobles had virtual monopolies on the best offices in the royal governments and in the military. Some received generous pensions from the crown. Noble sons and daughters received preferential treatment in the church and, like the clergy, the nobility in many places enjoyed widespread exemption from direct taxes. Although revenues from lands may have failed to keep pace with inflation in the sixteenth century, it is still important to remember that the nobility, which made up only about 2 percent of the population of Europe, controlled as much as half of the best land in many areas. So even though their incomes in many cases may have been falling during the period, they were still among the wealthiest people in Europe, and many rich commoners were eager to marry their daughters into the ranks of the nobility or to be made "noble" by royal favor.

Even though it was difficult even for a rich commoner to secure a patent of nobility, many prosperous merchants attempted to imitate noble lifestyles. The sons of the merchant elite as well as the nobility enjoyed hunting, dancing, jousting, and feasting. Merchants also emulated the social pretensions of the nobility. Indeed, with their sumptuous meals of meat soup, boiled beef, roasted mutton, capons fattened on oats, pigeon, fresh or salted fish, white bread, jams, juices, gravies, fruits, vegetables, and cheeses, all washed down by beer or watered wine, there was a great deal in a typical noble's gastronomic life to be envied.

Noblewomen, while hardly creatures of total leisure, still had much better lives than those below them, especially if their fathers and husbands were kind, something that could never be taken for granted. As with the women of other social groups, noble females were brought up to expect a far different destiny from noble males. Their lives would revolve around family and domestic life. Some would go into the church

as "brides of Christ." All women were taught that they held lower status than the males, for as the popular saying expressed it, "He is the sun and she is the moon."

Everyone in the nobility and the upper ranks of the merchant elite seemed to dress very sumptuously indeed when compared to the peasantry. Both men and women took to wearing jewelry, some of which was sown into their garments, as precious stones became more abundant in Europe following the voyages of discovery. Furs and fine fabrics, eventually including silk, made the "men in tights" (actually hose) of the era and their sumptuously clad and bejeweled ladies of lace and brocade appear to be figures worlds apart from the woolen-clad poor people who surrounded them and even the armies of servants who cooked for them and waited upon them. Clearly, the nobility of Europe were a privileged elite who often loved to display their power, status, and wealth in increasingly conspicuous consumption. Their "honor" demanded no less of them.

The Clergy

Also set apart from the roughly clad hordes of poor working people were the members of the first estate—the clergy—"those who pray." They were first, theoretically, in the medieval social hierarchy because they were considered to be closest to God. They were to pray, dispense charity, do good works, and sacrifice worldly pleasures for the sake of everyone's salvation. Therefore, they, like some in the second estate, were exempted from taxation by the state. They had their own legal code (canon law) and court system, which punished clerics less severely than secular courts punished the laity for similar crimes. Only the celebrant could receive both the cup and the bread during the Eucharist, among other signs of God's favor.

The clergy made up from 2 to 4 percent of the population at the beginning of the sixteenth century. This made them a relatively large group of people to have so many privileges in a culture where so many had so little except hard work and deprivation. Like the laity, the clergy were divided along class lines. While those at the higher levels had large incomes, many priests, especially those in rural parishes, were paid very poorly.

The clergy were made up of two main groups: the secular clergy, or those who were in the world, and the regular clergy, who followed a religious rule and were either cloistered monks or worked among the laity as friars. The clergy was technically a male monopoly; women were not candidates for ordination. Even cloistered nuns had to receive the sacraments from males. The higher ranks of the secular clergy administered the church's elaborate sacramental system: baptism, confirmation, penance, the Eucharist, ordination (for the clergy only), marriage (for the laity only), and final rites. The seven sacraments were considered outward signs of God's favor and were essential in order to achieve salvation. They helped instill a feeling of God's presence in the world and bound people of all stations into a sacred community of believers throughout the European world. They provided important rites of passage for all stages of a Christian's life on earth. The Latin of the Roman church and the Greek and Slovonic of the Orthodox church exposed Christians to common religious languages and rituals, which further enhanced the feeling of community for the majority who accepted the tradition. There were also those who secretly rejected many aspects of the church's tradition, but they were usually in the minority and ran great risks.

The secular clergy consisted of two groups: an upper and a lower clergy. The upper clergy was made up of priests and bishops. By the Renaissance, deacons and subdeacons were considered steps toward the priesthood. The lower clergy or those in minor orders consisted of doorkeepers, acolytes, lectors, and exorcists. The lower clergy were not often scrutinized carefully upon entrance and not bound by a permanent commitment to celibacy. Many in fact were married. They were set off from the world by their haircut (tonsure), which was short with a bald spot at the back of their heads. Members of the lower clergy could leave minor orders simply by growing their hair out. If they stayed in the service of the church, they shared in many of the clergy's privileges, such as the right to be tried for crimes in church rather than secular courts.

Much more was expected of the higher grades of the secular clergy than from those in the lower ranks. They were to be recognized by their tonsure and sober clothing. Since the eleventh century the church frowned upon sexual activity carried out by members of the higher clergy. Candidates for the priesthood were to be at least twenty-five years old, unmarried, of good moral character, educated, and have a reliable means of support. Those who lacked a church job of sufficient income could earn additional revenue in an "honorable profession" such as that of teacher or chaplain. All these requirements could be waived or ignored by securing a papal dispensation. Married priests or priests with concubines could still be found, especially in rural parishes.

The regular clergy followed such monastic rules as poverty, chastity, obedience, and humility. Some lived in cloistered religious communities behind walls away from the hustle and bustle of the workaday world. There they could experience lives of quiet devotion with usually seven occasions for prayer throughout the day from early in the morning to sunset. There was also time for study and manual work. This life was open to both men and women, although male houses always outnumbered female, and convents required male clerics to say Mass. Monks and friars were tonsured and wore distinctive clothing, from the black robes of the Augustinian friars to the white robes of the Cistercians monks. Nuns also had short hair and wore distinctive habits and head coverings, which visibly separated them from their lay sisters. Convents were the only places where European women in significant numbers could utilize fully their intellectual and administrative gifts. Intellectually inclined male clerics not only had their monasteries, but also the universities, which excluded women with only a few rare exceptions.

Although membership in the religious orders was theoretically open to all, men and women from rich families dominated their ranks. Most monastic houses for women required a form of dowry or deposit. In fifteenth-century Florence, the average deposit for future nuns was 435 florins (more than sixteen times what the average journeyman made in a year). While it was still usually less expensive to become "a bride of Christ" than to marry a mortal man, convents were havens for the daughters of the privileged. Male clergy also came pre-dominantly from the ranks of the nobility and the patriciate. Some came by choice, whereas others were sent into the church in order to avoid dividing inheritances or straining family resources.

Most clerics seemed to have kept their vows despite the popularity of stories of lascivious monks, friars, nuns, and priests, written by writers such as Giovanni Boccaccio (1313–1375) in his *Decameron Tales*, Geoffrey Chaucer (c. 1340–1400) in his *Canterbury Tales*, or Marguerite of Navarre (1492–1549) in her *Heptameron*. Regional studies have indicated that 80 to 90 percent of the clergy in 1500 remained continent. The lifestyles of the clergy varied enormously, from begging friars and monastic houses that practiced severe discipline and where food was modest, to Chaucer's drawn-from-life "regal" prioress, who ate "so primly and so well." Those at the top of the clerical hierarchy such as bishops, cardinals, and popes lived in splendor comparable to the great secular lords whose refined manners they emulated. The princes of the church were also waited upon by hosts of servants. Although the church had its share of problems, as we shall see, the surviving records indicate that the overwhelming majority of the sixteenth-century clergy lived lives of relative holiness despite the envy of some laity, who were all too willing to believe the worst of the first estate.

Further Reading

GENERAL SOCIAL HISTORY

Peter Burke, *Popular Culture in Early Modern Europe* (1978).

Roger Chartier, ed., *Passions of the Renaissance* (1989).

Natalie Davis, *Society and Culture in Early Modern France* (1975). A collection of her essays.

Lucien Febvre, *Life in Renaissance France*. Ed. and trans. by Marian Rothstein (1977).

Carlo Ginzburg, *The Cheese and the Worms: The Cosmos of a Sixteenth-Century Miller*. Tr. by John and Anne Tedeschi (1982).

George Huppert, *After the Black Death: A Social History of Early Modern Europe* (1986). An extremely valuable synthesis.

Henry Kamen, *The Iron Century: Social Change in Europe, 1550–1660* (1971). Still a valuable survey.

THE PEASANTRY

Wilhelm Abel, *Agricultural Fluctuations in Europe: From the Thirteenth to the Twentieth Centuries* (1980).

Andrew Appleby, *Famine in Tudor and Stuart England* (1978).

Natalie Davis, *The Return of Martin Guerre* (1983). A fascinating true story of a peasant imposter.

Jan de Vries, *The Dutch Rural Economy in the Golden Age, 1500–1700* (1974).

Emmanuel Le Roy Ladurie, *Montaillou: The Promised Land of Error* (1978). An intriguing account of life and heresy in a fourteenth-century French village.

———, *The French Peasantry, 1450–1660* (1987).

———, *The Peasants of Languedoc* (1969).

Thomas Robisheaux, *Rural Society and the Search for Order in Early Modern Germany* (1989).

Warren Sabean, *Power in the Blood: Popular Culture and Village Discourse in Early Modern Germany* (1984).

Richard Wunderli, *Peasant Fires: The Drummer of Niklashausen* (1991).

WOMEN AND GENDER

Bonnie Anderson and Judith Zinsser, *A History of Their Own: Women in Europe from Prehistory to the Present*. 2 vols. (1988). Although a general survey, it has a great deal to say about women in the Renaissance period.

Natalie Zemon Davis and Arlette Farge, eds., *A History of Women in the West*, vol. 3, *Renaissance and Enlightenment Paradoxes* (1993). Seventeen very important essays.

Barbara Hanawalt, ed., *Women and Work in Preindustrial Europe* (1986). Ten significant essays.

Constance Jordan, *Renaissance Feminism: Literary Texts and Political Models* (1990).

Margaret King, *The Death of the Child Valerio Marcello* (1994).

———, *Women of the Renaissance* (1991). A very important overview with particular attention given to women in Italy.

Thomas Kuehn, *Law, Family, and Women: Toward a Legal Anthropology of Renaissance Italy* (1991).

Gerda Lerner, *The Creation of Feminist Consciousness* (1993).

Ian MacLean, *The Renaissance Notion of Woman* (1980).

Marilyn Migiel and Julianna Schiesa, eds., *Refiguring Woman: Perspectives on Gender and the Italian Renaissance* (1991). A collection of diverse essays.

Merry Wiesner, *Women and Gender in Early Modern Europe* (1993). A fine survey.

———, *Women in the Sixteenth Century: A Bibliography* (1983).

———, *Working Women in Renaissance Germany* (1986).

JEWS

Salo Baron, *A Social and Religious History of the Jews*. 2nd ed. 14 vols. (1952–1969).

Robert Bonfil, *Jewish Life in Renaissance Italy* (1994).

R. Po-chia Hsia, *The Myth of Ritual Murder: Jews and Magic in Reformation Germany* (1988).

———, *Trent 1475: Stories of a Ritual Murder Trial* (1992).

——— and Hartmut Lehman, *In and Out of the Ghetto: Jewish-Gentile Relations in Late Medieval and Early Modern Germany* (1994).

Jonathan Israel, *European Jewry in the Age of Mercantilism, 1550–1750* (1985).

Heiko Oberman, *The Roots of Anti-Semitism* (1981).

Brian Pullan, *The Jews of Europe and the Inquisition of Venice, 1550–1670* (1983).

Raymond Waddington and Arthur Williamson, eds., *The Expulsion of the Jews: 1492 and After* (1994). Important essays.

AFRICANS AND OTTOMANS

Franz Babinger, *Mehmed the Conqueror and His Time* (1992).

Stanford Shaw, *Empire of the Gazis: The Rise and Decline of the Ottoman Empire, 1280–1808* (1976).

John Thornton, *Africa and Africans in the Making of the Atlantic World, 1400–1680* (1992).

Andrew Wheatcroft, *The Ottomans* (1994).

URBAN LIFE

Robin Briggs, *Communities of Belief: Cultural and Social Tensions in Early Modern France* (1989).

James Farr, *Hands of Honor: Artisans and Their World in Dijon, 1550–1650* (1988).

Barbara Hanawalt, *Growing Up in Medieval London: The Experience of Childhood in History* (1993).

Lewis Mumford, *The City in History* (1961).

Gerald Strauss, *Nuremberg in the Sixteenth Century* (1976).

Lee Palmer Wandel, *Always Among Us: Images of the Poor in Zwingli's Zurich* (1990).

THE CAPITALISTS

Janet Abu-Lughad, *Before European Hegemony: The World System 1250–1350* (1989).

Felix Gilbert, *The Pope, His Banker, and Venice* (1980).

Harry Miskimim, *The Economy of Early Renaissance Europe, 1300–1460* (1975).

Richard de Roover, *The Rise and Decline of the Medici Bank, 1397–1494* (1966).

THE NOBILITY

Davis Bitton, *The French Nobility in Crisis, 1560–1640* (1969).

Kristin Neuschal, *Word of Honor: Interpreting Noble Culture in Sixteenth-Century France* (1989).

Ellery Schalk, *From Valor to Pedigree: Ideas of Nobility in France in the Sixteenth and Seventeenth Centuries* (1986).

Lawrence Stone, *The Crisis of the Aristocracy, 1558–1641* (1965).

THE CLERGY

John Bossy, *Christianity in the West: 1400–1700* (1985).

K. J. P. Lowe, *Church and Politics in Renaissance Italy: The Life and Career of Cardinal Francesco Soderini (1453–1524)* (1993).

Joseph Lynch, *The Medieval Church: A Brief History* (1992).

Francis Oakley, *The Western Church in the Late Middle Ages* (1979).

Paolo Prodi, *The Papal Princes. One Body and Two Souls: The Papal Monarchy in Early Modern Europe* (1982).

Larissa Taylor, *Soldiers of Christ: Preaching in Late Medieval and Reformation France* (1992).

Thomas Tentler, *Sin and Confession on the Eve of the Reformation* (1977).

John Thomson, *Politics and Princes 1417–1517: Politics and Polity in the Late Medieval Church* (1980).

Notes

1. Cited in Bonnie Anderson and Judith Zinsser, *A History of Their Own: Women in Europe from Prehistory to the Present*, 2 vols. (New York: Harper, 1988), vol. 1, p. 88.
2. Cited in Jonathan W. Zophy, *Patriarchal Politics and Christoph Kress (1484–1535) of Nuremberg* (Lewiston, N.Y.: Edwin Mellen Press, 1992), p. 41.
3. Ibid., p. 39.
4. Castiglione, *The Book of the Courtier*, tr. by George Bull (Baltimore, Md.: Penguin, 1967), p. 216.

3

THE *STATES OF EUROPE*
ON THE EVE
OF THE REFORMATION

European people's first allegiance was usually to their families and then, perhaps, to their parish church. Local communities such as villages or neighborhoods or even entire towns also commanded loyalties. Yet Europe also had its share of large territorial states, especially in the north. The great drama of the Reformation was acted out initially against the background of emerging territorial monarchies. Northern monarchs attempted to assert more and more of their authority against the power of their feudal nobility. Instead of relying on feudal levies for the bulk of their military power, Renaissance princes employed mercenaries in increasing numbers. Royal bureaucracies and legal systems also expanded. Not just content with expanding their royal prerogatives within their states, European monarchs vied with each other for economic and political advantages. War was seen as an instrument of foreign policy. The result was a continuation of international instability which would persist throughout the Reformation era.

France under François I
(r. 1515–1547)

France entered the sixteenth century as one of the strongest of the European monarchies. In 1494 and again in 1499 it had invaded Italy to press, among other things, its claims to Naples. By 1504 the Spanish house of Aragon, which controlled the great port city, had driven the French out of Naples. Nine years later they were forced out of Italy altogether by the Swiss, who then took control of Milan. In 1515 François I of the house of Valois came to the French throne and renewed French interests in Italy. His particular aim was the rich duchy of Milan then controlled by the Swiss. Making an alliance with the Venetians, the aggressive, young French king crushed the Swiss at the battle of Marignano in September of 1515. Milan was then brought under the authority of the French crown.

It appeared François I's reign had begun auspiciously. He had also asserted his authority over the French nobility. With the exception of the duke of Bourbon, all the great feudal lords had been either subordinated to royal authority or allied to the king's cause through marriage or mutual affiliation. The French king won the loyalty of his nobles by showering them with gifts, honors, pensions, positions, and tax relief. Although his will dominated in government, the French nobility were made to feel an important part of an expanding monarchy and a glittering court with its elaborate entertainments.

François's court at times included his

brilliant older sister, Marguerite of Navarre (1492–1549), who was later found to be the author of the *Heptameron*, a witty collection of tales. She and her cultivated mother, Louise of Savoy, helped to give the king a taste for the finer things in life. He became a generous patron of the arts, bringing, among others, Leonardo da Vinci (1452–1519) to France. The leading French Greek scholar, Guillaume Budé (1468–1540), was made secretary to the king and master of the rapidly growing royal library at Fontainebleau. François I also built a spectacular series of palaces and gardens, some of them south of Paris in the Loire Valley. With such a king, France seemed on the verge of great things, even if the toiling masses below seldom benefited from the royal splendor.

Jean Clouet, *François I of France*. Louvre, Paris, France. Giraudon/Art Resource.

England under Henry VIII (r. 1509–1547)

England too had an able and aggressive young prince with expensive tastes. A handsome redhead, King Henry VIII was a vigorous athlete, musician, and something of an intellectual. He was surprisingly well-read in theology and the "new learning" of some of the humanists. Henry was married to Catherine of Aragon (1485–1536), the pious daughter of Queen Isabella of Castile and King Ferdinand of Aragon. She had previously been married to his older brother Arthur (d. 1502), but the connection with mighty Spain was too important to abandon, so Henry's father, Henry VII, shrewdly negotiated a second marriage. Like François of France, Henry Tudor relished extravagant display. Their sumptuous meeting in June 1520 at the Field of Cloth and Gold was described by contemporaries as the eighth wonder of the world. One of the observers from Venice commented wryly: "These sovereigns are not at peace . . . they hate each other cordially."[1]

The cordial hatred between Henry and François was part of an old rivalry between the English and French realms. Early in his reign in 1511, Henry had joined his father-in-law, Ferdinand of Spain, the warrior-pope Julius II (r. 1503–1513), and Holy Roman Emperor Maximilian I in a league designed to drive the French out of Italy. Eager for military glory, the young king led a French army into France in 1512, won the battle of Spurs, and seized Tournai. When his treacherous allies deserted him, Henry sued for peace in 1514 and agreed to accept an annual payment in return for relinquishing Tournai. When François I renewed French aggression in Italy in 1515, Tudor England backed Spain in the wars that followed between the Habsburgs and the Valois. Not

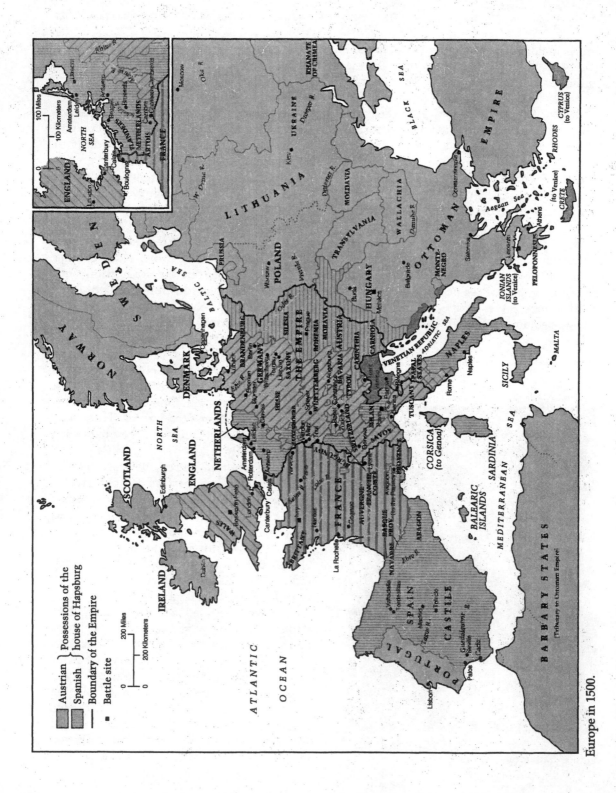

Europe in 1500.

Legend:
- Austrian ⎫ Possessions of the
- Spanish ⎬ house of Hapsburg
- Boundary of the Empire
- ■ Battle site

Scale: 200 Miles / 200 Kilometers

Inset scale: 100 Miles / 100 Kilometers

until 1526 did Henry make peace with François.

Henry VIII was assisted in his diplomatic maneuvering by Thomas Wolsey (c. 1472–1530), the archbishop of Canterbury. The ambitious son of a butcher, Wolsey had been named lord chancellor in 1515 and was determined to pursue an opportunistic line in foreign policy. At times, the able Wolsey emerged as the chief actor in English politics as the king occasionally withdrew into his interests and pleasures such as dancing and hunting. Like his master, Wolsey could be arrogant, extravagant, and ruthless. They made a formidable, if dangerous, team.

Henry could not play as complete an autocrat as François of France because he was forced to share power with a representative body known as Parliament. Made up of ecclesiastical and feudal magnates (the House of Lords) and knights and wealthy merchants (the House of Commons), Parliament in the fourteenth century had gotten a considerable say in the financial affairs of the monarchy. It was also seen as an instrument of making the king's will known to his subjects. By and large, Henry VIII got along well with Parliament and with the great noble families who vied with each other for power and preferment. Although its early sixteenth-century population (2.3 million) was only about one-eighth that of France (16.4), England under Henry VIII was a force to be reckoned with.

Spain

During a great deal of the Middle Ages, the Iberian peninsula had been under Muslim control. As the Christians gradually pushed the Muslims into the single kingdom of Granada in the south, they had forged a number of separate kingdoms. The strongest of these were brought together in 1469 by the marriage of Queen Isabella of Castile (1451–1504) to King Ferdinand of Aragon (1452–1516). Although Isabella and Ferdinand enjoyed a generally strong partnership, they never fully integrated their separate realms. Laws, government, currency, and language remained distinct to each kingdom. They did collaborate on their campaigns against Islamic Granada. By 1490 the Christians had virtually surrounded the city of Granada. In January of 1492, the Muslim king surrendered the keys to the city to Isabella and Ferdinand.

To further increase their power and promote religious unity, the monarchs petitioned the papacy to establish the Holy Office of the Inquisition in 1478 for Castile. The Inquisition was a church court which was used to examine the faith and morals of people in an area believed to be infected with heresy (literally "treason against God"). Spain was unique in Europe in having a fairly large Muslim population of nearly a quarter of a million. It also had a Jewish population of perhaps 100,000. Isabella had long protected Jews in Castile, but found herself under increasing pressure to force their conversion or expel them in the wake of the conquest of Granada. In March 1492, a royal edict ordered all of Spain's Jews to convert to Christianity or leave. At least 40,000 fled. Those who remained were closely supervised by the Inquisition. Islam remained legal in Castile and Granada for another ten years.

When Queen Isabella died in 1504, Castile was inherited by her son-in-law Philip the Handsome and her daughter Juana the Mad. Isabella had already laid the groundwork for Spain's vast colonial empire in the Americas by supporting the efforts of Christopher Columbus (1446–1506). In 1516 sixteen-year-old Charles of Habsburg inherited both Castile and Granada from his grandparents. The biggest threat to his authority in Spain came in the spring of 1520 when he faced a revolt of the towns and villages of Castile known as the revolt of the *comuneros* (commoners). Charles was accused of having turned over too much of his authority in Castile to his Burgundian courtiers and allowed too many foreigners to establish themselves on Castilian land. While firmly putting down the commoners and another rebellion in Valencia, King Charles put an end to foreign exploitation in Castile. Increasingly, he came to rely on Spanish officials and institutions such as the Spanish parliament (the Cortes). With vast amounts of gold and silver pouring in from Spain's empire in the New World, King Charles brought Spain into the forefront of European powers.

The Holy Roman Empire

In 1519 King Charles of Spain added to his responsibilities by being elected to succeed his grandfather Maximilian I (r. 1493–1519) as Holy Roman emperor. The Holy Roman Empire of the German nation was the largest state in Europe, encompassing most of central Europe. Its roughly fifteen million inhabitants spoke a variety of languages and dialects, though various forms of German predominated. In contrast to the hereditary monarchs of England, France, and Spain, the Holy Roman emperors were formally elected by a powerful group of seven elector-princes. The elective principle had become fixed in 1356 when the Emperor Charles IV of Luxembourg-Bohemia (r. 1347–1378) issued a written constitution for the empire known as the Golden Bull. By its terms, the archbishops of Mainz, Trier, and Cologne, the king of Bohemia, the duke of Saxony, the margrave of Brandenburg, and the count palatine of the Rhine were to serve

as imperial electors and make up the first house of the Imperial Parliament (Diet).

The electoral princes were virtually sovereign in their own lands and could, for example, mint their own coins. Their privileges were reconfirmed in Frankfurt on the Main River in the center of Germany at the election of each new emperor. The empire was a complete patriarchy; only males could be elected as emperor or serve as one of the seven powerful electors. The second house of the Imperial Diet was made up of the non-electoral princes such as the duke of Bavaria and the margrave of Hesse. The third house was filled with representatives of the towns, who in 1489 as part of a political reform movement had finally gotten a vote in imperial affairs. Since the merchant capitalists of the towns had long helped pay for many of the functions of the imperial government, they had long been keen about getting a vote as well as a voice. Although Holy Roman emperors had a great deal of prestige as descendants of such legendary monarchs as Charlemagne, Frederick Barbarossa, and Otto I, they were, in fact, dependent on their princely and merchant subjects for special revenues and military resources. There was no imperial tax of any substance and no standing army.

In reality the Holy Roman Empire was a loose confederation of over 300 virtually autonomous principalities and towns. During the Renaissance, the Austrian house of Habsburg usually succeeded in getting its sons elected as Holy Roman emperors time and time again. Since 1273 nearly every emperor was a Habsburg, a dynasty that made their influence felt throughout Europe by their remarkable success in marrying well. The Habsburgs prospered by the old motto: "Others may fight and die, thou happy Austria marry!" Among the many able Habsburg dynasts, few were ever as successful as Charles's grandfather Maximilian, "an odd little man, whose chin stuck out like a shelf."[2]

In 1491 Emperor Maximilian began negotiating a double marriage treaty with Isabella and Ferdinand of Spain. His daughter, Margaret, married the Spanish heir, Juan, while his son, Philip, married Juan's unstable sister, Juana. Although Juan died shortly thereafter, Philip and Juana (later called the Mad) produced a son, Charles, who inherited Spain, Austria, the Low Countries, and the inside track on his Habsburg grandfather's imperial title. A second grandson, Ferdinand, was engaged to King Vladislav of Hungary's daughter Anna, thus adding Habsburg claims to both Hungary and Bohemia.

As Holy Roman emperor, Maximilian attempted to strengthen the power of the crown, a move strongly resisted by the German princes. Their vision of reform was quite different from that of Maximilian, who frequently found himself short of cash and was constantly borrowing money from German bankers. On one occasion, the burghers of Augsburg threw dung at his imperial but improvident majesty. Other Germans rather admired Maximilian for his patronage of the arts and interest in ideas, even if some of them were rather grandiose for his limited resources. The emperor did succeed in reducing the power of the rival Wittelsbach dynasty in Bavaria (succession war of 1503–1505).

In the elaborate chess game that was European power politics, Maximilian attempted to stop French advances in war-torn but prosperous northern Italy. He also tried to stop the French from gobbling up the rich farmland and commercial centers in the Low Countries. He had less success with the Swiss Confederation, which won its independence from imperial authority in 1499. Maximilian also dreamed of mounting a crusade against the Ottoman Turks.

His grandson, Charles V (r. 1519–1556), was a conscientious and somber young man who wanted to use his imperial office to strengthen his efforts to dominate Europe and Italy. For their part, the German princes were determined to maintain their own privileges and not let Charles's courtiers from the Netherlands and Spain exploit German resources for the good of the emperor's wider interests. An English observer thought that twenty-one-year-old Charles showed a good mind and a solid grasp of foreign affairs at his first Imperial Diet in 1521. However,

> His appearance was against him. A prominent, misshapen jaw and irregular teeth disfigured his features and detracted from the considered judgment he showed in his speech. With his pale blue eyes and dead-white complexion he was far short of handsome, but he had finally managed to grow a beard and was said to possess the vigor of a grown man.[3]

Charles V never became a typical heavy-drinking, playful German prince. Having been raised in the Low Countries and then becoming king of Spain, among sixty other titles, he soon found himself overwhelmed by a host of problems all over his far-flung dominions. Although he had several wives in the course of his long reign, he did not compare with his Tudor and Valois rivals as a womanizer. François I was particularly notorious for his lechery. Recognizing that Spain was the key to his empire, Charles returned there in 1522 to crush the revolting Castilian towns and stayed until 1529. He became fluent in Spanish and developed a deep understanding of Spanish traditions and customs. Germany moved to the periphery of his concerns, except for his need to secure funds for his wars with the French over Italy and his need to secure his eastern flank from the incursions of the Ottomans.

Charles V's brother Archduke Ferdinand (1503–1564) served as his regent in the Holy Roman Empire and was given much of the responsibility for dealing with the crisis sparked by Martin Luther. Much less somber than his older brother, Ferdinand also worked hard to assimilate German traditions and customs and to make the German princes and rich burghers feel comfortable in his presence. Even when religious differences threatened to rip apart the Holy Roman Empire, Ferdinand enjoyed a high level of personal popularity and respect.

The Netherlands

Charles V had been born in Ghent, Flanders. After his father's death and because of the mental illness of his mother, Charles was raised by his aunt, Margaret of Austria, regent of the Netherlands. As a youth he was also influenced by one of his tutors, Adrian of Utrecht, a representative of the reform-minded modern devotion movement, who helped instill in him a lasting piety. In 1522, partly through Charles's influence, Adrian succeeded Leo X (r. 1513–1522) as pope. Charles's first major title was as duke of Burgundy, which he assumed in 1515. Two years later he left for Spain to assume his throne there. His interests in the Netherlands were served by his capable aunt, Margaret of Austria, until her death in 1530. She was followed by his half sister, Mary (1505–1558), the widow of King Louis of Hungary (d. 1526), a cultured and strong-willed leader. The Habsburg efforts to centralize their holdings in the Low Countries and efforts to increase taxation created mounting tensions, which would erupt in 1566 during the reign of Charles's son Philip II (1527–1598)

Scandinavia

The Scandinavian countries of Denmark, Norway, and Sweden were not nearly as populous as the monarchies to the south. As late as the 1630s, Sweden and Denmark had but 900,000 and 800,000 people, respectively. Norway's population is estimated "to have been at about 200,000 in the 1520s and 450,000 by 1645."[4] Agriculture dominated the area's economic life, although fishing was vital to Norway and mining was gaining importance in Sweden. Denmark was the most urbanized and densely populated of the kingdoms which since 1389 had been allied in the Union of Kalmar, organized by the astute Queen Margaret of Denmark (1353–1412).

The Roman Catholic church had become the largest holder of arable land throughout Scandinavia, controlling roughly 40 percent of the good farm land in Norway, a third in Denmark, and 21 percent in Sweden. The rest of the arable land was distributed between the crown, the nobility, and (most remarkably) burghers and peasants, who held an unusually large amount of arable land by European standards. For example, peasants and burghers held about 36 percent of the farmland in Norway.

By 1500 the previous domination of the Hanseatic League, the once powerful trading association of about 200 far-flung towns, had come to be challenged by the Dutch, who paid special dues to the Danish king. Tensions between the councils of the Scandinavian states escalated throughout the late fifteenth century and well into the sixteenth. The clash of wills and interests finally led the Danish King Christian II (r. 1513–1523) to impose his authority over the Union of Kalmar by force in 1520. His execution of scores of leading members of the Swedish nobility led the Swedes to repudiate the Union of Kalmar in 1523. Christian II was deposed in 1523 and replaced by his uncle Frederick I (r. 1523–1533). Norway remained yoked to Denmark, but Gustavus Vasa (r. 1523–1560) became king of Sweden. This resulted in separate Scandinavian monarchies going their own way into the crises of the early Reformation.

Eastern Europe

Eastern Europe was formed by the crown lands of Poland, Bohemia (including Moravia, Silesia, and Lusatia), and Hungary. They had developed vigorous parliamentary regimes in which the upper nobles formed an effective counterweight to their kings. Large numbers of Polish and Bohemian nobles owned their lands outright and had developed a tradition of political independence even in the face of Ottoman threats. Allied with the crown against the Reformation, except in Bohemia, was a politically powerful and wealthy church hierarchy. Bohemia had experienced the first reformation in Latin Christendom with the Hussite revolt of 1419 to 1436, which had been triggered by the martyrdom of the charismatic Czech reformer Jan Hus in 1415 at the great Church Council of Constance. This topic will be presented in greater detail in the next chapter.

In all three kingdoms, the nobles had come to assume a great deal of power. In addition to their considerable landholdings, the nobles of Bohemia, Hungary, and Poland had the right to elect or at least confirm the king's elevation. As in the Holy Roman Empire, kings needed the consent of the nobles to raise tax revenues. Powerful nobles dominated the highest offices, including the judiciary (the senate in Poland). In Poland and Hungary, the upper nobles also controlled provincial administration. The diffusion of power between the king and the nobility often made it difficult to achieve consensus on the proper course of action for Poland. Disagreements among the elite did little to improve conditions for the Polish peasantry, who were bound to the soil by an act of the Polish senate in 1511. This was at a time when serfdom had almost completely vanished in the West.

Although the onset of the Reformation was delayed in Hungary and Poland because of the opposition of their sovereigns, given the decentralized nature of power in those kingdoms, it is hardly surprising that Protestantism developed in eastern Europe. Borders can seldom contain ideologies, especially ones as well developed as Calvinism, which in fact came for a while to be the religion of a majority of Hungarians. Because of its western border with Lutheran Saxony, Poland was exposed to Lutheran ideas almost from the inception of the movement.

Russia

As for Poland's neighbors to the east, the Grand Princes of Moscow had been forced to pay heavy tribute to the nomadic descendants of Genghis Khan (1160–1227) until 1480 when Ivan III, the Great (1462–1505), threw off the Mongol yoke and abolished tribute. Ivan then annexed the Hanseatic trading city of Novgorod in the north and parts of Poland and Lithuania. Preferring diplomacy and intrigue to war, Ivan achieved a great deal of state-building with a minimum of bloodshed. Not only did he ward off the pretensions of his four brothers, the tall and fierce Ivan also married his son to the niece of the last Byzantine emperor. The marriage bolstered his claims to the vacant Byzantine throne.

As with his counterparts in France, Ivan also tried to reduce the power of his nobility and strengthen the personal institutions of his government. His policies were carried on with considerable success by his son Vasili III (r. 1505–1533). Vasili has been overshadowed by the spectacular careers of his father and his son and successor, Ivan IV, the Terrible (r. 1533–1584). Despite the improved organization and expansion of the Muscovite state, the Russians were still not strong enough to become major players in the mostly Western drama of the Reformation, even had they not been preoccupied with their own affairs and borders. As Eastern Orthodox Christians, the Russians were somewhat immune to the disorders plaguing the Latin church in the West. Vasili III was a genuinely pious Orthodox Christian who believed that the true center of Christendom had moved from Rome to Constantinople to Moscow, especially since 1453 with the Islamic conquests. Neither he nor his even more autocratic successor were about to allow problems in the Western church to influence them in the slightest.

Italy

"The home of the Renaissance" had suffered cruelly at the end of the fifteenth century from the ambitions of a series of unwanted guests. In contrast to the emerging territorial states to the north, Italy was still a land of dozens of small principalities and city-states, with a few large states such as the duchy of Milan, the kingdom of Naples and Sicily, the Papal States, and the prosperous republics of Florence and Venice. Queen Isabella of Castile's ambitious husband, Ferdinand of Aragon, was in control of Sardinia and Sicily and coveted Naples. Large French armies marched up and down the peninsula in 1494–1495 and 1499. Although only a few

major, pitched battles were fought, the French invasions changed forever the nature of Italian politics. Holy Roman Emperor Maximilian I also had his Italian ambitions and he certainly did not want his Valois rivals to have the upper hand in the Italian north. The divisions in Italy were an invitation to invasion and foreign domination in the dog-eat-dog world of early modern politics.

When King Louis XII (r. 1498–1515) ascended the French throne he felt determined to assert his claim to the rich duchy of Milan in the Po River Valley. Louis's grandmother was the daughter of the last Visconti duke, Giangeleazzo (1476–1494). In his eyes the Sforza family then in control of Milan were usurpers with no legitimate claim to the Milanese throne. The extravagant Ludovico il Moro (r. 1494–1500) had taken power as regent for his teenage nephew. Although Ludovico and his talented wife, Beatrice d'Este of Ferrara (1475–1497), had established one of the more spectacular Renaissance courts, graced by the likes of Leonardo da Vinci, his double-dealing had earned the wrath of the French and many in Italy. After having invited the French to invade in 1494, Ludovico had turned against them and sided with their enemies. Louis XII was determined to win a reputation for himself as a warrior and, among other things, punish the treacherous duke.

Having secured diplomatic support from the Papal States, then under the rule of the devious and corrupt Alexander VI (r. 1492–1503), Florence, and Venice, Louis launched his invasion in the fall of 1499. Ludovico's forces collapsed quickly after heavy artillery bombardment and the desertion to the French of two of their top commanders. Ludovico fled to Austria to attempt to hire fresh mercenaries. Back in Italy, he lost the battle of Novara on April 8, 1500. Ludovico's Swiss mercenaries, disgruntled over disruptions in their sched-

Renaissance Italy

uled payments, refused to fight at Novara against their fellow Swiss in the employ of the French. Hired troops have always been primarily motivated by money and are notoriously fickle. As the astute political theorist Niccolò Machiavelli (1469–1527) observed, "gold is not sufficient to find good soldiers, but good soldiers are easily sufficient to find gold."[5]

Ludovico was later again betrayed by his hired help, who sold him to the French. They in turn shipped him off to France where he died eight years later in a French dungeon. As for King Louis XII of France, he marched further south after signing a Treaty of Granada with the artful Ferdinand of Aragon (one of Machiavelli's models for *The Prince*). Louis and Ferdinand agreed in November 1500 to partition Naples between them rather than fight over it. Emperor Maximilian I was embroiled with his mighty subjects in Germany, who were quarrelling with him about sharing power in competing visions of imperial reform. He could do nothing to stop his rivals in Italy. The active and huge port city of Naples fell easily to the French and Spanish, but soon the victors began to argue over the fruits of conquest. By January 1, 1504, the Aragonese had driven the French out of Naples.

The papacy had been the most immediate benefactor of the French invasion of 1499. Using French and Swiss cavalry, Cesare Borgia (1476–1507) had managed to conquer the Romagna north and east of Rome and began to threaten prosperous Florence. Cesare was the most unsavory of Pope Alexander VI's children. He had been made a cardinal at age fourteen, but lacked even the slightest inclination for church work. Instead, his indulgent father used the resources of the church to provide Cesare with a French royal bride and land in central Italy to create a permanent duchy for him where none existed. At the height of his power, Cesare's father died, only to be eventually succeeded by the Borgias' greatest enemy, Giuliano della Rovere, known as Pope Julius II (r. 1503–1513), the warrior-pope. Without papal income, Cesare's empire quickly collapsed and he was imprisoned in 1504. He died three years later in Spain. Cesare's lack of scruples and vicious personality also influenced Machiavelli in his thinking about Renaissance princes as strange combinations of lions and foxes.

With the death of Alexander VI and the fall of his son Cesare, Pope Julius II became a dominant figure in Italian politics. Although in his early sixties, "Papa Terrible" (as he became known for the dread he inspired) possessed incredible reserves of energy and was determined to expand the power of the Papal States in central Italy. He made a show of force in Romagna and Emilia and bound those principalities to him before marching against Bologna, which surrendered to him in November 1506. Machiavelli, as a representative of the Florentine government, accompanied Julius on several of his campaigns and came away impressed with the foxy old papal lion. Julius then joined the French, Emperor Maximilian, and Ferdinand of Aragon in the League of Cambrai (November 1508) against

Unknown, *Portrait of Cesare Borgia*. Accademia Carra, Bergamo, Italy. Alinari/Art Resource.

the arrogant Venetian republic. The French feared Venice as an important rival for influence in northern Italy; the emperor was still smarting after having lost Trieste and Fiume to the Venetians after his own ill-fated invasion of Italy in 1508. Maximilian hoped to use Trieste and Fiume to challenge Venetian trade in the Adriatic. For his part, Pope Julius wanted to reduce Venetian influence in the Romagna. As for the Aragonese, they were eager to regain the seaports in the kingdom of Naples which the Venetians had occupied.

With such a powerful combination arrayed against them, even the wealthy Venetians were unable to mobilize sufficient land forces, although Venice remained a naval power to be reckoned with. Venice was crushed on land at Agnadello in May 1509 and forced to cede all their mainland possessions. Having consolidated his hold over the Romagna, Julius II now used his influence in an effort to unite the Italians against the French, his recent allies. His "Holy League," designed to liberate Italy from the French "barbarians," included such non-Italians as Ferdinand of Aragon, the Swiss, and Henry VIII of England. The French fought the Aragonese and papal forces in April 1512 outside Ravenna. Although they won the bloody battle, it cost them their top general, Gaston de Foix, and they took heavy casualties. Gunpowder weapons and better-cast cannons had increased the lethality of warfare. Sensing the vulnerability of the over-extended French, the Swiss rushed down the Saint Gotthard Pass through the Alps and stunned the French at Novara. Ludovico il Moro and Beatrice d'Este's son was made puppet duke of Milan, which the Swiss controlled to expand their trade with Italy.

The French invasions also had an impact upon the great art and commercial center of Florence. Since 1502 the Florentine republic, dominated by wealthy merchant families and guildsmen, had limped along under the nominal leadership of Piero Soderini (1452–1522). In August 1512 the Aragonese moved up from the south and captured little Prato, not far from Florence, from the retreating French. Florence was de-fended from the Spanish by a militia force that had been recruited by Niccolò Machiavelli. In the face of disciplined Spanish infantry, the Florentine militia fled in disarray. If mercenaries were often unreliable, so too, at times, were citizen militias, especially when badly led and up against seasoned and relatively well trained regular troops. The result was that Piero Soderini's republic was overthrown.

The Spanish decided that stability would best be assured by a restoration of the Medici banking family, which had dominated Florentine political life for much of the fifteenth century and been such important patrons of the arts. The Medici clan was now led by the two remaining sons of Lorenzo de' Medici (1449–1492), Cardinal Giovanni de' Medici and his younger brother Giuliano (r. 1512–1516). When Pope Julius II died in February 1513, Giovanni de' Medici succeeded him as Pope Leo X (r. 1513–1521). Even as pope, Leo X continued to exert authority in Florence, using his nephew Lorenzo (1492–1519) as his surrogate. Such a great distraction probably did little to help the pleasure-loving pope in dealing with the call for reform and the subsequent crisis involving an obscure theology professor in remote Saxony named Martin Luther.

Chronology

1340–1384	Reign of Margaret of Denmark.
1356	Golden Bull of Nuremberg.
1453	Fall of Constantinople to Mehmed the Conqueror.
1469	Marriage of Isabella of Castile to Ferdinand of Aragon.
1485–1509	Reign of Henry VII in England.
1492	Fall of Granada; expulsions of Jews from Spain; first voyage of Christopher Columbus.
1493–1519	Reign of Maximilian I as Holy Roman emperor.
1494	Invasion of Italy by King Charles VIII of France.
1499	Invasion of Italy by King Louis XII of France.
1500	Defeat of Ludovico il Moro at Novara; Treaty of Granada partitions Naples between the French and the Aragonese.

1502–1512	Piero de Soderini in power in Florence.		**1513**	Death of Julius II; beginning of reign of Pope Leo X.
1503	Death of Pope Alexander VI (Borgia); beginning of reign of Pope Julius II.		**1515–1547**	Reign of François I of France.
1504	Fall of Cesare Borgia; French driven out of Naples; death of Isabella of Castile.		**1515**	Battle of Marignano; French take Milan.
1505–1533	Reign of Vasili III.		**1516**	Death of Ferdinand of Aragon; Charles of Habsburg becomes king of Spain.
1509–1547	Reign of Henry VIII in England.			
1510	Holy League in Italy against France.		**1519**	Death of Maximilian I; Charles of Habsburg becomes Holy Roman emperor.
1511	Polish peasants bound to the soil.		**1523**	Christian II of Denmark deposed; breakup of the Union of Kalmar; Gustavus Vasa becomes king of Sweden.
1512	Medici returned to power in Florence.			

Further Reading

GENERAL

Richard Bonney, *The European Dynastic States 1494–1660* (1991).

Joycelyne Russell, *Peacemaking in the Renaissance* (1986).

FRANCE

Christopher Allmand, *Power, Culture, and Religion in France c. 1360–1550* (1989).

Frederic Baumgartner, *France in the Sixteeenth Century* (1995).

———, *Louis XII* (1994).

Richard Jackson, *Vive Le Roi: A History of the French Coronation Ceremony from Charles V to Charles X* (1984).

R. J. Knecht, *Renaissance Warrior and Patron: The Reign of Francis I*, 2nd ed. (1994).

Howell Lloyd, *The State, France and the Sixteenth Century* (1983).

J. H. M. Salmon, *Society in Crisis: France in the Sixteenth Century* (1975).

ENGLAND

S. B. Chrimes, *Henry VII* (1973).

John Guy, *Tudor England* (1988).

J. J. Scarisbrick, *Henry VIII* (1968). Still the leading biography.

Arthur Slavin, *The Tudor Age and Beyond: England from the Black Death to the End of the Age of Elizabeth* (1987).

Lacey Baldwin Smith, *Henry VIII: The Mask of Royalty* (1971).

SPAIN

Felipe Fernández-Armesto, *Ferdinand and Isabella* (1975).

Stephen Haliczer, *The Comuneros of Castile: The Forging of a Revolution, 1475–1521* (1981).

Peggy Liss, *Isabel the Queen: Life and Times* (1992).

A. W. Lovett, *Early Habsburg Spain, 1517–1598* (1986).

John Lynch, *Spain under the Habsburgs*, vol. I, *Empire and Absolutism, 1516–1598*, 2nd ed. (1981).

THE HOLY ROMAN EMPIRE

Manuel Fernández Alvarez, *Charles V: Elected Emperor and Hereditary Ruler* (1975).

Gerhard Benecke, *Maximilian I (1459–1519), An Analytical Biography* (1982).

Karl Brandi, *The Emperor Charles V*, tr. by C. V. Wedgwood (1939).

F. R. H. Du Boulay, *Germany in the Late Middle Ages* (1983).

Michael Hughes, *Early Modern Germany, 1477–1806* (1992).

Joachim Leuschner, *Germany in the Late Middle Ages* (1980).

Jonathan Zophy, *An Annotated Bibliography of the Holy Roman Empire* (1986).

———, ed., *The Holy Roman Empire: A Dictionary Handbook* (1980). Succinct essays and bibliographies by thirty contributors.

THE LOW COUNTRIES

Sherrin Marshall, *The Dutch Gentry, 1500–1650: Family, Faith and Fortune* (1987).

James Tracy, *Holland under Habsburg Rule 1505–1566: the Formation of a Body Politic* (1990).

Jan de Vries, *The Dutch Rural Economy in the Golden Age, 1500–1700* (1974).

NORTHERN AND EASTERN EUROPE

Peter Brock, *The Political and Social Doctrines of the Unity of the Czech Brethren in the Fifteenth and Early Sixteenth Centuries* (1957).

R. J. W. Evans and T. V. Thomas, eds., *Crown, Church and Estates: Central European Politics in the Sixteenth and Seventeenth Centuries* (1991). A challenging collection of essays.

David Kirby, *Northern Europe in the Early Modern Period: the Baltic World, 1492–1772* (1990).

Paul Knoll, *The Rise of the Polish Monarchy* (1972).

Nancy Shields, *The Making of the Muscovite Political System, 1345–1547* (1987).

Peter Sugar, *Southeastern Europe under Ottoman Rule, 1354–1804* (1977).

ITALY

Denys Hay and John Law, *Italy in the Age of the Renaissance* (1989).

Michael Mallett, *Mercenaries and Their Masters: Warfare in Renaissance Italy* (1984).

Garrett Mattingly, *Renaissance Diplomacy* (1955).

Christine Shaw, *Julius II, The Warrior Pope* (1993).

Notes

1. Cited in J. J. Scarisbrick, *Henry VIII* (Berkeley: University of California Press, 1968), p. 79.
2. Cited in Jonathan W. Zophy, *Patriarchal Politics and Christoph Kress (1484–1535) of Nuremberg* (Lewiston, N. Y.: Edwin Mellen Press, 1992), p. 28.
3. Cited in Ibid., p. 72.
4. Figures cited in Michael Metcalf, "Scandinavia, 1397–1560," in Thomas Brady, Heiko Oberman, James Tracy, eds., *Handbook of European History*, 2 vols. (Leiden: E. J. Brill, 1994 and 1995), II, 525.
5. Cited in Sebastian de Grazia, *Machiavelli in Hell* (Princeton, N.J.: Princeton University Press, 1989), p. 167.

4

THE CALL FOR REFORM

Europe in 1500 was in a delicate state of equilibrium. Economic uncertainties, political upheavals, and social tensions permeated European society. The maldistribution of privilege and wealth rankled many. Great enmity had developed between artisans and wealthy merchants. They in turn resented the privileges of the nobility, some of whom were jealous of the growing wealth of some of the leading merchants. Nearly every economic, social, political, and religious group had its own reform program. No element of European life seemed to be immune from criticism. Complaints about corruption in the Roman Catholic church had been reverberating through Europe for centuries, even though many people were satisfied with the performances of their local clergy. Since religion was so central to the lives of sixteenth-century Europeans, it was in the church that the call for reform had its greatest impact.

Late Medieval Critics of the Church

The fourteenth century was an age of disasters for medieval Europe. One of the first was the movement of the headquarters of the Roman Catholic church from Rome to Avignon in 1305. The popes stayed at Avignon until 1376 in what the influential Ital-

ian humanist Francesco Petrarca (1304–1374) dubbed the "Babylonian Captivity of the church of God," an allusion to the period in which the Hebrews of the Old Testament had been held captive in Babylon.

The fourteenth century "Babylonian Captivity" began in the reign of Pope Boniface VIII (r. 1294–1303), who wanted to increase papal revenues and expand papal power. His plans for a strengthened papal monarchy ran afoul of two equally ambitious sovereigns: King Philip IV the Handsome of France (r. 1285–1314) and King Edward I of England (r. 1272–1307). Both were engaged in expensive efforts to expand their realms and were seeking new sources of revenue to pay for a war against each other. They decided to access the wealth of the church by taxing the clergy in their lands and they did not bother to seek papal approval. Incensed by such audacity, Pope Boniface issued the bull *Clericus laicos*, which forbade taxation of the clergy without papal approval and threatened both kings with *excommunication* if they did not stop. To be excommunicated was to be deprived of the blessings of the sacraments and guaranteed damnation. It was a threat that Boniface's great papal heroes Gregory VII (r. 1073–1085) and Innocent III (r. 1198–1216) had used to force several medieval monarchs to change their policies on a number of occasions.

Since the heyday of papal power in the high Middle Ages (eleventh through thirteenth centuries), circumstances had changed most notably in the rise of power of the territorial state. Philip and Edward had achieved a great deal more control over their feudal vassals than had the contemporaries of Gregory and Innocent. In fact, by and large the nobility of France and England supported their sovereigns' defiance of the authority of the pope. King Philip stopped all papal revenues from leaving his kingdom for Rome and Boniface was forced into a humiliating retreat.

Several years later Boniface felt strengthened by the enormous success of the church jubilee celebrations for the year 1300, which brought large numbers of devout pilgrims to Rome and swelled papal revenues enormously. In 1302 he issued the papal bull *Unam Sanctam* in which he asserted the fullness of papal power and proclaimed "that all human creation be subject to the pope of Rome."[1] Alarmed by these new papal pretensions, Philip decided to take the offensive in turning French public opinion against Boniface. He summoned representatives of the clergy, nobility, and merchants and accused the pope of such hideous crimes as practicing black magic, sodomy, murder, and keeping a demon as a pet. The king's agents had been spreading similar wild stories about Boniface for years, so it is not surprising that the representative of the French estates should have agreed to support their king in his struggle with the "evil pope."

Philip followed up on his carefully orchestrated propaganda campaign against the papacy by dispatching armed men to Italy to confront Boniface at his villa outside Rome. After pillaging the papal residence,

Philip's men tried to force the aging pontiff to return with them to France to stand trial for his "crimes." Although Boniface was rescued from French hands three days later, he never recovered from the shock and humiliation and died a few weeks after his ordeal. Philip quickly took advantage of the vacant papal throne by supporting the election of a Frenchman, Clement V (r. 1305–1314). Two years later Clement moved the papal headquarters from often turbulent and faction-ridden Rome to Avignon, a sleepy town on the Rhone River very near the borders of France.

Clement V's successors remained in Avignon for the next seventy years, building up a new papal infrastructure of churches, offices, and palaces. New revenues were needed to finance this building boom as well as to pay for mercenaries in order to reassert papal authority over abandoned Rome. The church had to make up for revenues lost in central Italy. This put enormous pressure on the papacy to continue the practice of selling church offices (*simony*). Noble families throughout Europe were eager to place their younger sons in sometimes lucrative church jobs whether or not the young men in question had a religious vocation or not. Sometimes individuals held several offices (pluralism) and *benefices* (an endowment that supported an office) at the same time. Multiple offices led to the problem of absenteeism and the hiring of deputies to perform the actual duties. The upper ranks of the clergy had come to be dominated by the wealthy and socially prominent elite.

THE WESTERN SCHISM (1378–1417)

Finally, in 1376 Pope Gregory XI (r. 1370–1378) brought the papacy back to Rome. Appalled by the turbulent conditions in Rome, Pope Gregory planned to return the papacy to Avignon, but died before he could complete the move. He was succeeded by an Italian reformer, Pope Urban VI (r. 1378–1389). Urban attempted to curb the power and wealth of the cardinals, many of whom resisted his efforts. A group of primarily French cardinals declared Urban's election invalid because of mob duress and elected Robert, cardinal of French-speaking Geneva in Switzerland, as pope and returned with him to Avignon. Urban VI refused to accept his deposition or the validity of the new election. He appointed a group of new cardinals to replace those who had left. Thus began the great Western Schism, which did much more damage to the church than had the Captivity.

For the next thirty-seven years, the Roman Catholic church was torn between a succession of rival popes each claiming to be the lawful successor to St. Peter, the first bishop of Rome, while damning his rival as the anti-Christ. Excommunications were hurled back and forth between Rome and Avignon for decades. Such churlish behavior only added to the confusion of many western Europeans. Painful choices had to be made about which pope to support. France backed the French popes at Avignon, as did Aragon, Castile, Naples, Navarre, Portugal, Scotland, and Sicily. Since England was fighting France in the Hundred Years' War (1337–1453), it stayed loyal to the popes in Rome, as did parts of the Holy Roman Empire, Ireland, Flanders, and northern and central Italy. Some individuals and states shifted from one side to another as it suited their particular interests. Many wondered if their immortal souls might be in danger should the sacraments in their church be performed by a false priest ordained by a false bishop loyal to a false pope. A quiet feeling of disgust settled on Europe like a fog.

As the schism dragged on with no end in sight, thoughtful Christians began to suggest that the only solution was for a general church council to meet and settle the matter. Neither the pope in Avignon or the one in Rome would agree to break the stalemate and allow their clerical "inferiors" to decide the matter in convocation. The situation got even worse in 1409 when 500 prelates meeting at a council at Pisa decided to depose both sitting popes and elect a new one. Neither the Roman pontiff nor the one in Avignon would accept deposition or recognize the authority of the council. So for a short period, Europe had three popes, each claiming to be the only supreme head of the church on earth. Three such popes were not three times better than one.

Finally, the Holy Roman Emperor Sigismund of Luxembourg (r. 1411–1437) reluctantly agreed to break the impasse and in 1414 summoned important church leaders from all over Europe to the Swiss town of Constance for a great council that lasted until 1418. At Constance, assembled church dignitaries voted to depose all of the existing popes and elect a new pope, Martin V (r. 1417–1431). Although none of the existing popes wanted to step down, none of them had the necessary political and financial support to stay in power. The Western Schism had ended, but not without having done irreparable harm to the Roman Catholic church.

MARSILIUS OF PADUA (c. 1280–1342)

Even before Emperor Sigismund decided to act, serious questions about the governance of the church and its relation to the state had been raised by the physician-philosopher Marsilius of Padua. Very little is known about his life other than that he had been trained in medicine before becoming rector of the University of Paris in 1313, one of the highest administrative offices. At Paris, he completed his most important work, *The Defender of the Peace*, in 1324.

Marsilius was deeply concerned about the recent confrontation between Philip IV and Boniface VIII as well as a contemporary challenge to the election of Holy Roman Emperor Lewis of Bavaria (r. 1314–1346) by Pope John XXII (r. 1316–1334), who supported a Habsburg rival. Marsilius was also influenced by the three-decades-long struggle of the city of Padua to bring the clergy under civil control. He wrote *The Defender of the Peace* in an effort to find "tranquility . . . the highest temporal good . . . the truth which leads to the salvation of civil life, and which is also of no little help for eternal salvation."[2]

His fundamental idea was that all coercive power on earth lay with "the people"; the people as "human legislator" were the source of all worldly authority, not the "head bishop" in Rome. Therefore, the church must be subject to the state, which has the greater responsibility for maintaining law and order. Marsilius also asserted that a general church council, rather than the pope, should govern the church because councils represented the body of the faithful better than a single man. Since these ideas were considered by leading papal supporters to be subversive, Marsilius was forced to flee from his university post in Paris and take refuge with Emperor Lewis of Bavaria, who was pleased to have such a prominent intellectual confirm his feeling that he was superior to the pope.

The Defender of the Peace had an immediate and lasting impact. The work was condemned by the pope in 1326, but translated into French and Italian in 1363. An English translation appeared in 1535 and a German version came out in 1545. Its conclusions were often shared orally for their shock value or used by conciliar thinkers to bolster their position during the schism. Many of those who pressured Emperor Sigismund to convene the Council of Constance used arguments similar to those advanced by Marsilius. When popes, cardinals, and writers concerned about preserving the social order wished to condemn heretics such as John Wycliffe, Jan Hus, and Martin Luther, they charged them with having gotten their ideas from the "accursed Marsilius."[3]

JOHN WYCLIFFE (c. 1320–1384)

Among those intellectuals influenced by the ideas of Marsilius of Padua was a mild-mannered Oxford professor named John Wycliffe. Wycliffe came from a modest landed family in Yorkshire and came to have a distinguished academic career at Oxford, England's oldest university. He earned a B.A. in divinity there in 1368, and then a doctorate in 1372. Although granted a number of church positions, Wycliffe was a frequently absent cleric. He neglected his flock for his greater passion for scholarship. Oxford was his true home and Wycliffe loved being a professor.

His intensive studies of the Bible and scholastic theology led him to a number of the same conclusions as Marsilius of Padua and the equally controversial English Franciscan William of Ockham (c. 1290–1349). He agreed to some degree with William's nominalist position that universal ideas were not things (*res*) in the Platonic sense, but rather names (*nomen*) for abstractions which may or may not be ultimate realities. This theory of knowledge (also called the modern way or *via moderna*) had implications for theology. William of Ockham and John Wycliffe thought that religious belief had to be based largely on faith and that God's will is inscrutable and His power limitless.

Wycliffe also asserted that the lawful exercise of lordship, or dominion over men and women, depends on the righteousness of the person who exercises it. Like the non-theologically trained Marsilius of Padua, the Oxford don appealed to the authority of Scripture and secular authority rather than to canon law and papal power. Pope Gregory XI (r. 1370–1378) complained that Wycliffe was attempting "to overthrow the status of the whole church" by teaching the "opinions and ignorant doctrine of Marsilius of Padua."[4]

Wycliffe's disenchantment with the papacy had only been increased by the outbreak of the Western Schism in 1378 and the financial demands that Pope Gregory made upon the English clergy to support him in his war with the Milanese. In his published work from Oxford, Wycliffe attacked the wealth and worldliness of the Latin church, thus tapping into the anticlericalism that lurked below the surface in all European societies. In his revolutionary tract *On Simony*, Wycliffe argued that the church is essentially spiritual in nature and therefore has no right to extensive property and power in the secular world. Asserting that the church had grown rich at the expense of the poor, he concluded that the sale of church offices was the root cause of church corruption. Wycliffe also objected to elaborate church ceremonies, rites, and rituals as unnecessary. For him, salvation comes not through the sacraments, but through divine grace and mercy alone.

From the perspective of the Roman Catholic leadership, Wycliffe failed to appreciate the church's need for income if it was to render necessary services and maintain its independence from competing secular authorities who coveted church lands. Without continuing income, how was the church to care for the poor or run hospitals? The threat to their own lives of privilege, the sometimes opulent lifestyles which included handsome palaces and dozens of assistants and servants, must have been clearly understood if not openly acknowledged. Wycliffe was seen as more than a misguided, impractical intellectual; he was viewed as a dangerous heretic who infects others and threatens social order. Wycliffe's ideas were condemned as heretical by the English bishops, but he found protection for a while from John of Gaunt, duke of Lancaster and brother of King Edward III (r. 1327–1377). The unscrupulous Gaunt had his own interests in attacking the wealth and power of the English church.

John of Gaunt later deserted Wycliffe when he began to publish his Marsilian theory that the church was a community of true believers and to question *transubstantiation* (which asserts that the bread and wine are transformed into the body and blood of Christ in the Eucharist, while retaining their outward appearance). Wycliffe's reputation as a troublemaker was enhanced by the English Peasants' Revolt of 1381, which some unfairly blamed him for because of his attacks on authority. He was placed under house arrest at the rectory at Luttersworth in 1382, where he died and was buried in 1384. In 1428 after additional condemnations by the Council of Constance and elsewhere, the bishop of Lincoln had Wycliffe's bones dug up and cast into the river Swift.

Despite these efforts to eradicate his memory and his writings, Wycliffe continued to exert an influence on English church life. His English translation of the Bible proved popular even after his death. Wycliffe's followers were called "Lollards" by their enemies for their use of English in church services rather than the accustomed sound of Latin. They managed to survive as an underground movement despite persecutions sanctioned by King Henry IV (r. 1399–1413) after 1401. Although it is difficult to assess the impact of Lollardy on the sixteenth-century Reformation, there is no question that many of Wycliffe's ideas were similar to those raised by Martin Luther, John Calvin, and others.

JAN HUS (c. 1372–1415)

Wycliffe's most influential immediate disciple proved to be a Czech cleric named Jan Hus, who was burned to death as an infamous heretic by the reform Council of Constance. What had he done to deserve such a death voted for by even some of those who agreed with Marsilius of Padua? The search for answers goes back to Hus's youth as a poor peasant lad encouraged by his mother and a local priest to escape from a life of rural poverty in southern Bohemia by entering the service of holy mother church. As a boy, he had excelled in school; his superior intelligence was obvious. In 1390 Jan enrolled in the recently founded Charles University in Prague, the capital of Bohemia. Universities had proven to be useful institutions for improving minds and training professionals. By the time of the Renaissance, progressive rulers all over Europe were eager to add to their status by establishing them. At Prague, Hus proved his mettle on the advanced level and earned his M.A. in 1396 and an appointment to the faculty, where the handsome Hus became an exceptionally eloquent and popular lecturer, the standard method of instruction.

Partly in order to advance his career, Hus became a priest in 1400. In studying for the priesthood, the young Czech became a serious student of the Bible. He wrote of this new sense of purpose: "When the Lord gave me knowledge of the Scriptures, I discarded from my mind all foolish fun-making."[5] Already well known as a dynamic university lecturer, Hus now gained additional fame as a preacher, who dared to preach in the vernacular and not just in Latin. Useful political connections followed, and in 1401 he be-

came the confessor to Queen Sophia of Bohemia. She also came to hear him preach at the new Bethlehem Chapel in the heart of Prague.

His talent, fame, good appearance, and influential patrons might have eventually made him a privileged man in the church, but Hus's mind was increasingly disturbed by the radical notions of John Wycliffe and others, especially the dangerous idea that all church doctrines should be based on the Bible. The marriage between Anne of Bohemia and King Richard II of England had increased the traffic in people and ideas between the two lands and their universities. Czech students such as Jerome of Prague studied at Oxford and shared their copies of Wycliffe's writings with Hus. Hus wrote of his debt to Wycliffe:

> I am attracted by his writings, in which he makes every effort to lead all men back to the law of Christ, and especially the clergy, inviting them to abandon pomp and dominion of the world, and live, like the apostles, according to the law of Christ.[6]

Many of Hus's German colleagues on the faculty were appalled by his echoing of Wycliffe's call for fundamental changes in the church. The dispute over reform threatened to tear apart the university, particularly as it also began to touch on the subject of who was to control the university itself as well as the Roman Catholic church in Bohemia. Hus had become the most prominent faculty spokesperson for the cause of the Czech-speaking students.

Finally, in January 1409 King Wenceslaus IV, Emperor Sigismund's brother, and a supporter of Hus and moderate reform, issued a decree that gave the Czech-speaking student "nation" at the university three votes for every German one, a complete reversal of the previous situation. The Czechs were now poised to take control of the university after years of German domination. This sudden change and the fear that Hus was a dangerous radical resulted in many of the German students and faculty leaving Prague and founding a new university 150 miles away in Leipzig at the invitation of a Saxon duke. On October 17, 1409, the new Czech national hero, Jan Hus, was elected rector of the Charles University at Prague, its highest administrative office.

Despite his great popularity and new position, Hus still had his enemies among the local clergy, and they urged Archbishop Zbynek to proceed against him as a dangerous heretic in the Wycliffite mold. He was in fact the most prominent defender of Wycliffe's ideas in Prague and had called for vernacular translations of the Bible and lay communion with cup and bread. Hus had spoken and written in favor of Wycliffe's notion of the universal priesthood of all believers, the idea that each person has a direct spiritual relationship with Christ, who is seen as the sole head of the church. To some, this doctrine threatened the power of ordained clergy as intercessors between the laity and God and made the hierarchy of church office holders appear unnecessary. Zbynek also charged Hus with teaching that papal excommunications were invalid and that priests in mortal sin could not effectively administer the sacraments (Donatism). Donatism had been officially condemned in the fourth century as heresy.

Hus also preached against the sale of *indulgences*, which were relaxations of some of the penalties in purgatory for sin. The church taught that most people are not ready for heaven or not sinful enough for hell when they die. Instead, a truly penitent sinner goes to a cleansing place known as purgatory to have the soul purified in preparation for admission to heaven. Indulgences were being sold to finance a crusade against the Christian king of Naples, a political rival of one of the schismatic popes.

Hus's preaching against indulgences not only threatened one of the papal revenue streams, but also that of King Wenceslaus, who had been assured a percentage of the profits for the indulgences sold in Bohemia. The king's former support of Hus evaporated rapidly. In July 1410, Zbynek ordered Wycliffe's books burned and excommunicated Hus.

Hus continued his call for reform. The archbishop retaliated by placing the whole city under interdict on June 20, 1411. The interdict was a general form of excommunication which closed all churches, and stopped all baptisms, marriages, and church burials. It threatened everyone in Prague with eternal damnation. Not wishing to cause such great harm to Prague, Hus left the city in October 1412 at the suggestion of King Wenceslaus. For the next year and a half, he preached and wrote in his homeland of southern Bohemia, winning many new friends and followers to the cause of church reform. During this period he also wrote a major treatise, *On the Church* (1413), which summed up many of his major ideas and was the chief source for his condemnation at the Council of Constance.

Hus was summoned to the great reform council at Constance by his king's brother, Emperor Sigismund, who promised Hus that he would not be harmed. Hus was well aware of the risks of going to a church council and, therefore, made the appropriate farewells and arrangements at home. Since he did not think of himself or Wycliffe as heretics and was confident of his persuasive abilities, Hus was eager to discuss his views with a group, which would include some of the most progressive churchmen of his day. Despite the emperor's promises, Hus's teachings were condemned and he was imprisoned shortly after his arrival in Constance in October 1414. He languished there until June 1415 when he was finally brought before the council meeting in the great cathedral and allowed to speak before the same churchmen who had already condemned his writings. When Hus tried to explain the nature of his views about the church, he was shouted down by outraged churchmen. He complained to no avail, "In such a council as this, I had hoped to find more propriety, piety, and order."[7]

For the next four weeks, enormous pressure was placed on the condemned Czech to recant or deny his teachings. Brought to the cathedral of Constance for a final time on July 15, 1415, Hus was given one last chance to save his life if he would recant. Refusing, he was stripped of his clerical vestments, and a paper crown with three demons painted on it was put on his head with the words "We commit thy soul to the devil." Hus was then led to the town market square and burned alive. Fire was thought of as a cleansing element and to burn an unrepentant heretic like Hus was the only way to clean his soul and stop the spread of his contagious "infection." Shortly before his death, Hus was heard to say, "In the truth of that Gospel which I have written about, taught, and preached, I now die."[8]

Nine months later Jerome of Prague, Hus's colleague and friend, was also burned at the stake. Four hundred and fifty-two Bohemian nobles sent an indignant protest to the council and the emperor. Sigismund, angered by this challenge to his judgment, foolishly replied that he would very soon "drown all Wycliffites and Hussites." This was too much of an insult for the Czechs to bear from an emperor who had executed two of their national heroes. Rebellion soon raged throughout Bohemia, and King Wenceslaus was unable to restore order.

Emperor Sigismund and Pope Martin V proclaimed a crusade against the Hussites, who found superb military leadership in Jan Zizka (1376–1424). Crusade after crusade was defeated by the resourceful Czechs, even after they had split into two major factions: the *Utraquists*, who believed in lay communion in both kinds (bread and wine), and the *Taborites*, who recognized only the two biblically based sacraments of baptism and the Eucharist and wanted simple, early church-style ceremonies. Finally in 1434, the Utraquists decisively defeated the Taborites and got the Council of Basel to allow them to continue celebrating the Eucharist, with the laity receiving both the bread and the wine. Having been unable to enforce uniformity in church doctrine by the sword, church leadership had negotiated a unique settlement that kept Bohemia nominally under the spiritual direction of Rome.

The Failure of Reform Councils

The Council of Basel (1431–1449) in Switzerland, while achieving a measure of reconciliation with the Hussites, failed to substantially reform the church as had the councils at Pisa and Constance. Enthusiasm was already waning for the theories of the conciliarists, especially in the face of continued papal opposition. Even though the Council of Constance had decreed that a general church council derives its authority directly from Christ, and therefore the entire church was bound by its decisions, the pope elected by that council believed in papal supremacy and did his best to undermine the conciliar theories of Marsilius of Padua and others.

The Council of Constance had also declared in 1417 that the general council should meet frequently (*Frequens*), but popes stopped calling councils on a regular basis after Basel. The papacy also failed to implement most of the reform measures called for at Constance and elsewhere. The Council of Florence (1439–1442) did conduct important negotiations with the Eastern Orthodox church, but failed to achieve much in the way of reform. Even the progressive humanist Aeneas Silvius, when he became Pope Pius II (r. 1458–1464), condemned councils in his bull *Execrabilis*:

> The execrable and hitherto unknown abuse has grown up in our day, that certain persons, imbued with the spirit of rebellion, and not from a desire to secure a better judgment, but to escape the punishment of some offence which they have committed, presume to appeal from the pope to a future council, in spite of the fact that the pope is the vicar of Christ.[9]

Although Pius II was not unaware of the need for reform, he was obsessed with the idea of mounting a crusade against the Ottomans who had taken Constantinople in 1453 and were beginning to threaten to overrun all of eastern Europe. He failed to convince the crowned heads of Europe to support a new round of crusading and died frustrated. Frustration was nothing new to many others in the fifteenth century, such as the friar Girolamo Savonarola, who urgently renewed the call for reform.

Savonarola (1452–1498) versus Pope Alexander VI (r. 1492–1503)

In 1496 the charismatic Dominican preacher Savonarola wrote in his *A Compendium of Revelations*:

> I continually set forth three things: first, that the renovation of the church would come about in these times; second, that all of Italy would be mightily scourged before God brought about this renovation; third, that these two things would come about soon.[10]

Savonarola's call for reform was a culmination of a long spiritual journey that began when he rejected the wishes of his parents and entered a Dominican friary in Bologna after having been rejected by a daughter of one of Italy's wealthiest merchant families, the Strozzi. Girolamo also came from a prominent family; his father was a court physician at Ferrara. After studying theology at Bologna and Ferrara, Savonarola came to San Marco's convent in Florence as a teacher and a preacher.

The gaunt, young ascetic found Renaissance Florence to be incredibly beautiful, but also shockingly sinful and worldly. Too him it seemed as if the prosperous Florentines worshipped money and art rather than God. Finding his voice as a popular preacher, Savonarola became disgusted by the extravagance and sensuality of the Medici and spoke of the fall of tyrants and the need for justice for the poor and oppressed. He also preached the need for a reformation of the clergy. The Roman church, he said, was "full of simony and evils" brought on in part by the "tonsured ones" and those of "lukewarm piety."[11]

Beginning in August of 1490, Savonarola began preaching dire warnings of coming disasters and urged the Florentines to repent of their sins. In his Lenten sermons of 1494, he called for the building of another Noah's ark against the floods to come. Then the Dominican, who had been prior of San Marco's since 1491, claimed to have had a vision in which he saw a hand bearing a flaming sword inscribed with the words: "The sword of the Lord will be over the earth swiftly and soon."[12] When news reached Florence in September 1494 that King Charles VIII (r. 1483–1498) had crossed the Alps and arrived in Italy with the largest army seen there since the days of the ancient Romans, the Florentines were terrified. It seemed to many that Savonarola's dark prophecies were coming true.

When Charles VIII entered Florence on November 17, 1494, it was the popular preacher who twice met with the young king and begged him to spare the city on the Arno which had just exiled its Medici rulers. The French decided not to sack the city and departed eleven days later. Florence became a less autocratic republic with greater representation on its ruling Great Council of 3,000 members. Savonarola proclaimed that "Florence will be even more glorious, richer, and more powerful than she has ever been."[13] He wanted to make Florence a "godly city," purged of its vices and sins and rendering justice to the downtrodden. Toward that end, in 1496 the Dominican sponsored a great "burning of the vanities" in which gambling equipment, jewelry, cosmetics, false hair and pads, musical instruments, and lewd books were put to the torch. Even a few paintings by the great Renaissance master Sandro Botticelli (c. 1444–1510), a pious follower of Savonarola's, were thrown on the bonfires.

Savonarola dreamed of not only cleansing Florence, but also of reforming the church as a whole, beginning at the top with the corrupt Pope Alexander VI. He called upon King Charles VIII to depose the Borgia pope. Alexander was born Rodrigo Borgia to a grasping Spanish family, many of whom had come to Rome to enrich themselves during the reign of Rodrigo's uncle Pope Calixtus III (r. 1455–1503). Rodrigo was a bright and talented young man who rose rapidly in church preferment under the benevolent patronage of his uncle. He was named a cardinal at age twenty-six and became papal vice-chancellor during the reign of Pope Pius II. Although Rodrigo behaved with discretion for the most part, Pius II did have to admonish him in June 1460 for having indulged in "licentious dances" and an "orgy" in Siena with several married women. As the pope, himself a former rake, wrote: "Our displeasure is beyond words. . . . A cardinal should be above reproach."[14]

This reprimand failed to harm Borgia's career or slow up his increasingly sensual appetites. He continued to enjoy the trust of a series of popes and to become one of the wealthiest men in Rome. The papacy itself reached a low ebb during the reign of Pope Sixtus IV (r. 1471–1478). Pope Sixtus resented bitterly the pretensions of the Medici and replaced them as papal bankers with the rival Pazzi family. Sixtus feared that Lorenzo de' Medici planned to expand Florence at the expense of the Papal States and gave his blessing to a plot to assassinate Lorenzo and his brother Giuliano during the celebration of High Mass in the cathedral of Florence in 1478. The assassins succeeded in murdering Giuliano, but Lorenzo escaped with wounds and rallied the Florentines to punish the conspirators, who included Archbishop Francesco Salviati and Francesco Pazzi. The archbishop and Pazzi were both hanged from the windows of the Florentine town hall. Other plotters were brutally murdered by angry mobs.

Pope Sixtus then retaliated by excommunicating Lorenzo de' Medici, imposing an interdict on Florence, and invading Tuscany with his Neapolitan allies. Florence fought off its attackers and two years later signed separate treaties with Naples and the Papal States. Among those concerned with ending the war with Florence was the vice-chancellor Rodrigo Borgia, who had become the second wealthiest member of the College of Cardinals. A contemporary wrote of him:

> He is a fluent speaker, writes well—though not in a literary style, is extremely astute and very energetic and skillful in business matters. He is enormously wealthy, and through his connections with kings and princes, commands great influence. He has built a beautiful and comfortable palace. . . . His revenues from his papal offices, his abbeys in Italy and Spain, his three bishoprics of Valencia, Portus and Cartagena, are vast. His office of Vice-Chancellor alone yields him 8000 gold

Arnolfo di Cambio, *Palazzo Vecchio* (Town Hall). Florence, Italy, Alinari/Art Resource.

ducats annually. His plate, his pearls, his shirts embroidered with silk and gold, his books are of such quality as would befit a king or a pope.[15]

Indeed, Borgia used his vast wealth in several efforts to bribe his way onto the throne of St. Peter's. He finally succeeded in August 1492 in outbribing his competitors and securing the papal tiara. An extremely elaborate coronation celebrated his accession to the papal fullness of power. As pope, Borgia used the additional wealth and prestige of the papacy to advance the careers of his four living children by his favorite mistress, the former inn-keeper Vanozza Catanei. Although some reports indicate that she lived like a queen, Vanozza stayed in the background for the most part and signed her letters to her papal daughter Lucretia, "Your fortunate and unfortunate mother."[16] Lucretia (1480–1519) was well educated and used as a pawn by her father, who contracted three successive political marriages for her. The last, in 1501 to Alfonso d'Este, made her duchess of Ferrara, where she proved to be a tasteful patron of the arts.

The worst of the papal brood was the vicious Cesare, who had been made a cardinal at age fourteen and then created duke of Valentinois. Following the murder of his oldest son with Vanozza, Juan, duke of Gandia, in June 1497, a temporarily penitent Pope Alexander VI vowed to cleanse the church of its accumulated moral lassitude. A commission of six cardinals was appointed to draw up a draft plan for the reformation of the church. Simony was especially to be condemned. Concubines were to be dismissed and frugality enforced upon the cardinals. All this would have meant a complete reversal of Alexander's way of life and the way he took care of himself and his family.

The bull authorizing those reforms was never issued; instead, Alexander VI excommunicated his harshest critic, Savonarola. He had earlier ordered "the meddlesome friar" to stop preaching. Enraged by the pope's efforts to silence him and scandalized by reports that the pope and his family had been involved in crimes ranging from incest to murder, Savonarola only intensified his verbal attacks on Alexander. Not only was the friar excommunicated in 1497, the pope threatened to place Florence under an interdict if Savonarola was allowed to preach again. Many among the Florentine elite, already jealous of the preacher's power over the people and fearing the loss of some of their favorite pleasures if his efforts to create a republic of virtue succeeded, began to plot Savonarola's fall.

Savonarola's popularity was undermined by a whisper campaign launched against him by his enemies. A severe economic crisis in the winter of 1497–1498 added to the city's misery. In the spring of 1498 rival Franciscans challenged Savonarola to an ordeal by fire. He was going to have to prove his faith by agreeing to walk on hot coals. When the day of the promised spectacle arrived, there were procedural arguments between the Franciscans and the Dominicans which resulted in a cancellation of the promised fire walk. Egged on by Savonarola's political enemies and disappointed that they had been denied a public entertainment, an angry mob turned against their former hero and called for his arrest. The government acted quickly in seizing the opportunity to rid themselves of the sincere but fanatical reformer. Savonarola was arrested and condemned to death by hanging. On May 23, 1498, after days of torture, Savonarola and two young supporters were hanged in the public square, the site of the famous "burning of the vanities." Alexander VI's fervent prayer had been answered.

The Importance of Printing

Although the papacy had hit a new low in sleaze during the reign of Alexander VI, many people in other parts of Europe had no idea that bull fights had been fought in the Vatican square and that the pope had openly celebrated the various marriages of his talented daughter Lucretia in the papal palace. Only later when Johannes Burchardus, Alexander's master of ceremonies, retired to Germany and published his *Diary* were some of the worst suspicions of those away from the papal court confirmed with juicy details. Burchardus, like other writers of the early sixteenth century, was able eventually to reach a much larger audience than even prominent fourteenth-century authors because of the remarkable impact of the printing press.

Moveable type did not appear in Europe until the time of Johann Gutenberg (c. 1398–1468) of Mainz, Germany. The son of a goldsmith, Gutenberg discovered an alloy of tin, iron, zinc, and lead that could be poured into iron and copper molds to form letters that would not shrink or twist upon cooling. The letters could be arranged and rearranged in various combinations to print books, which could now be produced for a fraction of the cost of producing hand-copied manuscripts. The demand for printed books proved to be insatiable and printing presses spread throughout Europe like wildfire. By 1480, there were over 380 working presses in Europe and by 1500 some nine million copies of forty thousand different titles were in circulation. Such was the piety of the day among the literate that half of the newly printed books were religious in subject matter. Many of them were written by the humanists and some of them contained urgent calls for a reform of the church.

The Challenge of the Humanists

Humanism was a movement that encouraged the study of classical learning in order to foster individual and societal improvement. In the process of trying to recapture something of classical literature, humanists sharpened their linguistic and rhetorical skills and used them as part of the larger movement for a reform of the church. For example, the Italian humanist Lorenzo Valla applied philological skills to biblical studies with the aim of providing a better and clearer source text. Like Savonarola, preachers such as Johann Geiler von Kaysersberg added emotional force to the call for reform. Erasmus of Rotterdam not only produced a valuable new translation of the New Testament, he also spoke to a wide range of issues involving the need for reform. Humanists like Johann Reuchlin attempted to stimulate an interest in Hebrew studies as a way of finding new understandings of Christian truth. Reuchlin stayed loyal to the Roman Catholic church, as did Erasmus.

LORENZO VALLA (c. 1407–1457)

Lorenzo Valla was one of the most able humanists to emerge from the Italian Renaissance. A native of Rome and the son of an ecclesiastical advocate, he studied under Vittorino da Feltre (1378–1447), the most celebrated schoolmaster in Renaissance Italy, and showed his unusual aptitude for Greek and Latin. He later taught eloquence at the universities of Pavia and Rome before becoming secretary to King Alfonso the Magnanimous of Naples. At the end of his life, he became secretary to Pope Nicholas V

(r. 1447–1455) and then Pope Calixtus III (r. 1455–1458), where he was instrumental in establishing the great Vatican Library.

Intellectually fearless, Valla sparked controversy throughout his career. In his *On Religious Vows*, Valla attacked the special claims to piety made by some members of religious orders. In discounting the merit of vows and emphasizing spiritual devotion over ritual action, he wrote, "It is not the external man but the inner one who pleases God."[17] In *On Free Will* Valla denied the possibility that faith could be reconciled with reason. Instead, he promoted an emphasis on faith and love, which he sharply contrasted with the intellectual approach taken by scholastic theologians such as Saint Thomas Aquinas. "I would prefer that those who are called theologians would not depend so much on philosophy or devote so much energy to it."[18]

In his *On the False Donation of Constantine* of 1440, Valla demonstrated through historical, linguistic, and logical analysis that the first Christian emperor could not possibly have been the author of the document which allegedly transferred the territorial sovereignty over the Western Roman Empire to the papacy. Valla's scholarship revealed that a number of terms used in the "Donation" were not in use until at least a century after the time of Constantine. He wondered: Would Constantine give up the best part of his empire? If the emperor did so, why is there no proof that it was received? The papacy was stung by this revelation and Pope Felix V (r. 1439–1449) summoned Valla to Rome, but he wisely elected to stay in Naples under the protection of King Alfonso, an enemy of the pope's.

Applying his critical methods to the Bible, Valla produced a highly influential *Annotations on the New Testament*, which demonstrated many errors in Saint Jerome's Vulgate translation of the Bible, the official

Bible of the Roman Catholic church, which he criticized as "barbarous." Jerome (c. 340–420) was one of the most celebrated biblical scholars of his day and one of the most important of the Latin fathers of the early church. Valla defended his own work stoutly by writing:

> If Jerome came back to life, he would correct what has been vitiated and corrupted in some places. . . . To say it briefly: If I emend the text, I do not emend Scripture but a translation of it. In doing so, I am not scornful, but rather pious, and I merely offer a better version than the previous translator.[19]

Valla's *Annotations* was known only in manuscript form to a limited circle until published by Erasmus in 1505. Erasmus then used Valla's work in producing his own remarkable translation of the New Testament in 1516, which in turn influenced the German translation by the reformer Martin Luther. Both Luther and John Calvin praised his work, while his writings were placed on the Index of Prohibited Books. Undaunted by his foes and protected by powerful patrons during his own lifetime, Valla defied his contemporary critics:

> I have published many books, a great many, in almost every branch of learning. In as much as there are those who are shocked that in these I disagree with certain great writers already approved by long usage, and charge me with rashness and sacrilege, what must we suppose some of them will do now![20]

JOHANN GEILER VON KAYSERSBERG (1445–1510)

Although the writings of intellectuals such as Lorenzo Valla were familiar to only a few among the elite, popular preachers such as Girolamo Savonarola and Johann Geiler von Kaysersberg initially reached a much larger

and more varied audience with their calls for reform. Geiler became the most famous preacher north of the Alps on the eve of the Reformation and his witty barbs had a devastating effect. He was raised by his grandfather in the town of Kaysersberg in Alsace after the death of his father, a city clerk, in a hunting accident. Following a brilliant student career at the University of Freiburg, Geiler was invited to stay on as a professor. After five years of teaching, he left for Basel, where he obtained a doctorate in theology in 1475. Brought back to Freiburg by the demand of students, Geiler was elected rector of the university in 1476.

Despite his successful academic career, he yearned for the pulpit rather than the lectern. In the pulpit, Geiler knew that he could reach a much broader spectrum of society than he could in the university. He eventually accepted an endowed position as the people's priest and preacher at the cathedral in Strasbourg, a bustling Alsatian imperial city. Increasingly, preaching was becoming a popular activity and a number of churches in the Holy Roman Empire had established endowed preacherships. While upholding many traditional church practices and doctrines, Geiler ridiculed the wrangling of various schools of Scholastic theology as cats "dragging a piece of cloth to and fro." He was even more indignant over the moral laxity of both the clergy and the laity. In his popular sermons Geiler attacked a host of church abuses, such as simony, in no uncertain terms: "If someone wants to become pope, he need only bribe the cardinals."[21]

A REFORM BISHOP: GUILLAUME BRIÇONNET (c. 1470–1534)

It should also be remembered that despite his outspokenness, Geiler enjoyed the full support of his local bishop. Many princes of the church shared the concerns of some of the humanists about problems in the church and some used their powers to combat abuses and encourage reforms in their dioceses. Guillaume Briçonnet provides an excellent example of a reform-minded prelate. He was the illegitimate son of a cardinal who turned to an ecclesiastical career after the death of his wife. Briçonnet first began his reform efforts as abbot of Saint-Germain-de-Prés and then continued them as bishop of Meaux, outside Paris.

Protected for a while by Queen Marguerite of Navarre, sister of King François I, he castigated the worldliness of the clergy: "Some have fallen so low that they lavish on their hunting dogs the care they should give to souls."[22] Among those Briçonnet brought to Meaux was the great humanist textual critic Jacques Lefèvre d'Etaples (c. 1460–1536), who was put in charge of clerical discipline. Nevertheless, without the help of a reform papacy and full political support, there were serious limits to what could be done on the local level. At one point, hostility to Briçonnet's reforms was so great that he was fined for having allowed "heresy" to spread in his diocese. For a while he fled to Strasbourg, where he came to know and influence a number of individuals who became prominent in the Reformation, including the reformers of Geneva, Guillaume Farel and John Calvin.

DESIDERIUS ERASMUS (c. 1467–1536)

Erasmus was the humanist reformer who ultimately exerted the most influence on the coming of the Reformation. According to an old saying: "Erasmus laid the egg which Luther hatched." Although this is far too simplistic an assertion, there is no question that the so-called "prince of the humanists" was a potent intellectual voice at the beginning of the sixteenth century whose call for reform had a great impact.

Why was he so influential? Why did popes, emperors, kings, princes, and universities seek to honor him? Why did so many take his call for reform seriously? His importance is all the more amazing when one considers that he began life in less than the best of circumstances. Desiderius was the illegitimate son of a priest. His father, Gerhard, was the ninth son of a family who hoped he would advance their prospects by entering the priesthood. His mother, Margaret, was the daughter of a physician. She placed him and an older brother at a school in Deventer, a major center of the Brothers and Sisters of the Common Life. Later Erasmus studied at a Brethren School at Bois-le-Duc for two years.

Shortly after becoming an orphan, he was placed by his guardians in a friary of the Order of Augustinian Canons Regular. Six years later Erasmus accepted ordination as a way out of the friary. In 1494 he became secretary to the bishop of Cambrai and then went on to study at the College de Montaigu in Paris. He departed without taking a degree and complained about the college's "stale eggs and stale [scholastic] theology."[23] The year 1499 found him in England as a tutor, where he heard the influential humanist John Colet (1466–1519) lecture on the apostle Paul. Colet urged him to study Greek as a preparation to the serious study of theology. How else can one enter into the mental world of the New Testament? At this time Erasmus also began his great friendship with Thomas More (1478–1535), who became the most celebrated of the English humanists and King Henry VIII's friend and chancellor.

Returning to the Continent, Erasmus settled first in Paris and then in Louvain, where he helped to organize a trilingual college. In 1500 he published 800 Latin *Adages*, a collection of wise sayings culled from the classics. The *Adages* was his first great success because it made some of the wit and wisdom of the ancient Greeks and Romans accessible to a wider audience. The *Adages* were followed by his *Handbook of the Christian Soldier* (1503). In the *Handbook*, Erasmus called on his fellow Christians to rise from their concerns for this world to concentrate more on spiritual matters:

> I do not disapprove in any way of the external ceremonies of Christians and the devotions of the simple-minded, especially when they have been approved by the authority of the church, for they are signs of support for piety. . . . But to worship Christ through visible things for the sake of visible things and to think of this as the summit of religious perfection . . . would be to desert the law of the gospel, which is spiritual.[24]

The Handbook was followed by editions of the Roman Stoic Cicero's letters and those of Saint Jerome, the church father who had produced the great translation of the Bible known as the Vulgate. As a biblical scholar, Erasmus also published a critical edition of Lorenzo Valla's *Annotations on the New Testament*. This work helped him produce his own translation of the New Testament, which rolled off the presses in 1516. He thought that training in languages should be required of all theologians. "Our first care must be to learn the three languages, Latin, Greek, and Hebrew, for it is plain that the mystery of all Scripture is revealed in them."[25]

From 1506 to 1509 Erasmus worked as a tutor in Italy and immersed himself deeply in classical studies while drawing inspiration from the important work of Italian humanists. Back in England in 1509, he penned his most popular writing, *Praise of Folly*. In this work he attempted to criticize abuses in the church and society and to promote greater spirituality in religion. The witty Dutchman lambasted "the cheat of pardons and indulgences" and those who wor-

Hans Holbein the Younger, *Erasmus Writing*. Louvre, Paris, France. Giraudon/Art Resource.

shipped the Virgin Mary "before the Son." Even the papacy failed to escape his censure, although he was usually careful about challenging the teaching authority of the church: "Now as to the popes of Rome, who pretend themselves Christ's vicar, if they would but imitate his exemplary life, poverty, and contempt of the world."[26]

Similar criticisms can be found in his 1517 satire, *Julius Excluded from Heaven*, in which Julius III, the swaggering warrior-pope, is prevented from entering paradise to which he claimed to have the keys. Erasmus denied writing it, but scholars later found a draft in his handwriting. By then intellectuals inside the Holy Roman Empire had already been immersed in controversies involving the humanist Johann Reuchlin and the dissident friar Martin Luther. As a critical but loyal son of the church, Erasmus wanted no part of the great disputes which threatened to rip Christendom asunder.

THE REUCHLIN AFFAIR

The connection between humanism and the Reformation is also illustrated by the career of the German humanist Johann Reuchlin (1455–1522). Reuchlin was a native of Pforzheim and had been educated by the Brethren of the Common Life and later at the universities of Basel, Freiburg, Orléans, Paris, and Tübingen, where he also taught Greek and served as a magistrate. Like many other northern humanists of his generation, Reuchlin made several trips to Italy, where he came to know the famous Neoplatonic philosophers Marsilio Ficino and Giovanni Pico della Mirandola. He was also an admirer of the leading German Neoplatonist Nicholas of Cues (1401-1464). Nicholas was also dedicated to church reform and as bishop of Brixen tried to enforce discipline upon the clergy of his diocese in the 1450s. He later left Brixen for Rome to serve the humanist Pope Pius II.

As for Johann Reuchlin, he found employment as chancellor to the duke of Württemberg in southern Germany. A professional lawyer, Reuchlin also served as head jurist of the Swabian League (a military alliance of cities and princes) between 1502 and 1512. His last years were spent as a professor of Greek and Hebrew at the universities of Ingolstadt and Tübingen. He became particularly fascinated by the study of Hebrew, which he thought brought him close to the mind of God. After all, Moses and the other Old Testament prophets predate Christ and the New Testament. Reuchlin concluded that Old Testament writers had transmitted many divine truths orally through seventy wise men in an unbroken tradition. This wisdom had been embodied by medieval Jewish thinkers as part of the mystical book known as the *Cabala*. Because of the many references in the *Cabala* to the Messiah, or chosen one, Reuchlin argued

that the great Jewish mystical book supported Christian revelation and was well worth studying along with the Talmud.

To help other Christians read Hebrew sources, the mild-mannered humanist published a Christian-Hebrew grammar, *The Rudiments of Hebrew,* in 1506. It was the first reliable manual of Hebrew grammar to emerge from the pen of a Christian intellectual. In 1517 Reuchlin published *On the Cabalistic Art,* in which he sought to demonstrate that Greek Pythagorean theories and Talmudic and Cabalistic works harmonize with many Christian beliefs. His studies came to the attention of a recent convert from Judaism to Christianity, Johann Pfefferkorn (1469–1523), who was making a name for himself by attacking the new interest of Renaissance humanists in Hebrew writings.

In his polemical work of 1511, *A Mirror for Jews,* Pfefferkorn argued that all Hebrew books should be confiscated. Tragically, he received support for this absurd notion from some of the Dominicans of Cologne, who feared that humanism was undermining traditional scholastic understandings of Christianity. Consequently, heresy proceedings against Reuchlin were initiated by the inquisitor of Cologne. It should be remembered that the great scholastic Thomas Aquinas had studied with the learned Dominican teacher Albert the Great at Cologne. Less intellectually secure men than Thomas or Albert now felt that a great tradition was being challenged by Reuchlin, who seemed to be pushing the humanist notion of "to the sources" (*ad fontes*) to dangerous limits, such as suggesting problems in the Vulgate translation of the Bible. Anti-Semitism also played a great role in the attacks on Reuchlin and his sympathy for "Jewish studies."

The Reuchlin-Pfefferkorn matter reached the attention of Holy Roman Emperor Maximilian. In 1510 Maximilian had ordered four universities and three independent scholars, including Reuchlin, to write expert opinions about whether Jewish books should be tolerated. Reuchlin repeated his assertion that Christian scholars should make an intensive study of Hebrew texts. Pfefferkorn then attacked Reuchlin directly in a pamphlet accusing him of ignorance. Although he dreaded the continuing public controversy, Reuchlin felt compelled to defend his reputation and vindicate his orthodoxy. He fired back a treatise aimed directly at Pfefferkorn and also published a collection of testimonials on his behalf titled the *Letters of Famous Men* (1514).

Those testimonials inspired a group of Reuchlin's admirers to make their own satirical contribution. In 1515 Crotus Rubianus and Ulrich von Hutten published a collection of forty-one *Letters of Obscure Men*. The letters, ostensibly written in deliberately faulty Latin in support of a Cologne Dominican opponent of Reuchlin, ridiculed the ignorance and foolishness of those who followed Pfefferkorn's lead. Yet they also contained anti-Semitic jibes such as the charge

that Pfefferkorn "still stank like any other Jew."[27] The *Letters* also contained many nasty jokes about women, since misogyny was as much a staple of humanist culture as anti-Semitism. The *Letters of Obscure Men* proved so popular that a second edition of sixty-two letters appeared in 1517, the year of Martin Luther's "Ninety-five Theses against Indulgences."

All this had little impact upon Maximilian, who was growing increasingly alarmed by the even greater crisis stirred up over indulgences, which soon overshadowed the Reuchlin affair. Nevertheless, in an effort to try to reduce the level of contention, the emperor ordered in 1519 that all Hebrew books be confiscated. The next year Pope Leo X ordered Reuchlin fined and silenced, reversing a ruling of 1514 which had not found him to be heretical. Although brokenhearted by these blows to his life's work, Johann Reuchlin was a dutiful son of the church and obeyed the pope's order. He died a mere two years later. By then the call to reform had set off an uproar that threatened to destroy much of Christendom.

Chronology

1294	Beginning of the reign of Pope Boniface VIII.
1302	Boniface VIII issues *Unam Sanctam*.
1303	Humiliation and later death of Boniface VIII.
1305	Pope Clement V moves the papacy to Avignon.
c. 1320	Birth of John Wycliffe.
1324	Marsilius of Padua publishes *The Defender of the Peace*.
1337	Hundred Years' War begins.
1347	Beginning of the Black Death.
c. 1372	Birth of Jan Hus.
1376	Papacy returns to Rome.
1378	Western Schism begins.
1381	Peasants' Revolt in England.
1384	Death of John Wycliffe.
c. 1407	Birth of Lorenzo Valla.
1409	Jan Hus becomes rector of the Charles University in Prague; Council of Pisa (3 popes).
1410	Jan Hus excommunicated.
1413	Hus publishes *On the Church*.
1414–1418	Council of Constance.
1415	Burning of Jan Hus at Constance.
1416	Burning of Jerome of Prague.
1417	Western Schism ended by election of Pope Martin V.

1431–1449	Council of Basel.
1434	Utraquists defeat the Taborites at the battle of Lipan.
1436	Peace with Hussites.
1439–1442	Council of Florence.
1445–1450	Invention of moveable type by Gutenberg.
1445–1510	Life of Johann Geiler von Kaysersberg.
1450–1536	Jacques Lefèvre d'Etaples.
1452	Birth of Savonarola.
1454	Gutenberg printed Bible.
1455–1522	Life of Johann Reuchlin.
1460	Pope Pius II condemns conciliarism in *Execrabilis*.
c. 1467–1535	Life of Erasmus.
c. 1470–1534	Guillaume Briçonnet.
1488–1523	Ulrich von Hutten.
1492–1503	Reign of Alexander VI (Borgia) as pope.
1494	Savonarola in power in Florence; Sebastian Brant's *Ship of Fools*.
1498	Death of Savonarola.
1503–1513	Lateran Council; reign of Julius II as pope.
1506–1520	Reuchlin Affair.

Further Reading

GENERAL

Anthony Black, *Council and Commune: The Conciliar Movement and the Fifteenth-Century Heritage* (1979).

C. M. D. Crowder, ed., *Unity, Heresy, and Reform, 1378–1460* (1977). Valuable collection of sources.

Peter Dykema and Heiko Oberman, eds., *Anticlericalism in Late Medieval and Early Modern Europe* (1993). A collection of essays.

James Farge, *Orthodoxy and Reform in Early Reformation France: The Faculty of Theology of Paris, 1500–1543* (1985).

Denys Hay, *The Church in Italy in the Fifteenth Century* (1977).

Anne Hudson, *The Premature Reformation. Wycliffite Texts and Lollard History* (1988).

Howard Kaminsky, *A History of the Hussite Revolution* (1967).

Richard Kieckhefer, *Unquiet Souls: Fourteenth-Century Saints and Their Religious Milieu* (1984).

Gordon Leff, *Heresy in the Later Middle Ages: The Relation of Heterodoxy to Dissent, c. 1250–1450* (1967).

Louise Ropes Loomis, *The Council of Constance* (1961).

Alister McGrath, *The Intellectual Origins of the European Reformation* (1987).

Francis Oakley, *The Western Church in the Later Middle Ages* (1979).

Heiko Oberman, *Forerunners of the Reformation: the Shape of Late Medieval Thought*, 2nd ed. (1981).

———, *Masters of the Reformation: the Emergence of a New Intellectual Climate in Europe*, tr. Dennis Martin (1981).

R. R. Post, *The Modern Devotion: Confrontation with Reformation and Humanism* (1968).

Yves Renouard, *The Avignon Papacy, 1305–1403* (1970).

Miri Rubin, *Corpus Christi: the Eucharist in Late Medieval Culture* (1991).

Joachim Stieber, *Pope Eugenius IV, the Council of Basel, and the Secular and Ecclesiastical Authorities of the Empire* (1978).

Gerald Strauss, ed. and tr., *Manifestations of Discontent in Germany on the Eve of the Reformation* (1971). An important collection of source materials.

Phillip Stump, *The Reforms of the Council of Constance, 1414–1418* (1994).

R. N. Swanson, *Church and Society in Late Medieval England* (1989).

Norman Tanner, *The Church in Late Medieval Norwich, 1370–1532* (1984).

Larissa Taylor, *Soldiers of Christ: Preaching in Late Medieval and Reformation France* (1992).

Thomas Tentler, *Sin and Confession on the Eve of the Reformation* (1977).

J. F. A. Thompson, *Popes and Princes, 1417–1517* (1980).

Brian Tierney, *Foundations of the Conciliar Theory* (1955).

Donald Weinstein and Rudolf Bell, *Saints and Society: The Two Worlds of Western Christendom, 1000–1700* (1986).

INDIVIDUAL REFORMERS

E. Jane Dempsey Douglass, *Justification in Late Medieval Preaching: A Study of John Geiler of Keisersberg* (1968).

Anthony Kenny, *Wyclif* (1985).

John O'Malley, S. J., *Giles of Viterbo on Church and Reform: A Study in Renaissance Thought* (1968).

Matthew Spinka, *Jan Hus: a Biography* (1968).

Donald Weinstein, *Savonarola and Florence: Prophecy and Patriotism in the Renaissance* (1970).

PRINTING

Roger Chartier, *The Order of Books: Readers, Authors, and Libraries in Europe between the 14th and 18th Centuries* (1994).

Miriam Chrisman, *Conflicting Visions of Reform: German Lay Propaganda Pamphlets, 1519–1530* (1995).

———, *Lay Culture, Learned Culture: Books and Social Change in Strasbourg* (1982).

Mark Edwards, Jr., *Printing, Propaganda and Martin Luther* (1994).

Elizabeth Eisenstein, *The Printing Press as an Agent of Change*, 2 vols. (1979).

Lucien Febvre and Henri-Jean Martin, *The Coming of the Book: The Impact of Printing, 1450–1800* (1976).

HUMANISM AND HUMANISTS

Roland Bainton, *Erasmus of Christendom* (1969).

Manfred Fleisher, ed., *The Harvest of Humanism in Central Europe* (1992). A valuable collection of wide-ranging essays by various scholars in honor of Lewis Spitz, Jr.

Lisa Jardine, *Erasmus, Man of Letters* (1991).

James McConica, *Erasmus* (1991).

Heiko Oberman, *The Impact of the Reformation* (1994). Has several particularly important essays on Reuchlin.

James Overfield, *Humanism and Scholasticism in Late Medieval Germany* (1985).

Erika Rummel, *Erasmus and His Catholic Critics*, 2 vols. (1989).

———, *The Humanist-Scholastic Debate in the Renaissance and Reformation* (1995).

Richard Schoeck, *Erasmus of Europe: The Making of a Humanist 1467–1500* (1990).

J. Kelley Sowards, *Desiderius Erasmus* (1975).

Lewis Spitz, Jr., *The Religious Renaissance of the German Humanists* (1967).

Notes

1. Cited in Warren Hollister, et al., eds., *Medieval Europe: A Short Sourcebook*, 2nd ed. (New York: McGraw-Hill, 1992), p. 216.
2. Cited in Steven Ozment, *The Age of Reform 1250–1550: An Intellectual and Religious History of Late Medieval and Reformation Europe* (New Haven, Conn.: Yale University Press, 1980), p. 150.
3. Cited in Marsilius of Padua, *The Defender of the Peace*, tr. with an introduction by Alan Gewirth (New York: Harper and Row, 1956), p. xix.
4. Cited in William Estep, *Renaissance and Reformation* (Grand Rapids, Mich.: William Eerdmans, 1986), p. 62.
5. Cited in Theodore Rabb, *Renaissance Lives: Portraits of an Age* (New York: Pantheon Books, 1993), p. 20.
6. Ibid., p. 22.
7. Cited in J. W. Zophy, "Hus," in Jonathan W. Zophy, ed., *The Holy Roman Empire: A Dictionary Handbook* (Westport, Conn.: Greenwood Press, 1980), p. 228.
8. Ibid.
9. Cited in C. Warren Hollister, et al., eds., *Medieval Europe: A Short Sourcebook*, 2nd ed. (New York: McGraw-Hill, 1992), p. 245.
10. Cited in Erika Rummel, "Voice of Reform from Hus to Erasmus," in Thomas Brady, Jr., Heiko Oberman, and James Tracy, eds., *Handbook of Eu-*

ropean History 1400–1600: Late Middle Ages, Renaissance and Reformation, 2 vols. (Leiden: E. J. Brill, 1994 and 1995), vol. 2, p. 76.

11.   Cited in Ibid.
12.   Cited in Donald Weinstein, *Savonarola and Florence* (Princeton, N.J.: Princeton University Press, 1970), pp. 69–70.
13.   See Kenneth Bartlett, ed., *The Civilization of the Italian Renaissance: A Sourcebook* (Lexington, Mass.: D. C. Heath, 1992), pp. 331–336.
14.   Cited in E. R. Chamberlin, *The Bad Popes* (New York: Dial Press, 1969), p. 161.
15.   Ibid., p. 166.
16.   Ibid., p. 174.
17.   Cited in Erika Rummel, "Voice of Reform," in Brady, Oberman, and Tracy, eds., *Handbook*, vol. 2, p. 65.
18.   Ibid.
19.   Ibid., p. 66.
20.   Cited in Werner Gundersheimer, ed., *The Italian Renaissance* (Englewood Cliffs, N.J.: Prentice Hall, 1965), p. 56.
21.   Cited in Erika Rummel, "Voices of Reform," in Brady, Oberman, and Tracy, *Handbook*, vol. 2, p. 78.
22.   Ibid., p. 81.
23.   Cited in De Lamar Jensen, *Renaissance Europe: Age of Recovery and Reconciliation*, 2nd ed. (Lexington, Mass.: D. C. Heath, 1992), p. 383.
24.   Cited in Erika Rummel, "Voices of Reform," in Brady, Oberman, and Tracy, eds., *Handbook*, pp. 84-85.
25.   Ibid., p. 85.
26.   Cited in Lewis Spitz, ed., *The Protestant Reformation* (Englewood Cliffs, N.J.: Prentice Hall, 1966), p. 21.
27.   Ulrich von Hutten and others, *Letters of Obscure Men*, tr. by Francis Griffin Stokes, intro. by Hajo Holborn (Philadelphia: University of Pennsylvania Press, 1964), p. 157.

5

MARTIN LUTHER'S REVOLT

The Man with Seven Heads

The call for reform was renewed by Martin Luther, a man who some said had seven heads. After all, he was a well-published and beloved university professor, a friar, a priest, a heretic (to some), an outlaw, a family man, and a dedicated church reformer (to some). His ideas helped unleash complex economic, intellectual, political, and social forces which are still being felt today. A prolific author, he is one of the first persons in European history whom we can come to know in some detail. The story of his life is intertwined with that of the first phases of the movement known as the Reformation. How did this come to be? Who was this man with seven heads?

MARTIN LUTHER'S BACKGROUND

Martin Luther came from an ambitious, hard-working family. His grandfather had been a peasant. His father, Hans, left farm work to become a copper miner, and eventually rose to become a part owner of six mines and two copper smelters. Mining was a growth industry in the period, although its expansion ultimately contributed to problems of deforestation and pollution. Hans Luther had married slightly above his station; his wife, Margaret, was a member of a well-educated middle-class family—the Lindermans. When Martin was born on November 10, 1483, as the second son, Hans had not yet launched his successful mining career and was desperately searching for work in the mines.

Hans Luther eventually prospered in the rough life of the mines near Mansfeld in Saxony, but life in the Luther household could be difficult. Martin Luther later remembered being beaten by his mother until he bled for "stealing a nut from the kitchen table."[1] He was also punished severely by his father for a boyhood prank, but such discipline was common in a patriarchal age. To be sure, young Martin found a measure of tough love in that hardworking family, as did his four sisters and four brothers.

Luther's parents were determined that at least several of their sons should receive good formal educations as preparatory to prosperous careers. Should young Martin become, say, a lawyer, he would then be able to assure his parents' future and take good care of them in their dotage. This was the plan when Martin was enrolled in the Latin School in his home town of Mansfeld in 1492. Five years later he was sent to school in Magdeburg and a year later to an even better one in Eisenach, where he encountered the dedicated cleric Johann Braun, who became his most important early role model.

Hans Brosamer, "Martinus Luther Sieben-kopfe." Title page to Johann Cochlaeus's *Sieben Kopfe Martin Luther* (1529). Foto Marburg/Art Resource.

In 1501 Martin Luther entered Erfurt University and applied himself to the traditional liberal arts curriculum, receiving his B.A. degree in 1502 and his M.A. in January 1505. Although he still dreamed of becoming a clergyman, Martin dutifully began his legal studies in the spring of 1505. On July 2, 1505, while returning to law school from a home visit, he was nearly hit by a bolt of lightning. He took a vow, "Help me, St. Anne. I will become a monk."[2] Luther apparently felt he needed all the help the patron saint of miners could give him because he was about to disappoint his miner father and enter an Augustinian Hermit monastery back at Erfurt. A practical man of business, Hans Luther had invested a great deal

in the education of his son. Hans now worried that his investment would be wasted if Martin became another poorly paid member of the clergy and therefore less able to provide for him in his old age.

Less than a year later, an extremely terrified Martin Luther celebrated his first Mass as an ordained priest in the chapel of the Augustinian cloister at Erfurt. He felt unworthy of handling the body and blood of Christ. The celebration was witnessed by his still simmering father and several of his father's cronies. Luther expressed his feelings of unworthiness but explained to his father that he felt compelled to enter the monastery because of his experience with the thunderstorm. Hans Luther countered, "Let us hope it was not an illusion and a deception. Have you not also heard that parents are to be obeyed?"[3] Still the prosperous Hans could not resist showing off by presenting the monastery with an exceptionally generous present of twenty gulden (nearly 20 percent of a typical worker's annual wages).

Despite his pain at the anger his vocational choice had caused his earthly father, Martin Luther persevered in his efforts to achieve religious satisfaction by following a grueling routine in the monastery. His ecclesiastical superior and confessor, Johann von Staupitz (c. 1460–1524), became worried about his brilliant but obviously troubled young colleague. He urged the congenial Luther to continue his academic studies and try his hand at teaching and administrative work. Staupitz also sent Luther as a representative of his order to Rome in the fall of 1510. While Luther found his trip to Rome and his studies to be stimulating, he was still "yearning for Grace."

On October 19, 1512, Master Luther became Doctor Luther, having received his doctorate in theology. By then he was already well on his way toward becoming one of the most popular professors at Elector Frederick the Wise's University of Wittenberg, a university founded in 1502, the year of Luther's baccalaureate degree from Erfurt. Duke Frederick of Electoral Saxony (1463–1525) was almost as proud of his new university as he was of his fabulous collection of relics, one of the finest in Europe, and the charismatic Luther soon became one of his star faculty members even before his early publications on grace after the Indulgence Controversy of 1517 made him famous throughout the Holy Roman Empire.

THE INDULGENCE CONTROVERSY

At age thirty-four Martin Luther was convinced that he had finally figured out how people's souls were saved. This had been a question that had long troubled him, since he lived in a world where early death was common and most people felt burdened by guilt for their sins. Like many others in the early sixteenth century, Luther was obsessed with religion, worried about his own salvation, and afraid of an angry God.

His duties as a professor of theology at the University of Wittenberg, however, had forced him into a serious examination of the writings of the apostle Paul as well as the Psalms. Luther had become especially intrigued with Paul's letters to the Romans and the concept of "the righteousness of God." Perhaps Luther had been viewing the salvation question from the wrong direction, as his mentor Johann von Staupitz had suggested.

Luther assumed that because God is righteous, He, therefore, must punish sinful humanity. As he explained later, "Far from loving that righteous God who punished sinners, I actually hated Him."[4] Then he began to realize that because his "righteous God" is righteous, He mercifully chooses to give some of us the saving gift of faith even

though none of us is worthy. In the words of Paul, Luther's great biblical hero, "the just shall live by faith" (Romans 1:17).

Although this discovery of a loving rather than a hateful God changed Luther's entire outlook on life and brought him immense joy, it also brought him into serious trouble with many of his superiors in the hierarchy of the Roman Catholic church. Martin Luther was certainly not the first theologian to argue for the importance of faith rather than good works as a means of achieving grace. By some estimates at least forty-three other theologians had come to a position somewhat similar to Luther's on the importance of faith for salvation, including the patron saint of his order, Augustine of Hippo in Africa (354–430), and his mentor, Staupitz.

However, the views that Luther now held on the subject in October of 1517 were those of a minority of Catholic theologians. Most still argued for the importance of doing good works in order to earn salvation. Furthermore, the doctrine of good works was tied to the often lucrative, papal-controlled practice of selling indulgences.

Indulgences seem to have begun innocently enough as gifts of money to charity as an expression of gratitude for forgiveness. They soon became a way to relax or commute the "satisfaction" or penance imposed as an outward sign of sorrow for sins. The medieval church made a distinction between guilt and punishment for sin. Guilt was atoned for by Christ, but penance could be ordered by a priest. Indulgences were a convenient method for having some of the penalties for sin reduced. They also served as a valued reward for those going on crusade to the Holy Land.

During the thirteenth century, theologians in the service of the papacy formulated the conception of a "treasury of merits." This was a storehouse of the good works of Christ, the saints, and all worthy Christians that the pope could redistribute by means of indulgences. That is to say, Christ and the saints had been better than they needed to be to achieve salvation and therefore some of their "excess merit" could be transferred to the spiritual bank accounts of penitent sinners. These indulgences would be used to lessen punishment in purgatory still left after the priest had pronounced absolution. Purgatory, which had been so imaginatively described by Dante in his *Divine Comedy*, was the place where sinners went to expiate sins before going on to heaven.

Many people did not comprehend all the subtleties involved in the church's shifting teachings about indulgences and how the sacrament of penance operated. Some confused eternal punishment with the temporary punishment of purgatory and actually thought they could buy salvation for themselves and, after the fifteenth century, for the dead as well. Some viewed the purchase of an indulgence as a good work sufficient to expiate all sins. As one bold sinner claimed, because I have purchased this indulgence, I can "sleep with" the Virgin Mary and still go to heaven![5]

Since Martin Luther now thought that God saved men and women through his gift of faith, what use were indulgences? As he wrote in his "Ninety-five Theses on the Power and Efficacy of Indulgences" of October 31, 1517, "any truly repentant Christian has a right to full remission of penalty and guilt, even without indulgence letters."

Luther was horrified that so many seemed to be gulled by the sales techniques of crass indulgence sellers such as the cherubic Dominican Johann Tetzel (d. 1519). Tetzel would have been completely at home in our own more material age, outrageously peddling automobiles on television in a voice as loud as his sports coat. Modern advertisers can only marvel at his favorite jingle for selling indulgences:

> As soon as a coin in the coffer rings,
> Another soul from purgatory springs![6]

What Professor Luther failed to understand completely when he wrote his "Ninety-five Theses" was that Tetzel was at work because of a complicated transaction involving some of the most politically and economically powerful families in Europe. Tetzel was working for Albrecht of Hohenzollern (1490–1545), archbishop of Mainz, Magdeburg, and administrator of Halberstadt. Albrecht was the youngest son of Elector Joachim I of Brandenburg, and his family had borrowed a great deal of money from the Fugger family banking house of Augsburg. The Hohenzollerns wanted to advance Albrecht's ecclesiastical career because that would greatly increase their family's power, prestige, and ultimately their wealth. The purchase of the archbishopric of Mainz meant that the Hohenzollerns controlled half of the four electoral votes needed to become Holy Roman emperor. The Hohenzollerns would eventually become kings of Prussia and emperors of a unified Germany in 1871.

Pope Leo X (r. 1513–1521), scion of another great banking clan, the Medici, had revived a plenary Jubilee Indulgence sale inaugurated by his predecessor, the warrior-pope Julius II, Michelangelo's great patron, in order to continue the extraordinarily expensive rebuilding of St. Peter's basilica in Rome. Because the Hohenzollerns had shelled out something in the neighborhood of 34,000 ducats for several bishoprics and other favors for the underage Albrecht, that good man of business Pope Leo had graciously allowed half of the proceeds from the sales of this jubilee indulgence to go to the Hohenzollerns and the official papal bankers, the Fuggers of Augsburg. Here, of course, we have an unusually spectacular example of the sale of church offices (*simony*) and the holding of more than one office by a single individual (*pluralism*). Simony and pluralism were corrupt church practices which had been condemned for over a century before Luther's theses at the Council of Constance and elsewhere.

As a somewhat naive professor at a backwater German university, Martin Luther was not aware of all the complex negotiations involved in Tetzel's sales campaign and all of the powerful vested interests involved. In fact, he rather innocently sent a copy of his "Ninety-five Theses" to Archbishop Albrecht, who later proved to be a sympathetic and reform-minded churchman. However, Luther was suspicious enough about the financial aspects of indulgences to raise the question in his "Theses": Why doesn't the wealthy pope "build this one basilica of St. Peter with his own money rather than with the money of poor believers?"[7]

Martin Luther had intended the "Ninety-five Theses" to touch off an academic debate, but never dreamed they would lead to a full-scale movement that became known as the Reformation. However, within weeks of their initial distribution in Wittenberg, the theses had been translated from German into Latin and distributed all over the Holy Roman Empire and eventually beyond. Luther's "Theses" had hit an incredibly sensitive nerve that set off a great storm of controversy.

THE REBEL

In April of 1518, Martin Luther journeyed to the center of Germany to attend a convention of Augustinian Hermits at the lovely old town of Heidelberg on the Neckar River. Having prepared a more sharply focused "Twenty-Eight Theses on Indulgences," he was eager to defend himself and to share his recently discovered concepts of "salvation by faith alone" and the "sole authority of Scripture" for doctrine. Rather than being disciplined by his order and cowed into silence, Luther was cheered by his fellow Augustinians, a number of whom later became part of the first generation of Evangelical clergy, as Luther's followers were known. A Dominican present at Heidelberg, Martin Bucer, became the leading light of the Reformation in the mighty imperial city of Strasbourg. Johann Brenz, a student at Heidelberg, was also impressed by Luther's performance at the disputation. He later became the leading reformer in the duchy of Württemberg.

Although Luther had already become somewhat of a German folk hero in the empire, the great church bureaucracy in Rome was slower to react. After all, Leo X, who said at his accession to the throne of St. Peter, "God has given us the papacy, let us enjoy it," had numerous pleasures to divert him from his spiritual duties.[8] He was an especially avid hunter and spent a great deal of time traveling from one papal hunting lodge to another. However, as the son of the banker Lorenzo de' Medici, Leo was financially astute enough to know that Luther's attack on indulgences, if left unchecked, represented a serious threat to the church's revenue streams. As sales of indulgences threatened to drop off, the pope understood it was no longer just a matter of "the envy of the monks ... [Luther] will feel differently when he is sober."[9] Accordingly, on August 7, 1518, Pope Leo X ordered the dissident professor to come to Rome for a hearing.

At this critical juncture Martin Luther asked his prince, Frederick the Wise, for guidance. Reassured by his court chaplain and confessor, George Spalatin (1484–1545), that Luther was no heretic, Frederick al-

Raphael, *Pope Leo X and the Cardinals Guilio de' Medici and Luigi del Rossi.* Galleria Palatina, Palazzo Pitti, Florence, Italy.

lowed the controversial professor to stay in Wittenberg. He also used his influence as one of the seven electors of the Holy Roman emperor and one of the leading lay Christians in the empire to arrange for Luther's hearing to take place on German soil. Not wishing to offend such a pious and powerful prince, Leo X graciously consented to allow the Wittenberg theologian to meet with his envoy, Thomas de Vio, Cardinal Cajetan (1469–1534), at Augsburg in October 1518.

Although apprehensive, Luther was looking forward to this opportunity to meet with the distinguished church administrator and authority on the writings of the great scholastic theologian Thomas Aquinas. Luther was well acquainted with medieval scholastic thought from his days at Erfurt and was eager to debate his new evangelical theology with the learned cardinal. Meeting

at the palace of the Fuggers in the heart of Augsburg where the Dominican vicar-general Cajetan was staying in comfort, the two theologians did not hit it off. The academic Luther wanted to debate, whereas Cardinal Cajetan the church official demanded submission. This the courageous and stubborn German theologian would not agree to. When friends informed the Wittenberger that he was going to be arrested, Luther wisely left Augsburg for the relative safety of nearby Nuremberg, where he had already impressed a number of members of the town's elite business and humanist circles with his sincerity, good humor, and bravery.

When Luther returned to Wittenberg, he found that Frederick the Wise was disappointed with the results of the interview with Cajetan; however, Luther could continue to teach at the university and live in Wittenberg at the Augustinian cloister. Frederick hoped that the controversy would die down in time and Luther agreed to refrain from public disputation and publications on indulgences. However, what neither one of them could foresee was that larger forces had been unleashed by the controversy over indulgences, forces which no human could control. First, however, Frederick had to deal with a new crisis caused by the death of the Holy Roman Emperor Maximilian I in Austria on January 12, 1519.

CHOOSING A NEW CAESAR

As one of the seven electors of the emperor, Frederick had to help decide who was to replace the affable Maximilian as the heir to the Roman caesars of antiquity, the "descendants of Aeneas," as imperial propagandists argued. Among the candidates were three young kings: Charles I of Spain (b. 1500), François I of France, and Henry VIII of England. All three of these energetic, young Renaissance princes had much to recommend them, but they all had liabilities as well. Charles was Maximilian's grandson, but he already ruled in Spain, which he had inherited from his other grandparents, Isabella of Castile and Ferdinand of Aragon. Charles also had inherited rule over the Low Countries, where he had been raised and educated. Some politicians, including Pope Leo, feared that Charles' election would give the house of Habsburg too much power.

Much the same could be said of electing the ambitious François of France. If the Valois candidate won the imperial title, it would create an empire to rival Charlemagne's (c. 742–814). Few outside the French kingdom wanted that reality. Henry Tudor's candidacy was not really taken seriously as he had no real support among important German princes. Pope Leo was increasingly apprehensive about either a Habsburg or Valois election because both threatened him even in Italy, where Charles was also king of Naples and François ruled Milan.

In desperation the pope now urged Frederick the Wise himself to make a run for the office. The pious Saxon duke was not likely ever to pose a threat to papal power in Italy. Furthermore, Leo told the Saxon that if Frederick would agree to serve as emperor he could choose "any personal friend" and the pope would make that person a cardinal and endow him with an archbishopric. Should that "personal friend" be Martin Luther, two vexing problems might be solved at once. After all, would Archbishop Martin continue to challenge the authority of holy mother church?

What Pope Leo failed to reckon with was that Frederick was indeed wise enough not to want to rise above his level of competence. He was perfectly happy as the bachelor duke of Saxony with his relic collection and a congenial mistress. Elector Frederick

certainly did not want to inherit the dynastic responsibilities of the emperor, nor did he have the personal resources to fulfill those obligations. As a Saxon duke, Frederick had a degree of privacy; as an emperor, he would be continuously in the spotlight. Frederick wisely declined the pope's generous offer.

The imperial electors were thus forced to choose between Charles and François, accepting huge bribes from both. The Habsburg bribes were funded by the Fuggers of Augsburg, those aggressive papal bankers. On June 28, 1519, they announced that Charles of Habsburg, who had at least some "German blood in him," was their unanimous choice as Holy Roman emperor. Charles promised to respect the "imperial privileges of his German subjects," appoint only Germans to imperial offices, hold imperial diets only on German soil, and revive both the Imperial Council of Regency and the Imperial Supreme Court.[10]

Luther's Rebellion Intensifies

The election of Charles of Habsburg, a staunch supporter of the church, may have solved Frederick the Wise's personal dilemma, but it did little to take care of the problem of Martin Luther. In fact, matters got worse when Luther and several of his colleagues agreed to a debate over their new theology with an ambitious professor from the University of Ingolstadt, Dr. Johann Eck (1486–1543). The debate was held at the University of Leipzig in early July. Eck was a skillful debater, who had earlier been one of the first prominent academic theologians to justify capitalistic practices and was handsomely rewarded for his efforts by a number of grateful patrons, including the Fuggers.

Now Eck had a golden chance to defend the truth, earn additional celebrity, and win favor with Rome by crushing the

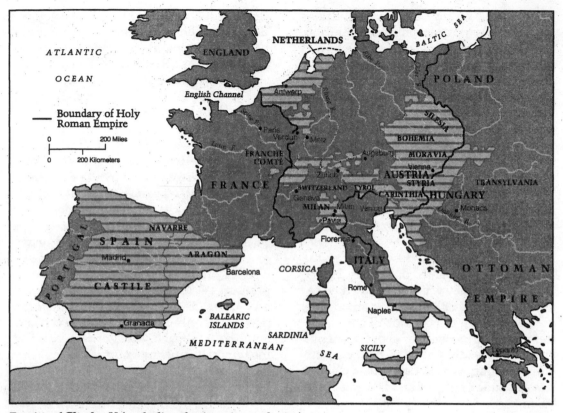

Empire of Charles V (excluding the American colonies).

rebellious Wittenberg professor in academic debate. The Wittenberg debate team was at first led by Luther's senior colleague Andreas Bodenstein von Karlstadt (c. 1480–1541). Luther had already convinced many of his colleagues and students at Wittenberg of the soundness of his position on "justification by faith." However, when Bodenstein seemed to be losing the debate to the wily Eck at every turn, Luther took over for his outmatched friend. Even the brilliant Luther proved to be no contest for Eck, who forced Luther to admit that his doctrines shared a striking number of similarities with those of the convicted heretic Jan Hus. Luther ended up conceding that "We are all Hussites."

Eck's Hussite strategy was a master stroke, for the University of Leipzig had been founded by faculty and students who had fled the University of Prague during the early days of the Hussite revolt a century earlier. Memories of that painful emigration still lingered in the minds of those descendants of refugees who were judging the debate. Getting Luther to admit to "Hussite tendencies" in Leipzig was like getting someone to admit to sympathy with the devil. No wonder Luther lost the debate.

Johann Eck was able to follow up on his debate triumph over Luther by being charged with the responsibility to draft the papal bull *Exsurge Domine* ("Arise Lord"), which gave the Wittenberger sixty days to recant or face excommunication. *Exsurge Domine* was published on June 15, 1520, and included several others against whom Eck had grudges, such as the humanists Ulrich von Hutten and two of Nuremberg's more prominent citizens—the city secretary, Lazarus Spengler (1479–1534), and the patrician humanist Willibald Pirckheimer (1470–1530). Hutten was on Eck's "hit list" because of his defense of Johann Reuchlin, the controversial humanist who advocated Hebrew studies. The Nurembergers were there because of a sprightly little satire, "Cutting Eck Down to Size," which had appeared anonymously earlier in the year. Professor Eck thought Pirckheimer had written it and that Spengler, who had written the first lay defense of his friend Luther, had gotten the satire published. Attacking two of Nuremberg's favorite sons was excessive and contributed to that town's growing dissatisfaction with the Catholic church. The response of Luther's students in Wittenberg to the papal bull against their hero was to use the bull and other papal decrees as kindling for an openly defiant bonfire.

The Leipzig Debate had already convinced Professor Luther that he was hopelessly at odds with the hierarchy of the church, but that he owed a duty to his protectors and followers to make his evangelical position perfectly clear. He therefore responded with a number of major writings in 1520 addressed to the German laity in which he spelled out his concerns about a number of church doctrines. In his *Appeal to the German Ruling Class*, Luther clarified his conception of the "universal priesthood of all believers" by reemphasizing that we all have a direct relationship with God. According to Luther, baptized believers are in a sense "priests of equal standing" and because of that they should "bring about a genuinely free council" to address the evils that have befallen Christendom which the

pope refused to deal with.[11] He also declared in this essay that the parish clergy should be allowed to marry, an argument that would also have revolutionary implications.

In his *Babylonian Captivity of the Church of God*, Luther made public his rejection of confirmation, marriage, holy orders, and supreme unction as sacraments on the grounds that they had no basis in the Scriptures. Here Luther was attacking the heart of traditional Roman Catholic piety and practice, the very rituals that had bound the Christian community together. For him, doctrine must clearly be supported by the Bible. If that was not sufficiently outrageous for his enemies, Luther went on in his *Treatise on Christian Liberty*, which was addressed to Pope Leo, to describe the liberating effect upon the Christian of faith in Christ. He argued that "faith alone, without works, justifies, frees, and saves."[12] As for good works, they "do not make a man good,

Lucas Cranach the Elder, *Luther as an Augustinian Monk* (1520). Engraving. Foto Marburg/Art Resource.

but a good man does good works." These writings were widely published and made Luther and his ideas even more widely known in Germany. Even in a predominantly oral culture, the printing press was making its impact known.

LUTHER VERSUS CHARLES V: THE 1521 DIET OF WORMS

His Holiness Pope Leo in Rome was not persuaded by Luther's writings to change his beliefs and launch a reformation of the church; in fact, he was further convinced that Luther was indeed a "dangerous and notorious heretic" who deserved excommunication and eternal damnation. Accordingly he initiated a bull of excommunication, *Decet Romanum Pontificem* ("It is Fitting that the Pope"), and expected that Charles V, the newly elected emperor, would carry it out.

This provided a bit of a dilemma for the newly crowned Charles, who although a loyal and convinced Catholic knew that the pope had not favored his election as Holy Roman emperor. Charles also knew that he could not afford to offend Luther's protector, Frederick the Wise, or indeed too many of the other German princes, for he needed their continued support for his wars with the French and for a new threat—the Ottoman Turks. The feared Ottomans were already pressing relentlessly up the Danube River and into Charles' Austrian crown lands. His spies had informed him that he would require a great deal of German help to defeat the mighty Ottomans, who had also found vigorous new leadership in the form of Süleyman the Magnificent (r. 1520–1566). Süleyman was a man of immense talents and varied interests. Trained as a goldsmith and a poet, he became an important patron of the arts and a highly suc-

Bernhard Strigel, *Portrait of Emperor Charles V as a Young Man.* Galleria Borghese, Rome. Alinari/Art Resource.

cessful lawgiver. Süleyman was also determined to make a great name for himself as a conqueror and the Habsburg lands seemed like inviting targets.

Therefore, Charles V's primary objective at his first German Diet was to win friends and influence people, even though he spoke not a word of German. He needed the help of the rich Germans against the threat posed by Sultan Süleyman and the "Turkish plague," as the Nuremberg diplomat Christoph Kress (1484–1535) characterized the Ottomans. So Charles did not feel in a position to turn down Frederick the Wise's polite request that Dr. Martin Luther be given a hearing at the Imperial Diet meeting in Worms in January 1521. The Diet was supposed to have met in Kress's Nuremberg, but an outbreak of the plague there resulted in the meeting site being shifted to the episcopal town of Worms on the Rhine.

Martin Luther dutifully journeyed to Worms, where he took advantage of the presence of some fine Jewish scholars to receive help with his Hebrew. He planned to produce a new translation of the Bible; however, despite his adequate knowledge of New Testament Greek, he still struggled with his Hebrew and the mysteries of the Old Testament. Although Luther was never a full-fledged humanist, he did agree with them that it was essential to get as close to the original sources (*ad fontes*) as possible. Luther was, therefore, an advocate of language studies—one of the central themes of Renaissance humanism.

On April 17, 1521, Luther made his first appearance at 4 P.M. before the assembled magnates of the empire at the bishop of Worms' palace. When asked if he would retract the contents of his published works, the usually bold Wittenberger, to the surprise of many, asked for a recess to consider his response. Screwing up his courage, Luther returned to the Diet late the next afternoon and informed the jewelled and handsomely robed representatives of the imperial ruling classes that:

> Unless I am convinced by the testimony of the Holy Scriptures or by some other clear, distinct reason—for I do not believe in the Pope or in councils alone, since they have been often shown to err and contradict themselves—then I am bound by those passages from Scripture that I have quoted. As long as my conscience is bound by the Word of God, I cannot and will not recant because acting against conscience is nei-

> ther safe nor sound. Here I stand. I can do no other. God help me. Amen.[13]

Martin Luther had affirmed before an audience of the most powerful men in the empire the essence of what he had been sharing with his students and colleagues for several years now. He had put his trust completely in his own interpretation of Scripture over the teaching authority of the pope and the entire hierarchy of the Catholic church. He would follow the dictates of his own conscience rather than obey a pope whom he viewed as a fallible human.

The recently excommunicated professor found himself at odds with the authorities of the state as well, for in his response to Luther given the very next day, Emperor Charles V declared:

> After the impertinent reply which Luther gave yesterday in our presence, I declare that I now regret having delayed so long the proceedings against him and his false doctrines. I am resolved that I will never again hear him talk. He is to be taken back immediately according to arrangement of the mandate with due regard for the stipulation of his safe-conduct. He is not to preach or seduce the people with his evil doctrines and is not to incite rebellion.[14]

Young Charles of Habsburg was not going to "deny the religion of all his ancestors for the false teachings of a solitary monk."

Charles was a shrewd enough politician to delay signing an edict against Luther and his followers until after he had secured financial support for his wars against the French and the Ottomans. His advisors had informed him that the Wittenberger was enormously popular with people all over Germany and with intellectuals throughout Europe, thanks to the thousands of printed copies of his writings that were already in circulation. With help against his enemies assured, Charles issued an edict from Worms on May 8, 1521, that made the professor an outlaw and commanded Charles's subjects not to aid him or his followers. Furthermore, "no one shall dare to buy, sell, read, preserve, or print any of Martin Luther's books."[15]

ANTICLERICALISM

Unfortunately from the emperor's point of view, the enforcement of the Edict of Worms against Luther proved impossible. Because he had touched such a culturally significant nerve with his attack against indulgences, which in turn played into a long-standing tradition of anticlericalism, Luther and his writings had attained enormous popularity by the close of the Diet of Worms in the spring of 1521. As the papal representative Girolamo Aleander (1480–1542) informed his master in Rome, ". . . all of Germany is in an uproar. Nine-tenths put up the battle cry, 'Luther!' and the other tenth 'Death to the papal court!'"[16]

Although Aleander's claims were greatly exaggerated, there was no question that in the spring of 1521, the now outlawed Wittenberg professor had become a German national hero, even if not always a clearly understood one. For example, some humanists initially thought the Wittenberger was one of them, but he was not a humanist in all respects. Luther's fundamental concern was for changing the way that humans understood their relationship with God. He thought that human will had nothing to do with salvation. For Luther it was God's decision, not ours, who is to be given the gift of saving faith. Pressured to prove he was not a Lutheran, in 1524 the great humanist Erasmus challenged Luther's theology of predestination in a pamphlet entitled *On the Freedom of the Will*. Luther responded in Au-

gustinian terms with a 1525 tract, *On the Enslaved Will*.

In 1521 many, including Erasmus, thought of Martin Luther as a German folk hero who wanted to clean up the church and liberate the empire from the "money grubbing rapacity" of the Italian-dominated clerical hierarchy. Indeed, if anything can be said to have unified the early Reformation, it was anticlericalism. Anticlericalism is a difficult concept for modern people to grasp partly because in a modern congregation there is little particular reason to be jealous of the privileges of the ministers or priests. In fact, the salaries of most modern clerics are far less than the average income of the laity in many Christian churches. In the sixteenth century, a typical priest made more money and lived a better lifestyle than most of his parishioners. For example, the clergy were exempt from taxation and were not citizens of towns, which meant that they avoided such unpleasant civic obligations such as sentry duty on the town's walls in bad weather.

Clerical celibacy was another sore point. Some clerics sought intimacy with the wives of parishioners; others kept concubines. Tales of lusty priests seducing women were a staple of European literature, as the highly popular writings of Giovanni Boccaccio and Marguerite of Navarre illustrate, and those who could not read relished gossip about lascivious priests, monks, and nuns. Yet real cases of clerical misconduct caused a great deal of anguish, anger, and resentment, even for those who knew that most clerics kept their vows. To many Europeans, even if they liked the clergy they knew personally, the clergy as an abstract body often were considered arrogant, fat, lazy, and lecherous. Although these prejudices did not square with reality in many cases, they were widely held.

LUTHER AT THE WARTBURG CASTLE, MAY 1521 TO MARCH 1522

As for Martin Luther, after the Diet of Worms he had seemingly vanished from the public scene. Frederick the Wise, hoping that his star professor's appearance before the emperor would end the controversy, had a alternate plan in case things went wrong. Duke Frederick's back-up strategy was that Luther would be taken to one of Frederick's more hidden fortresses, the Wartburg, and kept quiet while things cooled down in the empire. The workaholic Luther, disguised as Knight George, kept himself busy at the Wartburg by completing the draft of a translation of the New Testament into highly readable German. It took Luther until 1534 to complete his German Bible because his Hebrew was not as strong as his Greek. Luther's German translation was an enormous intellectual and literary success. Although not the first German Bible, it acquired an enduring popularity and thus helped put the Word of God into the hands of more people than ever before thanks to the printing presses that churned out numerous editions.

Luther's stay at the Wartburg was interrupted by disturbances at Wittenberg in December of 1521. The Reformation had continued in his absence as colleagues such as the brilliant humanist Greek scholar Philip Melanchthon (1497–1560) had, among other things, celebrated the first evangelical Lord's Supper. That is, Melanchthon had distributed the wine as well as the bread to the laity, as Luther had recommended in his 1520 pamphlet, *On the Babylonian Captivity of the Church*. Although much of the liturgy remained the same, the Lutherans argued that the Mass was not a sacrifice and that Christ's body and blood were present "in, with, and under the elements," but that the bread and wine remained bread and wine.

Some, however, like his colleague Andreas Bodenstein von Karlstadt, thought the pace of reform was too slow and wanted even more changes to be made. The unstable atmosphere was also intensified by the street corner preaching of one of Luther's former students, Marcus Stübner, joined by two illiterate weavers from the nearby town of Zwickau. Luther did not rule out the possibility that God might speak through the common man, but he wondered why it was that so many self-proclaimed prophets later proved to be "drunks and liars." Why would God work through them when he could use someone like Professor Luther as his spokesperson? Actually, since the Scriptures, as interpreted by well-educated clergy like himself and his good friend

Lucas Cranach the Elder, *Luther as an Augustinian Monk* (c. 1522–1524). Courtesy of the Germanisches Nationalmuseum, Nuremberg, Germany.

Philip Melanchthon, now spoke so clearly, was there really much of a need for such "prophets"?

As for Professor Bodenstein, he had obviously been carried away with enthusiasm and was persuaded to moderate his course. Luther did preach publicly against the Zwickau "prophets" and urged his followers to moderate their zeal. Such was Luther's stature that a few well-chosen words from him were sufficient to restore a measure of tranquility to Wittenberg. He then promptly returned to the Wartburg Castle until March of 1522 when a new round of excess zeal led by the recently married Bodenstein compelled him to return and take leadership of the Reformation in Wittenberg from those whom he dubbed "false brethren." Bodenstein now left Wittenberg for a pastorate in Orlamünde, where he could carry out his own more radical reform program free from the authority of Luther and his cautious prince, Frederick the Wise.

The Knights' Revolt of 1522 to 1524

Despite the bombast of some of his utterances, Luther was at heart a conservative law-and-order man. He had been alarmed that some wanted to use a sword to spread the Reformation and the Gospel. One of those would-be "swashbuckle Reformers" was the Imperial Knight Franz von Sickingen, who offered his sword to Luther in 1521 at the Diet of Worms. Luther politely but firmly declined the offer, but did dedicate one of his writings to Sickingen. The paladin had been converted to the cause of reform by his friend Ulrich von Hutten (1488–1523), the humanist-knight. One of the authors of the *Letters of the Obscure Men*, Hutten had many grievances with the Catholic church and favored the subordination of the papacy to the emperor.

FRANZ VON SICKINGEN (1481–1523)

Like many other members of the lower nobility in the Holy Roman Empire, Hutten and Sickingen had seen their land-based fortunes decline as part of the general economic changes Europe underwent at the beginning of the sixteenth century. With the value of their land holdings falling and expenses—because of inflation—rising, some nobles became robber knights attacking merchants' caravans. Others, like Sickingen, also became soldiers of fortune, selling themselves and their military skills to the highest bidder.

Sickingen had begun his career as a robber baron by attacking the towns of Frankfurt on Main, Metz, and Worms. In April 1515, Emperor Maximilian I declared him to be an outlaw but failed to take the necessary actions to enforce that declaration. The emperor was unwilling to punish the lower nobility, many of whom had friends and relatives at court, in part because he needed some of them as line officers. Military expertise was a valuable commodity. Sickingen soon found his services as a fighter in demand by both King François I of France and his rival Charles of Spain. He accepted the Habsburg's higher bid, but his campaign of 1521 in the first Habsburg-Valois War proved a disaster. The imperial government then defaulted on a loan of 76,000 gulden and Sickingen had to send home many of his unpaid troops with empty promises of future repayment.

During this difficult period in his life, Sickingen was converted to the cause of Martin Luther by a fellow knight, Ulrich von Hutten. Both had been disgusted by attacks against their intellectual hero Johann Reuchlin by the Dominicans of Cologne. They were both envious of the wealth of the Italian-dominated church. When Luther refused Sickingen's offer of military protection, the knight decided on his own means of reform, which included attacking the wealth of the archbishop of Trier in western Germany.

In August 1522, Sickingen launched an attack on the episcopal city of Trier, which found its own champion, ironically, in the form of the pro-Lutheran Margrave Philip of Hesse (1504–1567). Philip, known as the Magnanimous, admired Luther, but like the reformer was appalled at the idea of a violent Reformation and the threat to property posed by Sickingen and his raiders. As a staunch law-and-order man who recognized the threat to privilege posed by the knights, Philip moved to help the archbishop of Trier and others crush Sickingen and his followers. Sickingen's forces were soon driven back from the old episcopal city on the Mosel River.

Sickingen and many of his allies soon found themselves retreating to their home castles, which fell one by one to the artillery of the allied princes and in central Germany to the forces of the Swabian League of princes and cities. Sickingen was killed in 1523 during the siege of his castle at Land-stühl. His confederate Hutten fled to the reformer Huldrych Zwingli's Zurich in Switzerland, where he died of syphilis.

Encouraged by the success of the offensive against Sickingen, the army of the Swabian League of towns and princes assembled an army of 1,500 cavalry and 15,000 foot soldiers at Dinkelsbühl in the summer of 1523. The army was commanded by the able and ruthless George Truchsess von Waldburg (1488–1531). They began attacking robber baron castles in Franconia one by one. Thirty in all were destroyed by the forces of the Swabian League. The war against the knights proved a dress rehearsal for the even more destructive Peasants' War soon to follow. These bloody episodes began the awful linkage between Reformation ideas, social upheaval, and political violence, connections which blighted the course of the Reformation.

Chronology

c. 1460–1525	Life of Johann von Staupitz.
c. 1480	Birth of Andreas Bodenstein von Karlstadt.
1483	Birth of Martin Luther at Eisleben.
1486	Birth of Johann Eck.
1497	Birth of Philip Melanchthon.
1505	Thunderstorm and Luther's entrance into an Augustinian monastery at Erfurt.
1507	Luther celebrates his first Mass as a priest.
1512	Luther completes his doctorate in theology.
1513–1521	Reign of Pope Leo X (Giovanni de' Medici).
1517	The Ninety-five Theses against Indulgences.
1518	Luther meets with Cardinal Cajetan at Augsburg.
1519	Election of Charles of Habsburg as Holy Roman emperor; Leipzig Debate with Johann Eck.
1520	Pope Leo X's bull *Exsurge Domine* gives Luther sixty days to submit; Luther publishes a series of revolutionary pamphlets.
1521	The Diet of Worms; Luther at the Wartburg; Tumult at Wittenberg.
1522	Franz von Sickingen's campaign against Trier.
1523	Franconian robber knights crushed by Swabian League.

Further Reading

MARTIN LUTHER: BIBLIOGRAPHIES

Kenneth Hagen, et al., *Annotated Bibliography of Luther Studies*, 3 volumes to date (1977–).

Jonathan Zophy, "Martin Luther, 1483–1546," *Research Guide to European Historical Biography*, vol. 7 (1994).

LUTHER BIOGRAPHIES

Roland Bainton, *Here I Stand: A Life of Martin Luther* (1950).

Heinrich Bornkamm, *Luther in Mid-Career, 1521–1530* (1983).

Martin Brecht, *Martin Luther*, 3 vols. (1985–1992). The leading biography.

A. G. Dickens, *The German Nation and Martin Luther* (1974).

Mark Edwards, Jr., *Luther and the False Brethren* (1975).

———, *Luther's Last Battles* (1983).

Richard Friedenthal, *Luther: His Life and Times* (1967).

Leif Grane, *Martinus Noster: Luther in the German Reform Movement, 1518–1521* (1994).

Eric Gritsch, *Martin—God's Court Jester* (1983).

H. G. Haile, *Luther: An Experiment in Biography* (1980).

James Kittelson, *Luther the Reformer* (1986).

Walter von Loewenich, *Martin Luther* (1986).

Bernhard Lohse, *Martin Luther: An Introduction to His Life and Work* (1986).

Peter Manns, *Martin Luther: An Illustrated Biography* (1982).

Heiko Oberman, *Luther: Man between God and the Devil* (1989).

John Todd, *Luther: A Life* (1982).

LUTHER'S THOUGHT

Paul Althaus, *The Theology of Martin Luther* (1966).

Gerhard Brendler, *Martin Luther: Theology and Revolution* (1991).

J. Cargil Thompson, *The Political Thought of Martin Luther* (1984).

Brian Gerrish, *Grace and Reason: A Study in the Theology of Luther* (1962).

Scott Hendrix, *Luther and the Papacy* (1981).

Alister McGrath, *Luther's Theology of the Cross* (1985).

Gordon Rupp, *The Righteousness of God* (1953).

David Steinmetz, *Luther in Context* (1986).

SOME OF LUTHER'S EARLY ASSOCIATES

Calvin Pater, *Karlstadt as the Father of the Baptist Movement: The Emergence of Lay Protestantism* (1993).

Ronald Sider, *Andreas Bodenstein von Karlstadt* (1974).

David Steinmetz, *Misericordia Dei: The Theology of Johannes von Staupitz in Its Late Medieval Setting* (1968).

THE KNIGHTS' REVOLT

William Hitchcock, *The Background of the Knights' Revolt, 1522–1523* (1958).

Hajo Holborn, *Ulrich von Hutten and the German Reformation* (1937).

Notes

1. Cited in Heiko Oberman, *Luther: Man between God and the Devil*, tr. Eileen Walliser-Schwarzbart (New Haven, Conn.: Yale University Press, 1989), p. 87.
2. Cited in James Kittelson, *Luther the Reformer: The Story of the Man and His Career* (Minneapolis, Minn.: Augsburg, 1986), p. 50.
3. Cited in Eric Gritsch, *Martin—God's Court Jester: Luther in Retrospect* (Philadelphia: Fortress Press, 1983), p. 7.
4. Cited in Hans Hillerbrand, *The Reformation: A Narrative History Related by Contemporary Observers and Participants* (New York: Harper and Row, 1964), p. 27.

5. Ibid., p. 43.

6. Cited in Kittelson, *Luther*, pp. 103–104.

7. Martin Luther, "Ninety-five Theses," in Helmut Lehman and Jaroslav Pelikan, eds., *Luther's Works*, 55 vols. (St. Louis and Philadelphia: Concordia and Fortress Presses, 1955–1975), vol. 31, p. 33.

8. Cited in E. R. Chamberlin, *The Bad Popes* (New York: Dial Press, 1969), p. 248.

9. Cited in Roland Bainton, *Here I Stand: A Life of Martin Luther* (New York: Abingdon, 1950), p. 85.

10. Cited in Jonathan Zophy, *Patriarchal Politics and Christoph Kress (1484–1535) of Nuremberg* (Lewiston, N.Y.: Edwin Mellen Press, 1992), p. 64.

11. Cited in Lewis Spitz, ed., *The Protestant Reformation* (Englewood Cliffs, N.J.: Prentice Hall, 1966), p. 55.

12. Ibid., pp. 63–67,

13. Cited in Oberman, *Luther*, p. 39.

14. Cited in Hillerbrand, *Reformation*, p. 94.

15. Ibid., p. 100.

16. Cited in Kittelson, *Luther*, p. 158.

6

THE SPREAD
OF LUTHERANISM

A New Pope and New Hope, 1522–1524

While the Knights' Revolt was brewing, Pope Leo X died and the College of Cardinals elected the reform-minded Adrian of Utrecht as his replacement to the throne of St. Peter. A native of the Low Countries, Adrian was the only non-Italian to be elected in the sixteenth century and the only non-Italian to serve in that office until John Paul II of Poland was elected in 1978. Adrian had been a professor of theology and an administrator at the University of Louvain in the Netherlands before joining the service of the Habsburgs. Emperor Maximilian I hired him in 1507 to tutor his grandson and heir, Charles. Charles loved his tutor and had him promoted to a series of high church offices in Spain. In 1517, at the behest of Charles as king of Spain, Leo X made Adrian a cardinal.

As pope, Adrian VI recognized the need for reform in the church. Although he had supported the condemnation of Martin Luther's teachings by the theological faculty of his former university at Louvain, Adrian opposed the corruption found in the College of Cardinals, as well as pluralism, simony, and nepotism. Even though Adrian's call for a general church council to

reform abuses and clarify doctrines was rejected by those afraid of change, the pope did appoint a Reform Commission and was prepared to act on their recommendations when he died of the plague in 1523 after a promising reign of just twenty months. Few realized then that when Adrian VI died, the best hope for a peaceful Reformation died with him. Many in Rome hated Adrian's threat to the status quo and openly celebrated his demise. Although Adrian's successor, Clement VII, was a Medici, he lacked his family's characteristic boldness and thus had no stomach to take on the vested interests that were determined to block change.

THE DIETS OF NUREMBERG, 1522–1524

Back in Germany, three successive Imperial Diets met in the town of Nuremberg between 1522 and 1524. They were all presided over by the emperor's younger brother, Archduke Ferdinand (1503–1564), because Emperor Charles V had pressing business to attend to in Spain and elsewhere. Although educated in Spain, the affable Ferdinand made every effort to learn German and become "one of the boys" with the hard drinking and partying princes of the empire. This was in direct contrast to his more somber older brother, who always seemed stiff and remote to many and became more and more a Spaniard as he aged rapidly.

The three Imperial Diets at Nuremberg also had pressing business, including the "Luther affair" and the enforcement of the Edict of Worms against Luther. However, other matters took priority, for the Ottomans had taken the important fortress city of Belgrade in the Balkans in 1521 and the island of Rhodes in the eastern Mediterranean. If Christendom fell to the Ottoman crescent, it might not really matter whether or not the Edict of Worms against the Lutherans had been enforced or whether capitalist monopolies had been crushed. Archduke Ferdinand found himself in a weak position for pressing the German powers to eliminate the Lutherans. The Habsburgs had to move cautiously. When Ferdinand tried to get the estates to take decisive action against the Lutherans, they answered with lists of grievances against the church and called for a general council to reform the church. The 1524 Diet of Nuremberg decreed that "until a church council should meet, the holy Gospel should be preached according to old and established interpretations."[1] The language was sufficiently vague to allow the followers of Luther and other reformers additional time to continue to win converts despite the horrors associated with the Peasants' Revolts which raged throughout the German speaking world from 1524 to 1526.

THE SPREAD OF LUTHERANISM: THE CASE OF NUREMBERG

After a Religious Debate, the government of Nuremberg officially adopted Lutheranism in March 1525. This meant that one of the largest of the towns in the empire had become an outpost of Wittenberg in the heart of Germany. As the storage place of the imperial jewelry and regalia and host of three

successive Imperial Diets, as well as the seat of the Imperial Council of Regency and the Imperial Supreme Court, Nuremberg was virtually the capital city of the Holy Roman Empire. Therefore, its adoption of Lutheranism put the Catholic Habsburgs in an extremely awkward position. Understanding how this came to be is important for comprehending the rapid spread of the Reformation, even if other communities adopted the reform for somewhat different reasons and under a bewildering variety of circumstances. Most of the empire's large towns witnessed some sort of reform movement.

The way towards Reformation in Nuremberg had been paved for the introduction of evangelical ideas by an elite humanist group made up of members of the town's intellectual and business elite. It included the patrician Willibald Pirckheimer, the city secretary Lazarus Spengler, the artist Albrecht Dürer, and several leading members of the ruling city council. Therefore, some of the wealthiest and most prominent men in Nuremberg had an early exposure to the ideas of Martin Luther, who twice visited the city in 1518 and made several important friends. In addition to his attacks on clerical abuses, Luther's message offered hope for the release from the burdens of guilt imposed by traditional Catholic beliefs and practices such as regular confessions of sins. As Albrecht Dürer put it:

> In my opinion, it is exactly here that Luther has helped to clarify the situation by making it a point to trust God more than oneself, worldly works, and the laws of human beings. . . . For I believe it is wrong to confuse individuals with a sense of sins, errors, and doubts.[2]

Luther's emphasis on salvation through faith struck a positive chord in the hearts and minds of many Nurembergers. Many also liked his notion of vocation, which stressed that all honest work is useful in serving God. It is little wonder that a number of Nuremberg craftspeople such as the cobbler-poet Hans Sachs saluted Luther as the "Wittenberg nightingale." The lawyer Christoph Scheurl declared in 1520 that "the patriciate, the multitude of other citizens, and all scholars stand on Luther's side."[3] That is why, between 1520 and 1522, the city government appointed a series of church officials who had either been Luther's students at Wittenberg or had been converted by his writings. The most prominent of them was Andreas Osiander (1496–1552), who became the pastor of the town's major church and the leading theological advisor to the government.

The appointment of Lutheran preachers not only helped consolidate the hold of Luther's ideas upon the people of Nuremberg, but it also allowed the city government to assert its independence from the pope and its nearby ecclesiastical overlord, the bishop of Bamberg. For centuries, Nuremberg had struggled to become free of the political authority of the neighboring margraves of Brandenburg-Ansbach. A similar pattern developed with respect to the church. In 1474 the city gained the right to nominate candidates for the position of provost at each of its two major parish churches. In 1514 Pope Leo X granted the Nuremberg government full patronage rights over all the city's churches. With the adoption of Lutheranism in 1525, the Nuremberg merchant oligarchy had assumed complete ecclesiastical sovereignty, including the right to supervise the cloistered clergy inside the city and its territory. If the paternalistic patriarchs of the city government could regulate all aspects of the social life of the town, should they not be able to control the religious life of their citizens as well? It was an opportunity for power too tempting to miss and Nuremberg's

city council seized the chance which Luther's revolt had brought them.

Not everyone in Nuremberg was pleased with the adoption of the reform. Many of the city's monks and nuns resented bitterly the efforts in the spring of 1525 to close their cloisters. The most spirited resistance to the Reformation was offered by the nuns of St. Clara's Convent, led by the learned Abbess Charitas Pirckheimer (1466–1532), the sister of the prominent humanist Willibald Pirckheimer and a skilled Latinist. She used all her political connections and passive resistance to keep her convent open despite Nuremberg's official adoption of Lutheranism. Several daughters of prominent Lutheran politicians had to be dragged from the convent. Finally, the diplomatic Philip Melanchthon interceded on behalf of the nuns after meeting with Charitas. He recommended that the town fathers proceed more carefully with the nuns of St. Clara's, whose piety and learning he admired. Melanchthon recommended that the nuns not be allowed to take new members or receive their Franciscan preachers, but that essentially they be left alone. The Nuremberg government followed Melanchthon's advice and the convent survived until 1590.

The German Peasants' War, 1524–1526

The often fragile nature of social relations in the first decades of the sixteenth century and the potential for class warfare were illustrated by the German Peasants' War. Frequent late medieval agrarian revolts had established a tradition of peasant insurrection. Clerical and noble landlords had ruthlessly exploited their farm workers and violated village rights and customs. Commoners also complained that they were denied access to the markets of their choice, or were forced to sell to their lords at unfairly low prices. Some areas were overpopulated and some territories such as Alsace, Franconia, and the Upper Rhine suffered failed harvests for nearly two decades. Because a largely agricultural-based economy seldom produced much beyond subsistence, the hunger, disease, ignorance, and collective misery in the 1520s was alarming.

Political grievances were also a major factor in the Peasants' Revolt. The rising territorial states often replaced local communal self-government with the rule of district officials. To create a uniformity of administration and legal practice, customary law was being replaced by Roman law, changes that many peasants found unsettling. Efforts were made in some areas to bind the peasants to the land by reimposing serfdom. New taxes on beer, wine, milling, and slaughtering of farm animals were also deeply resented, as was the insistence of some church officials on the payments of *tithes* (the tenth of one's income) even during times of poor harvests.

The beginnings of the Reformation in Germany only intensified feelings of anticlericalism among the peasantry and some artisans in the towns. Martin Luther's emphasis on the universal priesthood of all believers gave new importance to the role of the laity in the affairs of the church. Some working people interpreted Luther's call for Christian liberty as an invitation to take more control over their own lives. Reform propagandists popularized the ideal of "Karsthans," the evangelical peasant who stood closer to God than a priest. The challenge to the authority of the Roman Catholic church resulted in some villages insisting on the right to elect their own clergy. Peasants also began to justify their demands not only in terms of traditional law, but also in terms of divine law and Scripture. Even

Albrecht Dürer, *Market Peasants* (1512). Woodcut. Foto Marburg / Art Resource.

some of the so-called "simple folk" of Germany had a sense that change was possible.

THE OUTBREAK OF THE REVOLT, MAY 1524

Astrologers had long predicted that 1524 would be a year of disasters, and for once they were right. This notion was supported by the popular saying, "He who does not die in 1523, does not drown in 1524, and is not killed in 1525 can truly speak of miracles."[4] On May 30, 1524, subjects of the Black Forest abbey of St. Blasien rebelled against their overlord, declaring that they would pay no more feudal dues and render no more feudal services. This was followed by work stoppages at Stühlingen in the southern Black Forest on June 24. Here the peasants were incensed by Count Sigismund's restrictions on self-government in the peasant communities. When the count refused to negotiate in good faith, peasant groups, led by the former soldier Hans Müller, began to march through the Black Forest, raising the standard of rebellion. The rebels found sympathy and ready allies among the citizens of the town of Waldschut, led by their reformminded pastor, Balthasar Hubmaier, the future Anabaptist leader.

The revolt soon spread throughout many parts of southern Germany. Both Archduke Ferdinand of Austria and the Swabian League found it impossible to take immediate steps against the dissidents, for nearly all available military forces were committed to the second Habsburg war with France in northern Italy. The Swabian League was bogged down by its cumbersome organizational and financial structure, and Catholic members of the league suspected that towns friendly to Luther, such as Nuremberg, were secretly plotting with the peasant rebels. Although some town artisans were supportive of the peasants, their governments were not. They began sending the Swabian League military aid and money. The league eventually sorted out some of its internal problems and created an effective command structure under George Truchsess von Waldburg, their commander during the war against the Franconian knights of 1523. Then came the news that the Habsburgs had won the Battle of Pavia and captured the French king on February 24, 1525. That allowed some of the Habsburgs' allies to transfer military resources to Germany. With the arrival of fresh troops from the end of the second Habsburg-Valois War, the Swabian League was ready to strike with nearly full force against the rebellious peasants.

THOMAS MÜNTZER (c. 1490–1525)

While the privileged orders were organizing their forces, the radical reformer Thomas Müntzer was hard at work among the dissidents in the Klettgau region for eight weeks. A Saxon native, he had studied at Leipzig, Frankfurt, and Mainz. As early as 1518, he became a partisan of Martin Luther. With the Wittenberger's help, Müntzer secured a pastorate in the town of Zwickau, where he came under the influence of Nicholas Storch, one of the "Zwickau prophets." Increasingly radicalized and frustrated by the slow pace of reform, Müntzer was ousted from Zwickau in April 1521. He fled to Prague, where he also got in trouble with local authorities. In the spring of 1523, Müntzer secured a pastorate at the town of Allstedt in Saxony.

There he fully developed his sense of himself as an Old Testament-style prophet. He began to openly challenge the more conservative Martin Luther for being "slavishly bound to the Gospel" and for not recognizing the continuing revelation of the Holy Spirit.[5] His sermons became increasingly apocalyptic as he foresaw the destruction of the godless by the elect of God and the coming of the reign of Christ on earth. Duke Johann of Saxony, who attended one of his sermons in July 1524, was alarmed by Müntzer's radicalism and ordered him to leave his pastorate. He fled to Mühlhausen, where an ex-priest named Heinrich Pfeiffer was leading a revolution.

Under the spell of Pfeiffer and his associates and his own arrogance, Müntzer now saw the rebellious peasants and their urban artisan allies as God's chosen instruments for the war of the godly against the godless. He moved to Thuringia and then to Saxony, urging the peasants in sermons and pamphlets that now was the time to strike. Urged on by Müntzer, Pfeiffer, and others during February and March of 1525, major peasant armies developed in Upper Swabia, Franconia, and Thuringia. Groups of rebels began seizing lands, burning castles, and looting churches and monasteries. Fearing destruction, several town governments co-operated with peasant bands.

The Swabian League under George Truchsess von Waldburg led the counterattack in Franconia. Waldburg's ferocity had been increased by the gruesome death of his cousin Count Ludwig von Helfenstein, who had been forced to walk through a gauntlet of peasant spears along with thirteen other nobles and ten of their servants. Helfenstein and the others were then executed while his former servant Jäcklin Rohrbach piped a tune. When Waldburg captured Rohrbach, he had him bound to a tree by an iron chain long enough to allow the captive to move two feet from the tree. Wood was then piled around the tree and the piper was slowly roasted to death.

Elsewhere, the Evangelical Philip of Hesse and the convinced Catholic Duke George of Saxony joined forces on May 15, 1525, to attack rebellious peasants at Frankenhausen, near Luther's birthplace. Thomas Müntzer hurried to Frankenhausen with 300 reinforcements, but even his presence and fiery oratory could not save the day for the outgunned peasants. The bloody Battle of Frankenhausen ended in a complete rout of the peasants and the end of the Peasants' War in Thuringia. The victors arrested Müntzer, viciously tortured him, and later executed him and fifty-two other peasant leaders.

THE END OF THE 1524–1526
PEASANTS' WAR

The Swabian League defeated peasant armies at Königshofen (near the Tauber River, due west of Nuremberg) on June 2 and at Ingolstadt on June 4. Even with some professional military help, the rebels were no match for the better-trained, more powerful, and determined forces arrayed against them. After being crushed in battle, the armies of poor people were often subject to brutal reprisals including exile, fines, blindings, torture, and imprisonment. Margrave Casimir of Brandenburg-Ansbach (1481–1527) was particularly cruel in his treatment of vanquished rebels. He ordered the blinding of sixty rebels at Kitzingen and had to be restrained from doing further damage by his brother, George, who pointed out to him that if Casimir blinded too many of his subjects he would have no one left to wait upon him or work his fields.

George, known for his piety, also persuaded his more temperamental brother that the real cause of the peasants' revolt in Franconia was the lack of uniformity in preaching. George recommended that "unlearned and unsuitable preachers be exiled" and replaced with "pious, honorable Christian preachers who would preach the Word of God purely and cleanly."[6] By this George meant Lutheran preachers. Casimir was eventually persuaded to go along with his brother's plan and on August 30, 1525, he issued an edict exiling all Catholic clergy from Brandenburg-Ansbach and replacing them with Lutherans. Thus another important territory had been converted to Lutheranism by the actions of its rulers.

Some of the victors, such as Christoph Kress of Nuremberg and one of the Swabian League's military advisors, tried to restrain their more zealous colleagues because many "knew how these people [the peasants] were brought to rebellion and the insufferable burdens with which they have been oppressed."[7] Moderation was also urged because they recognized how much their privileges depended on the hard work of the poor. Kress was able to get punishments lessened, including those levied on the towns of Dinkelsbühl, Heilbronn, Rothenburg on the Tauber, and Windsheim, which Margrave Casimir accused of having collaborated with the rebels. Nuremberg, which had officially adopted Lutheranism after a public debate on March 1525, even loaned some of its smaller neighbors the money to pay their fines to the Swabian League.

Peace came last to Austria, where a rebellion had first broken out in Brixen on May 9, 1525. The rebels plundered religious houses and noble castles and joined in opposition to the payment of church tithes. They elected Michael Gaismair, the bishop of Brixen's former secretary, as their leader. Gaismair proved a surprising combination of practical military strategist and utopian dreamer. Later, outside of Salzburg, he called for the establishment of a Christian, egalitarian, democratic republic that would care for the poor, ensure speedy justice for all, effect coinage and tax reforms, and guarantee the free preaching of the Word of God. By July 1526, forces from the Swabian League and the archbishop of Salzburg defeated Gaismair's motley army. Gaismair escaped to anti-Habsburg Venice, where a Habsburg agent assassinated him in 1532.

The Peasants' War of 1524 to 1526 resulted in the death of approximately 100,000 peasants and artisans. Most of the dead were males, but a few females, such as the runaway serf Margaret Rennerin, joined in the fighting. Sixty women rebels were known to have stormed a convent at Windsheim on May 5, 1525. Other women cooked, did laundry, nursed the wounded, sold goods, and tended camp for the peasant armies. Some worked as prostitutes. Most of the wives and daughters of warring peasants stayed at home and worked the land in their husband's or father's absence. Many were left with a great sense of loss and betrayal.

MARTIN LUTHER AND THE PEASANTS' WAR

As a child of working people, Martin Luther was sympathetic to the injustices under which many men and women labored. However, he was as opposed to peasant violence as he was to knightly violence. For him, social and economic grievances were to be addressed peacefully and out of Christian love. When the rebels refused to lay down their weapons, he became convinced that the devil was at work among the rebels and in anger he wrote *Against the Robbing and Murdering Horde of Peasants* in May 1525. Luther urged the authorities "to slay, stab, and smite" the rebels lest even more bloodshed follow as the rebellion spread.[8] Of course, the frightened authorities needed no exhortation from Luther to take stern measures against the rebels.

Some peasants felt betrayed by Luther and returned to their traditional Catholic beliefs. Promises to address peasant and artisan grievances at the next Imperial Diet were never kept. The rich and the powerful seldom concern themselves with the problems of the humble folk. In contrast, Martin Luther continued to be concerned about the oppression of the working people and had high hopes that the message of the Gospel about love and charity would lead to an improvement in the way the ruling classes treated those below them on the social scale. His belief was that better Christians would make better masters.

Katherine von Bora (1499–1550)

In the midst of the great crisis of the Peasants' War, the celibate ex-friar Martin Luther married a former nun, Katherine von Bora. At age ten she had been placed in a convent by her recently remarried father, who found, as had so many others, that unwanted children could become "brides of Christ" for smaller dowries than more earthly bridegrooms and their parents usually required. Katherine was not completely fulfilled by convent life, for when she read Luther's writings against clerical vows and monastic celibacy she decided to flee the cloisters. Katherine and eleven of her fellow nuns hid in empty barrels used for transporting smoked herring and bravely made their escape on the eve of Easter 1523.

Three of the nuns were taken in by their families, but Katherine and eight of her "sisters" ended up at Luther's Wittenberg. Runaway nuns who were not great beauties or lacked disposable wealth were becoming an increasingly difficult problem for the early Reformation. Efforts to marry Katherine failed and after two years in Wittenberg, Luther decided to marry her himself. He figured it was a good way to please his father, "spite the devil, and upset the pope."[9] As for Katherine, she liked Luther enough to marry him and eventually grew to love him deeply.

Learning to cherish the forty-two year-old professor who had spent so much of his adult life in all-male schools and monasteries proved at times to be a difficult task for Katherine. Luther had failed to change the straw in his bedding for a full year prior to their wedding night. The straw was so worn that it decomposed beneath the weight of their lovemaking, which the formerly celibate ex-monk enjoyed enormously. He boasted to friends about his newly discovered, mid-life sexuality: "I now go to bed each night with a beautiful woman and that is my Katie."[10] Six children followed in rapid succession from this union.

Martin Luther proved to be a tenderhearted, loving husband and father who shared in parental responsibilities to an unusual degree. The reformer was one of the

Lucas Cranach the Elder, *Portrait of Katherine von Bora*. Uffizi, Florence, Italy. Alinari/Art Resource.

first husbands to publicly advocate a form of partnership in marriage. He admired his wife's resourcefulness in stretching his modest academic salary so that he could entertain visiting dignitaries and homesick students alike. Katherine took in paying boarders and ran a successful small farm. She brewed excellent beer that Luther enjoyed immensely, though in moderation. Although usually deferring to her more learned husband, she was not afraid to speak her own mind at times, even when she disagreed with him.

Partly through his association with Katherine and his daughters, as well as through contacts with educated noblewomen with whom he corresponded, Luther came to appreciate some of women's gifts. He even became one of the first prominent advocates of elementary schooling for girls and helped women find jobs as elementary school teachers. He continued, however, to see women as equal to men "only in Christ." In this world, women were best confined to the domestic sphere, and they were not to assume too many public responsibilities, according to Luther. For example, he admired Argula von Grumbach (b. 1490) for defending him in writing to the faculty of Johann Eck's University of Ingolstadt, but he still did not want even a learned woman like her or Katherine Zell of Strasbourg to be ministers. At his cherished home, Martin Luther remained a benevolent patriarch to the end.

The Emergence of Evangelical Politics

Although religious motivations had been an important factor in the origins of the Reformation, political considerations became a crucial factor in determining the very survival of the various reform movements inside the empire and in the Swiss Confederation. Had Charles V exercised the kind of direct power over his subjects in Germany that he did in Spain, Luther would most likely have been burned as a heretic and his movement suppressed in its infancy. Even the parallel Swiss reform movements of Huldrych Zwingli and his colleagues in Bern and Basel would probably not have been able to hold out had they been completely surrounded by hostile Catholic forces. Further complicating the situation in the empire was the real threat posed by the advancing armies of the Ottomans. Therefore, the decentralized structure of the Holy Roman Empire and the military and political developments of 1526 and after were of critical importance for the spread of the reform movements.

THE DIETS OF SPEYER, 1526 AND 1529

As Martin Luther was experiencing the joys and sorrows of wedded life, the estates of the Holy Roman Empire met in the episcopal town of Speyer on the Rhine in late June 1526. Again Archduke Ferdinand presided in place of his absentee brother; again reports reached the dignitaries that the "Grand Turk" was once more on the march. More towns and principalities had turned "Evangelical," so many that Ferdinand had to agree to permit "each one to live, govern, and carry himself as he hopes to answer it to God and His Imperial Majesty."[11] In other words, the principle of "he who rules, his religion" (*cuius regio, eius religio*) would be the order of the day until the long-awaited general church council could meet.

Again the main reason for the compromise was the need to gain support for the war against the Ottomans, who now threatened central Hungary, defended by its king and Ferdinand's brother-in-law, Louis II. On August 23, the Diet of Speyer voted to dispatch 24,000 troops (a great force by sixteenth-century standards) to aid Louis against the Ottomans. However, it was too little, too late: Sultan Süleyman's forces crushed the Hungarians and killed King Louis on August 29 at Mohács, along with 500 of his nobles and nearly 16,000 troops. Hungary was devastated and all of Europe now seemed exposed and vulnerable. Fortunately for the Habsburgs, the Ottomans were unable to follow up on this great victory. Noble Ottoman landowners, who served as officers, were obligated to return to their estates at regular intervals to supervise their underlings. This made sustained campaigning over long periods of time an impossibility.

Although the Ottomans did not continue their advance into central Europe, the Evangelicals proceeded to gain converts and to consolidate gains already made. Martin Luther aided the spread of the reform movement by continuing to publish tracts explaining his theology. He also composed hymns mostly based on the Psalms, which enriched Evangelical worship. Perhaps his best-known musical composition is "A Mighty Fortress Is Our God," a hymn based on Psalm 46. The Reformation thus kept spreading in repeated bursts of art (chiefly woodcuts), printed pamphlets, sermons, song, and, above all, word of mouth. If many Germans felt repressed by guilt, they found a form of liberation in Luther's emphasis on the righteousness of God.

As for Luther's opponents, they were embarrassed when segments of Charles V's army in Italy viciously sacked the city of Rome in the summer of 1527. Imperial paymasters had failed to pay Charles's mercenaries in time, and some of them decided to enrich themselves in Rome on the wealth of the church. Pope Clement was a virtual prisoner until order could be restored. That loyal son of the church, Charles V, while deploring the lack of discipline in his army, took advantage of the situation to broker a new understanding with the pope, who had been allied against the emperor's ambitions in Italy.

By the time the German estates met again at Speyer in March of 1529, the Habsburgs were determined to deal harshly with the Evangelicals, who seemed in a weaker position than in 1526. By 1529 the Ottoman threat was widely known to be so grave that few would support Philip of Hesse or Duke Johann of Saxony (1468–1532) in threatening to withhold aid for the war against the Ottomans if the religious rights of the Evangelicals were not respected. Johann, known as the Constant, had replaced his brother Frederick (d. 1525) as duke of Saxony and was a committed supporter of Martin Luther. Taking advantage of divisions among the Evangelicals, the Catholic majority voted to revoke the compromise of 1526 on religion and return to "the ancient usages and customs until a general council should meet."

Led by Philip of Hesse, Johann of Saxony, Christoph Kress of Nuremberg, and Jacob Sturm (1489–1553) of Strasbourg, the stunned Evangelicals protested the revocation of "he who rules, his religion" on April 30, 1529. The protest was denied by both Ferdinand and later by Charles V in Spain, but the label "Protestants" remained. The emperor even placed a protesting Evangelical delegation sent to him in Spain under house arrest. Relations between the Evangelicals and the Habsburgs were clearly eroding.

Fearing that the Habsburgs and the German Catholics were going to move against them militarily, Philip of Hesse and others began planning a Protestant military alliance. It seemed to the energetic Philip that theological unity among the Protestants would help facilitate political unity. Therefore, he invited the major Protestant theologians in the empire and Switzerland to come to his town of Marburg for a conference that started on the first of October. Most of the major evangelical theologians of the day accepted, including Martin Luther and his friend Philip Melanchthon. At Marburg, Luther met for the first time the famous leader of the Reformation in Zurich, Huldrych Zwingli. Zwingli had begun his own independent movement for reform at the same time as Luther's revolt. An intensely political theologian, he had extended his influence into other parts of Switzerland as well as into the Holy Roman Empire.

Despite their enormous egos, the Protestant theologians did manage to find many areas of doctrinal agreement, but they could not agree on the subject of the Eucharist. Luther continued to argue for a real presence of Christ in the sacrament; Zwingli favored a symbolic interpretation, and neither would budge on that key issue. They agreed to disagree on the Eucharist and to go their separate ways. Luther never fully trusted Zwingli and believed he was really a radical at heart like Bodenstein. By the time preparations were underway for the next Imperial Diet at Augsburg in the summer of 1530, the Protestants had achieved neither a theological nor a political unified front. They were, however, pleased with the news that at least the Ottomans had failed to take Vienna in the fall of 1529. Most of the politically sophisticated people in the empire recognized that if the Ottomans took well-fortified Vienna, they could easily penetrate into the heart of Germany itself.

The Augsburg Confession of 1530

With the Ottomans now concentrating on taking the rest of Hungary from its new king, the emperor's brother Ferdinand, Charles V announced that he would come to Augsburg, Germany, to preside over the next meeting of the Imperial Diet. Charles was determined to deal with the Protestants, but he took a more conciliatory tack this time, addressing Johann of Saxony, for example, as "Dear Uncle." Although many remained skeptical about the emperor's tolerance for varying religious ideas, others were hopeful that if Charles would only give the Protestants a fair hearing, he would discover what good Christians they were and let them live in peace. The problem, of course, was that Charles had no intention of letting his German subjects reject the pope's authority and, by extension, his own. Emperors saw themselves as representatives of Christ; Charles's grandfather, Maximilian, had dreamed of combining the imperial and papal crowns.

PHILIP MELANCHTHON (1497–1560)

Some took Charles at his word that "animosities would be set aside, all past errors left to the judgment of our Savior, and every man given a charitable hearing."[12] Johann of Saxony decided to take Charles seriously and ordered his theologians to draw up a statement of their Protestant beliefs, called a "confession." The chief author of the so-called Augsburg Confession was Philip Melanchthon, Luther's colleague and close friend. Born in Bretten near Karlsruhe, Melanchthon was the son of an armor manufacturer. After the death of his father in 1507, the direction of Philip's education was assumed by his uncle, the talented humanist Johann Reuchlin. After studies at Heidelberg (B.A., 1511) and Tübingen (M.A., 1514), Melanchthon joined the faculty of the University of Wittenberg in 1518 as an instructor in Greek and the classics. There he became a close friend of Martin Luther, despite the difference in their ages.

In 1521 Philip Melanchthon published the first edition of the *Loci Communes*, a much-admired basic text for teaching Evangelical theology. Melanchthon was a much more systematic thinker and writer than Luther, who compared his own writings to "grapeshot." Luther very much appreciated his colleague and said of him, Master Melanchthon "towers above" the doctors of theology. Luther knew his views were well represented by his brilliant colleague. Furthermore, Melanchthon could work inside the walls of Augsburg, unlike Luther, who was still an outlaw and had to wait impatiently for news of events from the relative safety of another Saxon castle at Coburg.

The conciliatory Melanchthon worked diligently to provide a confessional statement that surprised Emperor Charles with its mildness. The Zwinglians and others also presented separate theological statements to the emperor. Charles, not willing to play the role of arbitrator of theological disputes, appointed a committee of "qualified theologians" led by Luther's great debate opponent at Leipzig, Johann Eck, to examine the Lutheran statement of belief. Two weeks later Eck returned a 351-page rebuttal to Melanchthon's "Confession." Eck's language was so polemical and abusive that Emperor Charles ordered it toned down and refused to allow the Protestants to see it until it was revised. The emperor still needed Protestant support for his war against the feared Ottomans.

Finally on August 3, 1530, Eck's truncated thirty-one-page report, known as the *Confutation*, was read and it completely maintained the existing papal status quo. Speaking as a stern but kindly father figure, Charles insisted that the Protestants must accept the *Confutation*, renounce their heresies, return to the holy church of Rome, or face his righteous wrath. The Protestant diplomats responded that they must first be allowed to study Eck's report before they could respond. His patience at an end, the emperor refused them even this courtesy and insisted on their immediate obedience to his will.

The Protestants stalled for time and warded off various imperial efforts to divide them with gifts and promises. Many, like the disappointed Elector Johann of Saxony, simply left the Diet early and in disgust. Although those who remained did vote to supply the Habsburgs with 40,000 infantry and 8,000 cavalry, the Protestant minority refused to abandon their new religious understandings and prepared to organize themselves militarily in case the emperor decided to back up his April 15, 1531, deadline for submission with force. The emperor's threats had only served to stiffen the Protestant backbone, although some like the Nurembergers still hoped the situation would not degenerate into a religious civil war.

THE FORMATION OF THE SCHMALKALDIC LEAGUE

The failure of the Diet of Augsburg to heal the religious divisions in the empire led to a renewed effort on the part of Landgrave Philip of Hesse and others to form a military alliance among Protestants "in defense of the Gospel." Philip and a number of others believed that if the emperor refused to allow his subjects to worship freely, he could be resisted by them as "lesser magistrates," who were also ordained by God if below the emperor in status. Even that committed monarchist Martin Luther was now persuaded that he might have to drop his opposition to taking up arms against the emperor if Charles persisted in his efforts to destroy the religious faith of his Protestant subjects. However, Luther still hoped desperately, even as late as 1542, that peace might prevail. He wrote the Protestant princes:

> Even if somebody were to kill my father or brother, I am not judge or avenger. What need is there for laws and authorities, what need for God, if everybody wanted himself to be judge, avenger, even God over his neighbor, especially in worldly matters.[13]

By then a majority of Protestants had agreed at the town of Schmalkalden in the winter of 1530–31 to form a military league to protect each other. Eight Protestant princes led by Philip of Hesse and Johann of Saxony and ten cities led by Strasbourg and Ulm had agreed that:

> Whenever any one of us is attacked on account of the Word of God and the doctrine of the Gospel, all the others shall immediately come to his assistance as best they can.[14]

There were some important defections from this show of Protestant military solidarity. Mighty Nuremberg and some of its satellite towns refused to commit themselves to the

Schmalkaldic League. Nuremberg was joined in its refusal by its princely neighbor, Brandenburg-Ansbach, now ruled solely by the Lutheran Margrave George. Philip of Hesse and Johann of Saxony still hoped that the Nurembergers and Margrave George would change their collective minds and join the Schmalkaldic League at a later date.

Luther's Declining Years, 1530–1546

People aged much more rapidly in the sixteenth century than they do now. Indeed, the average life expectancy then was only about half of what it is now in the United States, where many people expect to live well beyond their seventies. Luther had just turned forty-eight when the Schmalkaldic League was formalized in January 1531. A lifelong workaholic with fluctuating mood swings, he would deteriorate steadily in the last two decades of his life while continuing to be a caring family man, pastor, and professor. Luther had long been a man who seemed to be caught in the tensions between God and the devil. Often in his last years, the devil seemed to be getting the upper hand.

Martin Luther's decline reflected the continual pressures of events in his own life and the life of the world around him. Every year seemed to bring a new load of sorrows. His father died in 1530, followed rapidly, as so often is the case, by the death of his mother in 1531. Even the news that Emperor Charles had agreed to summon a church council within a year and stop his Imperial Supreme Court from proceeding against Protestants or their lands failed to lessen Luther's gloom or improve his health. The emperor had made these concessions to the Protestants because he again needed their help in defending Vienna from the Ottomans. Protestant aid arrived in time to help the Imperials defeat the Ottomans at Grens, sixty miles southeast of Vienna. In

June 1533 Sultan Süleyman agreed to a peace treaty with the Habsburgs. Perhaps this time the peace would hold.

As for Martin Luther, his spirits eventually rose again as he fathered several more children, in whom he delighted, and managed to complete his German translation of the Bible in 1534. His completed Bible was a great literary success and helped make him one of the "fathers" of the modern German language. Prior to Luther's day, German was a polyglot language—written and spoken in a bewildering array of dialects. Luther's writings were so popular and written in such a delightful style that later generations of Germans favored his method of using the language. He outpublished his rival reformers by a wide margin. Thus Luther became one of the German equivalents to Geoffrey Chaucer for English, John Calvin and François Rabelais for French, and Miguel Cervantes for Spanish. If he had done nothing else, the German writings of Martin Luther would have earned him a prominent place in history.

Yet Luther continued to be troubled by the fact that not everyone agreed with his religious teachings or seemed to have been transformed by them. Even his catechisms designed for young and old had failed to substantially alter the sinful behavior of many, or so the often ailing Luther complained. As the reformer aged he had increasingly identified himself with his biblical hero, the Apostle Paul. Like Paul, Martin Luther felt he had made clear some of God's greatest mysteries. Were people so steeped in pride and sin that they refused to accept the truth now that it had been so wonderfully revealed to them?

THE BIGAMY OF PHILIP OF HESSE

While fighting off painful attacks of uric acid stones, Luther was troubled by reports of the radical and violent Anabaptist takeover of the city of Münster in western Germany. His theological quarrels with opponents and some of his own colleagues in reform continued. In 1540 Luther's secret support for the bigamy of Philip of Hesse was made public and the reformer was mortified. Philip's sixteen-year-old political marriage to Christina, daughter of the Catholic Duke George of nonelectoral Saxony (1471–1539), had never been a happy one. Although Philip had ten children with Christina, he often complained of her "coldness, smell, and drinking." Philip was a man of enormous sexual appetites and had further satisfied himself with numerous liaisons with various ladies of the court, despite frequent pangs of conscience. Now in late 1539 he was feeling the first symptoms of syphilis, the same disease that had killed his father. The leader of the Schmalkaldic League had also fallen in love with one of the ladies of the court, seventeen-year-old Margaret von der Saal, and wanted to marry her.

Landgrave Philip unburdened himself to Luther and several of his ministerial colleagues, including Martin Bucer, the kindly and influential Strasbourg reformer. Earlier in 1526 when Philip wanted to marry another of his favorites, Luther had flatly said no. This time the pastors counseled Philip that a bigamous marriage was better than a divorce. After all, numerous Old Testament patriarchs had several wives and other German princes like Luther's patron Frederick the Wise had enjoyed irregular unions. The problem was that bigamy was against imperial law, so Philip was admonished to keep his second marriage a secret and to give Margaret the status of "concubine" in public.

When the landgrave failed to keep his second marriage of 1540 a secret, both he and the pastors were publicly humiliated. Worse yet, Philip had to promise Emperor Charles that he would retire from religious

politics in exchange for immunity from prosecution on the bigamy matter. Just six years earlier, the landgrave had been instrumental in restoring the Protestant Duke Ulrich of Württemberg to his duchy and further spreading Protestantism. The Schmalkaldic League, which Philip had played a major role in creating, had lost a pillar of strength, and Luther had been part of an attempt to cover up a sordid affair.

LUTHER AND THE JEWS

Things went from bad to worse for Martin Luther when his beloved fourteen-year-old daughter Magdalena died in 1542. "I wish that I and all my children were dead!" he exclaimed publicly a few months after her death as plague raged through Wittenberg.[15] Increasingly the aging Luther was convinced that the Final Judgment was coming and that the sinful world would be destroyed. In his frustration, sorrow, anger, and rage, he now lashed out against the Jews in vitriolic pamphlets such as *On the Jews and Their Lies* (1543). There he urged the authorities "to burn their synagogues and books, expel them from the cities and commerce if they refuse to convert."[16]

Luther also railed against the Anabaptists, Antinomians (those who denied the need for adherence to the law), Sacramentarians, the Ottomans, and the papacy, publishing *Against the Papacy at Rome Founded by the Devil* in 1545. He also failed to recognize the significance of the opening of the long sought reform council in 1545 by Paul III (r. 1534–1549), the reform pope. Luther dismissed the gathering of church leaders at Trent as "too little, too late." As we shall see, Luther was completely mistaken.

Of all the harsh polemics in Luther's last years, his tirades against the Jews are particularly unsettling, even without considering to what horrible use they and those of others were put by Adolf Hitler and his partners in the twentieth-century European Holocaust. Here were the toxic fruits of religious fanaticism, bigotry, and cultural, if not racial, anti-Semitism. What is also tragic about Martin Luther's tirades against the Jews is that he had once been a good friend to a number of Jewish communities. In one of his writings, in 1523, he had reminded his growing audience *That Jesus Christ Was Born a Jew.* In an age where many blamed Jews instead of Romans for the death of Christ and believed lies about Jews sacrificing Christian children in ritual murder, Luther had once been a brave defender of Judaism, although he had always believed that Jews were "money grubbers."

With his health in decline, fearful of the Second Coming, and terribly frustrated by the failure of his missionary efforts, Martin Luther indulged in typical expressions of anti-Semitism common to his culture. Although he never urged people to form vigilante mobs to punish "stubborn Jews who fail to embrace the truth of the Christian Gospel while there is still time," Luther failed to intervene when his pious but heavy drinking patron Duke Johann Frederick of Saxony (r. 1532–1547) exiled the Jews from his lands in 1536.[17] This was the beginning of a hardening of his heart against the Jews, which continued to his final moments. In his last sermon, preached at Eisleben on February 15, 1546, Martin Luther proclaimed that "the Jews are our enemies, who do not cease to defame Christ and would gladly kill us all if they could." However, "we want to practice Christian love toward them and pray that they convert."[18]

Overcome by feelings of weakness, Luther cut short his sermon and retired to his sickbed. There he said "yes" to his colleagues who asked him if he would "stand firm in Christ and the doctrine" he had preached. Three days later at 3 o'clock in the morning, Martin Luther's great heart burst.

The man with seven heads was dead at age sixty-three. The Reformation, which he had been so instrumental in launching, would continue to spread even to the northern lands of Scandinavia and beyond.

Lutheranism in Scandinavia

While Philip Melanchthon and other associates of Luther struggled to lead the Lutheran movement in the Holy Roman Empire, Lutheranism also became entrenched in the Nordic lands. Early in Luther's career as a reformer, the last ruler of Scandinavia under the Union of Kalmar, Christian II of Denmark (r. 1513–1523), permitted Lutheran theologians to teach at the University of Copenhagen. Angered by his cruelty and despotic ways, Swedish barons led by Gustavus Vasa successfully revolted against Christian in 1520. They had been outraged by the execution of more than eighty leading members of the Swedish lay and ecclesiastical aristocracy in Stockholm in November 1520. The martryed nobles had called for Sweden's separation from the Danish crown. By 1523 Sweden was reestablished as an independent kingdom.

Christian's similar efforts to weaken the Danish aristocracy led to his replacement as king by his uncle, Duke Frederick of Schleswig-Holstein. Since King Frederick I (r. 1523–1533) was also favorably disposed to Lutheranism, more Lutheran preachers poured into the kingdom. They were led by Hans Tausen, who had studied at Luther's Wittenberg, and later Johann Bugenhagen (1485–1558), a native of the Baltic island of Wollin, who became the pastor of the city church in Wittenberg and a close friend of Martin Luther. A systematic organizer of churches, Bugenhagen helped organize the Evangelical movement in many parts of northern Germany and in Denmark between 1528 and 1543. He also made considerable contributions to the organization of social welfare in Scandinavia. Lutheranism proved exceedingly popular to Scandinavians who had grown tired of political instability and theological wrangling.

Frederick I followed the lead of his subjects and in 1526 openly broke with Rome and allowed the introduction of the Lutheran liturgy into church services. His son and successor, Christian III (r. 1533–1559), was already a staunch Lutheran when he came to the throne. Declaring himself to be the supreme authority in church matters, Christian encouraged the Norwegians to adopt Lutheranism. Not wanting to have their religious beliefs imposed upon them by their neighbors, some Norwegians resisted. Since diversity in religious opinion was not long tolerated in sixteenth-century Europe, Catholic Norwegians found themselves under great pressure to convert to the Lutheran state church. Eventually, all pockets of Roman Catholic resistance were eliminated, and Norway became a bastion of Lutheranism in the north.

The Lutheran Reformation took even longer to become entrenched in Sweden among the common people. Sweden's king, Gustavus Vasa (r. 1523–1560), coveted the wealth of the Roman Catholic church and wanted the right to appoint its bishops. Breaking with Rome would allow him to do that and he could justify it as good for the souls of his subjects. Shrewdly, Gustavus encouraged reformers such as Olaus Petri (1493–1552), another former Wittenberg student, to evangelize and win converts. Later Petri would fall into disgrace for opposing the king's autocracy. His younger brother, Laurence (1499–1573), was more submissive and became the Lutheran archbishop of Uppsala.

After years of careful preparation, King Gustavus Vasa assumed the headship of the church in Sweden in late 1539. Lutheranism offered kings what distant Rome could not: full sovereignty over church and state. Fortunately for monarchs, its doctrines also had broad popular appeal. Gustavus and his theological allies completed the reform in stages. By the Diet of Västeras of 1544, the Lutheran takeover was complete and legalized by royal decree. Sweden became a leading center for Lutheranism. His descendant, Gustavus II Adolphus (r. 1611–1632), would try to defend Protestantism during the Thirty Years' War.

Chronology

1520	Sweden breaks away from Christian II of Denmark.
1522	Adrian VI elected pope.
1523	Clement VII elected pope; Diet of Nuremberg defers action against the Lutherans.
1524	Erasmus publishes *On the Freedom of the Will*; beginnings of Peasants' Revolt.
1525	Battle of Pavia (capture of François I); death of Elector Frederick the Wise, succeeded by his brother Johann; Luther publishes *Against the Robbing and Murdering Hordes of Peasants*; Luther marries Katherine von Bora; Nuremberg turns Lutheran; death of Thomas Müntzer.
1526	Diet of Speyer adopts formula "he who rules, his religion"; Ottomans victorious in Hungary; Denmark breaks with Rome.
1527	Troops of Charles V sack Rome; frequently ill Luther

	composes hymn "A Mighty Fortress Is Our God."
1529	Evangelical Protest at the Diet of Speyer; Marburg Colloquy; Ottomans at Vienna; Luther's German catechism.
1530	Presentation of the Augsburg Confession; formation of the Schmalkaldic League.
1532	Ottomans driven back from Austria; Religious Peace of Nuremberg.
1533–1559	Reign of Christian II; Norway becomes Lutheran.
1534	Publication of Luther's complete German Bible; Philip of Hesse and others restore Protestant Ulrich of Württemberg to his duchy.
1535	Münster Anabaptists.
1539	Sweden, under Gustavus Vasa, breaks with Rome.
1540	Bigamy of Philip of Hesse revealed; Mark of Brandenburg becomes Lutheran.
1542	Death of Magdalena Luther.
1543	Increasingly ill Luther publishes *On the Jews*.
1544	Diet and Ordinances of Västeras complete Swedish reform.
1545	Paul III opens the Council of Trent; Luther publishes *Against the Papacy at Rome Founded by the Devil*.
1546	Death of Luther at Eisleben.

Further Reading

EARLY REFORMERS

Roland Bainton, *Women of the Reformation in Germany and Italy* (1971). Has useful profiles of Katherine von Bora and others.

James Estes, *Christian Magistrate and State Church: The Reforming Career of Johannes Brenz* (1982).

Clyde Manschreck, *Melanchthon, the Quiet Reformer* (1968).

C. A. Maxcey, *Bona Opera: A Study in the Development of the Doctrine of Grace in Philip Melanchthon* (1980).

R. Emmett McLaughlin, *Caspar Schwenckfeld, Reluctant Radical: His Life to 1540* (1986).

THE SPREAD OF THE REFORMATION

Miriam Chrisman, *Conflicting Visions of Reform: German Lay Propaganda Pamphlets 1519–1530* (1995).

Susan Karant-Nunn, *Zwickau in Transition, 1500–1547: The Reformation as an Agent of Change* (1987).

Bernd Moeller, *Imperial Cities and the Reformation* (1972).

Steven Ozment, *The Reformation in the Cities: The Appeal of Protestantism to Sixteenth-Century Germany and Switzerland* (1975).

Paul Russell, *Lay Theology in the Reformation: Popular Pamphleteers in Southwest Germany, 1521–1525* (1986).

Robert Scribner, *For the Sake of the Simple Folk: Popular Propaganda for German Reformation* (1981).

THE REFORMATION IN NUREMBERG

Harold Grimm, *Lazarus Spengler, A Lay Leader of the Reformation* (1978).

Gerald Strauss, *Nuremberg in the Sixteenth Century*, 2nd ed. (1976).

THE PEASANTS' WAR, 1524–1526

Peter Blickle, *Communal Reformation: The Search for Salvation in Reformation Germany* (1992).

———, *The Revolution of 1525*, tr. Thomas Brady, Jr, and H. C. Erik Midelfort (1981).

Lawrence Buck, "The Peasants' War," in J. Zophy, ed., *The Holy Roman Empire: A Dictionary Handbook* (1980).

Walter Klaassen, *Michael Gaismair* (1978).

Keith Moxey, *Peasants, Warriors, and Wives: Popular Imagery in the Reformation* (1989).

Tom Scott and Bob Scribner, eds., *The German Peasants' War* (1991). An excellent collection of primary sources materials with very useful introductions.

Tom Scott, *Freiburg and the Breisgau: Town-Country Relations in the Age of Reformation and ·Peasants' War* (1986).

Bob Scribner and Gerhard Benecke, eds., *The German Peasant War 1525: New Viewpoints* (1979).

Kyle Sessions, ed., *Reformation and Authority: The Meaning of the Peasants' Revolt* (1968). Primary and secondary materials.

THOMAS MÜNTZER

Michael Baylor, ed. and tr., *Revelation and Revolution: Basic Writings of Thomas Müntzer* (1993).

Abraham Friesen, *Thomas Muentzer, A Destroyer of the Godless* (1990).

Eric Gritsch, *Thomas Müntzer* (1989).

Tom Scott, *Thomas Müntzer* (1989).

POLITICS OF THE EARLY REFORMATION

Thomas Brady, Jr., *Turning Swiss: Cities and Empire, 1450–1550* (1985).

Karl Brandi, *The Emperor Charles V* (1939).

Paula Sutter Fichtner, *Ferdinand I of Austria* (1982).

Hans Hillerbrand, *Landgrave Philip von Hesse* (1967).

Stanford Shaw, *Empire of the Gazis: The Rise and Decline of the Ottoman Empire, 1280–1808* (1976).

Jonathan Zophy, *Patriarchal Politics and Christoph Kress (1484–1535) of Nuremberg* (1992).

SCANDINAVIA

E. H. Dunckley, *The Reformation in Denmark* (1948).

Ole Peter Grell, "Scandinavia," in Andrew Pettegrew, ed., *The Early Reformation in Europe* (1992).

———, ed., *The Scandinavian Reformation: From Evangelical Movement to Institutionalisation* (1995). An important collection of essays by various authors.

Grethe Jacobson, "Nordic Women and the Reformation," in Sherrin Marshall, ed., *Women in Reformation and Counter-Reformation Europe* (1989).

Michael Roberts, *The Early Vasas: A History of Sweden* (1968).

Notes

1. Cited in Jonathan Zophy, *Patriarchal Politics and Christoph Kress (1484–1535) of Nuremberg* (Lewiston, N.Y.: Edwin Mellen Press, 1992), p. 90.
2. Albrecht Dürer, *The Writings of Albrecht Dürer*, William Conaway, ed. and tr. (New York: Philosophical Library, 1958), p. 157.
3. Cited in Gottfried Seebass, "The Reformation in Nürnberg," in Lawrence Buck and Jonathan Zophy, eds., *The Social History of the Reformation* (Columbus, Oh.: Ohio State University Press, 1972), p. 22.
4. Cited in Lawrence Buck, "The Peasants' War," in Jonathan W. Zophy, ed., *The Holy Roman Empire: A Dictionary Handbook* (Westport, Conn.: Greenwood Press, 1980), p. 365.
5. Cited in David Hockenbery, "Müntzer," in Zophy, ed., *Holy Roman Empire*, p. 329.
6. Cited in Tom Scott and Bob Scribner, eds., *The German Peasants' War: A History in Documents* (Atlantic Highlands, N.J.: Humanities Press, 1991), p. 330.
7. Cited in Zophy, *Patriarchal Politics*, p. 120.
8. Cited in Kyle Sessions, ed., *Reformation and Authority: The Meaning of the Peasants' Revolt* (Lexington, Mass.: D. C. Heath, 1968), p. 39.
9. Cited in Roland Bainton, *Women of the Reformation in Germany and Italy* (Minneapolis, Minn.: Augsburg, 1971), p. 26.
10. Cited in Jonathan Zophy, "We Must Have the Dear Ladies: Martin Luther and Women," in Kyle Sessions and Phillip Bebb, eds., *Pietas et Societas: New Trends in Reformation Social History* (Kirksville, Mo.: Sixteenth Century Journal Publishers, 1985), p. 143.

11. Cited in Zophy, *Patriarchal Politics*, p. 137.
12. Ibid., p. 165.
13. Ibid., p. 183.
14. Ibid., p. 188.
15. Cited in Mark Edwards, Jr., *Luther's Last Battles: Politics and Polemics, 1531–1546* (Ithaca, N.Y.: Cornell University Press, 1983), p. 15.
16. Cited in Heiko Oberman, *Luther: Man between God and the Devil*, tr. Eileen Walliser-Schwartzbart (New Haven, Conn.: Yale University Press, 1989), p. 290.
17. Edwards, *Last Battles*, pp. 124–136.
18. Cited in Oberman, *Luther*, p. 294.

7

ZWINGLI, SWISS REFORM, AND ANABAPTISM

Almost at the very moment that Martin Luther was embroiled with the church in a debate over indulgences, a similar controversy was raging in Zurich, Switzerland, involving the priest Huldrych Zwingli. A few years later, a classically trained humanist named Conrad Grebel performed the first known adult baptism and initiated the so-called Anabaptist movement, which was violently opposed by Zwingli and his supporters. Despite condemnations from both Protestants and Roman Catholics, the Anabaptist movement spread into central and eastern Europe, although seldom numbering more than 1 percent of the population. After Zwingli's death in 1531, the leadership of the reform movement in Switzerland passed to his successor, Heinrich Bullinger, and to Johann Oecolampadius in Basel before being overshadowed by the powerful movement led by John Calvin in Geneva.

Huldrych Zwingli (1484–1531)

EARLY YEARS

Huldrych Zwingli began life in the rural canton of Glarus in the Swiss Confederation a mere seven weeks after the birth of Martin Luther. His father was a relatively prosperous free peasant, eager to provide his sons

with the best available education. At age five, young Huldrych was sent to live with his uncle, the vicar of Wesen. His uncle taught him some Latin and then sent him off to grammar school in Basel. When he was twelve, Zwingli transferred to a school in Bern. In 1498 he enrolled at the university of Vienna, whose faculty included the renowned humanist Conrad Celtis. Zwingli had also become interested in the classics and had become a fine musician as well. A virtual one-man band, Zwingli played the lute, harp, viol, reed pipe, and cornet (a precursor of the trumpet).

After four years in the stimulating atmosphere of Vienna, Zwingli transferred to Basel, where he earned his B.A. in 1504 and his M.A. two years later. He was then ordained a priest and became the parish priest of the town of Glarus, where he remained until 1516. To secure his post in Glarus, Zwingli had to buy off a papally appointed competitor for the large sum of 100 florins. While being a conscientious pastor to his congregation in Glarus and several surrounding villages, Zwingli also continued his scholarly pursuits. He studied the Bible diligently, as well as the classical writings and the work of Greek and Latin church fathers. Zwingli also tried to learn Hebrew.

The young priest greeted the writings of Erasmus with great enthusiasm, even making the trip to Basel to meet his intellectual hero in person in 1516. He wrote the humanist later:

> When I think of writing to you, Erasmus, best of men, I am frightened by the brilliance of your learning, but I am encouraged at the same time by the charming kindness you showed me when I came to see you at Basel not long ago at the beginning of spring. It was no small proof of a generous nature that you did not disdain a man with no gift of speech and an author quite unknown.[1]

Over time Zwingli's self-confidence grew, as did his understanding of the biblical materials and ancient languages.

Like his hero Erasmus, Zwingli found a great deal to criticize in the church, although he was much more willing to challenge the authority of the pope than the Dutchman. Zwingli eventually became an outspoken advocate of reform, taking lively interest in Swiss political and military affairs. On several occasions he served as a military chaplain to groups of Swiss mercenaries fighting in various battles against the French for control of Milan. Zwingli showed great courage under fire and came to despise the mercenary system, which corrupted young Swiss when it failed to disable or maim them. Military camp life in the early sixteenth century was very ill disciplined. Army camps were filled with excessive drinking, gambling, and prostitution. When Zwingli returned from the Battle of Marignano of 1515, he began preaching against the evils of the lucrative mercenary system.

In 1516 Zwingli added to his duties by being named rector of the monastic church at nearby Einsiedeln, a position he held for two years. Since Einsiedeln was a center of pilgrimages, he was able to witness how many pilgrims actually came to worship relics and saints. Although Zwingli made his own pilgrimage in 1517, the year of Luther's "Ninety-five Theses," he was increasingly concerned about what he considered abuses in the practices of the church. At Einsiedeln, Zwingli also became involved in a controversy over indulgences with a Franciscan, Bernardin Samson. This controversy did not reach the proportions that Luther's did, but it shows that different people in different areas had come to agree with Erasmus that indulgences were a "cheat."

NOT A FRIVOLOUS MUSICIAN: ZWINGLI IN ZURICH

In October of 1518 the chance for an even more influential post opened up—that of cathedral priest at the Great Minster in the prosperous trading city of Zurich. With a population of about 7,000, Zurich was considerably larger than the small towns and villages Zwingli had previously served. The ambitious young cleric was keenly interested in the job, but reports circulated against him. Although people in Zurich praised Zwingli for his learning, there were reports that he was "pleasure-seeking and worldly." Even his musical inclinations were viewed with suspicion as "frivolous." Worse, there was a report that Zwingli had "seduced the daughter of an influential citizen" of Einsiedeln.[2]

Zwingli met the charges head-on. He wrote to the appointment committee that "some three years ago I firmly resolved not to touch any woman, since Paul stated that it is not good to do so." He admitted that he had slept with the daughter of a barber and that the child she awaited might well be his. He claimed that she had seduced him "with more than flattering words" and that she had sexual relations "with several clerical assistants." As for his music, "I play for myself and delight in the beautiful harmony of melodies and do not desire any recognition."[3] The canons were apparently impressed with Zwingli's defense, for on December 11 of 1518, they offered him the position over a Swabian competitor, who kept a concubine, had six children, and held several benefices. What happened to the barber's daughter and her child back in Einsiedeln is not known.

THE ADOPTION OF THE REFORM BY ZURICH

Zwingli went on to become an enormously popular preacher and to launch the Swiss Reformation. The citizens of Zurich found that he had an attractive personality, a quick wit, a fine intellect, and a beautiful voice. He soon earned a reputation as a charismatic preacher, whose call for reforms met with a sympathetic response in part because people genuinely admired and respected the messenger despite his previous moral lapses. His stature as a religious and political leader also grew as he became more serious and purposeful. During his first year in Zurich, a ferocious plague hit the city and killed almost a fifth of its population. Among the victims was one of Zwingli's brothers. Zwingli bravely ministered to the sick until catching the illness himself. Surviving the plague, he became a much more earnest and dedicated man with an even greater sense of purpose.

In his early years in Zurich, Huldrych Zwingli read Martin Luther's writings intently and preached directly from the New Testament. In the spring of 1522 some of his parishioners, moved by the emphasis of his sermons on "the Word of God which clearly allows the eating of all foods at all times," broke the church's prohibition against eating meat during Lent. Although Zwingli kept the Lenten fast himself, he defended those who had not from his pulpit and in several of his pamphlets. He wrote in one of them: "If you want to fast, do so; if you do not want to eat meat, don't eat it; but allow Christians a free choice."[4] The ruling Small Council of Zurich issued a decree that the fast be maintained, but it suggested that the matter needed further discussion. Zwingli, a shrewd political animal, had carefully cultivated friendships with many key members of both the council of fifty and the larger council of 200. He understood clearly that reform would not be possible without the support of Zurich's political and economic leadership. In Zwingli's view, both the clergy and the government derive their authority from God; therefore, both the preachers and the magistrates must make sure that God's authority is established over the community.

A public debate was held on January 29, 1523, between Zwingli and Johann Faber, representing the bishop of Constance, who had jurisdiction over Zurich. Zwingli presented sixty-seven articles for reform, which among other things objected to the powers assumed by the pope, argued that the Mass was a symbolic meal of remembrance, and opposed such traditional practices as clerical celibacy, fasting, monasticism, pilgrimages, indulgences, purgatory, and the worship of saints. For him the reformers were engaged in restoring the church to its original "purity" in accordance with what is described in the Acts of the Apostles. Upset by charges that he was a mere imitator of Luther, Zwingli stressed his own contributions to reform: "I began to preach the Gospel of Christ in 1516, long before anyone in our region had heard of Luther."[5] Indeed, Zwingli was much more concerned about the reform of society than Luther, who was more focused on the salvation of individuals.

Later public debates were held and the government of Zurich followed up by ordering other parish priests to follow Zwingli's lead. The collection of tithes was ended, clerical celibacy was denounced, and choral singing and images were removed from Zurich's churches. As Zwingli wrote, "the images are not to be endured, for all that God has forbidden, there can be no compromise."[6] The pattern of removing images as "idolatrous" was repeated in other Swiss cities and later in Calvinist churches. Given Zwingli's love of music, the limitation of congregational singing solely to the Psalms was a cross to bear, but he wanted to be consistent with his interpretation of the practices of the early church. He found some consolation in the arms of a widow with children, Anna Rhinehardt, whom he had secretly married in 1522. Their marriage was made public in 1524, a year before the Mass itself was abolished by order of the Small Council.

The reform Pope Adrian VI attempted to deal with Zwingli more diplomatically than his predecessor Leo X had dealt with Luther. He shared many of the same concerns and withheld papal condemnation. Tragically, Adrian died on September 14, 1523. His successor, Clement VII, was far too dependent on Swiss mercenaries to risk intervention in Swiss affairs. By then Zwingli's friends had spread the reform movement to Basel, Bern, Saint Gall, Schaffhausen, and as far north as Strasbourg. Recognizing the need for an international movement, Zwingli urged his colleagues to join Zurich in an alliance in "defense of the Gospel."

THE MARBURG COLLOQUY

In the autumn of 1529, Zwingli and several of his associates accepted the invitation of Landgrave Philip to attend a major meeting of reformers at Marburg in Hesse. It was the most important meeting of reform leaders held in the sixteenth century. Philip was hoping the conference would result in a common statement of doctrine and a military alliance of reform communities. He feared that Charles V would soon lead the Catholics in a crusade to exterminate the Evangelicals. Zwingli was joined by Luther, Melanchthon, Martin Bucer and Wolfgang Capito of Strasbourg, Johann Oecolampadius of Basel, Johann Brenz of Schwäbisch Hall, Andreas Osiander of Nuremberg, and several others. Never again would such a celebrated group of early sixteenth-century Evangelical theologians be gathered in one place at the same time.

The reformers did find they had a lot of common ground and some of them cemented lasting friendships. Unity dissolved, however, on the thorny issue of the Lord's Supper. All the reformers denied the sacrificial nature of the Catholic Mass and agreed that both the bread and the wine should be given to the laity. Yet Zwingli was unwilling to accept Luther's assertion that Christ was bodily present in the sacrament. He argued that the words "This is my body" were meant only symbolically. The Eucharist is a meal of remembrance; Christ is not present in any form. Neither side would budge from those positions. They finally agreed to disagree. Without complete doctrinal agreement, Luther would not support a military alliance with the Swiss, whom he suspected of secretly being too prone to radicalism and too closely related to the Anabaptists.

ZWINGLI'S LAST YEARS

Returning to Zurich, Zwingli was determined to pressure the five Catholic cantons in the central part of the Swiss Confederation to accept the reform. He believed Protestantism should be spread by any means necessary. At a January 1530 stormy session of the Swiss Parliament (Diet), Zwingli managed to get the Protestant majority to pass economic sanctions against the

Sixteenth-century portrait engraving of Huldrych Zwingli. Bibliotheque de l'histoire du Protestantisme, Paris, France. Giraudon/Art Resource.

Zurich council members and 25 Protestant ministers. Catholic soldiers found Zwingli's body, quartered and burned it, and scattered his ashes after mixing them with dung. Luther, who had never trusted Zwingli's political activism, was not overly surprised that Zwingli had died in battle.

Having taught the Protestants a bloody lesson, the Catholics wisely made no attempt to continue the offensive or to disturb the Protestants in their new worship practices. They knew the more populous Protestant areas could raise additional troops if pressured further. What they wanted was the freedom to continue their traditional religious practices. The Peace of Kappel of November 20, 1531, maintained the religious status quo in the Swiss Confederation. Catholic but not Protestant minorities were to be tolerated, and all entangling foreign alliances were forbidden.

Heinrich Bullinger (1504–1575)

Zwingli was ably succeeded by Heinrich Bullinger, who had been exiled from his pastorate at Bremgarten. A native of Bremgarten in the Aargau, Bullinger had earned his bachelor of arts and his master's degrees at the University of Cologne. He then became the head teacher at the abbey school of the Cistercian monastery at Kappel, where he reformed the curriculum of the Latin school along humanist lines. Converted to Protestantism, Bullinger reformed the monastery itself before leaving to take a pastorate in his home town.

Bullinger was an important and influential covenant theologian, who wrote a very valuable *History of the Reformation* and the Second Helvetic Confession (1566), which became one the most accepted of all the Reformed confessionals. A powerful intellect, Bullinger stressed the nature of the

Catholics. The Diet prohibited the sale of such basic commodities as wheat, salt, wine, and iron to the Forest cantons in the mountainous heart of Switzerland. Reformation doctrines had not found such fertile soil in the less urbanized, more mountainous portions of Switzerland, where parishioners were happier with their local clergy and less exposed to the new currents of thought which coursed through Swiss trade and university centers.

In October of 1531 the Catholics struck back with a military force of 8,000 marching on Zurich. Taken by surprise, Zwingli rushed to meet them with a much smaller army of about 1,500 troops. Seeing his badly outnumbered soldiers give way, Zwingli put himself in the center of the Protestant army and took a fatal sword thrust in his throat. With the death of their hero, the Protestant army broke ranks and fled from the field. They lost over 400, including 26 relationship between an all-powerful God and sinful humans. He also insisted that ordinary people needed to have the Bible interpreted for them by experts. His concerns were much more theological than political, so in time Zurich was eclipsed by Bern and then Calvin's Geneva as the center of Swiss Reformed Protestantism. Primarily through correspondence, Bullinger developed a close friendship with John Calvin, who respected his insights and abilities. Contemporaries viewed the sensible Bullinger as one of the leading lights of the reform.

Big Names in the Reform of Basel

The reform movement followed many different patterns in various places. At Basel, a major center of printing with a population of 9,000, the reform was led by Johann Oecolampadius (1482–1531), an able classical and Hebrew scholar. He had studied law at Bologna and theology at Heidelberg and Tübingen. Like Huldrych Zwingli, Oecolampadius was a great admirer of Erasmus and assisted him in the production of his Greek New Testament and an edition of St. Jerome's writings. In 1520 he entered a Birgitten monastery, but soon became disenchanted and left the following year. By 1522 he was in close contact with Zwingli and they developed a warm friendship. In June of 1523 Oecolampadius secured a position as a professor of theology at the University of Basel.

Oecolampadius also became the preacher at St. Martin's Church, where he enthusiastically promoted the reform. In Basel, the magistrates were much slower than they were in Zurich to adopt reform measures. Guild representatives proved particularly reluctant to go along with the religious changes proposed by Oecolampadius, fearing that the town's economic life might suf-

fer. With the help of Zwingli and reformers from Bern, the city council in February of 1529 finally made the break with Rome after a major outbreak of iconoclasm. Although Oecolampadius agreed with Zwingli on most points of doctrine, he felt church discipline should solely be a matter of pastoral concern. He was reluctant to use civic officials to enforce faith and morals. Oecolampadius also participated in the Marburg Colloquy and made a good friend of Luther's irenic colleague Philip Melanchthon.

A devoted son, he delayed marriage until after the death of his mother. In his forty-fifth year at the urging of the reformer Wolfgang Capito, he married Wibrandis Rosenblatt (1504–1564), the attractive widow of a Basel humanist, Ludwig Keller. She made him a most comfortable home and they had three children. Wibrandis was a gracious hostess, who also kept up a lively correspondence with the wives of other reformers. They had a lot in common as the first generation of pastors' wives since the early Middle Ages. The network established by the thoughtful Wibrandis was absolutely essential in helping Protestant women married to clergy adapt to their new role and responsibilities, which often included hosting religious refugees. Wibrandis was sensitive to many of the practical realities of the new situation for married clergy fostered by the Reformation. She also enjoyed the company of women and men of faith and intellect.

A year after Oecolampadius's death in 1531, Wibrandis married the humanist-reformer Wolfgang Capito, who had lost his first wife at nearly the same time she had lost her second husband. They moved to Strasbourg and had five children. Following Capito's demise in 1541, Wibrandis married her third reformer, Martin Bucer, whose wife had died of the plague. After his death in England in 1551, she moved back to the

Continent and eventfully died in reformed Basel of yet another outbreak of the dreaded plague. She was widely admired for her good sense, graciousness, problem-solving skills, and supportive nature.

The Rise of Anabaptism

The stress of the early reformers on the importance of reading Scripture gave rise to the problem that the Bible is a complex book that can be interpreted in different ways by different people. In Zwingli's Zurich, for example, a reading group led by Conrad Grebel came to the conclusion that there was no warrant in the Bible for infant baptism. In the Gospel according to Luke, John the Baptist had baptized Jesus as an adult, not as a child. If infant baptism is so essential, why was there no evidence of it in the first two centuries? Why is Scripture itself so silent about it?

CONRAD GREBEL (1498–1526)

Conrad Grebel, a member of a patrician family and a well-educated humanist, concluded that baptism was a sign or symbol of regeneration or the coming of faith by adults who had reached an age of accountability. Grebel and his associates were also concerned about the political activities of Huldrych Zwingli and his willingness to use the power of the state to spread the Gospel. He thought the church should be a voluntary community of believers; no one should be compelled by force to accept the truth of the Gospels. Furthermore, the church should not be an arm of the state or vice versa. Even at the Zurich Disputation of 1523, Grebel called upon Zwingli to repudiate not only the medieval church, but the authority of the city government over religious affairs as well. Since Zwingli had worked

long and hard to achieve political influence, he was not about to abandon his efforts at a state-sponsored reform movement.

Grebel and his followers went their own way in trying to establish a form of the church that closely resembled that described in the Acts of the Apostles. They used a simple form of service in private homes and celebrated the Lord's Supper as a meal of solemn remembrance. Grebel's followers tried to follow the Sermon on the Mount as closely as possible. Then, in January 1525, Grebel performed an adult baptism on George Blaurock as a public symbol of his coming into a new understanding (covenant) of God. Blaurock, a former priest, then baptized others.

Since the first group of people who were baptized as adults in 1525 had already been baptized as Catholic children, their enemies called them Anabaptists or Rebaptists. This brought them under the penalty of Roman law, which prescribed death for those who rebaptize. The Romans tended to view religion as a community rather than an individual matter. The Anabaptists, who believed that like the early Christians they were destined to suffer, called themselves "Christians," "Saints," or "Brethren." They saw themselves as outside the mainstream of society or at least as an alternative to it. Inherent in Anabaptism was the idea that man's law had no force for those whom God had saved (*antinomianism*). Some Anabaptists taught that faith takes precedence over marital vows. They allowed even single women to convert and had some female prophets, such as Ursula Jost and Barbara Rostock, who were active in Strasbourg.

Tragically, the Anabaptist movement began in the midst of the Peasants' War in the Holy Roman Empire (1524–1526), which greatly added to the fears of the authorities about social upheaval. Although most Anabaptists were pacifists, enemies such as

Martin Luther believed they were "wolves in sheep's clothing." He linked them with fanatics like Thomas Müntzer and Hans Hut. In Zurich, Zwingli was distressed that his former disciple Grebel had moved so far from his teachings about the role of civil government and the importance of infant baptism. He believed false reports about their dissolute behavior and condemned them in a tract called *Against the Tricks of the Katabaptists.*

After a public disputation on adult baptism in Zurich, the city council ordered Grebel and his followers to leave the city. When Anabaptists continued to win converts in the countryside, the Zurich government on March 7, 1526, made rebaptism punishable by death according to Roman law. Grebel was imprisoned for five months before escaping. He died of the plague later in that same year. Other Anabaptists were arrested, burned at the stake, and sometimes symbolically punished by drowning, as was the case with most captured female Anabaptists. Yet the movement continued to attract new members, many of whom were impressed by the clarity of the Anabaptist message and the courage of the "suffering saints."

MICHAEL SATTLER (c. 1490–1527) AND THE SCHLEITHEIM STATEMENT

Michael Sattler was one of the bravest of the Anabaptist suffering saints. He had been a prior in a monastery near Freiburg in Breisgau before converting to Lutheranism. In 1525 Sattler arrived in Zurich and became an important convert to Anabaptism. After being expelled from the city, he became an evangelist outside Zurich and later in the Strasbourg area and then at Horb in Württemberg. In 1527 Sattler presided over a conference of Anabaptists meeting at Schleitheim near Schaffhausen in south Germany.

For that conference, he drew up a brief statement of basic Brethren beliefs for those at Schleitheim. It was never intended as a public confessional statement.

According to the Schleitheim Statement:

1. Baptism was to be given to all those who had learned repentance and amendment of life and who truly believed their sins were taken away by Christ.
2. After having professed to be brothers or sisters, all those who fall into error and sin shall be warned twice in secret and excommunicated upon the third offense.
3. Those who wish to participate in the Lord's Supper must first be baptized.
4. The baptized were to separate themselves from the "evil and wickedness, which the devil planted in the world."
5. A pastor in the church must have a good reputation with those outside the church. [Members of the Brethren were still being accused of having joined with rebellious peasants as did the radical theologian Thomas Müntzer].
6. No member of the church was to bear arms in any cause.
7. No member of the church was to take an oath.[7]

Although the Schleitheim Statement was not accepted as definitive by all Anabaptists, it does give us a sense of some of their early beliefs. Anabaptists came to see themselves primarily as local "gathered communities" and, therefore, they did not need a binding, public confessional declaration. They left that for the state churches of the larger Catholic and Protestant denominations.

Shortly after his return to Horb from Schleitheim, Sattler, his wife, and several others were arrested. The imperial authorities, fearing the continued spread of the Brethren, were determined to make an example of the unrepentant Sattler. After a two-day trial in which he defended himself and his beliefs with great courage and intelligence, the gentle Sattler was cruelly tortured by having pieces of his body torn with red hot tongs before he was burned at the stake. His devoted wife was drowned eight days later, after having turned down an offer of amnesty and a comfortable retirement home if she would recant.

BALTHASAR HUBMAIER (c. 1480–1528)

Balthasar Hubmaier helped provide intellectual leadership for the early Anabaptists. A gifted former student of Luther's opponent at Leipzig, Johann Eck, Hubmaier earned a doctorate in theology and became a chaplain and vice-rector of the University of Ingolstadt by 1515. He left the university for an important cathedral pulpit at Regensburg and then, after a controversy over pilgrimage revenues, a more modest one at Waldshut on the Rhine. Impressed by the writings of Zwingli, he made his own intensive studies of the New Testament and came to the conclusion that there was no basis for the practice of infant baptism. In April 1525 he had himself baptized by an associate of Grebel's. After resigning his clerical position, Hubmaier was chosen by his congregation to continue as their minister. He also married Elizabeth Hüglein.

Later that year he responded to Huldrych Zwingli's published attacks on the Brethren with a highly influential book, *Concerning the Christian Baptism of Believers*. This became known as one of the most intelligently argued statements of the Brethren position on adult baptism. Forced to flee from Waldshut by Archduke Ferdinand, the Hubmaiers fled to Zurich, where he was arrested, tortured, and forced to recant his Anabaptist beliefs. He was then banished to Nikolsburg in southern Moravia, where he succeeded in converting two of the local barons, who encouraged him to continue his ministry. Thousands of others were converted by Hubmaier's congenial personality, incisive mind, and clear message.

Hubmaier continued his writing and was one of the first to call for religious toleration, thereby atoning to an extent for his own role in the expulsion of Jews from Regensburg earlier in his career. He disagreed with most other Anabaptists on support of the state and the necessity at times of defensive warfare. His views on baptism were circulated widely in Brethren circles. When his old enemy, Archduke Ferdinand, became king of Bohemia in February 1527 Moravia came under his authority. Hubmaier and his wife were soon arrested. Brought to Vienna, he was tortured and then burned at the stake after refusing to recant. His wife, Elizabeth, was drowned and another 105 of Hubmaier's followers were executed.

Charisma and Fanaticism at Münster

Despite the persecutions of the early Anabaptists, the movement continued to spread throughout the Holy Roman Empire and into the Low Countries, although it never numbered more than 1 percent of the European population during the sixteenth century. In an age that valued conformity and suspected all deviance from the norm, Catholics and other Protestants continued to believe the worst about the Anabaptists. A strange outbreak of fanaticism in the Westphalian city of Münster in 1534 seemed to support even the greatest fears that people like Martin Luther and others had about them.

After a period of unrest over plague, crop failures, and an unpopular bishop,

Münster's city council appointed Lutheran ministers to the town's parish churches in 1532. Protestants of all sorts flocked to the city as a safe haven. Among them were disciples of Jan Matthys, a fanatical Dutch baker. Claiming to be the prophet Enoch, Matthys preached that the Day of Judgment was coming and that the elect must prepare for Christ's return and the rule of the saints in the millennium. While most other Millenarians were pacifists, the tall and bearded Matthys preached that the elect must take up the sword against the ungodly. Several of his more enthusiastic followers had run naked through the streets of Amsterdam proclaiming the imminent coming of Christ. They were quickly seized and butchered.

Then in February of 1534 Jan of Leiden (c. 1509–1536), a tailor, arrived in Münster, which was to become the city of God proclaimed by his spiritual leader, Jan Matthys. The handsome, illegitimate son of a Dutch mayor, Jan of Leiden was sent to help prepare for the coming of the great prophet Matthys and his followers. In new elections, the municipal council was replaced by one dominated by "immigrants, shoemakers, tailors, furriers, and other artisans."[8] Conservatives who could fled the city, but were replaced by the coming of Matthys himself and more of his disciples. Münster was proclaimed to be the New Jerusalem, which would be spared when the rest of the world was destroyed at Easter. All those who accepted Matthys as their prophet were rebaptized, private property was abolished, and laws were promulgated for "perfection of the saints."

Franz von Waldeck, the former bishop of Münster, returned with a besieging army made up of Catholic and Protestant recruits. The rule of working-class fanatics in Münster frightened many throughout Europe,

who listened to the wild tales about the city with great fascination. Yet the New Jerusalem held out, protected by its thick walls and the desperate courage and faith of its defenders. Then Matthys had a vision that he claimed instructed him to leave the city's walls and attack the bishop, which would lead to a glorious victory. On Easter Sunday of 1534, Matthys was pierced by a spear while leading a small raiding party outside the protective walls of the city. Apparently, he had misinterpreted his vision.

The Fall of "King" Jan

With Matthys dead, Jan of Leiden moved quickly to take full control over Münster and reassure the faithful. First he ran naked through the streets, fell into a trance, and proclaimed himself to be the new prophet and king of Zion. He began to force the council to issue even more revolutionary decrees, including one which established Old Testament-style polygamy. Jan of Leiden himself led the way by eventually taking fifteen wives, including the lovely widow of Matthys. His loyal followers continued to defend the city, despite the hardships imposed upon them by the siege, such was their desperate faith in Jan of Leiden and their fear of the attackers' wrath. While others suffered, King Jan, his leading lieutenants, and their harems lived remarkably well.

After sixteen months of siege, Münster was finally taken. Its besiegers had been reinforced by the army of Philip of Hesse, a Protestant prince. Its defenders were starving and disease ridden except for their leaders, including King Jan. Most of the men, women, and children who remained alive in the town were ruthlessly slaughtered. Jan of Leiden was exhibited throughout north-

Heinrich Aldegrever, portrait engraving of Jan van Leiden (1536). Foto Marburg/Art Resource.

ern Germany before being mutilated with red hot tongs and hung with several of his associates in cages above the walls of Münster as a warning to others of the dangers of fanaticism and trust in false prophets.

Menno Simons (1496–1561)

Anabaptism survived the great trauma of the Münster episode because most of its leaders were not self-serving powermongers like Matthys or Leiden. The movement soon found renewed leadership under Menno Simons, an often self-effacing man of genuine faith and deep piety. Born in the Low Countries, Simons worked as a parish priest for twelve years before coming to the conclusion that many Catholic doctrines were insufficiently supported by Scripture. In 1527 he was shocked by the reports of the

execution of the first Anabaptist martyr in the Low Countries. While Simons could find no warrant for infant baptism in Scripture, he was not willing to take the risk of converting. Then came the terrible news of the debacle at Münster. Simons felt partly responsible for having "disclosed to some of them the abominations of the papal system."[9] Although terribly misled, the Münsterites had been willing to die for their version of the faith. Did he lack similar courage?

In October of 1536, Menno Simons was baptized and began a career as a highly influential Anabaptist preacher. When exiled from Groningen in 1539, he continued his ministry in the Dutch province of Friesland. Two years later, Simons was forced to flee to Amsterdam. Late in 1543 he left Holland for the north of Germany, where he would spend the rest of his life. Intent on calling the Brethren back to their original vision, the pacifist Simons expounded his views in a series of important books, including *Christian Baptism* (1539) and *Foundations of Christian Doctrine* (1540). He stressed the new birth in Christ of Brethren believers and the importance of living as Christ taught. For Simons, the church was an "assembly of the righteous" at odds with the world.[10] His voluminous writings were printed in many languages and he soon became the best-known Anabaptist theologian of the century. However, since many of the early Anabaptists had become suspicious of learned doctors after the extermination of the first generation of educated Anabaptist clergy such as Grebel, Hubmaier, Sattler, and Pilgram Marpeck, Simons downplayed his own academic background and intellectual tendencies. At one point he told his supporters that "Scripture does not need interpreting; it needs only to be obeyed."[11] His followers became known as Mennonites.

The Hutterites
and the Community of Goods

Many Anabaptists held that the Christian was only a steward and not the owner of the property she or he possessed. Christians should be compelled by brotherly and sisterly love to share with anyone in need, especially those of the same faith. Hutterites made the belief in the "community of goods" an indispensable mark of discipleship and the church.

The Hutterites trace their beginnings to Nikolsburg, Moravia, where under the leadership of Jacob Wiedemann they began to practice the sharing of goods in 1528. They were named after Jacob Hutter (d. 1536) from the Austrian Tyrol. He had been converted to Anabaptism by the preaching of Conrad Grebel's associate George Blaurock. A staunch pacifist, Hutter argued that the Anabaptists were a threat to no one: "we have no physical weapons, such as spears or muskets. We wish to show, by our words and deeds, we are true followers of Christ."[12] Despite such protestations, Hutter had to flee from persecution in the Tyrol. He and and a loyal band of followers arrived in Moravia in 1533. Hutter then began reorganizing the Moravian Brethren into tight-knit congregations with common ownership of all goods, as based on the Acts of the Apostles, the fifth book of the New Testament.

After Jacob Hutter's arrest and execution in 1536, the Hutterites found new leadership in Peter Riedemann, who wrote the influential *Confession of Faith*. Written while Riedemann was in prison in Hesse in 1545, the *Confession* became the definitive statement of Hutterite beliefs. Riedemann argued that only fallen persons have a desire to own things. God did not intend for humans to appropriate property for their own selfish purposes. A true Christian disciple will have no problem in forsaking private property. Despite continued persecutions, the Hutterites spread into Slovakia, Hungary, Transylvania, and the Ukraine. In the nineteenth century, many Hutterites moved to the United States in an effort to maintain their communal existence.

Believing in a voluntary association of the faithful as opposed to a state-supported church, the Hutterites, Mennonites, and other Anabaptist groups remained for the most part scattered, small, and struggling. No great prince offered them his or her protection. Most of their members remained working people. Although the Anabaptists never became a majority in any one area, they did make up 10 percent of the population of the Low Countries at one point. The movement spread into eastern Europe, throughout the Holy Roman Empire, and eventually to the Western Hemisphere. While trying to renounce the world, the Anabaptists usually became a force in promoting religious freedom. Their courage when persecuted and their usually gentle lives of faith eventually won a measure of acceptance from a world all too ready to fear that which was different.

Chronology

c. 1480–1528	Life of Balthasar Hubmaier.	c. 1490–1527	Life of Michael Sattler.
1482–1531	Johann Oecolampadius.	1496–1565	Menno Simons.
1484	Birth of Huldrych Zwingli.	1504–1564	Wibrandis Rosenblatt.

1504–1575	Heinrich Bullinger.
1519	Zwingli begins his ministry in Zurich.
1522	Breaking of the Lenten fast in Zurich.
1523	First Public Disputation in Zurich.
1524	The Mass abolished in Zurich.
1525	First adult baptisms in Zurich.
1527	Schleitheim Conference and Statement.
1528	Bern adopts the reform.
1529	Basel adopts the reform; Marburg Colloquy.
1531	Death of Zwingli; Peace of Kappel.
1534	Anabaptists take control of Münster.
1535	Fall of Münster; death of Jan of Leiden.
1536	Death of Jacob Hutter.
1540	Publication of Simon's *Foundation of Christian Doctrine*.
1545	Peter Riedemann's *Confession of Faith*.
1566	Publication of Bullinger's Second Helvetic Confession.

Further Reading

ZWINGLI

Ulrich Gäbler, *Huldrych Zwingli* (1986).

Charles Garside, Jr., *Zwingli and the Arts* (1966).

Gottfried Lochner, *Zwingli's Thought: New Perspectives* (1981).

G. R. Potter, *Zwingli* (1976).

W. P. Stephens, *The Theology of Huldrych Zwingli* (1986).

Robert Walton, *Zwingli's Theocracy* (1967).

Lee Palmer Wandel, *Always Among Us: Images of the Poor in Zwingli's Zurich* (1990).

BULLINGER

Aurelio Garcia Archilla, *The Theology of History and Apologetic Historiography in Heinrich Bullinger: Truth in History* (1992).

J. Wayne Baker, *Heinrich Bullinger and the Covenant* (1980).

Paul Rorem, *Calvin and Bullinger on the Lord's Supper* (1989).

EARLY SWISS REFORM

Irena Backus, *The Disputations of Baden, 1526 and Berne, 1528: Neutralizing the Early Church* (1993).

Hans Guggisberg, *Basel in the Sixteenth Century* (1982).

Lee Palmer Wandel, *Voracious Idols and Violent Hands: Iconoclasm in Reformation Zurich, Strasbourg, and Basel* (1995).

ANABAPTISM: GENERAL STUDIES

Michael Baylor, ed. and tr., *The Radical Reformation* (1991). A valuable collection of sources.

Claus-Peter Clasen, *Anabaptism: A Social History* (1972).

Kenneth Davis, *Anabaptism and Asceticism* (1974).

William Estep, ed., *The Anabaptist Story* (1975).

Hans Hillerbrand, *A Bibliography of Anabaptism, A Sequel* (1975).

Joyce Irwin, ed., *Womanhood in Radical Protestantism* (1979). Important essays.

Cornelius Krahn, *Dutch Anabaptism: Origin, Spread, Life, and Thought, 1450–1600* (1968).

Franklin Littel, *The Anabaptist View of the Church*, 2nd ed. (1958).

Michael Mullett, *Radical Religious Movements in Early Modern Europe* (1981).

Werner Packull, *Hutterite Beginnings: Communitarian Experiments during the Reformation* (1995).

———, *Mysticism and the Early South-German-Austrian Anabaptism Movement* (1977).

John Rempel, *The Lord's Supper in Anabaptism: A Study in the Christology of Balthasar Hubmaier, Pilgram Marpeck, and Dirk Philips* (1993).

James Stayer, *Anabaptists and the Sword* (1972).

J. Denny Weaver, *Becoming Anabaptist: The Origins and Significance of Sixteenth Century Anabaptism* (1987).

George Williams, *The Radical Reformation*, expanded 2nd ed. (1991).

INDIVIDUAL ANABAPTIST LEADERS AND VARIETIES

Stephen Boyd, *Pilgram Marpeck: His Life and Theology* (1992).

Cornelius Dyck, *An Introduction to Mennonite History*, rev. ed. (1981).

Hans-Jürgen Goetz, *Profiles of Radical Reformers* (1982).

Leonard Gross, *The Golden Years of the Hutterites* (1980).

H. Wayne Pipkin and John Yoder, *Balthasar Hubmaier, Theologian of Anabaptism* (1989).

Calvin Redekop and Samuel Steinter, *Mennonite Identity* (1988).

C. Arnold Snyder, *The Life and Thought of Michael Sattler* (1984).

Gary Waite, *David Joris and Dutch Anabaptism, 1524–1543* (1990).

Jerold Knox Zeman, *The Anabaptists and the Czech Reform in Moravia, 1526–1628: A Study of Origins and Contacts* (1969).

Notes

1. Cited in Andrew Johnson, *The Protestant Reformation in Europe* (New York: Longman, 1991), p. 91.
2. Cited in Hans Hillerbrand, ed., *The Protestant Reformation: A Narrative History Related by Contemporary Observers and Participants* (New York: Harper and Row, 1964), pp. 114–115.
3. Ibid., p. 116.
4. Cited in Johnson, *Reformation*, p. 92.
5. Cited in Hillerbrand, *The Reformation*, p. 125.
6. Cited in Lee Palmer Wandel, *Voracious Idols and Violent Hands: Iconoclasm in Reformation Zurich, Strasbourg, and Basel* (New York: Cambridge University Press, 1995), p. 81.
7. Adapted from Lewis Spitz, ed., *The Protestant Reformation* (Englewood Cliffs, N.J.: Prentice Hall, 1966), pp. 89–96.
8. Cited in Hillerbrand, *The Reformation*, p. 254.
9. Ibid., p. 254.
10. Cited in Alister McGrath, *Reformation Thought: An Introduction*, 2nd ed. (Oxford: Blackwell, 1993), p. 202.
11. Quoted by John Roth, "Panel on Sixteenth-Century Confessionalism," Sixteenth Century Studies Conference, Toronto, Canada, October 28, 1994.
12. Cited in McGrath, *Reformation Thought*, p. 203.

8

JOHN CALVIN
AND CALVINISM

The reform movement in Switzerland found new and dynamic leadership in the considerable personage of John (Jean Cauvin) Calvin (1509–1564). A Protestant reformer of the second generation, Calvin was a brilliant theologian, a powerful preacher, a caring pastor, a skilled legalist, and something of an organizational genius. Not only did he accomplish a thorough reform of the city of Geneva, but Calvin used that Swiss city as a base from which missionaries were sent out to much of the rest of Europe. Calvinism eventually outstripped Lutheranism as the largest denomination within the ranks of Protestantism.

CALVIN'S EARLY YEARS

John Calvin began life in the town of Noyon in northern France. His mother, Jeanne, known for her beauty and her piety, was the daughter of a successful innkeeper. She died when John was only three. His notary father, Gerard, soon remarried, but little is known about his second wife. Young John was educated by private tutors and attended an endowed school in Noyon attended by the sons of the aristocratic Montmor family. He soon exhibited a keen intelligence and a facility with Latin.

Calvin's father, who had become secretary to the bishop of Noyon, used his connections to obtain a cathedral chaplaincy and other benefices for John, all of which supported his continued education. At the age of fourteen, Calvin was sent to a college of the University of Paris, with the Montmor boys as companions and schoolfellows. His radiant personality and fine manners helped make him a number of close friends and he excelled in his studies. He soon transferred to the College of Montaigu, where Erasmus had studied and complained about the food and the scholastic theology. Calvin found the environment there much more stimulating, partly because he came into contact with some of the finest minds in Paris including the great humanist and Greek scholar Guillaume Budé and the literary titan François Rabelais. A true intellectual, Calvin blossomed in the stimulating atmosphere of Renaissance Paris.

Calvin had been preparing for the priesthood, but in 1528, shortly after receiving his M.A. at age 18, he suddenly left Paris to study law at Orléans. By this time, his father was having difficulties in his relations with the cathedral chapter in Noyon over disputed accounting records. These problems apparently influenced Gerard Calvin to reconsider his son's future. Although he was more enamored of humanistic studies than the law, the dutiful son continued his study of law until his father's death in 1531.

He had completed all work for his license as a lawyer, but instead of practicing law, Calvin returned to Paris to continue his classical scholarship.

Immersing himself in Greek and Hebrew studies, John Calvin published his first book, a *Commentary on Seneca's Treatise on Clemency* in 1532. Calvin's work on the Roman Stoic reveals his impressive knowledge of classical literature and philosophy. Deeply religious, he was particularly attracted to the Stoic belief in divine providence. During this period, Calvin also underwent "a sudden conversion" to Protestantism. Forbidden Protestant books and ideas circulated widely among Calvin's friends. His father's problems with the church may also have played a part in his souring on the Catholic church and his decision to give up his benefices. He later wrote of his conversion: "And first, since I was too obstinately devoted to the superstitions of Popery to be easily extricated from so profound an abyss of mire, God by a sudden conversion subdued and brought my mind to a teachable frame."[1]

THE FLIGHT FROM PARIS

In 1533 John Calvin was forced to flee Paris. His friend Nicholas Cop, son of the royal physician and recently elected rector of the university, gave a convocation address at the opening of the fall semester that had a decidedly Protestant tone to it. Cop not only defended Marguerite of Navarre's mystical poem *The Mirror of a Sinful Soul*, which had been condemned by the faculty of theology, but he emphasized the role of grace in salvation. The brilliant Calvin was known to have helped Cop write the address and was advised to leave the city to avoid arrest. He spent the first half of 1534 at Saintonge in the home of a student friend whose parents had a good library.

When pranksters broke into the royal palace of King François I in October of 1534 and posted Protestant slogans on his bedroom door as well as throughout Paris, the king responded with even more persecutions of Protestants in France. Some of the posters called the Mass an "execrable blasphemy, pretending to be a sacrifice to God."[2] Calvin fled France for Strasbourg, where he met the talented reformers Martin Bucer, Matthew Zell, and Katherine Zell. He then moved on to Basel, which had become Protestant in 1529, and there met another important humanist turned reformer, Wolfgang Capito, who would later join Bucer and the Zells in Strasbourg. In Basel during March of 1536, Calvin published the first edition of his masterwork, *The Institutes of the Christian Religion*, which he spent the rest of his life expanding.

Calvin's Theology

A brilliant summary of Protestant theology, *The Institutes* helped establish Calvin at age twenty-six as one of the leading Protestant minds in Europe. He later translated it into French and kept expanding it in numerous editions until his death. Even the aging Martin Luther found the book most impressive. Its lucid and facile style had much the same influence on the formation of modern literary French as Luther's translation of the Bible had on German. Its success was rivaled only by the ribald writings of the ex-monk and humanist François Rabelais, Calvin's former associate. Like Luther, Calvin used the printing press to great advantage.

Probably Calvin's most significant contribution to the emergence of Protestant theology was his sublime conception of the majesty of God. For him the divine creator is so overwhelming and awe-inspiring that humans by contrast seem insignificant, sinful, and unworthy. Nevertheless, this majestic God is a God of love, who planned the whole universe to the end of time, selecting some humans for salvation and some for damnation. Like Luther, Calvin was strongly influenced by the writings of St. Augustine and gave priority to the role of God in the salvation of humanity. He believed that faith unites the believer to Christ and begins a process of regeneration which makes the believer more Christ-like.

Calvin described his doctrine of double predestination in the *Institutes* with great clarity, as the following illustrates:

> Predestination we call the eternal decree of God by which He determined in Himself what would have to become of every individual of mankind. For they are not all created with a similar destiny, but eternal life is foreordained for some and eternal damnation for others. Every person, therefore, being created for one or the other of these two ends, we say is predestined to life or to death.[3]

Although Calvin shared many of these ideas with other reformers, few had expressed Protestant beliefs with such lucidity and power. A prolific author, he supplemented the various editions of the *Institutes* with numerous biblical commentaries, polemics, treatises, and letters.

Calvin differed from both Luther and Zwingli in his understanding of the sacrament of the Eucharist. He took a position midway between Luther's conception of the real presence of God in the sacrament and Zwingli's symbolic presence. Instead, Calvin argued for a "spiritual" presence. He stressed that there is such a close connection between the symbol (the bread) and the gift which it symbolizes that we can "easily pass from one to the other. For why should the Lord put in your hand the symbol of his body, unless it was to assure you that you really participate in it?"[4]

With the first edition of *The Institutes* published, Calvin set out for Italy to visit the court of Renée, duchess of Ferrara and daughter of King Louis XII of France. Renée (1510–1575) was known for her learning and her sympathies with reformers. He stayed barely a month in Ferrara because Renée's more conservative husband, Duke Ercole I (d. 1559), refused to let her turn their court into a refuge for religious dissenters. Renée kept up a lifelong correspondence with Calvin; and when her husband died, she joined the Calvinists in France and provided safe havens for many of them. John Calvin then returned to France to bring a brother and sister to safety in Strasbourg, but was forced to take a detour by marauding troops involved in the third of the Habsburg-Valois wars (1536–1538) and ended up in Geneva in July of 1536.

THE CALL TO GENEVA

The Swiss city of Geneva, an active commercial town of 10,300 inhabitants, had become a center for religious refugees from France and Italy. It had previously been ruled by a rapacious bishop as a fief of the Holy Roman Empire. The duke of Savoy, whose territory surrounded the town, also claimed influence in the city. Nearby Bern had sent the preacher Guillaume Farel (1489–1565) to urge the Genevans to free themselves from the authority of both the bishop and the house of Savoy and save their souls by adopting the Protestant version of reform. This combination of religious and political motivations was too appealing to reject. After a public debate between Protestant leaders and Catholic clergy in June 1535, a majority of the male citizens voted to "abandon all papal ceremonies and abuses, images, and idols."[5] Yet the Genevans also resisted Farel's efforts to dampen their enthusiasm for amusements and make the city more "godly."

The fiery Farel wanted Calvin's help in further changing the community and begged him to stay. Contemplating a quiet life of scholarship, Calvin was reluctant to become involved in the turbulent waters of reform on a daily basis. Farel admonished him: "You are following only your own wishes, and I declare in the name of God Almighty, that if you do not assist us in this work of the Lord, God will punish you."[6] Overcome by guilt and a stoical sense of duty, Calvin agreed to stay and help Farel reform Geneva. He was made "Reader in Holy Scripture to the church of Geneva." With his encouragement, the Mass was replaced with simple services of prayer, sermons, and the singing of the Psalms. In January 1537 the hardworking and legalistic Calvin submitted his *Articles Concerning the Government of the Church*, a *Confession*, and a *Catechism*, for purposes of instruction.

Calvin and Farel proposed that his confession be made mandatory for all citizens by public profession and oath. They insisted that the reformed church had the right to scrutinize the lives of its members and to punish impenitent sinners. After considerable debate, these stern and intrusive measures were adopted by a majority of the city's ruling councils. Calvin also insisted that Geneva's existing ordinances against licentious dancing, card playing, theater-going, drunkenness, gambling, and swearing be enforced and applied equally to all, regardless of social standing. As one cynical wit commented, "You can do anything you want in Geneva as long as you do not enjoy it."[7]

Political leaders began hearing rumblings of discontent from some prominent Genevans who resented the power over their lives assumed by two French immigrants. Calvin and the councils began to disagree publicly on whether the church or the state should administer church discipline. The crisis escalated in February of 1538 when Calvin refused the government's order to administer the Lord's Supper in the Bernese manner with unleavened bread.

Calvin and Farel were expelled from the city on April 23, 1538.

The Reform in Strasbourg

They first went to Bern, then to Zurich, and finally ended up in Basel. Farel then accepted a call from his former parish at Neuchâtel and Calvin accepted one from his friend Martin Bucer to return to Strasbourg. Strasbourg was a busy and prosperous commercial town of about 20,000 people, located at the crossroads between Germany, France, Switzerland, and the Low Countries. As an imperial city, it technically owed allegiance to the Holy Roman emperor but was independent for all practical purposes. Strasbourg was one of the more than fifty imperial cities which had recognized the Reformation in the sixteenth century. As early as 1521 it had exhibited Lutheran sympathies. Later Strasbourg came under the influence of the moderate reformer Martin Bucer, who was sympathetic to a variety of Protestant views, including those of Huldrych Zwingli.

MARTIN BUCER (1491–1551)

A former Dominican friar with humanist leanings, Bucer had attended Martin Luther's 1518 meeting with the Augustinians at Heidelberg and been profoundly impressed. He left the monastery and became a priest at Landstühl, the parish of Franz von Sickingen, a knight. After the failure of Sickingen's Knights' Revolt, Bucer and his young wife, a former nun, moved to Weissenberg and later to Strasbourg in 1523. Supported by theologically sophisticated politicians such as the ex-cleric Jacob Sturm, the reformers eventually persuaded a reluctant city council to abolish the Mass in 1529. Like Zwingli, Bucer believed that the magistrates had the obligation to help reform the church.

Blessed with a fine mind and a unique vision, Martin Bucer tried to make Strasbourg a unique center of reform that was relatively open to a variety of religious opinions. Anabaptists, Spiritualists, and refugees from Catholicism such as the former abbot Peter Martyr Vermigli (1499–1562) found hospitality and sanctuary there. Vermigli claimed that Bucer's home was "like a hostel, receiving refugees for the cause of Christ."[8] Bucer did not think the breach with Rome had to be permanent and hoped that one day unity would be restored. Over time, he lost that hope, but continued to mediate between his fellow Protestants on various disputed points of doctrine. Bucer was ably assisted in his reform efforts by the humanist Wolfgang Capito, Caspar Hedio, and Matthew and Katherine Zell, among others.

KATHERINE ZELL (c. 1497–1562)

Katherine Zell was one of the most important female leaders of the early Reformation. Inspired by the writings of Martin Luther, Katherine had married the ex-monk Matthew Zell in 1523 in a service presided over by Martin Bucer. They became a ministerial team because of her strong religious interests and the admiration her much older husband had for her abilities. The daughter of a respected carpenter, Katherine had been tutored at home and possibly at a vernacular school. She developed a fondness for liturgical reform and theology. When her two babies died in infancy, she threw herself into her husband's ministry with great energy. She sheltered large groups of religious refugees, administered relief to the poor, visited the sick and infirm, wrote theological tracts, published hymns, and delivered a public address at the funeral of her husband in 1548, in an age when women were seldom allowed to speak in public.

Martin Bucer, Wolfgang Capito, and the Zells had a lot to teach John Calvin about how to be a successful pastor. Calvin served as the pastor of a congregation of fellow French refugees. He also attended Protestant meetings at Frankfurt on the Main, Hagenau, Worms, and Regensburg. There he met many of the leaders of German Protestantism, including Philip Melanchthon, whom he admired greatly, and Gasparo Contarini, the reform-minded cardinal. At age thirty Calvin also accepted Bucer's suggestion that he marry Idelette de Bure, the widow of a Dutch Anabaptist. The marriage proved a happy one, though both were troubled with ill health. She was further weakened by childbirth and the death of their only child and died six years later in 1549.

Calvin's Return to Geneva

Calvin reluctantly returned to Geneva in September of 1541 to complete his reform work. Genevan leaders had promised that this time they would fully support his disciplinary efforts and treat him with the respect he deserved. He was appointed pastor of St. Peter's parish and given a substantial salary and a large house. The ruling elite in Geneva had decided they needed the astute Calvin's firm hand in creating a truly reformed city and were willing to pay a high price to bring him back. Calvin's leadership was challenged in 1546 when a prominent member of the elite Small Council accused him of being "a wicked man, who preaches false doctrine." Calvin demanded a public apology and that his accuser march through the streets of Geneva in disgrace. This was done but other members of the Genevan old-guard rose up to challenge Calvin's authority from time to time. Calvin also found that he could not trust many of his ministerial colleagues, especially those who had remained in Geneva during his and Farel's exile.

THE MICHAEL SERVETUS CASE

Public opposition to Calvin within Geneva virtually came to a head in 1553 with the trial and burning of Michael Servetus (c. 1509–1553). Servetus was a Spanish scientist, lawyer, physician, and amateur theologian. He was the first person to postulate the pulmonary circulation of the blood. Turning to theology, Servetus was interested in building the Jewish case for Christianity. In his *On the Errors of the Trinity* (1531), Servetus seemed to cast doubt on the divinity of Christ, traditionally a sensitive issue for Christians. After failing to convince the reformers of Basel and Strasbourg of the correctness of his views, he was arrested by the Catholic Inquisition and condemned "as a case of total heresy." He later escaped from prison and arrived in Geneva on his way to refuge in Italy.

Servetus was recognized in Geneva and immediately turned over to the authorities for trial as a heretic. He had earlier sent Calvin a copy of the *Institutes* with the Spaniard's "corrections" written in the margins. After a lengthy trial at which Calvin testified and was counterattacked by Servetus, the Spaniard was found guilty and burned at the stake. Calvin graciously attempted to minister to him in his cell and recommended the less painful punishment of beheading but was overruled by the authorities. Calvin gained prestige with some for having moved against a talented but arrogant man believed to be a dangerous heretic. However, the death of Servetus appalled his former colleague Sebastian Castellio (1515–1563), who was banished

from Geneva in 1545 for his insistence on drawing a distinction between essential and nonessential doctrines. Castellio had also asserted that the biblical Song of Songs was a true love song and not an allegory.

Castellio argued in his 1554 treatise, *Whether Heretics Should Be Persecuted*, that to kill a man "is not defending a doctrine, it is merely killing a man." He understood that the root cause of intolerance was arrogance and pride:

> Men are puffed up with knowledge or a false opinion of knowledge and look down upon all others. Pride is followed by cruelty and persecution so that now scarcely anyone is able to endure another who differs from him. Although opinions are almost as numerous as men, nevertheless there is hardly any sect which does not condemn all others and desire to reign alone.[9]

Tragically, Castellio's words of wisdom were not heeded by Calvin or very many other leaders of the time. Religious toleration was not an acceptable concept for most in the sixteenth century, who saw only a lack of religious fervor in those willing to allow a range of religious thought. Such laxity, it was believed, jeopardized souls by exposing people to the risk of "false teachings." Heresy was thought to be a "cancer" that had to be eliminated at all costs. As for Castellio, he died a professor of Greek at Basel under suspicion in 1563, having dared to question such basic theological issues as predestination.

THE THREAT OF THE LIBERTINES

Two years after the execution of Servetus, Calvin faced his gravest political threat when a native Genevan, Ami Perrin, tried to take over the government of Geneva by force. Perrin was an influential member of the Small Council and an early supporter of Calvin's. However, he fell out with Calvin over the latter's insistence that church discipline should be enforced uniformly against all members of Genevan society. In 1546, Perrin's father-in-law, François Favre, also a member of the Small Council, had been excommunicated for immoral conduct. Perrin's wife, Francesca, also attempted to defy Calvin's insistence on equal justice for all and was exiled for disobeying some of Geneva's laws against dissolute public behavior.

Ami Perrin himself was arrested later in 1546 when it was discovered that he had entered into negotiations with the French king on his own authority. His political allies rallied behind him and he was acquitted and returned to office. In 1548 Perrin's faction was victorious in the elections for the town council. Calvin called them the "Libertines," and argued against their attempts to relax ecclesiastical discipline. An uneasy truce existed for seven years between Calvin's friends and foes on the city councils. The Libertines also broadened their support base in Geneva by stirring up resentment among the older inhabitants against the increasing number of religious refugees who were fleeing France in ever greater numbers.

When the Calvinists won the majority of seats on the Small Council in the spring of 1555, Perrin, who was then a captain of the town militia, attempted a coup against the government and called for the massacre of the French. His followers were promptly put down, but Perrin managed to escape from the city with three companions. This was the last great political challenge Calvin had to face in Geneva. He now felt secure enough to become a citizen of the city— eighteen years after he had first settled in Geneva.

DISCIPLINE IN CALVIN'S GENEVA

Always concerned with the practical aspects of reform, John Calvin helped establish what his Scottish disciple John Knox called "the most perfect school of life that was ever on earth since the days of the apostles."[10] Among the many things about Calvin's Geneva that Knox admired were its clean streets devoid of beggars and its well-organized churches. Calvin's legal training and orderly mind were invaluable in organizing the Genevan church and in dealing with societal problems. Calvin's *Ecclesiastical Ordinances* of 1541 established four orders of offices: pastors, teachers, elders, and deacons. Ministers were to preach the word, administer the sacraments (baptism and the Eucharist), and admonish their parishioners both publicly and privately. Teachers were to "instruct the faithful in sound doctrine." Elders were laymen whose primary function was to "oversee everybody" and maintain proper order and discipline. The deacons were to help the poor, comfort the sick, and care for widows and orphans. All these things were done with greater efficiency in Calvin's Geneva than almost anywhere else in Europe.

Discipline especially was rigorously maintained over all segments of society. The chief instrument of enforcement in Calvin's Geneva was the Consistory, made up of twelve elders and five pastors and presided over by a member of the Small Council. This made the Consistory at once an agency of both the church and the state. Calvin believed that both the magistrates and the ministers were agents of God with similar purposes, although different tools: "For the church has not the right of the sword to punish or restrain, has no power to coerce, no prison nor other punishments which the magistrate is wont to inflict."[11]

The chief difference between Calvin's Geneva and most other places in Europe was the thoroughness of the Genevan Consistory in attempting to enforce morality. Geneva's city fathers also tried to deal with some of the root causes of crime, such as poverty. Relief was carefully administered to the poor, for Calvin argued that "we should be moved to pity when we see any poor folks in adversity and provide for them according to our ability."[12] Even Geneva's prostitutes were organized under the leadership of a "queen" and carefully regulated with regular medical inspections after efforts to eliminate the practice failed.

CALVIN AND WOMEN

All these public functions, however, were carried out solely by men; even the "queen" of the prostitutes reported to a male official. A thorough patriarch, Calvin argued that in the early church "a woman was not allowed to speak in church, and also not to teach, to baptize, or to offer."[13] He was apparently unimpressed by the many women deaconesses in the early church or the significance of the prophet Joel's (2:28) statement that "your sons and your daughters shall prophesy." Biblical heroines such as Deborah and Judith were "exceptional women." Calvin did think that salvation was open to both sexes and approved of religious education for girls. Women were to read the Bible only in private, but he did allow female singing in church, despite the criticism of some members of the government.

Calvin held views on women rulers which were quite similar to his colleague John Knox, who got in considerable trouble with Queen Elizabeth I of England for his misogynist diatribe *Against the Monstrous Regiment of Women*. Calvin apologized to the powerful English queen for the tenor of Knox's comments, but his own thoughts in a letter to Heinrich Bullinger of April 28, 1554, reflect ideas similar to the Scotsman's. Calvin wrote:

> About the government of women I expressed myself thus: since it is utterly at variance with the legitimate order of nature, it ought to be counted among the judgements with which God visits us. . . . For a gynaecocracy or female rule badly organized is like a tyranny, and is to be tolerated until God sees fit to overthrow it.[14]

Obviously, Calvin was a shrewd enough political animal to not share his real thoughts on this subject with Queen Elizabeth, whose support he needed to help Calvinist communities elsewhere in Europe.

CALVIN THE MAN

During his lifetime Calvin acquired a reputation for severity and somberness. A closer examination reveals that his image as a "blue-nosed Puritan" is based more on polemics than reality. Although he was deeply concerned about sexual improprieties, particularly adultery, those who knew him well—such as his ministerial colleague and biographer Theodore Beza—found him to be a kind and gentle man with "a singular good wit greatly given to the service of God."[15] Beza pointed out that Anabaptists were exiled from Calvin's Geneva and not executed as they were in most other places. Despite his frail health and many struggles, Calvin was a good pastor, companion, and friend. As Calvin himself wrote in the *Institutes*: "We are nowhere forbidden to laugh or to be satisfied with food or to be delighted with music or to drink wine."[16]

Calvin's opportunities to delight in wine or music were limited by the many struggles of his life. His latter years were especially troubled by bouts of ill health and a number of scandals which plagued his family and friends. His brother's wife was found guilty of adultery with one of the reformer's servants and his stepdaughter Judith was also found guilty of adultery. Calvin viewed extramarital sex as a threat to society and all good order. He argued that "fornicators and adulterers should not be tolerated" because they "rob the honor of everything."[17] Calvin was also upset when Guillaume Farel, his former colleague, married a much younger woman when he was sixty-four. He worried about "what will the sneerers say, and what will the simple think, but that the preachers wish to have the law for themselves."[18]

For many years after his return to Geneva in 1541, Calvin had felt a strong sense of isolation. He found that he could not trust many of his ministerial colleagues, with the major exception of Pierre Viret (1511–1571). Viret had converted Lausanne to Protestantism and then joined Farel in the early reform in Geneva. Calvin's loneliness increased in 1549 with

Anonymous, *Portrait of John Calvin.* SEF/Art Resource.

the death of his wife, Idelette. He wrote of her, "I have lost the best companion of my life. . . . While she lived, she was the faithful helper of my ministry. . . . Her greatness of spirit means more to me than a thousand commendations."[19]

Theodore Beza (1516–1605) and the Genevan Academy

Although he never returned to France, Calvin kept a close eye on developments there and sent out teams of missionaries to his homeland. Many of those missionaries were trained in the Genevan Academy that Calvin founded in June 1559. Calvin also had a strong concern that the church be led by well-educated men. The Academy emphasized instruction in languages, the liberal arts, philosophy, and theology. Calvin recruited Theodore Beza, who came from the provincial French nobility, to serve as the Academy's rector. Calvin had first met Beza in 1529 when Calvin was studying law briefly in Bourges. Beza had received much of his legal training at Orléans, where Calvin had also studied law. Beza later earned a licentiate in law from Bourges. After a number of years pursuing humanist learning and worldly pleasure in Paris, Beza took a religious turn and visited Calvin in Geneva in 1548. He then joined Pierre Viret on the faculty of the Academy in Lausanne as a professor of Greek before agreeing to serve in Geneva. Beza may have had an even better command of Greek than Calvin. Like Calvin, he was a fine, largely self-taught theologian with a strong concern for helping others.

The Academy was divided into two sections: a high school and a college. To some extent, it was modeled after a very successful school at Strasbourg developed by Johann Sturm (1507–1589). Sturm was the leading educator in the Reformation period and was much admired by Martin Luther and many others. In the Genevan high school, young males were taught French, Latin, and Greek grammar and literature, as well as elements of logic. Students in the college learned Greek, Hebrew, philosophy, and theology. The Academy was supported by the public treasury and did not charge tuition. Many of its early students came from various parts of France, to which a number returned as Calvinist missionaries. By Calvin's death in 1564, the Genevan Academy enrolled 1,200 students in the high school and 300 in the college, which eventually became the University of Geneva. Its faculty included François Hotman, one of the foremost legal theorists of the century.

Theodore Beza, who continued to teach theology at the Academy between 1564 and 1595, was named by the dying Calvin to succeed him in Geneva as head of the Company of Pastors. Beza was highly respected as a biblical scholar and had completely absorbed and supported Calvin's theological system. His aristocratic background served him well with the social elite of Geneva and as a diplomat. Beza reluctantly became the leading force in the church of Geneva and helped spread international Calvinism.

The Spread of Calvinism

John Calvin's clearly articulated theology and well-organized churches had enormous appeal. Calvin and Beza continued to supply a steady stream of well-trained missionaries to start congregations in nearby France and elsewhere throughout Europe. Geneva offered itself as a successful model of a reform community, and its printing presses supplied an abundance of materials for the new centers of Calvinism. Calvin and Beza both kept up an active correspondence with those who were spreading the movement, including their close friend Pierre Viret, who became a leading missionary in France. Beza also served ably as a missionary and diplomat in France and attended a number of Calvinist religious conventions (synods) before he returned to succeed Calvin in Geneva.

Although France held a special place in the hearts of Calvin and Beza, they also encouraged missionary efforts in other parts of Europe. The clarity of the Calvinist organizational structure had great appeal in the Low Countries, especially in the French-speaking areas. A Belgic Confession of Faith was drafted as early as 1561. Later, as we shall see in Chapter 12, Calvinism will become deeply rooted in the Dutch-speaking portions of the Netherlands. In 1560 Elector Frederick III, count Palatine of the Rhine, converted to Calvinism and established his electorate as a major center of Calvinism inside the Holy Roman Empire. Three years later his theologians drew up the Heidelberg Catechism, which joined Heinrich Bullinger's second Helvetic Confession of 1556 as the most influential doctrinal guides for Calvinist congregations east of the Rhine. A Protestant academy founded at Heidelberg threatened to overshadow the Genevan Academy as a trainer of Calvinist missionaries.

A FAILED CALVINIST REFORMATION IN BRANDENBURG

In 1613 the Hohenzollern Elector Johann Sigismund of the Mark of Brandenburg attempted to convert his north German electorate from Lutheranism to Calvinism in a "second Reformation." Educated at Heidel-

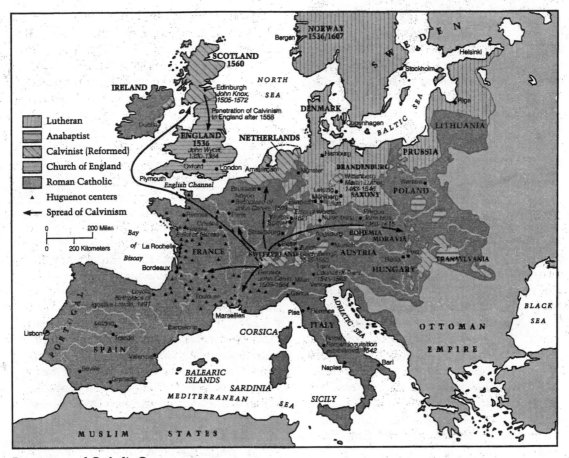

Protestant and Catholic Centers.

berg and Strasbourg, Johann Sigismund had become convinced of the superiority of Calvinism to Lutheranism. He thought that though Martin Luther "has done much to set the gospel free, yet he has remained deeply stuck in the darkness of the papacy."[20] Sigismund favored the Calvinist spiritual interpretation of the Lord's Supper and the less elaborate liturgy of the Swiss reformers. The Lutheran Mass was too close to that of the Catholics for Johann Sigismund's taste. Calvinist churches used hymns based on the Psalms and removed traditional art.

For political as well as religious reasons, the elector wanted to draw closer to the Calvinist Palatinate.

However, Elector Johann Sigismund's efforts to promote Calvinism failed; Lutheranism was too popular and too deeply entrenched into the fabric of society to be dislodged. Lutheranism had officially been adopted by the Mark of Brandenburg in 1540 under Johann Sigismund's grandfather, Joachim II (r. 1535–1571). He in turn had been strongly influenced by his mother, Electress Elizabeth (1485–1545), the sister of

Christian II, the Lutheran king of Denmark. Defying her philandering Catholic husband, Elizabeth had taken communion in both kinds during Easter of 1527 from a Lutheran minister. When he learned of his wife's defiance, Elector Joachim I considered divorcing her or incarcerating her for life. Elizabeth's uncle, Duke Johann the Constant of Saxony, offered her sanctuary, which she accepted, fleeing Berlin disguised as a peasant.

An enraged Joachim demanded that she be returned at once, but Johann the Constant refused. Joachim then appealed to the 1529 Diet of Speyer for the restoration of his "property." The Diet took no action against powerful electoral Saxony and Elector Johann wondered aloud whether it was "possible for a good Catholic to keep concubines while his legitimate wife had to be fed in Saxony."[21] The crisis continued as Joachim became the leader of the Catholic League of Halle, formed in opposition to the Protestant Schmalkaldic League. He also sought to bind his sons to Catholicism by threatening them with disinheritance in his will should they not be faithful to "the old Christian faith."

Meanwhile, the exiled electress lived on in poverty and battled mental illness. She stayed for a time with Martin and Katherine Luther. Her son, Joachim II, succeeded his father in 1535 and invited his mother to return. Elizabeth refused as long as he remained Catholic. Although long attracted to Luther's doctrines, Joachim II resented the reformer's continuing verbal attacks on his uncle, Archbishop Albrecht of Mainz. He also hoped that a general church council could achieve harmony between Lutherans and Catholics in the empire. However, the pressure of events soon got the better of his intention to achieve a degree of religious toleration.

Joachim's younger brother, Hans of Küstrin, embraced the reform and joined the Schmalkaldic League in 1538. Influenced by Prince George III of Anhalt, a fellow moderate and a recent convert to Lutheranism, and Philip Melanchthon, Joachim II issued a new church ordinance in 1540 that brought him reluctantly into the Protestant camp. His ordinance barely passed muster with the Wittenbergers and Joachim himself continued to collect relics. He continued his efforts at mediation and was a strong supporter of the 1541 Regensburg Colloquy between, among others, Philip Melanchthon and Cardinal Gasparo Contarini, a Catholic moderate reformer. In 1545 his brother Hans arrived in Lichtenberg with 500 horses to bring his mother back from exile. He paid her debts and settled her at Spandau. She was allowed the minister of her choice and freedom of worship. Her health failing, Elizabeth requested that Elector Joachim bring her to Berlin. There she died in that same year and was buried beside her Catholic husband from whom she had fled twenty-seven years earlier.

Despite Joachim II's best efforts to steer a course between Rome and Wittenberg and to work out a compromise with Emperor Charles V during the crisis of the Schmalkaldic War and its aftermath, Brandenburg became thoroughly Lutheran. When Johann Sigismund and his court tried to turn the electorate to Calvinism, he found fierce opposition not only from Lutheran pastors but also from their congregations. Neighboring Prussia, which the Hohenzollerns sought to incorporate into their holdings, also was firmly committed to Lutheranism. Therefore, Elector Johann Sigismund found that he could not force Calvinism down the throats of his subjects. He and his court worshipped as Calvinists, but the rest of the electorate stayed Lutheran.

CALVINISM TRIUMPHANT

Although Calvinism failed to dislodge Lutheranism from the Mark of Brandenburg, it continued to advance elsewhere on all fronts. Further to the east, for example, Calvinism had grown rapidly in Poland and in Hungary in the 1550s (for a while, it was the leading denomination in Hungary). Calvinism also had strong minority followings in Bohemia and England (the Puritans). Scotland became Calvinist (the Presbyterians) during the reign of Mary, queen of Scots, as will be discussed in Chapter 10. Emden in the Low Countries became almost a second Geneva, serving as a base for the spread of the reform. As various Calvinist groups and missionaries spread from Europe to the rest of the world, Calvinism became one of the strongest sets of traditions within Protestantism. Its appeal has proved universal and enduring. For such a slender man, John Calvin has indeed cast a wide shadow.

Chronology

1485–1545	Life of Elizabeth of Brandenburg.
1489–1565	Guillaume Farel.
1491–1555	Martin Bucer.
c. 1497–1562	Katherine Zell.
1509	Birth of John Calvin.
1511–1571	Life of Pierre Viret.
1516	Birth of Theodore Beza.
1523	Marriage of Matthew and Katherine Zell.
1528	Calvin earns his M.A. in the arts at Paris and begins law school.
1529	Strasbourg adopts the reform.
1532	Calvin publishes his *Commentary on Seneca's Treatise on Clemency*.
1533	Calvin forced to flee Paris.
1534	Affair of the Placards.
1535	Geneva adopts the reform under Farel and Viret.
1536	First edition of Calvin's *Institutes of the Christian Religion*; Calvin begins his ministry in Geneva.
1538	Calvin and Farel exiled from Geneva; Calvin begins his pastorate in Strasbourg.
1539	Calvin marries Idelette de Bure.
1540	Adoption of Lutheranism in Brandenburg.
1541	Calvin returns to Geneva; publication of the *Ecclesiastical Ordinances*.
1549	Death of Idelette Calvin.
1553	Trial and execution of Michael Servetus in Geneva.
1554	Castellio's *Whether Heretics Should be Burned*.
1555	Ami Perrin's attempted takeover of Geneva fails.
1556	Bullinger's Second Helvetic Confession.
1558	Theodore Beza and Pierre Viret flee Lausanne for Geneva.
1559	Founding of the Geneva Academy.
1560	Elector Frederick III of the Palatinate converts to Calvinism.
1563	Publication of the Heidelberg Catechism.
1564	Death of Calvin.
1605	Death of Theodore Beza.

Further Reading

CALVIN: BIOGRAPHIES

William Bousma, *John Calvin* (1988). The leading biography.

Alister McGrath, *A Life of John Calvin* (1990).

T. H. L. Parker, *John Calvin, A Biography* (1975).

Ronald Wallace, *Calvin, Geneva, and the Reformation* (1988).

François Wendel, *Calvin: The Origin and Development of his Religious Thought* (1963).

CALVIN'S THOUGHT

Jane Dempsey Douglas, *Women, Freedom, and Calvin* (1982).

Richard Gamble, ed., *Calvin and Calvinism*, 14 vols. (1992). A vast collection of scholarly articles.

Timoth George, ed., *John Calvin and the Church: A Prism of Reform* (1990).

B. A. Gerrish, *Grace and Gratitude: The Eucharistic Theology of John Calvin* (1993).

W. Fred Graham, *The Constructive Revolutionary: Calvin's Socio-Economic Impact* (1989).

Harro Höpfl, *The Christian Polity of John Calvin* (1982).

Elsie McKee, *Elders and the Plural Ministry: The Role of Exegetical History in Illuminating John Calvin's Theology* (1988).

William Naphy, *Calvin and the Consolidation of the Genevan Reformation* (1994).

Jeannine Olson, *Calvin and Social Welfare* (1989).

Robert Schnucker, ed., *Calviana: Ideas and Influence of Jean Calvin* (1988). Valuable essays by a variety of leading scholars.

David Steinmetz, *Calvin in Context* (1995).

John Lee Thompson, *John Calvin and the Daughters of Sarah* (1992).

Thomas Torrance, *The Hermeneutics of John Calvin* (1988).

OTHERS INVOLVED IN THE GENEVAN REFORM

Jerome Friedman, *Michael Servetus* (1989).

Robert Lindner, *The Political Thought of Pierre Viret* (1964).

Jill Raitt, *The Eucharistic Theology of Theodore Beza* (1972).

CALVINISM

Brian Armstrong, *Calvinism and the Amyraut Heresy* (1969).

Phyllis Mack Crew, *Calvinist Preaching and Iconoclasm in the Netherlands, 1544–1569* (1978).

Alastair Duke, Gillian Lewis, and Andrew Pettegree, eds. and trs., *Calvinism in Europe, 1540–1610: A Collection of Documents* (1992).

W. Fred Graham, ed., *Later Calvinism: International Perspectives* (1994). A valuable collection of essays.

Henry Heller, *The Conquest of Poverty: The Calvinist Revolt in Sixteenth-Century France* (1986).

Robert Kingdon, *Adultery and Divorce in Calvin's Geneva* (1994).

———, *Geneva and the Consolidation of the French Protestant Movement* (1967). By the leading authority.

John T. McNeill, *The History and Character of Calvinism* (1967).

Eric Monter, *Calvin's Geneva* (1967).

Richard Muller, *Christ and the Decree: Christology and Predestination in Reformed Theology from Calvin to Perkins* (1986).

Bodo Nischan, *Prince, People, and Confession: The Second Reformation in Brandenburg* (1994).

Andrew Pettegree, *Emden and the Dutch Revolt: Exile and the Development of Reformed Protestantism* (1992).

Minna Prestwich, ed., *International Calvinism, 1541–1715* (1985). Important essays by a variety of scholars.

Stephen Strehle, *Calvinism, Federalism, and Scholasticism: A Study of the Reformed Doctrine of the Covenant* (1988).

STRASBOURG

Jane Lorna Abray, *The People's Reformation* (1985).

Thomas Brady, Jr., *Ruling Class, Regime and Reformation at Strasbourg* (1978).

Amy Nelson Burnett, *The Yoke of Discipline: Martin Bucer and Church Discipline* (1994).

Miriam Usher Chrisman, *Strasbourg and the Reform* (1967).

James Kittelson, *Wolfgang Capito From Humanist to Reformer* (1975).

Elsie McKee, *Reforming Popular Piety in Sixteenth-Century Strasbourg: Katharina Schütz Zell and Her Hymnbook* (1995).

Lewis Spitz and Barbara Sher Tinsley, *Johann Sturm on Education: The Reformation and Humanist Learning* (1995).

W. P. Stephens, *The Holy Spirit in the Theology of Martin Bucer* (1970).

William Stafford, *Domesticating the Clergy: The Inception of the Reformation in Strasbourg 1522–1524* (1976).

Notes

1. Cited in Andrew Johnson, *The Protestant Reformation in Europe* (New York: Longman, 1991), p. 99.
2. Cited in Lewis Spitz, *The Renaissance and Reformation Movements* (Chicago: Rand McNally, 1971), p. 415.
3. John Calvin, *Institutes of the Christian Religion*, tr. by Ford Lewis Battles, ed. by John T. McNeill, 2 vols. (Philadelphia: Westminster Press, 1960), vol. 2, p. 926.
4. Cited in Alister McGrath, *Reformation Thought: An Introduction*, 2nd ed. (Oxford: Blackwell, 1993), p. 182.
5. Cited in De Lamar Jensen, *Reformation Europe: Age of Reform and Revolution*, 2nd ed. (New York: D. C. Heath, 1992), p. 136.
6. Cited in Hans Hillerbrand, ed., *The Protestant Reformation: A Narrative History Related by Contemporary Observers and Participants* (New York: Harper and Row, 1964), p. 179.
7. James Tillema, April, 1964.
8. Cited in Roland Bainton, *Women of the Reformation in Germany and Italy* (Minneapolis, Minn.: Augsburg, 1971), p. 88.
9. Cited in Lewis Spitz, ed., *The Protestant Reformation* (Englewood Cliffs, N.J.: Prentice Hall, 1966), p. 108.
10. Cited in John T. McNeill, *The History and Character of Calvinism* (New York: Oxford University Press, 1967), p. 178.
11. Cited in Alister McGrath, *Reformation Thought: An Introduction*, 2nd ed. (Oxford: Blackwell, 1993), p. 216.
12. John Calvin, *Sermons from Job*, tr. by Leroy Nixon (Grand Rapids, Mich.: William Eerdmans, 1952), p. 199.
13. Cited in Julia O'Faolain and Lauro Martines, eds., *Not in God's Image: Women in History from the Greeks to the Victorians* (New York: Harper and Row, 1973), p. 202.
14. John Calvin, *Letters of John Calvin*, ed. and tr. by Jules Bonnet, 4 vols. (Edinburgh, Scotland: Thomas Constable, 1855–1857), vol. 4, pp. 128–129.
15. Cited in Hillerbrand, *Reformation*, pp. 206–207.
16. Calvin, *Institutes*, vol. 1, pp. 720–721.
17. Calvin, *Sermons from Job*, p. 186.
18. Calvin, *Letters*, vol. 3, pp. 473–474.
19. Ibid., vol. 2, pp. 202–203.
20. Cited in Bodo Nischan, *Prince, People, and Confession: The Second Reformation in Brandenburg* (Philadelphia: University of Pennsylvania Press, 1994), pp. 94–95.
21. Ibid., pp. 120–121.

9

THE REFORMATION
IN ENGLAND TO 1558

King Harry's Trouble with Women

The word on the streets of Catholic Dublin in the summer of 1530 was that "King Harry of England was having trouble with his women."[1] People were referring, of course, to King Henry VIII of England, a remarkable Renaissance prince who had been seeking a divorce from his wife, Queen Catherine of Aragon (b. 1485), since 1527. Henry wanted a divorce, because after eighteen years of marriage he had been blessed with only one surviving child, a daughter, Mary (b. 1516). All the rest of his offspring died before birth or within a few days of their birth. Their deaths had confirmed Henry's fear that he had been living in sin, albeit with a woman who was a model of piety.

By the spring of 1527, the king had become convinced that God was denying him a son to punish him for having married his brother's widow. Even if Henry had been less of a misogynist, when he looked back into English history, he saw only one ruling female, and that was the "imperious" Matilda (1102–1167), daughter of King Henry I (r. 1100–1135), whose right to rule had been challenged by her more popular cousin Stephen of Blois (1135–1154). This contest for the throne eventually led to nine years of civil war that ended when Stephen was allowed the throne on the condition that upon

his death it go to Matilda's son, the future Henry II. By this time neither faction had been able to decisively defeat the other, and Stephen's only son had died.

Henry VIII, a talented lay theologian with a tender conscience, came to the conclusion that his marriage to Catherine was contrary to the injunction in Leviticus 20:21: "If a man takes his brother's wife, it is impurity; he has uncovered his brother's nakedness, they shall be childless." Queen Catherine was the widow of Henry's older brother Arthur (d. 1502), who had died of consumption four months after their marriage. Not wanting to lose Catherine's considerable dowry or the prestige of marrying into the house of Ferdinand and Isabella of Spain, Henry's father, the frugal King Henry VII, succeeded in convincing the Spanish to agree to the second marriage despite the fact that the twelve-year-old Henry was six years younger than his bride.

Henry VII also had to get a special papal dispensation from Pope Julius II to permit a marriage that so clearly violated the injunction in Leviticus. His theologians argued that Deuteronomy 25:5 permitted the nuptials:

When brothers shall dwell together, and one of them dies without children, the wife of the deceased shall not marry to another;

but his brother shall take her, and raise up seed for his brother.

At length the papacy was convinced to permit the marriage and Henry and Catherine were finally wed on June 11, 1509, a few weeks after the death of Henry's father.

The marriage was generally considered a happy one despite the age difference. Catherine was a good, well-educated, intelligent, and pious woman, and Henry was a remarkably talented young prince. Not only was he a warrior and a statesman, but he was a gifted athlete, an active hunter, a musician, and a poet. A loyal son of the church, he had been named "Defender of the Faith" by Pope Leo X in 1521 for his writings against Martin Luther. Now in 1527 his conscience was dis-

After Hans Holbein, *Henry VIII* (c. 1536). Photo courtesy of the National Portrait Gallery, London, United Kingdom.

turbed by his failure to have a son and heir. Perhaps the church had been wrong; perhaps he should never have violated Leviticus by marrying his brother's widow.

CARDINAL THOMAS WOLSEY (1471–1530)

King Henry now turned for help to his great friend and the head of his government, Cardinal Thomas Wolsey. A veritable mountain of flesh with a lively mind, Wolsey was one of the most talented men in England. The son of a successful butcher, Wolsey had gone on to a university career at Oxford and rose eventually to become a chaplain to King Henry VII. Following the death of the first Tudor king, Wolsey entered the service of Henry VIII and proved invaluable as a judge and councillor, despite his lack of a legal background. A gifted administrator whose talents allowed Henry to mix governing with the pleasures of the hunt and the dance, Wolsey eventually became head of the government as lord chancellor.

As the king's favorite, Wolsey also advanced in the church. By 1527 he was the greatest pluralist in the church, serving as papal legate, archbishop of York, and abbot of St. Albans. Wolsey also held three other bishoprics and three deputy bishoprics. He supplemented his already enormous income with bribes and extortions. Arrogant and sensual, Wolsey loved power, eating well, fornicating, and living sumptuously. The stately palace at Hampton Court west of London is one of his great monuments. Possessed of great wit and a gift for management, Wolsey knew that he still owed his fabulous rise to power and wealth to his king. Even his dazzling accomplishments in administration and foreign policy, where he had helped make England a power to be reckoned with on the Continent, would begin to pale if he failed Henry in the matter of the divorce.

"BREAKING UP IS HARD TO DO": THE PROBLEM OF THE DIVORCE

Getting the papacy to grant Henry an annulment of his marriage was going to be very difficult. As fate would have it, Emperor Charles V's army in Italy had just sacked Rome in the summer of 1527, and Charles was the nephew of Henry's queen. Pope Clement VII was still a virtual prisoner of Charles's army and Queen Catherine did not want her marriage to Henry Tudor to end. The thought that she had been "living in sin" with Henry for eighteen years appalled the queen, who was widely respected in England and elsewhere for her piety. Emperor Charles was not about to let the pope agree to the disgrace of his aunt even if it meant breaking up the English-Habsburg alliance.

Pope Clement VII was also not willing to admit that the original dispensation that had allowed Henry's marriage to Catherine was illegal. Such an admission would challenge the "fullness of power" (*plenitudo potestatis*) doctrine upon which great medieval lawyer-popes such as Innocent III (1161–1216) had built the authority of the papal monarchy. Even Wolsey did not seem to push the case as hard as he might have for fear of offending the Sacred College of Cardinals. After all, his sole remaining ambition was to become the next pope and he would need the good will of many of the cardinals. He did try to get the case transferred to England and his own jurisdiction. Although agreeing to this for a while to gain time, Pope Clement had no intention of giving up the power of the papal court over marriages, and he took the case back after failing to persuade Henry to drop the matter.

The case dragged on and on as Henry's and Catherine's relationship continued to deteriorate under the pressure of his eagerness to remove her as his queen. His desire to end the marriage was further fueled by an attractive, dark haired, younger woman with whom he had fallen in love and lust, Anne Boleyn (b. 1506). Having previously sampled the favors of Anne's married, older sister, Mary, Henry was keen to wed the bright-eyed, intelligent, sophisticated beauty with six fingers on one hand, who had picked up some of the graces of the French court. She held out the promise of sons and renewed youth for the middle-aged lion. Anne insisted on a clear understanding of marriage before sex, not wishing to be as easily discarded as other mistresses such as her sister had been. With great skill, she held the king at bay for over five years until a promise of marriage had been secured.

In his fury over Cardinal Wolsey's failure to achieve the divorce, Henry ruthlessly turned on his former favorite and stripped him of his office as lord chancellor in 1529. Even the cardinal's sudden gift of Hampton Court to the king failed to appease the wrath of the ruthless and morbid Henry. Only Wolsey's death of a heart attack a year later saved him from dying at the chopping block for "treason." In his play *Henry VIII*, William Shakespeare has Wolsey saying: "Had I served my God with half the zeal I served my king, he would not in mine old age have left me naked to mine enemies." Although the quote may not be historically accurate, the sentiment rings true.

REPLACEMENTS FOR WOLSEY

New helpers now emerged to assist the king in the running of England. To replace the worldly cardinal as lord chancellor, Henry selected Sir Thomas More (1478–1535), the gifted humanist and lawyer, celebrated author of the visionary *Utopia*, and veteran politician. What an ornament he would be to Henry's inner circle. More recognized the dangers of serving Henry as chancellor, but did not think he could turn down his sovereign. As a man of great conscience, Thomas

More was unwilling to become a tool in the process of disgracing Queen Catherine. He would serve his master in other ways for the time being, such as by persecuting Protestants and suppressing English translations of the Bible.

Help with the divorce problem now came from an ambitious young cleric named Thomas Cranmer (c. 1489–1553). A graduate of Cambridge University and sympathetic to Continental reform ideas, Cranmer proposed that the universities should rule on Henry's divorce case. This idea was tried, and although the king got a mixed verdict from the academicians, he was pleased with Cranmer's intelligence and willingness to be of service. Cranmer had also impressed Anne Boleyn, another advocate of church reform. She used her influence to have her lover appoint Cranmer archbishop of Canterbury following the death of William Warham in 1532. As archbishop, Cranmer dutifully pronounced the dissolution of Henry's marriage to Catherine of Aragon, and in June 1533, he married the king to Anne Boleyn.

THOMAS CROMWELL (1485–1540)

Thanks in part to the work of another shrewd servant of the crown, Thomas Cromwell, the king's marriage was widely accepted in England. A cloth worker's son who got into trouble as a teenager, Cromwell had been forced to flee England. He became a mercenary soldier in Italy, then turned to a prosperous career in international trade. The hardworking, ambitious, and talented Cromwell eventually returned to England and married a woman for her money, but proved a dutiful husband and son-in-law. Even after his wife's death, Cromwell continued to support his mother-in-law. In 1514 he entered the employ of Cardinal Wolsey, who recognized his considerable gifts and used him as an attorney and

his chief man of business. In 1523 he was elected to the House of Commons. A largely self-made lawyer, Cromwell was one of the few who stayed loyal to the great cardinal even after his fall. He soon entered into the king's service and eventually became the king's leading advisor and principal secretary.

It was the precedent-minded Cromwell who persuaded Henry VIII to make his reformation a legal one. Cromwell, a stout, sober student of the Bible, was convinced that England should break with the papacy. In so doing, Henry could not only obtain his divorce, but he could also enhance his power as well. Henry could become "supreme head of the church" in England and attain full sovereignty. In Cromwell's vision, England could become a godlier and more powerful state. This would also enhance

After Hans Holbein, *Thomas Cromwell*. Courtesy of the National Portrait Gallery, London, United Kingdom.

his own stature as the king's most "devoted servant."

EXPLOITING ANTICLERICALISM

Henry and Cromwell began their move toward Reformation by allowing their publicists to stir up additional anticlericalism, already a staple in many parts of England, as in other European lands. The corrupt pluralist Wolsey was an obvious target for ridicule. Yet it would take a considerable effort to turn public opinion in England away from the Catholic church, which was strong and vigorous for the most part.

The king's propagandists felt compelled to bring up a nasty case from 1514 involving a merchant named Richard Hunne, which still rankled many in England as a telling example of clerical abuse. Hunne had refused to pay the mortuary fee to a priest for burying one of his infant sons. The merchant was sued for this a year later in the bishop of London's court. Hunne countersued in the Court of King's Bench. Bishop Richard Fitzjames of London then instituted heresy proceedings against Hunne, accusing him of possessing a Lollard Bible and other forbidden writings.

On December 2, 1514, Hunne was sent to the bishop's prison and found two days later hanging from a beam. Hunne's jailer and a representative of the bishop of London were implicated in the merchant's death. To cover up their involvement, church officials argued that Hunne had committed suicide and continued their suit against his estate. They also had Hunne's body burned as a heretic. This raised an outcry with the public, and the jailer and the bishop's vicar were arrested. The jailer escaped from his holding cell and the vicar blamed him for murdering Hunne. The bishop of London pleaded immunity from punishment and begged Cardinal Wolsey to

protect him. The case had now gone to Parliament, which ordered the vicar to pay a huge fine. Wolsey pleaded for forgiveness and understanding for the church, but he also maintained that clerics must continue to be immune from civil punishment.

Other anticlerical tales were allowed to circulate during this period when Cromwell was working hard to cultivate public opinion in advance of the planned break with Rome. In 1529 Simon Fish's scurrilous anticlerical pamphlet, "The Supplication of Beggars," appeared. Fish wrote that monks were after "every man's wife, every man's daughter, and every man's maid."[2] Fish urged the king to prohibit clerical begging and allow the true Gospel to be preached. Anne Boleyn personally brought the former Oxford student's writings to the attention of the king, as she did other reformers' works.

Members of Parliament had also expressed anticlerical sentiments in 1529, when they attacked the privileges of church courts, pluralism, and nonresident bishops like Wolsey. The Richard Hunne case was brought up as a great symbol of church corruption. William Warham, archbishop of Canterbury, responded by holding several assemblies of the English clergy, who apologized for wrongdoings, declared Henry to be the English church's "supreme head and protector," and voted gifts of 118,000 pounds to help defray Henry's divorce expenses. Since the church already controlled about a fourth of the land in England, they could well afford to be generous in order to save their privileges.

The Legal Reformation

Thomas Cromwell was determined to make Parliament—and through it the public—full partners in Reformation. As a lawyer, he knew that to become permanent, the Reformation needed the force of law. It could not rely on just the whim of mercurial sovereigns such as King Henry VIII. Therefore Cromwell continued his efforts to make Parliament a major participant in the process of reform and to institutionalize the Reformation. In 1532 he succeeded in getting it to approve an "Act of Annates," which stopped certain church revenues from going to Rome. In March 1533 Parliament passed an "Act in Restraint of Appeals," which declared England to be "an empire" that did not need to appeal church legal matters to Rome. A new "Act of Succession" was also issued by Parliament to give precedence in inheritance to the children of Henry and his new bride, Queen Anne.

On September 7, 1533, Anne Boleyn gave birth to her first child—a girl named Elizabeth. She was to become, arguably, the greatest monarch in English history, but at the time of her birth her father was deeply disappointed and did not even bother to attend her christening. He still did not have the legitimate son he desperately wanted. Anne tried to reassure him that she was still young enough to have many sons. She also encouraged him on his path of Reformation. Among her carefully chosen chaplains was Matthew Parker (1504–1575), the future Protestant archbishop of Canterbury under Elizabeth.

The "Act of Supremacy" of 1534 made Henry "supreme head of the church in England." This was far more than Sir Thomas More could stand. He had already resigned his position as lord chancellor in May of 1532, deeply concerned about the direction Henry, Cromwell, Cranmer, and the queen were moving the kingdom. When he would not agree to recognize the succession of Elizabeth over Mary, Henry had him arrested for treason. He was executed on July 7, 1535, and his severed head was prominently dis-

played on London Bridge as a warning to any other subject who might put his loyalty to the pope above his obedience to the king.

More died blessing King Henry, his old intellectual friend whom he genuinely admired, and was joined in martyrdom by John Fisher, the bishop of Rochester, another prominent foe of the Reformation. More and Fisher were among the few who openly resisted Henry's break with Rome despite the high level of satisfaction with the old church. The king was so popular and powerful and anticlericalism was so strong that Cromwell was able to lead the kingdom away from the authority of Rome without much public protest.

In 1536 Cromwell took another major step toward reform on the Continental model by securing an "Act of Dissolution," which completed the process of closing 560 of England's monasteries begun under Wolsey as a fund-raising measure and ceded their lands to the crown. To add to the confusion, monks were still required to keep their vows. The spendthrift king was pleased at these additional revenues and promised to make up for the loss to various charities and schools. The further closing of the monasteries and continued agricultural problems in the north contributed to an uprising known as "The Pilgrimage of Grace." Although not as great a threat to law and order as the German Peasant Revolts of 1524 to 1526, Henry moved quickly to crush the rebellion of "priests and gentlemen" in the summer of 1536.

UNLUCKY IN LOVE:
HENRY'S MATRIMONIAL DIFFICULTIES

By 1536 the death of Catherine of Aragon removed the basis for Henry's quarrel with the papacy. It was also clear that the king was uncomfortable with some aspects of Protestant theology and practice. Some in the old church still hoped Henry might revert back to the authority of Rome. For that reason there was a two-year delay in publishing in England the 1536 bull that excommunicated the English king. Even before, Henry had turned against Anne Boleyn, who had miscarried a deformed male fetus in January 1536. The king now thought God had damned his second marriage, and charges of treasonous adultery and witchcraft were brought against Anne. She was executed at the chopping block inside the Tower of London on May 19, 1536.

Her replacement, the lovely but slight Jane Seymour (b. 1509), finally presented Henry with a son in 1537, the future King Edward VI. Sadly for Henry, Jane died shortly after giving birth. Thomas Cromwell, now earl of Essex, was increasingly concerned about the king's misgivings about the Reformation. He decided that a political marriage to a Protestant dynasty might be just the thing to help save the reform in England. Since no daughter of a staunch Protestant house was then made available to the aging British lion, Cromwell settled on Anne (b. 1515), eldest daughter of Duke Wilhlem of Cleves. The Erasmian Wilhelm joined Henry in having reservations about some aspects of both Protestantism and traditional Roman Catholicism. Cleves, like England, was at odds with Charles V; therefore, the marriage would help cement an anti-imperial alliance and at least not bring Henry any closer to Rome.

Since the sensual Henry was not about to marry a woman he had never seen, the king's favorite court artist, Hans Holbein of Augsburg, was dispatched to Cleves to paint Anne. The German was noted for the high quality of his portraits. Holbein's likeness sufficiently pleased the king that he allowed his ambassadors to finalize their negotiations, and Anne was sent to England by her brother to marry Henry in 1539. When

the two finally met, neither liked what they saw. Holbein's miniature portrait had hidden the effects of smallpox on Anne's complexion, and the king referred to her cuttingly as the "Rhenish mare." Anne of Cleves probably did not consider Henry much of a prize either, for he was already well into the process of moving from a svelte 32-inch waist to a gargantuan 52-inch waist. The marriage was quickly annulled, and Anne was given a handsome country estate and a sufficient income to live upon, lest her brother be incensed. She was also invited to court for holidays, treated as a beloved relative, and officially referred to as the "king's sister."

Someone had to bear the brunt of the king's wrath over the Cleves fiasco, and this time the talented Thomas Cromwell was the victim. Henry was eventually persuaded by Cromwell's enemies that he was a danger-

After Hans Holbein, *Anne of Cleves*. Photo courtesy of the National Portrait Gallery, London, United Kingdom.

ous heretic who must be removed from office. Despite his invaluable services to the crown and his fervent pleas for mercy, Cromwell was duly executed in the exact spot where Anne Boleyn had previously lost her head.

Disappointed in love for at least the fourth time, the aging king vowed never to marry and promptly fell in love with a lively young beauty, Catherine Howard. He married the high-spirited Catherine in 1540, shortly after Cromwell's execution. By then he had issued his "Six Articles" of 1539, which reaffirmed his essential Catholicism on such issues as clerical celibacy, the real presence of Christ in the sacrament, the withholding of the cup from the laity, and the importance of oral confession. The "Six Articles" were opposed by the secretly married Thomas Cranmer, but to no avail. For Henry, the Reformation had gone far enough and he wanted to revel in the robust sensuality of his pretty young wife.

Unfortunately for Henry, Catherine Howard found him insufficient to satisfy her sexual and romantic longings and she invited several of her former lovers to share her royal bed while Henry was away. Enemies of the Howard clan eventually dared to report Catherine's treasonable liaisons, and she was duly executed in 1542 along with several of her lovers. A year later Henry married his sixth and last wife, the matronly and charming Catherine Parr (1513–1548).

A cultivated woman of good sense, Catherine had been twice widowed before winning the affections of the declining and disappointed king. She proved to be a good companion to Henry and a good nurse, which he needed very much in his last four years of life as his world grew smaller. A Protestant sympathizer and a compassionate woman, Catherine also proved to be a wonderfully nurturing stepmother to Henry's children, who badly needed some stability

and maternal love after the deaths of so many of their mothers and stepmothers. Queen Catherine seems to have done a great deal to repair some of the psychic damage done to the royal offspring.

The Reformation under Edward VI (1537–1553)

When that master manipulator Henry VIII died in 1547, he was succeeded by his ten-year-old son, Edward. Although Edward was a bright youth with a great fondness for Protestant theology, England was in fact ruled by a Council of Regents led by the king's ambitious uncle, Edward Seymour (c. 1500–1552). The handsome Seymour, who soon became the duke of Somerset and lord protector, had the Catholic "Six Articles" repealed and with the support of the frail young king moved England solidly into the Protestant camp. Seymour was particularly zealous in attacking Catholic shrines. His brother, Thomas, quickly married Edward's Protestant stepmother, Catherine, and envied his brother's power. Being named an admiral in the English navy was insufficient to satisfy his grandiose dreams of power. The admiral's later "romping" with the fourteen-year-old Princess Elizabeth put her in a compromising position and was obviously an expression of his interest in promoting his own ambitions. Elizabeth's stepmother intervened after catching her husband kissing the princess in a more than stepfatherly manner and sent her to a safer haven elsewhere.

Despite these behind-the-scenes maneuvers, Edward VI's reign witnessed the full flowering of Protestantism in the realm. Archbishop Thomas Cranmer was now allowed to introduce his wife, a niece of the Lutheran reformer of Nuremberg Andreas Osiander, at court for the first time. Even more important, Thomas Cranmer was ordered to issue his Protestant manual of worship, *The Book of Common Prayer*. The "Act of Uniformity" of 1549 made the prayer book's use mandatory for religious services throughout the kingdom. Cranmer also published "Forty-two Articles of Religious Belief," which further clarified the triumph of Protestantism in England.

THE TYNDALE BIBLE

The use of the English Bible of William Tyndale (1494–1536) and Miles Coverdale (1488–1568) was now fully encouraged and Lollard descendants of John Wycliffe and others could openly read the Scriptures in English. Tyndale was the first person to translate the New Testament and the Pentateuch from their original languages into English. He was also the first to print an English version of the Bible. Ordained a priest, Tyndale was educated at Oxford, where he took his M.A. in 1515. He then moved to Cambridge before leaving seven years later for London. There Tyndale became immersed in the writings of Martin Luther and determined to make his own contribution to the cause of reform by making the Bible available to the laity.

Finding it impossible to work on an English Bible in England because of the prejudices against "Lollardy," Tyndale moved to Germany in 1524 and then to the Low Countries, where he published his new translations in 1525. His translations were widely circulated back in England despite official condemnation. Tyndale never lived to see the eventual royal acceptance of his work, for he was arrested by officials of the Holy Roman Empire in Brussels and burned at the stake for heresy in 1536. His loyal follower, Miles Coverdale, completed the English translation of the Old Testament. Their Bible became known as the Great Bible when printed by Thomas Cromwell and sanctioned by Henry VIII in 1539. An act of Parliament in 1543 restricted its use until the reign of Edward VI.

THE FALL OF EDWARD SEYMOUR

While the Protestant reform proceeded apace, Edward Seymour found himself in political difficulties. Unfortunately, he was not the most efficient of administrators and there were still many, especially in the north, who resisted the new religion. In 1549 a rebellion led by Robert Kett, a Protestant tradesman, broke out at Norwich and elsewhere. Seymour had continued Henry VIII's 1542 policy of debasing the coinage, which helped fuel inflation. The continuing problem of converting farm lands to more profitable sheep runs, which required less labor, also contributed to rural unrest. Usually a good soldier, Seymour gave the command to the earl of Warwick who put down the revolt, and Kett and 1,000 of his followers were executed. Seymour was blamed for a loss of nerve and the continuing economic problems and was replaced as head of the council of regency by John Dudley, another self-aggrandizing politician.

THE RISE AND FALL OF JOHN DUDLEY (c. 1502–1553) AND LADY JANE GREY (1537–1554)

Dudley, who became duke of Northumberland, had ousted Seymour in 1547, promising to improve administration, end public commotion, and halt Seymour's foreign adventures in Scotland and France. Seymour had wished to bring about the union of the English and Scottish crowns, one of Henry VIII's fondest wishes. France was allied with Scotland and determined to keep the Scots out of English hands. They sent a powerful army to defend Scotland's southern border in 1549 and inflicted a humiliating defeat upon England. Dudley also continued the Reformation knowing that the priggish and bigoted King Edward would never abandon his Protestantism and that too many powerful people in England agreed with the young king.

By the winter of 1553 it was becoming increasingly clear that the king was dying of what proved to be tuberculosis. Mary, daughter of Catherine of Aragon and a loyal Catholic, was to inherit the crown under the terms of the Succession Act of 1543 and Henry VIII's will. Her accession meant a Catholic restoration was certain. This placed John Dudley's future in question, and he took steps to ward off this potential disaster before the dying Edward expired. He married his oldest son, Guilford, to the convinced Protestant Lady Jane Grey, a theologically sophisticated sixteen-year-old Tudor cousin. King Edward, also wanting to avoid a Catholic restoration, agreed in writing to disinherit his sisters and left the crown to Lady Jane and her heirs before his death on July 6, 1553.

Dudley had thought of almost everything, except that he neglected to secure Princess Mary, around whom opposition could rally. She was removed from London by several Protestant politicians, who could not bear the thought that the legitimate succession should be violated and that the Dudleys would remain in power. John Dudley was believed to have been converting some of the wealth of the crown to his own personal use for some time and was disliked by some who were jealous of his power and talent. Mary's rescuers took her to Suffolk, where she was surrounded by loyal Catholic gentry. Her followers marched on London and the Dudleys and Lady Jane were arrested and later executed for treason. Mary exhibited a merciful heart in not executing a larger number of traitors.

At age thirty-seven, Mary became queen of England. Her heart was set on finding happiness for herself and her people. To do that, the religious history of her brother's six-year reign must be reversed. Roman Catholicism must be restored to England so that the souls of the English people could be rescued from eternal damnation.

The Reign of Mary I, Tudor, 1553–1558

Like all the children of Henry VIII, Queen Mary had been well educated in languages and was intelligent. She also had a good heart, strong religious convictions, and was very well intentioned. Unfortunately, Queen Mary was also very rigid and did not always receive or follow the best of advice. Her chief advisor was her cousin, Cardinal Reginald Pole (1500–1558), whom she made archbishop of Canterbury in place of the Protestant Thomas Cranmer. Pole was a well-respected churchman, but he, in his fervent zeal to restore what he considered to be the true faith, did not always exhibit the best of judgment in the face of the new realities in England. Cranmer was arrested for treason and burned at the stake as a heretic. Under judicial torture, he had recanted his Protestant beliefs and then denied his denial. When brought to the stake at Smithfield, he put his right hand in the flames so he could write no more recantations.

Reginald Pole and others urged Queen Mary to deal harshly with heretics. Pole, like Mary, was kindhearted and merciful, but as a matter of public policy he felt it was essential to exterminate heresy by publicly burning prominent Protestants as an example to others. Unfortunately for the archbishop's intended purposes, most of the Protestant leaders had already fled to the Continent upon the accession of Mary. The result was that most of the 287 or so Protestants executed for religious treason in the queen's six-year reign were comparatively small fish, with a few notable exceptions such as Thomas Cranmer and Hugh Latimer (1485–1555), the Protestant bishop of Worcester and a major figure in the reform. The queen's policy thus did not destroy English Protestantism as she had hoped, but earned her the unhappy title "Bloody Mary."

Even worse from the point of view of the public was Mary's decision to wed Emperor Charles V's son Philip rather than one of several English candidates. Mary wanted a staunch Catholic and the blond-haired, blue-eyed, devout, and intelligent Philip more than filled the bill. However, the proposed match touched off strong antiforeign feelings in the realm. Many could not stomach the notion of England's having "a Spanish king," and 3,000 joined Sir Thomas Wyatt (son of a famous poet of the same name) of Kent in attempting to overthrow the government. Wyatt's forces did succeed in penetrating into London in February of 1554 before their defeat. The ringleaders of the revolt were executed, as well as Lady Jane Grey and her husband, even though they had not been involved in the uprising. Wyatt had rebelled in the name of the queen's sister, Elizabeth, who disavowed the rebels and worshipped publicly as a Catholic.

At long last Philip of Spain arrived in England in July 1554 and the marriage was celebrated. Although the middle-aged Mary was very pleased with her younger and equally pious husband, their union was not blessed with children. Finally, in September 1554 Philip departed England to attend to business in Flanders. Two years later he succeeded his father as king of Spain. The disconsolate Mary was left eagerly looking for the signs of a child. She was also having difficulties with Parliament over her program for the restoration of Roman Catholicism.

After Antonio Moro, *Portrait of Mary I Tudor.* Bibliotheque Nationale, Paris, France. Giraudon/Art Resource.

Those who had purchased church lands had no intention of returning them to the church, but Mary was finally able to get Parliament to repeal many of the Reformation statutes passed under her late brother. She also appointed new Catholic bishops and made one of them, the vindictive Stephen Gardiner (c. 1497–1555), her lord chancellor. On the positive side, the queen completed some of the fiscal reforms begun by John Dudley.

For the most part, however, Queen Mary's six-year reign must be judged a failure. Her persecutions of Protestants and her unpopular marriage helped to undermine the cause of Roman Catholicism in England. She had no great successes in foreign policy, even having to abandon Calais to the French. The port of Calais was the last English toehold on the Continent after the close of the Hundred Years' War. Its loss in 1558 hurt English pride. Philip made only a brief return to England in 1557 and failed to impregnate Mary. She died of uterine cancer onNovember 17, 1558. Her good friend Cardinal Pole died twelve hours later. Neither

had lived long enough to permanently reestablish Catholicism as the official state religion of England. Their creation of Protestant martyrs and generally unsuccessful policies had in fact made the situation worse for practicing Catholics.

Chronology

1502	Catherine of Aragon marries Arthur Tudor of England, who dies four months later.
1509	Catherine marries King Henry VIII.
1514	Richard Hunne case.
1521	Henry VIII named a "Defender of the Faith" by Pope Leo X for his written attack on Martin Luther.
1527	Henry requests a papal annulment of his marriage to Catherine of Aragon.
1529	Cardinal Thomas Wolsey ousted as Lord Chancellor; first Reformation Parliament; Simon Fish's "Supplication of Beggars."
1531	Convocation of the English clergy declares King Henry VIII "Supreme Head of the Church" in England.
1532	Act of Annates; Thomas More resigns as chancellor.
1533	Act in Restraint of Appeals; Henry marries Anne Boleyn; birth of future Queen Elizabeth I; Act of Succession.
1534	Act of Supremacy.
1535	Executions of Sir Thomas More and Bishop John Fisher.
1536	Act of Dissolution of the monasteries; death of Catherine of Aragon; suppression of the Pilgrimage of Grace; death of William Tyndale.
1537	King Henry VIII marries Jane Seymour, who dies shortly after giving birth to future King Edward VI.
1539	Henry weds Anne of Cleves; English Bible sanctioned; Henry reaffirms Catholic doctrines by issuing "Six Articles."
1540	Aging Henry weds youthful Catherine Howard; execution of Thomas Cromwell.
1543	Henry VIII weds his sixth and last wife, Catherine Parr.
1547	Death of Henry VIII; accession of Edward VI; Council of Regency dominated by Edward Seymour.
1549	Act of Uniformity makes Archbishop Thomas Cranmer's *Book of Common Prayer* and "42 Articles" mandatory in English churches.
1551	Kett's Rebellion suppressed; John Dudley replaces Seymour as head of king's Council of Regency.
1553	Failing health of Edward VI; Guilford Dudley marries Lady Jane Grey; death of Edward VI; overthrow of Dudleys; accession of Queen Mary I.
1554	Thomas Wyatt's revolt; Queen Mary weds Philip of Habsburg; Parliament repeals the Act of Supremacy; England received back in the good graces of the Catholic church; Reginald Pole serves as archbishop of Canterbury; Philip leaves England.
1555	Persecutions of Protestants intensify; death of Hugh Latimer.

1556	Death of Thomas Cranmer.	**1558**	Calais lost to the French; deaths of Queen Mary and Cardinal Reginald Pole.
1557	Brief return of Philip II, now king of Spain.		

Further Reading

THE ENGLISH REFORMATION AND THE EARLY TUDORS

Susan Brigden, *London and the Reformation* (1989).

A. G. Dickens, *The English Reformation*, 2nd ed. (1989). Still one of the best overviews.

Eamon Duffy, *The Stripping of the Altars: Traditional Religion in England, 1400–1580* (1992). Argues that the late medieval English church was strong and vigorous.

G. R. Elton, *England under the Tudors*, 3rd ed. (1991).

———, *Reform and Reformation: England 1509–1558* (1977). Valuable surveys by a master historian.

Ronald Fritz, ed., *Historical Dictionary of Tudor England, 1485–1603* (1991). An outstanding reference work with contributions from a host of able scholars.

Charles Gray, *Renaissance and Reformation England, 1509–1714* (1973).

John Guy, *Tudor England* (1988). One of the best recent surveys.

Christopher Haigh, *English Reformations: Religion, Politics, and Society under the Tudors* (1993).

Felicity Heal and Rosemary O'Day, eds., *Church and Society in England: Henry VIII to James I* (1977).

Richard Helmholtz, *Roman Canon Law in Reformation England* (1990).

J. D. Mackie, *The Early Tudors, 1485–1558* (1994).

Richard Rex, *The Theology of John Fisher* (1991).

John Scarisbrick, *The Reformation and the English People* (1984).

Arthur Slavin, *The Precarious Balance: English Government and Society, 1450–1640* (1973). Still very sound.

Leo Solt, *Church and State in Early Modern England, 1509–1640* (1990).

Carl Trueman, *Luther's Legacy: Salvation and the English Reformers, 1525–1556* (1994).

Penry Williams, *The Tudor Regime* (1979).

Joyce Youings, *Sixteenth-Century England* (1984).

———, *The Dissolution of the Monasteries* (1971).

KING HENRY VIII

Carolly Erickson, *Great Harry* (1980).

Henry Kelly, *The Matrimonial Trials of Henry VIII* (1976).

Stanford Lehmberg, *The Later Parliaments of Henry VIII* (1977).

Helen Miller, *Henry VIII and the English Nobility* (1986).

Richard Rex, *Henry VIII and the English Reformation* (1993).

John Scarisbrick, *Henry VIII* (1968). Still the most important biography.

Lacey Baldwin Smith, *Henry VIII: The Mask of Royalty* (1971). A fascinating psychological study.

HIS QUEENS AND MINISTERS

R. W. Chambers, *Thomas More* (1958).

G. R. Elton, *Reform and Renewal: Thomas Cromwell and the Commonweal* (1973).

Antonia Fraser, *The Six Wives of Henry VIII* (1992).

Peter Gywn, *The King's Cardinal: The Rise and Fall of Thomas Wolsey* (1993).

E. W. Ives, *Anne Boleyn* (1986).

Richard Marius, *Thomas More, A Biography* (1985).

Garrett Mattingly, *Catherine of Aragon* (1944).

Lacey Baldwin Smith, *A Tudor Tragedy: The Life and Times of Catherine Howard* (1961).

Retha Warnicke, *The Rise and Fall of Anne Boleyn* (1989). Revises many of our understandings.

OTHER FIGURES IN THE REFORM

David Daniell, *William Tyndale: A Biography* (1994).

Thomas Mayer, *Thomas Starkey and the Commonweal* (1990).

Jasper Ridley, *Thomas Cranmer* (1962).

Donald Smeeton, *Lollard Themes in the Reformation Theology of William Tyndale* (1986).

THE REIGN OF EDWARD VI AND MARY I

Barrett Beer, *Northumberland, the Political Career of John Dudley* (1973).

Carolly Erickson, *Bloody Mary* (1978).

Dale Hoak, *The King's Council in the Reign of Edward VI* (1976).

W. K. Jordan, *Edward VI*, 2 vols. (1968, 1970).

David Loades, *The Reign of Mary Tudor* (1979). The leading study.

Alison Plowden. *Jane Grey and the House of Suffolk* (1986).

Notes

1. Quoted by Thomas Clarke, "Irish Awareness during the Reformation," paper presented at The Sixteenth-Century Studies Conference, St. Louis, Missouri, October 27, 1978.

2. Cited in Lewis Spitz, ed., *The Protestant Reformation* (Englewood Cliffs, N.J.: Prentice Hall, 1966), p. 150.

10

A TALE OF TWO QUEENS: ELIZABETH I OF ENGLAND AND MARY OF SCOTLAND

Queen Mary was succeeded by her twenty-four-year-old sister, Elizabeth, the daughter of Anne Boleyn. It was under Elizabeth I that the Reformation came to full flower in England. The Reformation in Scotland came to fruition during the reign of Elizabeth's staunchly Catholic cousin, Mary, queen of Scots. Nine years younger than Elizabeth, Mary of Scotland eventually became the leading candidate to succeed her unmarried cousin as queen of England. She dreamed of restoring Catholicism to both monarchies. The two queens found themselves locked in a dangerous competition.

The Young Queen Elizabeth

Like her sister, Mary Tudor, Elizabeth was well schooled in languages, knowing some Greek, Latin, French, and Spanish. Elizabeth had been tutored by, among others, Roger Ascham (1516–1568), a Cambridge scholar and one of the foremost pedagogues of the Renaissance. Ascham believed that Latin grammar and literature were the foundations of a sound humanist education. Elizabeth, his greatest pupil, demonstrated a keen mind and an aptitude for learning. Later she even learned to talk to her sailors in a language they could understand.

Unlike her older sister, Elizabeth had a talent for survival and could demonstrate great flexibility when needed. With the help of her stepmother, Catherine Parr, she had warded off the dangerous advances of Thomas Seymour as a teenager. Elizabeth had also survived the threat of confinement and possible death in the Tower of London during the reign of her sister when she had been accused of attempting to undermine the queen's restoration of Catholicism. Elizabeth had learned the lessons of caution and discretion at an early age. Such lessons served her well as queen.

The young queen also learned to judge character and not let emotions interfere with matters of state. Elizabeth usually made shrewd appointments to office. One of her best choices was of William Cecil (1520–1598), an experienced officeholder, as her principal secretary and later lord treasurer. Cecil, although a very able official, found he could never dominate the queen but that he could work most effectively with her. Although sometimes disagreeing with her on such matters as the need for Elizabeth to marry, he was always completely loyal to his prodigious sovereign and held her in deep affection and respect. His talented son, Robert (1563–1612), served both Elizabeth and her successor with distinction.

Both Elizabeth and Cecil were naturally cautious and careful in spending money, qualities essential in a modest monarchy with limited resources. England could hardly have stood another prodigal like Henry VIII. Although Elizabeth and the able Cecil usually agreed on the main outlines of policy, serving her was not without its moments of trauma. She was capable of serious outbursts of ill temper—some real, some staged. More problematic was Elizabeth's difficulty in making up her mind on a variety of issues. Possessed of a very complicated intelligence, she anticipated a myriad of ramifications to most policy decisions. Elizabeth also understood that many problems would solve themselves if one delayed taking action long enough. Still her labored style often frustrated her ministers, including her astute principal secretary from 1573 on, Francis Walsingham (1530–1590), who nevertheless remained in awe of her intelligence and vast knowledge.

THE ELIZABETHAN RELIGIOUS SETTLEMENT

Although frequently appearing indecisive, the astute young queen recognized early in her reign that the religious question had to be dealt with immediately. Religion was a crucial matter to most people in England and the country had already been through too many shifts between Catholicism and Protestantism, as had Elizabeth herself. There were many issues to be sorted out. If England returned to the Protestant fold, it would be threatened by potentially hostile Catholic powers such as France and Spain. Yet most of the English, including the queen, had no wish to continue their religious allegiance to Rome. What emerged was a compromise between the Marian exiles who returned after a period of association with Calvinist Protestants on the Continent and Elizabeth's own desire for a settlement that would be more centrist Protestant.

Elizabeth had Parliament recognize her as sole "supreme governor of this realm in all things ecclesiastical and temporal" in an "Act of Supremacy" of 1559. Unlike her more arrogant father, she refused the title of "supreme head" of the church since that dignity belonged to God alone. Parliament also issued an Act of Uniformity in 1559 which further reestablished a Protestant church, but a state church in which many Catholics could worship in relative comfort of conscience. Thomas Cranmer's "Forty-two Articles" of religious belief were trimmed to "Thirty-Nine Articles" and issued in 1563. Only the two Protestant sacraments of Eucharist and baptism were retained. The Act of Uniformity also mandated the use of a modified version of Cranmer's *Book of Common Prayer*. She named her mother's former chaplain, the moderate Matthew Parker, as archbishop of Canterbury.

The Elizabethan Settlement had features designed to appeal to both Catholics and Protestants. It permitted the clergy to marry as they did in Protestant lands, but it also continued the traditional episcopal system. Church ritual retained its ceremonial splendor, which Elizabeth enjoyed, but its theology embraced a number of evangelical innovations, such as the emphasis on salvation by faith over good works. Elizabeth's religious agreement, while leaning towards Protestantism, was moderate enough and sensible enough to please the overwhelming majority of her subjects.

The queen especially desired an end to religious wrangling and civil unrest. Not wanting to establish "windows into men's souls," Elizabeth settled for outward conformity and obedience to law. This she generally achieved, although her Reformation had too many elements of "popery" to please those mostly Calvinist Protestants who would "purify" the English church and society. They became known collectively as the *Puritans* and would increase in influence and numbers throughout her reign. A few Protestant extremists wanted to separate themselves completely from the church of England, but they too would have to bide their time.

Some uncompromising Roman Catholics also were not happy with aspects of Elizabeth's religious program, which they considered too Protestant. In 1570, Pope Pius V (r. 1566–1572) excommunicated the queen and absolved her subjects of their obligations to her. Nevertheless, most Catholics stayed loyal to the increasingly popular "Virgin Queen." Repeated attempts by some Catholic gentlemen to replace the "English Jezebel" with her Catholic cousin, Mary of Scotland, only served to further discredit the church of Rome and its more loyal adherents. Mary's execution in 1587 and the defeat of the Spanish Armada of 1588 sealed the fate of Catholicism in England. Elizabeth's government executed 183 religious dissidents, but those executions were not as unpopular as Mary's in part because they were spread over a forty-five-year reign. The well-intentioned but unfortunate Mary has had to bear the epithet "bloody," while her more popular sister's persecutions have been largely downplayed.

Gloriana: The Successful Queen

Elizabeth's enemies were faced with the great problem of her developing status as a beloved cultural icon and her considerable success as an administrator. Fiscally conservative, the queen usually managed to avoid bothering the all-male Parliament for additional revenues, which pleased them a great deal. "Gloriana" put herself on public display to great advantage with her brilliant speeches to Parliament, pageants, and processions around the country. Her subjects loved those glimpses of their glamorous queen and her brilliantly clad court. She was capable of personally charming almost anyone.

Beneath the style, there was also a great deal of substance. Elizabeth was able to sponsor new efforts at colonization, aid rebels in the Netherlands, defeat the Spanish invaders, subdue Irish rebels, enhance economic development, revise the laws dealing with poor relief, and offer encouragement to brilliant artists such as the matchless playwrights William Shakespeare (1564–1616) and Christopher Marlowe (1564–1593), and the poets Edmund Spenser (c. 1552–1599), and Mary (1561–1621) and Philip Sidney (1554–1586). Seldom had one European monarchy seen such a concentration of talent. Queen Elizabeth's usual course was to avoid costly foreign entanglements and military display, using her status as Europe's most eligible single female to neutralize potential aggressors. After all, why would anyone attack England if he had hopes of gaining it by marrying Elizabeth?

Elizabeth decided early in her reign that she would never share power and her bed with a man. She liked being a ruling queen and had no wish to run the risks of her mother, her stepmothers, and her sister—all of whom had suffered for the sake of their relationships. Physical problems may have compounded the issue. Elizabeth did enjoy both flirting and dancing, but had no desire to make herself vulnerable to another human being. She did have her court favorites—men such as Robert Dudley, son of the traitor John Dudley, the dashing Christopher Hatton, and Walter Raleigh (c. 1552–1618), the founder of a colony off the coast of North Carolina. Raleigh later wrote a *History of the World*, while in prison during the reign of James I. The married Dudley was a particular friend whom she

Federigo Zuccaro, *Portrait of Elizabeth I* (known as the "Sieve" Portrait). Pinacoteca Nazionale, Siena, Italy. Scala/Art Resource.

made master of her horses. When Dudley's wife died under mysterious circumstances in 1560, many believed the queen would marry her beloved "Robin." Wanting to avoid all hints of scandal, Elizabeth continued her friendship with Dudley, but remained perpetually single.

The decision to remain a single woman married to her career was unique for the period and provided its own set of pressures. Scurrilous gossip about the queen's personal life became a staple of Elizabethan life. Her advisors continually pressured her to marry and assure the succession. Elizabeth held them and her various suitors at bay, and demonstrated that England could prosper under its "Virgin Queen," even if one favorite, Robert Devereux, earl of Essex (1567–1601), had to be executed for treason.

Essex's treachery was particularly galling for he was the stepson of her beloved Robert Dudley and she had lavished favors upon him. A serious Irish revolt broke out in 1598, and Hugh O'Neill, earl of Tyrone (c. 1547–1616), defeated an English army at the Battle of Blackwater River. Elizabeth sent an army led by Essex to Ireland to quell the revolt. His command was a disaster; instead of fighting Tyrone, he lavished knighthoods on fifty-nine gentlemen against his instructions. Blaming his failures on the queen and her Privy Council, Essex returned to England without permission and later plotted to force the government to replace the trusted Robert Cecil with himself. One of Essex's supporters was the earl of Southampton, Shakespeare's great patron; both were found guilty of treason and executed.

For the most part, the queen's judgment of people was sound and her policies worked. England kept its independence and prospered under her rule. Embarrassing and soul-wrenching reversals on religious policy were avoided throughout her long reign. The aging Elizabeth was able to continue impressing many of her subjects and many of the crowned heads of Europe well into her sixties. Near the end of her rule in 1601 after some particularly stormy sessions of Parliament over the Essex crisis and various monopolies granted by the queen, the elaborately bejewelled Elizabeth informed her subjects:

> Though God has raised me high, yet this I count the glory of my crown, that I have reigned with your loves. . . . Your prosperity has been my chief concern. . . . My heart was never set on worldly goods, but only for my subjects' good.[1]

The sly Elizabeth was such a great actress and politician that it is likely she actually believed these words, as did many of those parliamentarians who heard them. Here was a performer worthy of the age of Marlowe and Shakespeare.

Mary Stuart and the Reformation in Scotland

As for Elizabeth's neighboring monarchy to the north, Scotland also experienced the rise of a Protestant movement. The way to Reformation in Scotland, as in England, was paved by anticlericalism, remnants of Lollardy, and to some extent Renaissance humanism. Lutheran ideas had infiltrated into Scotland during the reign of King James V (r. 1513–1542) despite the outlawing of Luther's writings in 1525 by the Scottish Parliament. The English Bible of William Tyndale was also popular in mountainous and rugged Scotland.

THE SPREAD OF PROTESTANT IDEAS

Part of the reason for the appeal of Protestant notions in Scotland was a high level of dissatisfaction with the Roman Catholic church. There was widespread resentment of its financial power, since the church held about a third of the landed wealth in Scotland at this time and its leadership insisted on strictly enforcing the payment of tithes. This wealth was enjoyed primarily by the upper clergy; an estimated 10,000 Scottish priests labored without regular church incomes (benefices). The higher clergy added to their unpopularity by tending to side with the crown in quarrels with the Scottish barons.

Disputes between the crown and the nobility grew more and more frequent as King James was followed in power by his French wife, Mary of Guise (1515–1560). A devout Catholic, Mary served as regent for her infant daughter, Mary, queen of Scots (b. 1542). The widowed queen was determined to bring Scotland more firmly into the orbit of her native France and her militantly Catholic family, the Guises. Most of the barons were equally determined to keep Scotland an independent kingdom.

Reformation ideas had been spread by attractive figures such as Patrick Hamilton (d. 1528). Hamilton was a humanist of noble blood and related to the king. He had studied at Paris, Louvain, and several places in Germany before becoming a teacher at the University of St. Andrews in 1523. There he openly taught Lutheran ideas until cited for heresy by the archbishop of St. Andrews. Hamilton found refuge in Luther's Wittenberg before returning to Scotland in 1528. He was then tried and burned for heresy, a grim lesson for other would-be Lutherans.

Despite the dangers of spreading Lutheranism, another charismatic preacher emerged in the person of the handsome George Wishart. Wishart had visited a number of Protestant communities on the Continent and had returned in 1543 to advocate many of the positions of Huldrych Zwingli. It was Wishart who converted John Knox (1513–1572) to Protestantism. Knox was a peasant's son who had become a disillusioned Catholic priest and would later become the charismatic leader of the Reformation in Scotland. In 1546 David Beaton, cardinal and archbishop of St. Andrews, had Wishart tried and burned for heresy. The cardinal was reported to have laughed out loud as the popular Wishart writhed in agony.

Determined on revenge, a number of Wishart's friends entered Beaton's castle at St. Andrew's in May 1546 and murdered the cardinal in his bedroom. The assassins then draped the cardinal's body, which they had urinated on, over his castle wall as a public expression of defiance. Holding the archbishop's fortress in the name of King Henry VIII of England, the rebels called John Knox to join them as their preacher. They held out until July 1547, when a squadron of French warships summoned by the queen-regent took over the castle and dispatched the rebels to French prison ships. Their preacher, John

Knox, was sentenced to life as a galley slave on French ships plying the Mediterranean.

THE RISE OF KNOX, THE "THUNDERING SCOT"

After serving as a bound oarsman for nineteen months, Knox managed to escape and made his way to England. There the "thundering Scot" became a very popular preacher during the reign of the Protestant Edward VI. With the Catholic Mary Tudor's accession in 1553, Knox fled England for the Continent and spent time at Frankfurt on the Main in Germany and the Geneva of John Calvin.

Knox was especially dazzled by Calvin's reformed Geneva. He was keen for a chance to reform his native Scotland along the lines laid out so successfully by John Calvin in Geneva. The problem was that Catholic women still ruled in England and Scotland. In chauvinist and Protestant anger, Knox published his "First Blast Against the Monstrous Regiment of Women." He declared that to "promote a woman to have rule in any realm is repugnant to nature, contumely to God, a thing most contrary to His revealed will and approved ordinance, and a subversion of all good order, equity, and justice." As for Mary of Guise, she was an "unruly cow saddled by mistake."[2]

Knox's flagrant display of misogyny did not sit well with Mary Tudor's successor, Elizabeth I, and she wrote John Calvin, rebuking him for the tirade of his Scottish disciple. An embarrassed Calvin apologized to the queen and assured her that Knox's comments were in no way directed at a Protestant queen such as herself. Elizabeth was somewhat mollified and agreed in 1559 to send an English army to drive the French out of Scotland. During the ensuing war, Mary of Guise died. Her forces were defeated by the English and their pro-Protestant Scottish allies. The Treaty of Edinburgh of July 6, 1560, which concluded the hostilities, assured the triumph of Protestantism. Catholicism was outlawed by an act of the Scottish Parliament on August 24, 1560.

As for John Knox, he had been called back to Scotland in 1558 by a delegation of Scottish Protestants. He soon became the enormously popular preacher at St. Giles' Cathedral in the heart of downtown Edinburgh. There his energetic preaching, punctuated by his habit of pounding his fists, reduced several pulpits to rubble. His congregations loved the show, but also found a great deal of substance in his sermons. A tireless worker of deep faith and courage, Knox also wrote a *Confession of Faith*, a *Book of Common Order*, a *First Book of Discipline*, and eventually *A History of the Reformation in Scotland*, which contributed to his reputation as one of the heroes of the movement.

MARY, QUEEN OF SCOTS

If John Knox was the greatest hero of the Reformation in Scotland, the lovely and talented daughter of Mary of Guise was his antagonist. Mary Stuart had been out of Scotland during most of the turbulent years of the Scottish Reformation. She had been married to the heir to the French throne, the future François II (r. 1559–1560), since 1548. Now in 1561 the eighteen-year-old widow with glorious auburn hair returned to Protestant Scotland to reclaim her throne. Intelligent and well educated, Mary was astute enough to recognize that she was going to have to accept Protestantism for the moment while worshipping privately as a Roman Catholic, much to the dismay of John Knox. However, beneath her surface charm, the steely Mary Stuart was determined to achieve a Catholic restoration.

Unlike Elizabeth I, who feared the possibility of being dominated by a husband,

French School, *Portrait of Mary Stuart, Queen of Scots*. Prado, Madrid, Spain. Alinari/Art Resource.

Mary wanted to remarry and have children. Her uncles proposed Don Carlos, son of Philip II of Spain. She declined the suggestion upon learning that Don Carlos was mentally unstable. Then a strange suitor from England appeared in the handsome personage of Robert Dudley, the earl of Leicester. Dudley had been Elizabeth of England's great favorite. Elizabeth probably was interested in having her beloved "Robin" as a spy in Mary of Scotland's bed. This possibility no doubt also occurred to Mary, who was not interested in marrying one of Elizabeth's ex-suitors, so instead she turned to another gentleman in Dudley's entourage, Charles Stuart, Lord Darnley (1545–1567).

Darnley had many qualities to recommend him. He was handsome and tall, which made him an ideal dance partner for a willowy queen such as Mary. Darnley was of royal blood, a grandson of King Henry VII, but most importantly to the devout Mary, he was a fellow Roman Catholic. He could be her partner in turning Scotland away from the Protestant plague. They were married in July 1565.

The prospect of a Catholic restoration horrified Mary's half brother, James Stuart, the earl of Moray, who raised the flag of revolt and was joined by a number of other Protestant lords. Moray's revolt failed and he and many of his co-conspirators fled to safety in England. Queen Mary promptly confiscated their lands and proceeded with her plans to restore Catholicism with the help of the pope and Philip II of Spain. However, her real partner in plotting was her secretary, an Italian musician named David Rizzio (c. 1533–1566). Shortly after her honeymoon, Mary had discovered that her passionate Darnley was "a man of mystery with no secret."[3] In short, she had been blinded by passion and had married a boring blockhead, something her royal cousin would never do. As early as 1558, Elizabeth had informed Parliament: "I have long since made a choice of husband, the kingdom of England."[4]

More and more, Mary turned to the agreeable company of the amusing Rizzio. Darnley grew insanely jealous and in March 1566 he and a number of henchmen broke in upon the pregnant queen and stabbed her suspected lover to death. Mary fled the crime scene at her palace of Holyrood House in Edinburgh on horseback not knowing if Rizzio's death would be enough to satiate the blood lust of Darnley. She eventually found a replacement for Rizzio in the arms of the dashing James, earl of Bothwell (c. 1536–1578), a Protestant. His charms and his willingness to convert to Catholicism were enough for Mary to fall passionately in love with him.

However, Mary still had a murderously jealous husband to deal with, as well as an infant son, the future King James VI of Scotland, who also became James I, king of England (b. June 1566). A skilled political actress herself, Mary fooled Darnley into thinking that she had forgiven him for the murder of Rizzio. The queen also tenderly nursed him as he tried to recover from a bout of venereal disease that had so disfigured his once handsome face that he wore a veil. However in February 1567, the house that Darnley was recuperating in blew up, and he was found strangled in the garden. Apparently Darnley had heard mysterious sounds of barrels of gunpowder being put into position and had attempted to escape by crawling out of his bedroom window.

Although legally acquitted of the crime, the queen's lover, Bothwell, was obviously guilty. When he quickly divorced his wife and married the queen in May of that year in a Protestant ceremony, it was more than John Knox and the Scottish people could bear. They flew to arms against the "wicked Jezebel" and her "evil lover." The queen's forces were soon defeated and Bothwell fled to the Continent. Mary was imprisoned for her role in the murder of Darnley, partly on the basis of possibly forged incriminating letters. She was also forced to abdicate in favor of her young son, with Moray being named as regent.

MARY'S LIFE AND DEATH IN ENGLAND, 1568–1587

In May of 1568 Mary managed a daring escape from prison and, deciding to try her luck with English gentlemen Catholics, she fled to England, where she was soon arrested upon the orders of her cousin and ri-val, Elizabeth I. Mary's arrival on English soil put Elizabeth in an awkward situation. She did not want to outrage Scottish Protestant sensibilities by attempting to restore the convicted Catholic murderess to her throne. Elizabeth also did not want to turn Mary over to her subjects for execution; the death of a fellow sovereign would establish a dangerous precedent.

The solution that Elizabeth came up with was to play for time, an approach she took to many problems. After all, Mary might catch a cold in a drafty English country house and die of natural causes. Maybe Mary was innocent of the death of Darnley and might one day be sent back to Scotland. Elizabeth ended up keeping Mary in forced detention in a succession of country estates for nineteen years. Mary was not permitted to leave England or to come to court. Elizabeth was not going to permit Mary to gain adherents at the center of power, nor was she going to risk face-to-face comparisons with her dangerous and glamorous cousin. On one occasion Elizabeth asked a courtier who had returned from a recent visit to Mary how the two queens compared in height. The embarrassed courtier grudgingly conceded that Mary was, indeed, somewhat taller than Elizabeth. Gloriana responded, "she is too tall; I myself am of a perfect height."[5]

Mary was kept in relative isolation and her host jailers were rotated lest they succumb to her fatal charm. She was never again to see her beloved Bothwell. The passionate earl died ten years later, having gone insane in a Danish prison.

The exiled queen grew increasingly impatient in her gilded cages. In 1571 she entered into a plot with a group of Catholics led by Thomas Howard, the duke of Norfolk. Norfolk wanted to marry the queen of Scots and return her to the throne of Scotland. In time, Mary would inherit the English throne as well. Others secretly hoped they could hasten the restoration of Catholicism by facilitating the death of Elizabeth. The marriage of Mary and Norfolk, supplemented by an invasion from Spain, was to signal an uprising of English Catholics. The Ridolfi Plot, named for one of its members, Roberto Ridolfi, a Catholic banker from Florence, soon fell apart and the duke of Norfolk was imprisoned and later executed in 1572 for treason.

In 1586 another Catholic conspiracy, this one led by Anthony Babington, was uncovered by Francis Walsingham's spies. This time Mary Stuart had agreed in writing to support the assasination of her cousin and replace her as queen of England. Obviously, Elizabeth could not ignore Mary's treasonous role. She reluctantly allowed her trial and execution at the chopping block in February of 1587. Mary had paid the ultimate price for her impatience. Consequently, King Philip II of Spain, a Catholic crusader, felt compelled to send his forces against England to attempt a forceable conversion, as we shall see in greater detail in Chapter 12.

Meanwhile, Mary's son, James, was raised as a Calvinist Protestant. James was as vain of his abilities as an amateur theologian as Henry VIII had been. It was James who later, as Elizabeth's successor, sponsored a beautifully lyric translation of the Bible—the so-called King James Bible. Some called him the "wisest fool in Christendom" for his arrogance. Be that as it may, the English and Scottish kingdoms, united after 1603, would move into the seventeenth century firmly in the Protestant camp.

Chronology

1528	Execution of Patrick Hamilton.
1533	Birth of Elizabeth Tudor.
1542	Birth of Mary Stuart; death of King James V of Scotland.
1546	Execution of George Wishart; murder of Cardinal David Beaton and seizure of his castle by Protestants.
1547	Recapture of the archbishop's castle; John Knox sentenced to French prison galleys.
1548	John Knox escapes from the galleys; Mary Stuart engaged to marry future King François II of France.
1554	Knox forced to leave Catholic England of Mary Tudor.
1558	Death of Queen Mary Tudor; accession of Elizabeth I; Knox publishes his "First Blast Against the Monstrous Regiment of Women" and returns to Scotland.
1559	Acts of Supremacy and Uniformity in England; civil war in Scotland; Protestants aided by Elizabeth I; Mary Stuart is queen of France.
1560	Death of Mary of Guise, Amy Rosbart Dudley, and François II of France; Catholicism outlawed by Scottish Parliament; Knox becomes preacher at St. Giles.
1561	Widowed Queen Mary Stuart returns to Scotland.
1564	Births of William Shakespeare and Christopher Marlowe.
1565	Queen Mary marries Henry, Lord Darnley.
1566	Darnley and others murder David Rizzio; Queen Mary gives birth to future Scottish and English King James.
1567	Darnley is murdered; Mary marries Bothwell; Scots revolt against Mary and Both-

	well; Bothwell escapes to the Continent; Mary forced to abdicate and name her son James VI as her successor; Mary imprisoned for the death of Darnley; birth of Robert Devereux.
1568	Mary escapes from Scotland to England; Queen Elizabeth of England keeps Mary in forced detention.
1571	The Ridolfi Plot against Elizabeth I.
1572	Execution of the duke of Norfolk.
1578	Death of the earl of Bothwell.
1585	Raleigh founds a colony on Roanoke Island, North Carolina.
1586	Babington Plot against Elizabeth I.
1587	Execution of Mary for plotting against Elizabeth.
1588	Defeat of the Spanish Armada.
1598	Death of William Cecil, Lord Burghley; Irish revolt.
1601	Execution of Robert Devereux, the earl of Essex.
1603	Death of Elizabeth I; accession of Protestant James I of England and VI of Scotland.

Further Reading

THE REFORMATION IN ENGLAND AFTER 1558

Stephen Brachelow, *The Communion of Saints: Radical Puritan Thought and Separatist Ecclesiology, 1570–1625* (1988).

James Bryant, *Tudor Drama and Religious Controversy* (1984).

Patrick Collinson, *The Religion of the Protestants: The Church in English Society 1559–1625* (1982).

Alan Dures, *English Catholicism 1558–1642: Continuity and Change* (1983).

Richard Greaves, *Religion and Society in Elizabethan England* (1981).

Norman Jones, *The Birth of the Elizabethan Age, England in the 1560s* (1994).

Diarmaid MacCulloch, *The Later Reformation in England 1547–1603* (1990).

Peter Marshall, *The Catholic Priesthood and the English Reformation* (1994).

ELIZABETH I

Susan Bassnett, *Elizabeth I: A Feminist Perspective* (1988).

J. B. Black, *The Reign of Elizabeth I, 1558–1603*, 2nd ed. (1994).

Carolly Ericson, *The First Elizabeth* (1983).

Christopher Haigh, *Elizabeth I: Profile in Power* (1988). Less admiring of her than most studies of the queen.

T. E. Hartley, *Elizabeth's Parliaments: Queens, Lords and Commons, 1559–1601* (1991).

Paul Johnson, *Elizabeth I: A Study in Power and Intellect* (1974).

Carole Levin, *The Heart and Stomach of a King: Elizabeth I and the Politics of Sex and Power* (1994). A fresh approach.

Wallace MacCaffrey, *Elizabeth I* (1994).

———, *Queen Elizabeth and the Making of Policy, 1572–1588*, 2nd ed. (1994). Meticulous scholarship.

John Neale, *Queen Elizabeth I: A Biography* (1934). Still valuable.

D. M. Palliser, *The Age of Elizabeth: England under the Later Tudors, 1547–1603* (1983).

Conyers Read, *Mr. Secretary Cecil and Queen Elizabeth* (1955).

Lacey Baldwin Smith, *Elizabeth I* (1975).

THE SCOTTISH REFORMATION

Frank Bardgett, *Scotland Reformed: The Reformation in Angus and the Mearns* (1992).

Keith Brown, *Bloodfeud in Scotland 1573–1625: Violence, Justice and Politics in an Early Modern Society* (1986).

Ian Cowan, *The Scottish Reformation* (1982).

Gordon Donaldson, *All the Queen's Men: Power and Politics in Mary Stewart's Scotland* (1983).

———, *The Scottish Reformation* (1960).

———, *Mary, Queen of Scots* (1974). Three studies by a leading authority.

Antonia Fraser, *Mary Queen of Scots* (1969). A lively account.

Richard Greaves, *Theology and Revolution in the Scottish Reformation: Studies in the Thought of John Knox* (1980).

Richard Kyle, *The Mind of John Knox* (1984).

Michael Lynch, *Edinburgh and the Reformation* (1981).

James McGoldrick, *Luther's Scottish Connection* (1989).

W. Stanford Reid, *Trumpeter of God: A Biography of John Knox* (1974).

Jenny Wormald, *Court, Kirk, and Community: Scotland 1470–1625* (1981).

OTHER TOPICS

Brendan Bradshaw, *The Dissolution of the Religious Orders in Ireland under Henry VIII* (London, 1974).

Patrick Collinson, *The Elizabethan Puritan Movement* (1990).

Felicity Heal, *Hospitality in Early Modern England* (1990).

Colm Lennon, *Sixteenth-Century Ireland* (1995).

Jennifer Loach, *Parliament under the Tudors* (1991).

Roger Manning, *Village Revolts: Social Protest and Popular Disturbances in England, 1509–1640* (1987).

Martha Skeeters, *Community and Clergy: Bristol and the Reformation c. 1530–c. 1570* (1993).

Glanmor Williams, *Renewal and Reformation: Wales c. 1415–1642* (1987).

Notes

1. Cited in Lacey Baldwin Smith, ed., *Elizabeth I* (St. Louis, Mo.: Forum Press, 1980), pp. 38–39.
2. Cited in Lewis Spitz, *The Renaissance and Reformation Movements* (Chicago: Rand McNally, 1971), p. 465.
3. Phrase used by Professor Norman Rich to refer to Louis Napoleon in a class at Michigan State University in the sring of 1966. I think it holds true for Darnley as well.
4. Cited in Helga Harriman, *Women in the Western Heritage* (Guilford, Conn.: Dushkin Publishing, 1995), p. 198.
5. Cited in Lacey Baldwin Smith, *Elizabeth Tudor: Portrait of a Queen* (Boston, Mass.: Little Brown, 1975), p. 73.

11

THE CATHOLIC
REFORMATION

It is relatively easy to get the impression from the anticlerical tone of much popular Renaissance literature and the propaganda of the reformers that almost everyone in Europe had serious grievances with the Roman Catholic church in the sixteenth century. Nothing could be farther from the truth. While perhaps as many as 40 percent of Europeans became Protestant, many areas remained Catholic and some sovereigns that had changed to Protestantism regretted it and returned to the umbrella of the papacy. A majority of Europeans seemed to find that the church of Rome met their spiritual needs. Many loved the rich ceremonial and liturgical life of the Catholic church; others admired the institution for its care of the poor and the sick; intellectuals continued to admire the rich theological tradition of Catholicism. Above all, most Europeans seemed to believe their souls had the best chance of being saved by staying Catholic and adhering to the church's teachings and sacraments.

It is interesting to note how many humanists stayed loyal to the church, even when they agreed with Luther and others that there was a great deal that needed to be changed about church thought and practice. As the learned jurist Ulrich Zasius put in a letter of 1519:

I agree with much in Luther and admire him. . . . But there are in his teachings some blemishes which I dislike. His assertion, for example, that we sin even when we perform a good work is a misplaced proposition. . . . He thinks it proved that the Pope is not universal bishop by divine right. I cannot say emphatically enough how much this displeases me.[1]

Others like Erasmus found the dogmatism and inflexibility of many of the early reformers to be offensive, and many other perceptive observers joined him in fearing that the reform movement would destabilize European society; in other words, the cure of radical reform might prove worse than the disease of church corruption and clerical abuses.

Reform in Spain

Looking back through history, thoughtful persons could observe that the Roman Catholic church has always had periods of trouble followed by periods of renewal. Even before Martin Luther's call for change, many Roman Catholics were actively working to reform the church. In Spain, for example, the scholarly Cardinal Francisco Jiménez de Cisneros (1436–1517) had imposed stricter discipline upon the clergy and helped wage war against heretics with the founding of the Spanish Inquisition in 1480. A relatively unknown Franciscan, Jiménez saw his career skyrocket when Queen Isabella of Castile found that his religious passion matched her own. He became her confessor and leading spiritual advisor. Through her influence Jiménez rose to become Grand Inquisitor, governor of Castile, and the first churchman of Spain as archbishop of Toledo.

As primate of Spain, Cardinal Jiménez took many paths to reform. To improve the quality of clerical learning, he founded the University of Alcalá near Madrid in 1509 and sponsored the publication of a Polyglot (multilingual) Bible with papal approval. The Polyglot Bible featured Hebrew, Greek, and Latin texts in parallel columns for ready comparisons. Jiménez also sponsored translations into Spanish of such great mystical works as Ludolf the Saxon's *Life of Christ* and Thomas à Kempis's *Imitation of Christ*. Both became major influences on the development of Ignatius Loyola, the founder of the Society of Jesus. Before his death, Jiménez had helped Spain become the center of a version of reformed Catholicism, a place where Protestants, fearful of the Inquisition, could make few inroads.

The price of attempting to create a religious monolith was terribly high. Forced to flee Spain rather than give up their religious and cultural traditions, thousands of people saw their lives destroyed. Thousands of Jews, Moors, Protestants, and others suspected of heresy were brought before the Inquisition and hundreds were executed by the royal government in horrific and elaborate public ceremonials. Many prominent churchmen and women had brushes with the terror of the Inquisition, including Ignatius of Loyola. Isabella's and Jiménez's attempts to purge Spain of non-Catholics left a terrible legacy and contributed in

many ways to the eventual decline of Spain. Even if other sovereigns had been willing to put their swords in the service of the Catholic church, it is doubtful that the Spanish situation could have been replicated anywhere else in Europe. The Catholic church in Spain had wealth and firm support from the crown.

Efforts at Reform in Italy

In Italy an informal group of dedicated clerics and some laymen and laywomen were worshipping together, sharing ideas, doing works of charity, and hoping for internal church reform. First founded in Genoa in 1497 by Catherine Fieschi (later Saint Catherine of Genoa), the Oratory of Divine Love spread to Rome early in the reign of Pope Leo X and later to other parts of Italy. Among its more prominent members were the poet Vittoria Colonna, Gasparo Contarini (later a cardinal), Gianpietro Carafa (later Pope Paul IV), Jacob Sadoleto (later a bishop), and Gaetano Thiene (one of the founders of the Theatines). They were disappointed that although the Fifth Lateran Council summoned to Rome by Pope Julius II in 1512 and continued by Pope Leo had identified many abuses in the church, so little was being done to implement the reforms recommended by the council. The first Medici pope, Leo X, seemed preoccupied with his pleasures (chiefly hunting and art) and hurling condemnations at the rebellious monk Luther.

Since the Roman Catholic church was structurally a monarchy, even though in theory all power came from God and was invested also in the "body of the faithful," the members of the Oratory realized that there were limits to what could be achieved at the grassroots level or even at their level of prominent laity and promising clerics.

Hopes for papal leadership were renewed in 1522 with the accession of Adrian of Utrecht, a Dutchman. As we have seen, Adrian was serious about change and appointed a reform commission, but died in 1523 before he could put its recommendations into action. His successor, the second Medici pope, Clement VII (r. 1523–1534), was too timid and vacillating to accomplish anything substantial in the way of reform. Although he was a man of some integrity and ability, he was overwhelmed by such challenges as the Sack of Rome of 1527 and the loss of Henry VIII's England.

NEW REFORM ORDERS: CAPUCHINS, THEATINES, AND URSULINES

The founding of new religious orders had traditionally been a source of renewal and reform in the Catholic church. Yet the Fourth Lateran Council in 1215 had discouraged the establishment of new orders as Pope Innocent III enhanced the papal monarchy and tightened his grip on all agencies of the church. In 1525 two members of the Oratory, Gaetano Thiene and Gianpietro Carafa, persuaded Pope Clement VII to allow the creation of a new order, called the Theatines. Thiene was a monk from Vicenza and the tempestuous Carafa was bishop of Chieti. The Theatines were a religious society made up of regular priests who took vows similar to those of monks and mendicant friars. In this way Theatines were able to continue their parish ministries while enjoying a more regulated devotional life. They concentrated on study, meditation, preaching, and good works and earned a great reputation as advocates of improvement.

Other new orders sprang up, including the Company of Saint Ursula, founded by Angela Merici of Brescia (1474–1540). Orphaned at age ten, she became a Franciscan tertiary when she was thirteen. *Tertiaries*

were laypersons attached to a religious house and following lives of austerity. At age twenty-three Angela had a vision that she would found a religious congregation devoted to service, teaching, and curing. After the death of her guardian uncle, she began her exemplary career of service and teaching among the poor of Brescia. In 1535 Merici founded the Company of Saint Ursula, named for the legendary British princess who was martyred while on the way to her wedding, allegedly along with 11,000 virgin companions. The Ursulines were to dedicate themselves as "consecrated virgins" to prayer and charitable work. They usually lived at home with their parents, wore no special habit, and concentrated on teaching young girls.

Not until four years after the death of their founder in 1540 were they officially recognized by the reform-minded Pope Paul III, with some alterations. The patriarchs who dominated the church wanted to keep religious women firmly under their control and protection. Some were concerned about safeguarding dowries and possible inheritances. Pope Paul made the Ursulines wear habits and in 1566 they were cloistered. In 1612 Pope Paul V ordered the Ursulines to follow the Augustinian rules. Even though the rules developed by Angela Merici were discarded and the Ursulines were put under masculine control, they continued to be a strong force for the education of women. Ursuline schools could be found all over Italy and elsewhere.

The Capuchins came out of the Franciscan tradition and were recognized as an independent order by Pope Clement VII in 1528. Matteo da Bascio (d. 1552) had gathered the first group of Capuchins and introduced wearing beards and the distinctive painted hoods (*capucchio*) from which the order derived its name. Bascio served only briefly as their vicar-general before returning to the Observant Franciscans. Bernardino d' Asti (1484–1554) eventually became the leader of the Capuchins and played a major role in drafting their constitution. His work was almost undone when his successor, Bernardino Ochino (1487–1564), fled to Geneva in 1542 and became a Protestant. Pope Paul III considered abolishing them, but a church investigation vindicated their orthodoxy. Their supporters included Vittoria Colonna.

Despite these difficult beginnings, the Capuchins managed to grow rapidly after 1574 when they were allowed to serve outside of Italy. They worked as military chaplains, preachers, and missionaries. More than any other group, they worked courageously with plague victims. They generally lived in small hermitages near the towns where they begged for their daily bread. Despite their austere lives and work among the poor, the Capuchins attracted a large membership. They numbered 8,803 by 1600; a century later there were 27,336 Capuchins.

Ignatius of Loyola (1491–1556) and the Society of Jesus

The most prominent of the new church orders that came into existence was the Society of Jesus, founded by the remarkable Ignatius of Loyola (Inigo López de Recalde). The last of thirteen children, Ignatius was born at the castle of Loyola in the Basque territory of northern Spain in the Pyrenees Mountains. He received the customary limited education of the lesser nobility before being sent to the household of the chief treasurer of King Ferdinand of Aragon at age thirteen. When his master died in 1517, the red-haired Ignatius entered into military service under the viceroy of Navarre.

Ignatius of Loyola served only a few months as a military volunteer until the Battle of Pamplona between France and Spain on May 20, 1521, when a cannon ball shattered his right leg and badly wounded his left. Because they grew crooked, Loyola's legs were set twice and rebroken twice, each time without the benefit of modern anesthetics. He was left with a limp for life and his brief stint as a soldier was over. While recuperating, Loyola found little pleasure in the chivalric tales that he once loved to read. Instead, he was forced to find consolation in reading the lives of saints. Ignatius's inner voice gradually brought him to the conviction that God wanted him to follow the way of St. Francis and St. Dominic.

Once his health was sufficiently restored, Loyola set out for the Benedictine monastery of Montserrat in Catalonia. He planned a pilgrimage to Jerusalem. After spending an entire night in vigil before a statue of the Virgin Mary, Ignatius put down his sword and dagger and took up instead a beggar's staff and clothing. He spent three days confessing his sins before heading to the small town of Manresa near Barcelona. An outbreak of the plague forced him to remain there for almost a year. At Manresa, Loyola was greatly influenced by Thomas à Kempis's *Imitation of Christ* and his own inner experiences in finding God. He used those experiences in writing his famous *Spiritual Exercises*.

The pilgrim finally arrived in the Holy Land in autumn of 1523, where he hoped to spend the rest of his life "helping souls." Because of pressure from Ottoman authorities, the Franciscans who were in charge of looking after Christian pilgrims told Loyola he would have to leave. Bitterly disappointed, he returned to Barcelona, where he studied Latin grammar with children less than half his age. Begging for his food, Ignatius shared what he had obtained with other

Juan Martinez, *St. Ignatius*. Sculpture. University Chapel, Seville, Spain. Foto Marburg/Art Resource.

street people. In 1526 he enrolled for theology classes at the University of Alcalá. Wearing his pilgrim's garb, Loyola continued his begging and began to teach people a version of his "Spiritual Exercises." Rumors began to circulate that he and his associates were "enlightened ones" (*alumbrados*), members of a suspect mystical movement. He was hauled before the Inquisition of Toledo, where he spent forty-two days in prison waiting for a verdict.

Declared innocent by the Inquisition, Ignatius continued his studies at the University of Salamanca, where he was examined for heresy by local Dominicans. Again found innocent, the Spaniard then tried his luck in Paris in 1528. He earned his licentiate in theology in 1534 and his M.A. in 1535.

Loyola was in Paris during the period of Nicholas Cop's controversial rectorial address and subsequent flight with Calvin, so very likely he was exposed to "Lutheran ideas." Protestantism in any form never had any appeal for Ignatius of Loyola.

THE FOUNDING OF THE SOCIETY OF JESUS

On August 15, 1534, Ignatius and six friends vowed to "spend their lives helping souls." One of them was Francis Xavier, who later became an incredibly successful missionary to the Orient; another was Diego Lainez, who succeeded Loyola as the second head of the Society of Jesus. These seven men formed the nucleus of what became one of the most influential religious organizations in history and profoundly changed the life of the Roman Catholic church.

Loyola guided all his fellow founding Jesuits, and several others who joined them, through his "Spiritual Exercises." In January 1537 Ignatius and his associates met in Venice, hoping to take a ship to Jerusalem. They spent their time in such charitable activities as nursing the sick, cleaning, removing garbage, digging graves, and burying the dead. Pope Paul III agreed to bless their trip to the Holy Land and provided funds. On June 24, 1537, Ignatius and six of his friends were ordained priests. The political situation in Palestine prevented them from making their journey, so instead Loyola and several others went to Rome to offer their services to Pope Paul III. The pope appointed several of them to teaching positions at the University of Rome. Ignatius helped many prominent persons through the "Exercises," including Cardinal Gasparo Contarini, who helped persuade the pope to sanction the Society of Jesus in September 1540.

Anonymous, *St. Ignatius before Pope Paul III*. Gesu, Il, Rome, Italy. Scala/Art Resource.

THE ORGANIZATION OF THE JESUITS

Ignatius of Loyola was elected as the first superior general of the Society of Jesus. By 1550, as membership expanded, the Society was grouped into four provinces—Italy, Portugal, Spain, and India. Each province was governed by a "provincial," who was responsible directly to Ignatius, who governed all other Jesuits. At the death of the superior general, the Jesuits would meet in General Congregation to elect his successor. The Jesuits set high standards for admission, wanting only men of sound intelligence, good character, and good health. They came from a variety of backgrounds as Loyola wished to combine diversity with quality. Under pressure from Pope Paul III in 1545, he reluctantly permitted a few "devout women" to join, but this experiment was abandoned two years later. In 1554, Juana of Austria (d. 1573), the deeply pious and talented daughter of Emperor Charles V, sometime regent of Spain, forced Ignatius to admit her as a secret member.

The Society placed great emphasis on the vow of obedience. Loyola admonished his fellow Jesuits that if the hierarchical church "defines anything to be black which to our eyes appears to be white, we must declare it to be black."[2] Members were to cut earthly ties and devote themselves entirely to the Society, whose primary purpose was "to help souls." Jesuits also took vows of chastity and poverty. After a difficult two-year period of testing, they were given rigorous academic training to help prepare them for careers as priests, preachers, teachers, chaplains, missionaries, diplomats, or in whatever way they might "serve the greater glory of God." If there were sufficient numbers of them, they might live in a house, but Jesuits were not cloistered like monks or nuns. The world was their home.

Although Ignatius of Loyola had no intention of being a church reformer, his leadership of the Society proved inspirational to many, as did his incredible manual of meditation, *The Spiritual Exercises*. Loyola helped the Jesuits ward off attacks from church leaders jealous of the Society's privileges or, like Pope Paul IV (Carafa), eager to control them. Because of his own prejudices, Paul IV was unhappy with Ignatius's willingness to accept former Jews, such as his successor, Diego Lainez, the son of a Jewish merchant from Castile. Paul confined the Jews of Rome to a ghetto in 1555.

The success of the Jesuits in all their various callings attracted criticism. The Society was particularly successful as educators. Their schools were much more innovative than most rival schools, dividing pupils into classes by age and ability, and using better catechisms, textbooks, and methods of examination. They were very involved in higher education as well. Loyola saw education as a key tool in the fight against heresy. As he wrote in a letter of August 13, 1554:

> The heretics have made their false theology popular and presented it in a way that is within the capacity of the common people.... Their success is largely due to the negligence of those who should have shown some interest; and the bad example and the ignorance of Catholics, especially the clergy, have made such ravages in the vineyard of the Lord.... To put a stop to these evils, we must multiply the colleges and schools of the Society in many lands.... We must write answers [to the Protestants] in pamphlet form, short, lively, and well-written. This must be done by learned men well grounded in theology, who can write for the multitudes.[3]

THE JESUIT LEGACY

By the time of Ignatius of Loyola's death in 1556, there were already thirty-five Jesuit colleges. The membership of the Society of Jesus itself had grown from the original seven to about 1,000 members. A number of these early Jesuits became leading theologians and debaters, such as Robert Bellarmine (c. 1542–1621) and Francesco Suárez (1548–1617). Jesuits also excelled as missionaries. For example, the dynamic Dutchman Peter Canisius (1521–1597) had enormous success in winning back many Protestants to Catholicism in the Holy Roman Empire and Poland. Canisius also wrote a catechism that became an extremely important learning tool as well as a crucial statement of Catholic belief.

Ignatius of Loyola's close friend Francis Xavier (1506–1552) converted thousands of Asians to Christianity despite numerous hardships. Xavier was particularly impressed by the Japanese: "they are a people of excellent morals—good in general and not malicious."[4] Ignatius had wisely advised Jesuit missionaries to learn the language of the country where they were living. The courage, faith, and hard work of Jesuit missionaries resulted in widespread conversions to Catholicism in Europe and throughout the world. In all, the Society of Jesus has been one of the greatest legacies of the period of the Catholic Reformation.

Teresa of Avila (1515–1582)

The Catholic church not only gained added strength from the creation of new orders, but it also witnessed a revival of existing orders. The Carmelites in Spain, for example, found vigorous new leadership during the sixteenth century in Teresa of Avila and Juan de la Cruz, her famous disciple. Teresa grew up in the fortified town of Avila as part of a prosperous merchant family. Her grandfather, Juan Sanchez, had converted from Judaism to Christianity, but still had been publicly shamed by being hauled before the Inquisition in Toledo. When she was thirteen, she suffered the death of her devout mother and the loss of her oldest sister to marriage. Teresa responded to these losses by running with a fast crowd and getting into minor forms of trouble.

Her worried and doting father reacted by placing her in a nearby Augustinian convent, known for its strict discipline. Teresa remained in the convent for a year and a half and thrived on its disciplined love. After a bout of illness and despite objections of her father, she joined a Carmelite house in Avila in 1535 and remained there for the next twenty-six years. At first her longing for her family made her confinement difficult, even though her convent allowed her numerous creature comforts. Teresa suffered persistent ill health until she was in her early forties. She also came under the influence of a Dominican priest, Domingo Banes, who taught her that God can be loved in and through all things. Reading St. Augustine's *Confessions* also had a serious impact upon her development.

After a series of visions that reprimanded her for her worldly concerns, Teresa decided to return to a life of austerity. In 1562, she left her monastery to embark on a life of service to others. With four companions, Teresa founded a new convent dedicated to St. Joseph in Avila, one which renounced worldly goods and followed a strict form of discipline. Although greeted with deep suspicion, Teresa eventually won the support of the reform-minded bishop of Avila, and her order of Discalced ("barefoot," to suggest a life of poverty) Carmelites was officially recognized in 1562.

During the remaining twenty years of her life, Teresa wandered throughout Spain establishing convents and reforming others. On her travels, she met Juan de la Cruz, a Carmelite monk who became her most ardent disciple. "Although he is small, he is great in the sight of God," she said of him.[5] He became spiritual director of the Discalced house of St. Joseph's in 1572, but was seized and thrown into prison for nine

months by his unreformed Carmelite brothers. Juan (1542–1591) was a major poet who also wrote some of the most inspiring works of mystical literature, including his *The Dark Night of the Soul*, *The Ascent of Mount Carmel*, and *The Living Flame of Love*.

Teresa's publications, such as her *Way of Perfection* and *Interior Castle*, also became religious classics. Her writings, including a partial *Autobiography*, tell of her own life of struggle, persecutions endured, her many doubts, and the triumph of her faith. In her 1562 *Autobiography*, she described one of her visions as follows:

> Almost always Our Lord appeared to me as He rose from the dead, and it was the same when I saw Him in the Host. Only occasionally, to hearten me if I was in tribulation, He would show me His wounds, and then would appear sometimes on the Cross and sometimes as He was in the garden. . . . I found myself dying of the desire to see God. . . . This love came to me in mighty impulses which robbed me of all power of action.[6]

For all her religiosity, she was also a sound woman of business and a born political intriguer. By the time of her death, Teresa had founded thirty reformed Carmelite houses, for both women and men. However, controversy swirled about her throughout her life because some church leaders, having been deceived by a number of frauds, doubted the nature of her visions. At several points, Teresa was even accused of "Lutheran tendencies." As she wrote, "I was startled by what the devil stirred up against a few poor little women."[7] Despite the attacks from her critics, she found great support from King Philip II, other Spanish grandees, and influential church leaders in Rome, who recognized her administrative and spiritual talents.

Always self-deprecating, Teresa of Avila would have been astonished that in

Bernini, *Ecstasy of St. Teresa*. S. Maria della Vittoria, Rome, Italy. Alinari/Art Resource.

1622 the church made her a saint. As she had written about her life in the community at Seville, "one of the things that makes me happy here is that there is no suggestion of that nonsense about my supposed sanctity."[8]

Pope Paul III and Reform

As important as the work of lay and clerical reformers was, the Catholic church would never have succeeded in undertaking such a thorough reform without the support of the papacy and many in the College of Cardinals. In 1534 Cardinal Alessandro Farnese, a smart and aging aristocrat, became Pope Paul III (r. 1534–1549). As a churchman who had first been made a cardinal during the scandalous pontificate of Alexander VI (Borgia), Paul was well aware of church corruption and the need for change in the face of the Protestant and Ottoman threats. Real-

izing that "fish stink from the head down," a reform commission of 1537 chaired by Contarini recommended a number of reforms in the College of Cardinals itself and the elimination of the selling of church offices, which had grown from 625 at the time of Sixtus IV (r. 1471–1484) to 2,232 by the time of Leo X (r. 1513–1521).

A conservative majority of the College of Cardinals, however, was unwilling to make the necessary changes and the papacy had become financially dependent on the revenues from venal offices. What was needed was an increase in the number of reform-minded cardinals and new sources of revenues. Paul III's first round of appointments to the College of Cardinals included no major reformers and two of his own grandsons, both teenagers. It seemed to many in Rome that Paul III was going to be just another nepotistic Renaissance pope determined to take care of his own family first. Yet in his next series of appointments, the pope promoted a number of earnest reformers to the cardinalate, including Gianpietro Carafa, Reginald Pole (archbishop of Canterbury under Queen Mary Tudor), Jacopo Sadoleto, Gasparo Contarini, and others. They pressured the pope to follow through on reform measures, despite the opposition of those in high places who had a large financial stake in existing practices.

AN IRENIC REFORMER:
GASPARO CONTARINI (1483–1542)

Gasparo Contarini was an especially fine choice for a cardinal's hat. The seventh son of an illustrious Venetian family, he studied philosophy at Padua before becoming a member of the Venetian government and diplomatic corps. He followed Emperor Charles V to Germany and attended the Diet of Worms of 1521. In 1528 Contarini represented Venice's interests at the court of Pope

Clement VII. Thus he was able to witness firsthand the rise of Protestantism and the papal response. While sympathetic to some of the ideas of the Protestants, Contarini remained a convinced Catholic who was committed to reason and peaceful reform. In 1535 although a layman, he left his position in the Venetian government to accept a cardinalate because he hoped he could do something worthwhile for the church in a time of great need.

Two years later Contarini presented the pope with a report on church reform, which was rejected by the majority of the papal court as impractical. Although disappointed, he continued to urge his friend Paul III to carry on with efforts at reform and even compromise with the Protestants. In 1541 Cardinal Contarini was named as legate to an important meeting at Regensburg with leaders of the Protestant movement. Sponsored by Emperor Charles V, the Regensburg Colloquy sought to find common theological ground between Catholics and Protestants. Working in harmony with Martin Bucer, Johann Eck, and Philip Melanchthon, Contarini was able to help draft a statement which contained both Catholic and Evangelical ideas. However, the temper of the times was such that the Regensburg formula was rejected by all groups. Contarini then served as a reform legate in charge of Bologna.

The Council of Trent, 1545–1563

Despite the failure of both Catholics and Protestants to accept the spirit of compromise manifest at Regensburg, Pope Paul III pressed on with his version of reform. In 1542 he established the Inquisition in Rome as recommended by the militant reformer Cardinal Carafa of Naples. Carafa served as its first inquisitor-general. The influence of the hardliner Carafa caused the vicar-gen-

eral of the Capuchins, Bernardino Ochino, to flee Italy, along with the prolific and skilled theologian Peter Martyr Vermigli. They both ended up as wandering preachers in various northern Protestant communities before Vermigli found a chair for a while in theology at Oxford during the reign of Edward VI.

Balanced against these important defections from Catholicism, Pope Paul III also chartered the Jesuits and the Ursulines. His most famous accomplishment was his calling of a general reform council of the church, which began meeting in the Italian Alpine town of Trent in March of 1545. Although Emperor Charles V had long called for a reform council, his rival, François I, and the French bishops were opposed, fearing the loss of the French church's privileges. Still hoping for peace between the great powers, Paul III had the vision and courage to go ahead with "a general, holy council" despite their political pressure and his fears of the Ottomans. "We must do this," he informed church leaders, because "all the world is in fear and sorrow."[9]

The opening sessions of the Council of Trent were attended by four legates and cardinals, four archbishops, thirty-one bishops, five generals of church orders, and fifty theologians and canonists. The ailing Luther, who had often called for such a reform council, called this one "too little, too late." The Wittenberger was wrong, for although the Council of Trent was forced to meet off and on for eighteen years before concluding, it proved to be the most important church council in a thousand years. Paul III had devised measures to control its voting and membership. Unlike the Council of Constance (1414–1418), the delegates at Trent voted as individuals, not as nations. This way the big Italian delegation made up the largest voting block and their loyalty to the papacy could generally be relied upon.

Titian, *Portrait of Pope Paul III*, Museo Nazionale di Capodimonte, Naples, Italy. Alinari/Art Resource.

Before Trent would finally conclude its important work in 1563, four popes would come and go, and the council would suffer many misadventures. Plague forced the council to adjourn to Bologna in March of 1547. When Carafa became Pope Paul IV in 1555, he refused to continue the council, believing that he as papal monarch could best revive the church. Paul IV issued his own reform decrees, such as the one setting up the Index of Prohibited Books in 1559. Paul's papal list of "unholy and dangerous books" included the complete writings of Calvin, Luther, Zwingli, Knox, and other reformers. It also condemned certain writings of Erasmus, Machiavelli's *The Prince*, Rabelais's *Pantagruel*, and the Koran.

Prohibited works listed between 1559

and 1596 also included Dante's *On Monarchy*; Boccaccio's *Decameron* (unless expurgated); four of the humanist Petrarca's sonnets; four of Lorenzo Valla's major works; the ribald Aretino's works; the poetry of the courtesan Veronica Franco; the Latin edition of Guicciardini's *History of Italy*; Castiglione's *The Courtier*; and many other Renaissance classics. Authors were condemned sometimes for their words and sometimes for their lives and in some cases for both. Although debate continues on how successful the Index was in helping to halt the spread of Protestant doctrines, there is no question that it had a chilling effect on the freewheeling exchange of ideas that had been such a stimulating part of the Renaissance.

THE CONCLUSION OF THE COUNCIL OF TRENT AND ITS IMPACT

With Carafa's death in 1559 and peace between Henri II of France and Philip II of Spain, the Council of Trent reconvened in 1562 with the blessing of Pius IV (r. 1559–1565), the new Medici pope. Under the aegis of the tactful Cardinal Morone, Trent finally came to closure in 1563. Among its great work was the reaffirmation and clarification of major church doctrines. There had been enormous confusion among Catholics about what exactly was the official church teaching about, for example, purgatory prior to the start of the Reformation. Different popes, councils, and theologians had said different things at different times. After Trent issued its concluding statements, the official church positions on such matters as the seven sacraments, transubstantiation, communion in one kind for the laity, auricular confession, celibacy, monasticism, purgatory, indulgences (reaffirmed, but sellers outlawed), the invocation of saints, and the veneration of saints were perfectly clear.

Trent declared that good works were necessary for salvation, but that faith was also crucial. The apostolic succession was reaffirmed. Scripture was to be valued equally with tradition as sources of doctrine. The authority of the church to interpret Scripture against the rampant individualism of Protestant interpreters was affirmed: "No one shall presume to interpret Scripture contrary to that sense which Holy Mother Church . . . has held and now holds."[10] The doctrinal statements of Trent concluded by making it clear to Protestants that they must accept the teaching authority of the church without deviation or be "accursed."

In the area of church practice, the Council of Trent admitted the existence of a great deal of corruption and issued stern measures to help clean it up. Pluralism, simony, nepotism, absenteeism, immorality, and ignorance among the clergy were all condemned and combatted. Pluralists had to give up their multiple benefices. Priests were ordered to reside in their parishes. Bishops were made more responsible for the discipline of their clergy. More masculine control was put over female religious orders and houses. To improve the education of the clergy, seminaries were to be established in each diocese. The supremacy of the pope over prelates increased. As King Philip II of Spain wryly commented, "I sent bishops to Trent and they came back parish priests."[11]

Although the church has had a long history of reform councils, what is particu-

Aerial view of St. Peter's Basilica (columns by Bernini, dome by Michelangelo). Vatican State. Alinari/Art Resource.

larly striking about the Council of Trent is how many of its decrees were in fact carried out and how much it changed the church despite pockets of resistance, often in rural parishes. While the sale of offices and pluralism were never completely eliminated, as illustrated by the case of the underage pluralist Joseph Clemens (1671–1723), archbishop of Cologne and a member of the great house of Wittelsbach, such abuses were substantially reduced.

Pius IV continued the spirit of reform by implementing the Tridentine reforms and by continuing the tradition of appointing reformers to high office, such as his talented nephew, Carlo Borromeo (1538–1584), who was made a cardinal and archbishop of Milan at age twenty-one. Borromeo's appointment initially looked like nepotism as usual, but he soon proved the cynics wrong with his administrative skills and devoted work among the poor. His reform activities included writing a very influential catechism and a very sensible redesign of the confessional, which allowed for greater privacy.

Stimulated by the work of the reformers and the new and revived religious orders, the Catholic church seemed ready for a new era of glory. Artists such as Michelangelo (1475–1564), Artemisia Gentileschi (1593–c. 1632), Gian Lorenzo Bernini (1598–1680), and Giovanni Palestrina (c. 1525–1594) were already transforming that feeling of renewed piety into a stunning series of artistic masterpieces as the Renaissance gave way to the age of the Baroque. The church had been reformed in head and numbers, while withstanding the first onslaughts of Protestantism and the Ottomans. Tragically, there were still convinced Catholics and Protestants who were willing to use any means necessary to promote their vision of the truth. The spirit of reason and compromise so wonderfully exemplified by Cardinal Gasparo Contarini was soon swept away and the age of religious wars launched in earnest.

Chronology

1436–1517	Life of Cardinal Francisco Jiménez des Cisneros.	1528	Clement VIII recognizes the Capuchins.
1474–1540	Life of Angela Merici.	1534–1549	Reign of Paul III.
1480	Spanish Inquisition established in Seville.	1537	Commission on Reform of the Church.
1483–1542	Life of Cardinal Gasparo Contarini.	1538–1584	Life of Carlo Borromeo.
1491	Birth of Ignatius of Loyola.	1540	Paul III charters the Jesuits.
1506–1552	Life of Francis Xavier.	1541	Regensburg Colloquy.
1512–1517	Fifth Lateran Council.	1542	Inquisition established in Rome; Bernardino Ochino flees to Geneva.
1515	Birth of Teresa of Avila.		
1517	Oratory of Divine Love begins in Rome.	1544	Chartering of the Ursulines.
1521–1597	Life of Peter Canisius.	1545	Opening of the Council of Trent.
1522–1523	Reign of Pope Adrian VI; Commission on Reform.	1555–1559	Reign of Pope Paul IV (Carafa).

1556	Death of Loyola; Diego Lainez elected as Jesuit general.	**1559–1565**	Reign of Pius IV.
1559	Establishment of the Index of Forbidden Books.	**1563**	The Council of Trent concludes.
		1582	Death of Teresa of Avila.

Further Readings

GENERAL

Michael Carroll, *Madonnas that Maim: Popular Catholicism in Italy since the Fourteenth Century* (1992). Use with care.

Louis Chatellier, *The Europe of the Devout: the Catholic Reformation and the Formation of a New Society* (1989).

N. S. Davidson, *The Counter-Reformation* (1987).

Jean Delumeau, *Catholicism Between Luther and Voltaire: A New View of the Counter-Reformation* (1977).

H. O. Evennett, *The Spirit of the Counter-Reformation* (1968).

Marc Forster, *The Counter-Reformation in the Villages: Religion and Reform in the Bishopric of Speyer, 1560–1720* (1992).

Barbara McClung Hallman, *Italian Cardinals, Reform, and the Church as Property* (1985).

Hubert Jedin and John Dolan, eds., *History of the Church*, Vol. 5, *Reformation and Counter Reformation* (1980).

Martin Jones, *The Counter Reformation: Religion and Society in Early Modern Europe* (1995).

Michael Mullett, *The Counter Reformation and the Catholic Reformation in Early Modern Europe* (1984).

Marvin O'Connell, *The Counter-Reformation* (1974). One of the more readable surveys.

John Olin, ed., *Catholic Reform from Cardinal Ximenes to the Council of Trent, 1495–1563: Illustrative Documents and a Brief Study of St. Ignatius Loyola* (1990).

——, ed., *The Catholic Reformation: From Savonarola to Ignatius Loyola* (1990). Useful collections of documents.

John O'Malley, ed., *Catholicism in Early Modern Europe: A Guide to Research* (1988). An invaluable collection of bibliographical essays by leading scholars.

Frederic McGinness, *Right Thinking and Sacred Oratory in Counter-Reformation Rome* (1995).

Nelson Minnich, *The Fifth Lateran Council (1512–17): Studies on Its Membership, Diplomacy and Proposals for Reform* (1993).

G. W. Searle, *The Counter Reformation* (1974).

Philip Soergel, *Wondrous in His Saints: Counter-Reformation Propaganda in Bavaria* (1993).

A. D. Wright, *The Counter-Reformation* (1982).

NEW RELIGIOUS ORDERS AND IGNATIUS OF LOYOLA

Wiliam Bangert, *History of the Society of Jesus* (1972).

Richard De Molen, ed., *Religious Orders of the Catholic Reformation* (1994). Scholarly essays by a variety of contributors.

John W. O'Malley, *The First Jesuits* (1993). An important survey.

A. Lynn Martin, *The Jesuit Mind: The Mentality of an Elite in Early Modern France* (1988).

W. W. Meisner, *Ignatius of Loyola: The Psychology of a Saint* (1992). A Freudian interpretation.

INDIVIDUAL REFORMERS

Gillian Ahlgren, *Teresa of Avila and the Politics of Sanctity* (1996).

Jodi Bilinkoff, *The Avila of Saint Teresa* (1989).

Robert Birely, *Religion and Politics in the Age of Counter-Reformation* (1982).

Philip Caraman, *St. Angela. The Life of Angela Merici* (1964).

Stephen Clissold, *St. Teresa of Avila* (1982).

John P. Donnelly, *Calvinism and Scholasticism in Vermigli's Doctrine of Man and Grace* (1976).

Elisabeth Gleason, *Gasparo Contarini: Venice, Rome and Reform* (1993).

Pamela Jones, *Federico Borromeo and the Ambrosiana: Art Patronage and Reform in Seventeenth Century Milan* (1993).

Philip McNair, *Peter Martyr in Italy: An Anatomy of Apostasy* (1967).

José Nieto, *Mystic, Rebel, Saint: A Study of St. John of the Cross* (1979).

Anne Jacobson Schutte, *Pier Paolo Vergerio; the Making of an Italian Reformer* (1977).

Carol Slade, *St. Teresa of Avila: Author of a Heroic Life* (1995).

George Tavard, *Poetry and Contemplation in St. John of the Cross* (1988).

THE INQUISITION AND INDEX

Paul Grendler, *Culture and Censorship in Late Renaissance Italy* (1981).

Henry Kamen, *Inquisition and Society in Spain in the Sixteenth and Seventeenth Centuries* (1985).

———, *The Phoenix and the Flame: Catalonia and the Counter-Reformation* (1993).

———, *The Spanish Inquisition* (1965).

William Monter, *Frontiers of Heresy* (1990).

Edward Peters, *Inquisition* (1988).

THE COUNCIL OF TRENT

H. O. Evenett, *The Cardinal of Lorraine and the Council of Trent* (1940).

Herbert Jedin, *History of the Council of Trent*, tr. by Ernest Graf, 2 vols. (1957–1961).

Notes

1. Cited in Hans Hillerbrand, ed., *The Reformation: A Narrative History Related by Contemporary Observers and Participants* (New York: Harper and Row, 1964), p. 428.
2. *The Spiritual Exercises of St. Ignatius*, tr. by Anthony Mottola (New York: Image Books, 1964), p. 428.
3. Cited in Hillerbrand, *Reformation*, pp. 446–447.
4. Cited in Theodore Rabb, *Renaissance Lives: Portraits of an Age* (New York: Pantheon Books, 1993), p. 107.
5. Cited in John O'Malley, *The First Jesuits* (Cambridge, Mass.: Harvard University Press, 1993), p. 76.
6. *The Life of St. Teresa by Herself*, tr. by J. M. Cohen (New York: Penguin, 1957), pp. 206–208.
7. Ibid., pp. 268–270.
8. Ibid., p. 19.
9. Cited in Hillerbrand, *Reformation*, pp. 460–461.
10. Cited in Alister McGrath, *Reformation Thought: An Introduction*, 2nd ed. (Oxford: Blackwell, 1993), p. 156.
11. Cited in DeLamar Jensen, *Reformation Europe: Age of Reform and Reconciliation*, 2nd ed. (Lexington, Mass.: D. C. Heath, 1992), p. 216.

12

AN AGE OF RELIGIOUS WARFARE, 1546–1660

The willingness to tolerate a diversity of opinion on some matters of religious doctrine and practice displayed by people like Cardinal Gasparo Contarini, Sebastian Castellio, or Marguerite of Navarre was not in tune with the prevailing sentiments of many in the sixteenth century. For many, to tolerate other opinions on matters of faith was a sign of weak religious convictions, or worse, a tendency toward heresy. Not only did the age suffer from an excess of religious and social intolerance, but there was a tendency on the part of many prominent individuals of the period to declare themselves correct on all major points of doctrine and to demonize their opponents. Martin Luther, for example, regularly referred to the pope as "the devil incarnate" and "a brothel keeper."[1] When some of his theological colleagues disagreed with him on points of doctrine which he considered clearly established, they were castigated as "false brethren" and sometimes worse. Luther's Catholic and Protestant opponents replied in kind. Even Philip Melanchthon, Luther's close friend and partner in reform, admitted that he was at times "a violent physician," while excusing his rhetorical excesses as caused by "the magnitude of the age's disorders."[2]

What made the bombast of the theologians particularly dangerous was that many of those in political power shared their intolerance of the ideas of others. Emperor Charles V, for example, referred to the Lutheran Reformation as an "evil movement, which seduces the people with false doctrines and incites rebellion."[3] While some political authorities saw in the Reformation an opportunity for them to take over church authority and property, others saw the reform movement as a threat to law, order, and their own power. Charles's son, Philip II of Spain, was typical of those who thought forced conversions were the only way to prevent souls from being damned for all eternity. Most Protestant princes agreed with Philip's position. Many on all sides of the Reformation were willing to use coercion as a way to solve religious and political problems. They believed that religious differences in a state caused factionalism and made the state ungovernable. Religious fanaticism coupled with political power proved to be an explosive mixture in the already fragile economic and social environment of the sixteenth and seventeenth centuries. The end result was wave after wave of widespread death and destruction.

The Empire Strikes Back: The Schmalkaldic War, 1546–1548

Having survived the tremors of the Peasants' War and the assault of the Ottomans on Hungary in 1526, Emperor Charles V was determined to deal firmly with the growing Evangelical movement. Landgrave Philip of Hesse, Duke Johann the Constant of Saxony, and Jacob Sturm of Strasbourg were equally determined to protect their new religious understandings by armed alliance against the emperor if necessary. The failure of peaceful efforts to come to terms with the emperor at the Diet of Augsburg of 1530 resulted in a meeting of Protestant leaders at the town of Schmalkald in the Thuringian forest in December of 1530. There eight princes and ten cities agreed to defend each other if attacked because of their religion.

The signatory powers had come to agree with Landgrave Philip of Hesse and others who argued that lesser magistrates had the right to resist the emperor if he refused to protect or abused the religious rights of his subjects. Some legal theorists asserted that, according to both canon and civil law, anyone who is attacked unjustly has the right to self-defense. Philip of Hesse concurred with that opinion: "Since I must protect my subjects . . . must I wait to protect them after they are dead; what good is that?"[4]

THE DEFECTION OF NUREMBERG AND BRANDENBURG-ANSBACH

Brandenburg-Ansbach and Nuremberg disagreed with the landgrave about their right to resist the emperor by force of arms. They refused to support their fellow Protestants by allying themselves against Charles V and the Catholics. Although unwilling to commit themselves to use the sword against their sovereign, they promised to study the matter and assist by legal means other Protestants who were being proceeded against by the Imperial Supreme Court. The magistrates of Nuremberg and some of their advisors still had grave doubts about whether it was lawful to resist their emperor

by violent means. Even Martin Luther, as a man of peace, still hoped the Evangelicals would not have to arm themselves against the emperor, whom many still viewed as a "father." As late as 1542 he warned the Protestant princes not to be so quick to take up the sword, even in a just cause. He informed the members of the Schmalkaldic League:

> Even if somebody were to kill my father or brother, I am not judge or avenger. What need is there for laws and authorities, what for God, if everybody wanted himself to be judge, avenger, even God over his neighbor, especially in worldly matters.[5]

The wealthy merchants in control of Nuremberg also worried that the formation of an anti-Catholic league would escalate tensions. Rising tensions might eventually result in a war that would destroy international trade, the basis of Nuremberg's prosperity. Brandenburg-Ansbach, Nuremberg's neighbor and ally, followed the imperial city's lead on this matter. Despite these important defections, the Schmalkaldic League was able to add additional members and become a force to be reckoned with.

A TRUCE WITH THE OTTOMANS

The Schmalkaldic League was saved from an immediate test of strength by the advance of the Ottomans toward Vienna in the summer of 1532. Horrified by the Ottoman advance, Emperor Charles arranged for a truce with the Protestants at Nuremberg. He agreed to summon a church council within a year, quash all cases against Protestants pending in the Imperial Chamber Court, and postpone the question of confiscated church property. In return the Protestants sent troops, weapons, and money to aid the Habsburgs in their campaign against the forces of Süleyman the Magnificent. The imperial forces defeated the Ottomans sixty miles southeast of Vienna at Grens. The sultan sent raiding parties throughout Austria, but withdrew the bulk of his army. In June of 1533 the Ottomans made peace with the Habsburgs, allowing Charles's brother, Ferdinand, to continue to hold the western part of Hungary in exchange for the payment of tribute to the sultan.

The Ottomans joined with sea raiders from Algeria and Tunisia in naval attacks on the Mediterranean coast of Italy and Spain. Charles V defended his empire and succeeded in capturing Tunis in North Africa in 1535. His great enemy, François I of France, shocked Europe by concluding a treaty with Sultan Süleyman that gave France the right to trade inside the Ottoman Empire. King François then marched into Savoy, which he claimed through his mother. His real objective was the rich duchy of Milan. Emperor Charles then counterattacked in French Provence and Languedoc. None of these attacks succeeded, and finally in 1538 the warring kings agreed to peace at Nice.

IMPERIAL INITIATIVES

The emperor then resumed his efforts to find a peaceful resolution to the religious differences in the Holy Roman Empire. He pressured the papacy to sponsor a general reform council, which finally bore fruit with the convening of the Council of Trent in 1545. Even before that, Charles had sponsored discussions between Catholic and Protestant theologians at Speyer, Hagenau, Worms, Leipzig, and Regensburg in 1540 and 1541. Although many areas of agreement were found, fundamental divisions remained.

In that same period, the truce with France collapsed as François I sent naval units to support the Muslims in their war in the Mediterranean and then sent French troops into the Low Countries. A Habsburg fleet was destroyed by a storm off the coast of Algiers in October 1541. Süleyman the Magnificent then resumed his conquests in western Hungary and the Danube valley. Inside the Holy Roman Empire, additional territories became Protestant and even the archbishop of Cologne, Herman von Wied, allowed Martin Bucer and Philip Melanchthon to introduce Protestantism into his lands in 1542.

Faced with enormous pressures on all sides, Emperor Charles managed to conclude a new alliance with King Henry VIII of England and attacked the duchy of Cleves, a recently acquired ally of the French. He then continued his offensive in the west, marching to within sight of Paris. A startled François I quickly agreed to peace at Crépy in September 1544. An armistice with the Ottomans soon followed.

When it became apparent that the Council of Trent was not going to solve the religious fissures in Germany, Charles concluded that it was time to use military force to hold his empire together while his truces with France and the Ottoman Empire held. The death of Martin Luther in February of 1546 removed a strong voice for peace in the empire and made the emperor doubly eager to strike rapidly should the Lutherans be in disarray. First, Charles shored up support among various Catholic princes in the empire, such as the powerful duke of Bavaria. Then Charles won the support of the ambitious Protestant Duke Moritz of ducal Saxony (r. 1541–1553) by promising him the electoral title, which then was lodged in the hands of his cousin, Johann Frederick (d. 1554), the heavy drinking duke of electoral Saxony. Moritz was soon called a "Judas" by his fellow Protestants.

THE BATTLE OF MÜHLBERG, 1547

Duke Moritz invaded electoral Saxony in November 1546, which caused Elector Johann Frederick to abandon his Schmalkaldic League allies in the south and rush to his homeland's defense. The gout-afflicted emperor was thus able to increase his forces and assume control of much of the Rhineland and southern Germany. Meanwhile, Johann Frederick was enjoying military success against both Moritz and King Ferdinand (Charles's brother). The emperor moved north to relieve Moritz and managed to surprise Johann Frederick at the Battle of Mühlberg on the Elbe River on April 24, 1547. The elector had only a third of his army with him and was captured during the battle. He was forced to cede his electoral title and much of his land to Moritz. Philip of Hesse surrendered a short time later. The Schmalkaldic League had been utterly humiliated, and the emperor seemed poised to realize his dream of forcing the Protestants to return to the church of Rome.

Titian, *Emperor Charles V at Mühlberg*. Prado, Madrid, Spain. Alinari/Art Resource. This is an idealized image because, in reality, Charles had to be carried on a litter throughout much of the campaign because of painful attacks of gout.

THE AUGSBURG AND LEIPZIG INTERIMS

The victorious emperor followed up his military success by presenting the Imperial Diet of Augsburg of 1547–1548 with a document known as the *Augsburg Interim*, which was to give the empire a temporary religious policy until the Council of Trent could complete its work. For the most part, it restated traditional Catholic doctrines, but offered a few concessions to the Protestants, such as permitting clerical marriages with papal dispensation and allowing for communion with both bread and wine. Although formally accepted by a majority of the estates at Augsburg, hardly anyone was satisfied with it. Pope Paul III felt too much had been conceded to the Protestants; militant Protestants considered it far too Catholic. Philip Melanchthon and Julius Pflug, the irenic Catholic bishop of Naumburg, at the urging of Duke Moritz of Saxony, drafted a more Protestant *Leipzig Interim*, but that too was rejected by the many hardliners on both sides.

SPLITS IN LUTHERANISM

The arguments over the Augsburg and Leipzig *Interims* marked the first major fissures in the Lutheran movement after the death of Luther. Philip Melanchthon was criticized severely for his willingness to compromise on what he considered nonessentials of doctrine and practice. For example, Melanchthon was willing to accept the episcopal system in the interest of religious peace. His opponents were led by a fiery Slav, Flacius Illyricus (1520–1575), and Nicholas von Amsdorf (1483–1565). Flacius was a former humanist educated at Venice, Basel, and Tübingen. He argued that there were no nonessentials in Lutheranism. Flacius soon left his position as a professor of Hebrew at Wittenberg for Magdeburg, where he became one of the most outspoken leaders of the Gnesiolutherans, or conservative Lutherans.

Nicholas von Amsdorf was born at Torgau in Saxony to a noble family. A nephew of Johann von Staupitz, Amsdorf earned his licentiate in theology from Wittenberg, where he studied under Martin Luther and Philip Melanchthon. One of the first converts to Lutheranism, Amsdorf accompanied Luther to the Leipzig debate in 1519 and to Worms in 1521 and served on the faculty of his alma mater. He later helped reform Magdeburg, Goslar, and Einbeck before becoming the Lutheran bishop of Naumburg/Zeitz in 1541. A close friend and advisor to Elector Johann Frederick, Amsdorf was driven into exile during the Schmalkaldic War. He considered Melanchthon too open to compromise. Therefore, he helped found a new university at Jena because he thought Wittenberg was too much under the influence of the "Philippists," as the supporters of Melanchthon were called.

The Schmalkaldic War and its aftermath had revealed the fragile nature of Lutheran unity. Another victim of the war and its aftermath was Katherine Luther. She had been forced to flee Wittenberg several times when it was threatened by imperial troops. Then in the fall of 1550, an attack of the plague hit Wittenberg and with two of her children, Katherine had set out for Torgau. Her horses bolted and she was thrown from her wagon into a ditch filled with cold water. Nursed for three months by her daughter, Margaret, age eighteen, Katherine Luther died on December 20, 1550. Her last known words were, "I will stick to Christ as a burr to a top coat."[6]

THE RELIGIOUS PEACE
OF AUGSBURG OF 1555

Meanwhile Emperor Charles found himself abandoned by his ally, Duke Moritz of Saxony. Moritz had become impatient with the emperor's refusal to release his father-in-law, Philip of Hesse, from prison in the Low Countries. More importantly, he found it difficult being accepted as the ruler of Lutheran Saxony while being known as the "betrayer of the Gospel." To demonstrate his Lutheranism, he called upon Philip Melanchthon to restore the University of Wittenberg along strictly Lutheran lines. Moritz helped revive the Schmalkaldic League by taking in new members and joining in an alliance with the new king of France, Henri II, who invaded the empire from the west and seized the fortress cities of Metz, Toul, and Verdun. In 1552 Duke Moritz, at the head of a Protestant army, marched on Charles V at Innsbruck. The imperial forces were taken by surprise and the emperor was forced to flee and agree to peace negotiations.

Worn out and bitterly disappointed by the failure of his imperial policies, Charles turned over German affairs to Ferdinand, his brother and successor. Earlier, he had attempted to bypass Ferdinand and have his son, Philip, succeed him in both Spain and the empire. Ferdinand, who had for so many years served his brother as regent in the empire, refused to accept this and threatened a Habsburg civil war. Charles backed down and agreed to support Ferdinand as the Habsburg candidate for the imperial dignity. It was King Ferdinand who presided over the Diet of Augsburg, which met from February to September 1555.

The recess of the Diet of Augsburg provided a measure of religious peace for the empire, which lasted almost until 1618. By its terms, the Lutheran estates in the empire were given legal recognition and permitted to retain all their acquired territories. Imperial cities that had adopted Lutheranism had to allow and protect the rights of minority Catholics to worship in the Catholic churches that had been reopened after the

1548 *Interim*. In princely territories, the ruler decided the religion of all his subjects. Only Catholicism and Lutheranism were recognized by the Religious Peace of Augsburg. Every ecclesiastical prince who became Protestant would forfeit his title, lands, and privileges.

Emperor Charles V was not happy with the concessions his brother had been forced to make to the Lutherans in the Holy Roman Empire, but his years of trying to hold his vast, multinational empire together had left him exhausted. A month after the Diet of Augsburg ended, the ailing emperor turned over his authority in the Low Countries to his son, Philip. In 1556 he became the first Holy Roman emperor to abdicate. He then turned over his Spanish possessions to Philip and retired to a palace near the Jeronimite monastery of Yuste in southwestern Spain, where he died two years later.

The Religious Wars in France

The Holy Roman Empire was not the only part of Europe to become a battleground because of religious differences. Hatred of religious pluralism was also a staple of French society and a matter of royal policy. Despite the vigorous persecutions of King François I and his son, Henri II, Calvinism made slow but steady progress in France. John Calvin had been sending out missionaries trained in Geneva for many years trying to convert his fellow French to his brand of Protestantism. Young Henri II was even less tolerant of the Huguenots (French Protestants, from the Swiss-German term *Eidgenossen*, or confederates) than his father had been. Upon coming to the throne in 1547, he had created a special committee (called the "Burning Chamber") of the Parlement of Paris to suppress heresy.

François Clouet, *Henri II of France*. Louvre, Paris, France. Giraudon/Art Resource.

THE REIGN OF HENRI II (r. 1547–1559)

Although he had been married at age fourteen to Catherine de' Medici, Henri's constant companion and most influential advisor was his beloved mistress, Diane de Poitiers, a well-read and politically astute woman. She viewed the Huguenots as representing a threat to her lover's authority and joined Charles de Guise, archbishop of Rheims, in urging Henri to be severe with them. In spite of these persecutions, the well-organized Huguenot movement continued to grow and came to include even members of the nobility, such as the king's cousins from the house of Bourbon. Because the king was distracted by yet another round of war with Habsburg Spain, suppression of the Calvinists proved impossible.

In 1559 King Henri II finally agreed to peace with Spain by signing the very important Peace of Cateau-Cambrésis. In order to create "perpetual peace," Henri's daughter, Elizabeth of Valois, was married to King Philip II of Spain, who had recently lost his second wife, Queen Mary Tudor of England. As part of the festivities surrounding the royal nuptials, a great tournament was held in late June in which King Henri, a veteran jouster, eagerly participated. On the last joust of the day, the king was struck in the eye by a piece of his opponent's shattered lance. Twelve days later Henri II died of complications from his wound.

THE POWER OF CATHERINE DE' MEDICI (1519–1589)

Henri's beloved and influential mistress, Diane de Poitiers, was dismissed from the court by order of Queen Catherine de' Medici, whose sickly fifteen-year-old son, François II (r. 1559–1560), took the throne. Educated by nuns, Catherine was the daughter of Lorenzo de' Medici (1492–1519), nephew of Pope Leo X. She became a dominant figure in the reigns of her three sons. Catherine shared many of the common prejudices against the Huguenots, who in 1559 had held a major synod, or convention. She also hoped that religious civil war could be avoided.

Queen Catherine was disappointed by the growing militancy displayed by both sides, as well as by the growing influence exerted over her young son by the house of Guise, fanatical champions of Catholic orthodoxy. Rumors circulated that the Protestants planned to burn down the city of Paris and, if that failed, to kidnap the king at Amboise and force him to recognize their reli-

gion or to abdicate in favor of the Bourbons. The conspiracy of Amboise was discovered, and its ringleaders were harshly punished in the spring of 1560. The incident left an important legacy of fear in the minds of many Catholics, including the queen mother.

THE SAINT BARTHOLOMEW'S DAY MASSACRE

When the young king died unexpectantly in December of 1560, the savvy Catherine was named regent for her nine-year-old son, Charles IX (r. 1560–1574). She supported a policy of moderation and easing of the persecutions against the Calvinists. The queen also sponsored discussions between Catholic and Protestant theologians at Poissy in 1561 and St. Germain-en-Laye early in 1562. Despite the clear presentations of Calvinist theology by Theodore Beza and the willingness of some moderate Catholics to compromise, neither group could find common ground on the nature of the "true church" and the importance of images. Extremism dominated as France drifted toward religious civil war. Because of apocalyptic fears, the failure of compromise, religious bigotry, and desires for power by various factions, a series of isolated clashes between Catholics and Protestants led to a general outbreak of religious warfare in 1562, which lasted, on and off, for the next ten years.

Finally by 1572, it appeared that both Protestants and Catholics were ready to end the bloodletting. The Peace of Saint Germain was to be followed by a great celebration on Saint Bartholomew's Day, August 24. There was much to celebrate, for the king's sister, Marguerite of Valois, had just married Henri of Navarre, the dashing young Huguenot leader. Surely this happy union would put an end to the religious civil wars in France.

The religious peace and the wedding of

Anonymous, *Portrait of Catherine de' Medici.*
Palazzo Medici Riccardi, Florence, Italy.
Alinari/Art Resource.

Marguerite and Henri attracted thousands of Huguenots to Paris, including their most influential leader, Gaspard de Coligny, admiral of France. Weddings between prominent families were great occasions. Coligny had been urging the king to intervene in the Low Countries against Philip of Spain. Assassins, possibly encouraged by Henri, duke of Guise, plotted Coligny's murder in revenge for his alleged agreement to the murder of Henri's father in 1563. The admiral's attackers initially succeeded only in wounding him, and the Protestant leaders demanded that the culprits be punished. On the night of August 23, fearing a Huguenot plot against the crown, King Charles gave the order to exterminate the Protestant leadership in Paris.

On the morning of Saint Bartholomew's Day, a detachment of the king's Swiss Guard led by the duke of Guise broke down the door to Coligny's house and murdered him in the ensuing scuffle. The duke of Guise then urged his followers to begin killing other nearby Huguenots: "kill them, kill them all, it is the king's command!"[7] The murder of Coligny sparked a general slaughter of Huguenots in Paris, which spread to the countryside over the next several weeks. Thousands were murdered. Henri of Navarre escaped the assassin's blade by promising to convert to Roman Catholicism. He was detained for three months in Paris, but eventually managed to escape to the countryside to rally the surviving Huguenot forces.

When news of the massacre reached Madrid, the usually dour Philip II could not repress a smile. In Rome, special church services were held to commemorate the massacre. However, many Catholics were appalled by the level of hatred and violence in France. Protestant leaders such as Elizabeth of England protested the new outbursts of religious and political violence in the French kingdom. Many Protestant propagandists blamed Catherine de' Medici ("the wicked Italian queen") for the massacre, but it is unlikely that she condoned such extensive atrocities after years of trying to maintain peace between Huguenots and Catholics and her general high level of political astuteness. Guilt probably added to the instability and poor health of King Charles IX, who died two years after the massacre.

THE REIGN OF HENRI III (r. 1574–1589)

Charles was succeeded by his twenty-three-year-old brother, Henri III. An intelligent prince, Henri was in much better physical health than either of his elder brothers and had commanded royal armies in victories over the Huguenots when he was only eighteen. In 1573 he had been elected king of Poland, but he was unhappy there and eagerly fled the country after learning of the death of his brother. As king of France, Henri resumed the war against the Calvinists, but in April 1576 he agreed to a truce that recognized the legality of Protestantism.

This unprecedented display of toleration gravely upset the duke of Guise and other hardline Catholics determined to exterminate the Huguenots. Eventually Henri of Guise formed the Catholic League with support from Spain and the papacy. It became a powerful force and helped to contribute to the next agonizing round of religious and civil wars. Some of the misery of the period is shown in the revival of flagel-lants, not seen in France in large numbers since the time of the Black Death in the middle of the fourteenth century.

In June of 1584, the duke of Anjou, younger brother of the king, died. Openly homosexual, Henri III showered his affections and favors—such as choice lands, titles, and honors—on a series of handsome young men. To pay for his extravagant court and the expenses of the civil wars, the intelligent but erratic king raised taxes on the already strained peasantry and confiscated the estates of some nobles. With the death of the last Valois heir, the Huguenot Henri of Navarre was next in line for the throne of France. Henri was the son of Antoine of Bourbon, king of Navarre, who vacillated between Catholicism and Protestantism. His mother, Jeanne d'Albret (1528–1572), daughter of Marguerite of Navarre, was a

Engraving of Flagellants (1583). Bibliotheque Nationale, Paris, France. Giraudon/Art Resource.

staunch Protestant. When chided by a papal legate for her support of the Huguenots, she responded, "Your feeble arguments do not dent my tough skull. I am serving God and He knows how to sustain his cause."[8]

POLITICAL THEORISTS

With Jeanne d'Albret's energetic son destined to inherit the throne of France, Protestant political theorists turned from justifying rebellion against royal authority to writing in praise of the monarch as the embodiment of sovereignty. For example, in *Six Books of the Commonwealth* (1576), the lawyer Jean Bodin argued that the chief end of the state was the preservation of peace, justice, and private property, which can best be done where sovereignty is not divided, as in a monarchy. Although "all princes of the earth are subject to the laws of God and of nature, and even to certain human laws common to all nations," they are not subject to the authority of others.[9] Moderate intellectuals called *politiques* ("politicals") hoped that a way could be found to assure religious coexistence between Catholics and Protestants.

One of the foremost of the *politiques* was Michel de Montaigne (1533–1592). Montaigne was the son of a prosperous merchant family in the area of Bordeaux. His father taught him to read, write, and speak Latin. Educated in the law, he became a magistrate in the Parlement of Bordeaux (superior court) until ill health forced him into a life of study and writing. He is best known for his series of *Essays*, which explored the human condition and acknowledged the limitations of human reason. In the face of the upheavals caused by the religious civil wars in France, Montaigne urged moderation, take the "middle way, wide and open."[10] Be yourself and let others be themselves was his plea. After an extended

Portrait of Montaigne (copy of a seventeenth-century original). Private Collection. Giraudon/Art Resource.

period of travel in Europe searching out the healing qualities of mineral baths, he returned to Bordeaux and served two terms as mayor.

THE WAR OF THE THREE HENRIES, 1587–1589

Tragically, Montaigne's pleas for toleration were ignored and France soon found itself in another nasty round of civil war. The ensuing conflict was known as the War of the Three Henries, named after its three major participants: King Henri III, Henri, duke of Guise, and Henri of Navarre. In the autumn of 1587, Huguenot forces led by Henri of Navarre routed a royal army at Coutras near Bordeaux. The scar-faced Henri of Guise had more success against Protestant mercenaries in the northeast, but was angered by the king's failure to send him royal troops. He then marched on Paris in May of 1588, forcing the king to flee to Chartres for safety. Wildly popular in the capital as the champion of militant Catholicism, Guise was proclaimed "king of Paris."

While Guise was planning his next move in consultation with the aging but still shrewd Catherine de' Medici, Henri III learned of the defeat of the Spanish Armada and determined to rid France of Guise and his Spanish backers. He invited Guise and his brother, the cardinal of Lorraine, to a secret meeting and had them murdered on December 22, 1588, as traitors to the crown. King Henri was in turn denounced as a tyrant and a traitor by the Catholic League and soon fled to the camp of his Protestant rival, Henri of Navarre, whom he agreed to accept as his heir. The king then met with his estates at Blois and presented them with a reorganized government. With the help of Navarre, Henri III planned to retake Paris, but he was assassinated on August 1, 1589, by a friar who thought the king was a traitor for being willing to accept a Protestant as his successor. The surviving Henri (Navarre) now declared himself to be king of France as Henri IV, but Paris refused to recognize his authority. Half of the kingdom was in the hands of the Catholic League and its Spanish allies.

HENRI OF NAVARRE AS KING OF FRANCE, 1589–1610

A five-year struggle followed as the Catholics and Spain were determined that a Huguenot would never be allowed to hold the throne of St. Denis. King Philip II of Spain dispatched his best general, Alexander Farnese, duke of Parma (1542–1592), from the Low Countries to France. He lifted Henri IV's siege of Paris in the summer of 1590. However, when Parma died from

wounds in battle in 1592, Spanish power in France ebbed. The king's pragmatic fifth reconversion to Catholicism in 1593 further undermined the Catholic League's willingness to resist Henri's authority. Thinking that "Paris is well worth a Mass," Henri realized that he could never truly be king of France if his religion was different from 90 percent of his subjects. The Catholic majority needed to have its fears of the Huguenot minority alleviated, or so the king was advised by his leading counselor, the duke of Sully, who remained a Protestant.

A short bundle of charm and vitality, the gallant king eventually became one of the most popular sovereigns in French history. He faced a mountain of debt, a country ravaged by two decades of civil war, and enemies on all sides. Even his Bourbon dynasty was not secure, as he and Marguerite of Valois had failed to conceive a son after twenty-one years of marriage. Henri petitioned Pope Clement VIII (r. 1592–1605) for both absolution and a divorce. Fearing a repeat of the English experience under Henry VIII, Jesuits in Rome persuaded the pope to grant both. In return, Henri promised to be a loyal servant of the church. In 1600 the king, notorious for his many love affairs, married Marie de' Medici of Florence in a politically motivated match. They eventually produced a legitimate male heir, the future Louis XIII.

Not until his long war with Spain had ended in 1598 and several of his rebellious nobles had been subdued by bribery and/or force was King Henri IV able to give a large measure of civil and religious liberty to his Protestant subjects. In his "Edict of Nantes" of 1598, Henri granted religious liberty to French Huguenots. They would be allowed 75 fortified towns plus other fortified places in which to exercise freedom of religion in addition to the right to worship in the lands of Huguenot nobles. Huguenots were declared eligible for public office and guaranteed the right to use schools and other facilities on an equal basis with Catholics. The Edict also declared Catholicism to be the official state church and restored to it its former income, possessions, and rights. Although it did not satisfy extremists, the Edict of Nantes was usually enforced by the king until his death in 1610. It did provide a strong measure of peace to a land long devastated by religious and civil war.

With the aid of his able superintendent of finances, the duke of Sully, Henri launched a major economic reform program. Government debt was reduced, tax collecting improved, roads and bridges were rebuilt, farm land was reclaimed, grain export restrictions were eased, and silkworm cultivation was introduced into southern France. The king genuinely hoped to improve the quality of life for the peasantry to the extent that every peasant family would have a chicken in the pot for Sunday dinner. This promise was never fulfilled for all areas, but it is significant that Henri and Sully made the effort. Few other sixteenth-century rulers were overly concerned about the welfare of the working masses. Little wonder that so many French people came to revere him as "Henri the Grand" and mourn his death to a monk-assassin, who apparently doubted the sincerity of his Catholicism.

Henri's reputation might have suffered had he realized some of his later military ambitions for expansion to the east. It is intriguing to note that at the time of his murder, Henri IV was planning to establish a sort of "united states of Europe." Given the state-building mentality of the time and the jealousy of French power, it is not likely that Henri could have achieved his grand design through diplomacy. To create such a confederation of territorial states by military means would have meant a series of bloody conflicts with the Habsburgs and others. The king's early death kept his subjects from paying the full price of their sovereign's ambitions.

Philip II's Crusades

Although many had doubts about the extent of Henri IV's commitment to Catholicism, no one had any about that of Philip of Habsburg's. Philip of Spain was the most powerful ruler of the late sixteenth century. His father, Charles V, had bestowed the lion's share of his vast empire upon Philip. In addition to mighty Spain, Philip had inherited

Titian, *Portrait of Philip II*. Prado, Madrid, Spain. Alinari/Art Resource.

the Burgundian Low Countries, Luxembourg, Franche-Comté, Naples, Sicily, Sardinia, Corsica, the Balearic Islands, Milan, and all of the Spanish holdings along the west coast of Africa and in the Western Hemisphere. In 1580 Philip conquered Portugal in the name of his Portuguese mother and added Portugal's huge eastern empire to his dominions. He also sponsored the colonization of the Philippines, which are still named after him. The introverted Spanish sovereign could claim legal authority over more of the earth's surface than any other monarch in history.

THE CHARACTER OF THE KING

Philip II of Spain was a very complex individual. Cautious, hardworking, and patient, he was notorious for his attention to details. Because he was afraid to trust his subordinates, almost every state document of importance passed through his hands, which made the inner workings of his government cumbersome indeed. He treated servants and nobles alike with equal courtesy. Devoted to his children, Philip of Spain was also a major friend of the arts and learning. Sofonisba Anguissola and Titian were just two of the many artists to benefit from his good taste and eye for talent. He also established academies to promote mathematics and the sciences.

At the core of Philip's being was a deep sense of religious duty. Religion was his solace from the deep tragedies of his personal life and the difficulties of his governmental responsibilities. In rapid succession he lost his mother, father, sister, four wives, one daughter, and four sons. His sense of obligation to Catholicism added additional burdens to his already troubled soul. Philip took it upon himself to use the wealth and power of his vast empire to restore the dominion of the Roman Catholic church over

as much of Europe as possible. Furthermore, he thought it was his divine mandate to protect Christendom from the forces of Islam.

WAR AGAINST ISLAM

Philip II distrusted the thousands of Moriscos (nominally Christian Moors) who lived in his southern Spanish provinces and had gradually been reverting to Islamic practices. On occasion, some Moriscos had aided some of the Muslim sea raiders. Philip and others feared that they would one day open the gates of Spain to the Muslims of North Africa. In January 1567, the king issued a royal decree ordering the Moriscos to cease practicing Islam and using the Arabic tongue. The Moriscos of Granada responded by revolting against the authority of Philip's government. Aided by Arab allies from Algiers and other Muslim lands, the rebellion dragged on for two years. Both sides committed unspeakable atrocities.

Finally, Philip's illegitimate half brother, Don Juan of Austria (1547–1578), succeeded in crushing the rebels. By a royal edict of 1570, the Moriscos of Granada were ordered to leave their homes and settle among the Christians of Castile and Aragon. In 1609 Philip issued an edict that expelled them from all of Spain.

Before that, the monarch had experienced an even greater triumph against the Ottomans at the naval battle of Lepanto, despite humiliating defeats in the Low Countries, England, and France.

In 1566 Sultan Süleyman the Magnificent died and was succeeded by his son, Selim II (r. 1566–1574), who was eager to get out from under his illustrious father's considerable shadow. To do that Selim thought he needed to make his own reputation as a conqueror. Selim's ambitions were opposed by an aggressive new pope, Pius V (r. 1566–1572), who called for a new crusade against the Ottomans. The pope's calls for holy war took on extra significance when Selim's forces conquered the island of Cyprus in 1570. Philip II joined with Venice and the pope in a new Holy League. A huge fleet was assembled under the command of Philip's half brother, Don Juan of Austria, in the fall of 1571.

On October 7 the Christian fleet engaged the Ottomans in the Bay of Lepanto off the east coast of Greece. The battle involved over 400 galleys and 160,000 participants. The Christians had 1,815 naval guns, which destroyed at least seventy Ottoman galleys. The battle raged for three hours and resulted in a major victory for the Holy League. Not until the seventeenth century would the Ottomans be able to resume their naval war against Christian Europe in the Mediterranean on a full scale. The youthful Don Juan became the romanticized military hero of the moment among Christians. His brother, Philip II, thought that God was indeed on his side and was encouraged by the great victory at Lepanto to attempt new crusades, this time against various Protestants, whom he also viewed as spawn of the devil.

THE REVOLT OF THE LOW COUNTRIES

The Spanish Lowlands (Netherlands) were the richest part of Philip II's vast empire. The Netherlanders had taken a large portion of the herring trade and international commerce from their rivals. Their farmers were some of the most efficient in Europe. However, Philip, unlike his father, Charles V, was considered to be an unsympathetic foreigner who taxed their prosperous trade and commerce for the benefit of Spain. Emperor Charles V, after all, had been born in Ghent and grown up in the Flemish-speaking provinces of Flanders and Brabant. Although Philip's policies were not that much different from his father's, the Netherland-

ers never trusted Philip as much as they had his predecessor. The area was already suffering through a series of economic and social crises in the 1560s when Philip II decided to move against Protestants. In 1566 he outlined his policy to the Spanish ambassador at Rome: "I neither intend nor desire to be the ruler of heretics. If things cannot be remedied as I wish without recourse to arms, I am determined to go to war."[11]

Philip's policy of repression touched off a war which resulted in the independence of more than half of the Low Countries. Tensions that had been slowly increasing between the king and his subjects escalated when the Habsburg king sponsored a much-needed reorganization of the church in the Netherlands in 1565. The existing structure was cumbersome and awkward and left a lot of freedom of action to local magnates, who enjoyed their privileges. Philip pressured the church to create fifteen new bishoprics, which was protested by a group of nobles led by William of Nassau, prince of Orange (1533–1584). In August petitions were sent to the king asking for an easing of the religious persecutions. When he refused, William of Orange and several others resigned from the Council of State.

In April 1566 a large body of the lesser nobles presented a request to Philip's regent and half sister, Margaret of Parma, that the king allow the States General to deal with the religious problem. During their interview with the regent, one of Margaret's counselor's referred to the rowdy nobles as "those beggars." The label was quickly adopted by the leaders of the opposition as an appropriate reflection of the contempt in which the Netherlanders were held by the ruling Spanish. In the summer of 1566, bands of rebels began desecrating Catholic churches, smashing stained glass windows, altar paintings, and statues.

Philip II dispatched the "Iron duke" of Alba (1507–1582) from Genoa to the Netherlands. Alba arrived in Brussels with an imposing army of 10,000 mostly Spanish and Italian troops in August 1567 and promptly set up a "Council of Blood," which took swift and brutal actions against suspected heretics. Margaret of Parma resigned, protesting Alba's severity. Alba was named to replace her and continued his reign of terror for six years. Thousands were put to death. The duke further antagonized the Dutch by levying a permanent sales tax.

William of Orange found refuge in Holland and Zeeland, where he led resistance to the authority of Alba. He proved a worthy opponent for the Spanish and came to be widely respected for his courage, intelligence, and tactical abilities. William married Charlotte de Bourbon, the daughter of a French duke, who made a fine home for his children from two previous marriages and ran his estates with great efficiency. He was also aided by daring Dutch privateers, called "Sea Beggars," who attacked the coastal towns and crippled Spanish shipping and communications. Alba was recalled in 1573, but the revolt continued under other governors when the rebels refused to lay down their arms, even though Philip offered to cease the hated sales tax.

In 1578 the king turned to his talented young nephew, Alexander Farnese (1545–1592), the son of Margaret of Parma. An able diplomat, Parma managed in 1579 to persuade ten of the southern provinces to reaffirm their loyalty to Philip II and "maintain good government and the Catholic church" in the Union of Arras.[12] William of Orange countered by organizing the seven northern states into their own Protestant Union of Utrecht, which continued the revolt with great vigor. William was assassinated by a hireling of Philip II in the summer of 1584. The rebels found capable new leaders such as William's son, Maurice of Nassau (1567–1625), and the shrewd lawyer Jan van Oldenbarneveldt (1547–1619).

The Dutch rebels also persuaded Elizabeth I of England in 1585 to send them an army of 6,000 men under the command of her favorite, Robert Dudley, earl of Leicester. Elizabeth had been sending the rebels money, and at times she allowed the "Sea Beggars" to use English ports. The fall of Antwerp and Brussels to the Spanish made the situation appear even more threatening. Leicester had to be withdrawn a year and a half later for incompetence, one of the queen's rare lapses in her judgment of men and situations. Despite the mixed blessings of English help, the Dutch under Maurice of Nassau succeeded in driving out the last remnants of the Spanish forces. Finally in 1609, eleven years after Philip II's death, Spain agreed to a twelve-year truce. The full independence of the Calvinist "United Provinces" was formally recognized in 1648 as part of the general treaties at the conclusion of the central European phase of the Thirty Years' War (1618–1648). Philip II's agents were able to preserve Catholicism only in the southern provinces of the Low Countries.

As for the United Provinces, they soon became the world's leader in commercial activity. In the course of the long war with Spain, they had seized the richest part of the Portuguese empire in the East Indies. The products of the East poured into Dutch ports and were exchanged for goods from all over Europe. Dutch ships were some of the best designed in the world and could carry more than any of their competitors. The French finance minister, J. B. Colbert, estimated that the Dutch came to control 75 percent of Europe's merchant marine by the second half of the seventeenth century. Quality products manufactured in the Low Countries were also in high demand, including new optical instruments. Amsterdam became a major center of finance.

The wealth of the Netherlands was reflected in the high levels of patronage and support for major artists such as Judith Leyster (1609–1661), Frans Hals (c. 1581–1666), Jan Vermeer (1632–1675), Rembrandt van Rijn (1606–1669), and many others. Rembrandt is often considered the greatest painter of the seventeenth century and one of the very best of all time. Dutch artists painted not only religious subjects, but also portrayed the lives of people of all stations. Obviously the expanding merchant class had plenty of money to invest in art. With the innovative ideas of the jurist Hugo Grotius (1583–1645) in international law and Baruch Spinoza (1632–1677), a Jewish lens grinder, in philosophy, along with numerous scientific and technological breakthroughs, the seventeenth century proved

Rembrandt van Rijn, *Self-Portrait* (c. 1657). Kunsthistorisches Museum, Vienna, Austria. Foto Marburg / Art Resource.

to be a golden age for the enterprising Dutch.

THE SPANISH ARMADA OF 1588

The most grandiose of King Philip II's crusading efforts was his attempt to restore wayward England to the Roman Catholic fold. His first move had been to marry England's Catholic queen, Mary Tudor. This was done in 1554, two years before the start of his own rule over the Spanish empire. Mary's marriage to the future king of a feared and hated rival power and her bloody persecutions of English Protestants diminished her popularity and that of her beloved church in England. Moreover, the marriage failed to produce a Catholic heir. When the unhappy Mary died in 1558, Philip sought to continue his influence in England by trying to court Mary's sister and successor, Elizabeth.

For her part, Elizabeth was determined to marry no one as we have seen. She loved being queen and having power. Marriage to an ambitious consort meant giving up or sharing power. She loved being a sovereign and saw no reason to give up her freedom and authority. Therefore, the "Virgin Queen" refused to marry despite the pressures of her advisors such as William Cecil, who were desperate that she marry in order to produce an heir. Philip of Spain was too important a suitor to spurn outright, so Elizabeth strung him along for a number of years as she would do other suitors throughout her long reign. By the 1570s, Philip was fully aware that she would never marry and instead sought other means for bringing England back to Catholicism. He was encouraged by Catholic exiles and others to liberate England from the Protestant "Jezebel."

Philip's anger at Elizabeth was only increased by her aid to his rebellious Dutch subjects and by the attacks on his shipping by English privateers such as Francis Drake (c. 1540–1596) and John Hawkins (1532–1595). When a Spanish fleet defeated a French fleet in the Azores in 1583, its commander, the marquis of Santa Cruz, urged Philip to follow up his success by launching a naval offensive against England. The cautious Spanish monarch was tempted but thought he still lacked sufficient resources to be successful in such an elaborate enterprise. When Elizabeth sent an army to the Low Countries in 1585 and aided the Huguenots in France, Philip felt compelled to order Santa Cruz and the duke of Parma to draw up their plans for an invasion of England.

With the execution of Mary Stuart, queen of Scots, on February 7, 1587, Philip had an additional excuse for launching his invasion. The staunchly Catholic Mary had been Elizabeth's heir, but with her death a Protestant succession through Mary's son, James, who was being reared a Calvinist in Edinburgh, seemed likely. Mary had encouraged a number of conspiracies against her cousin's life during her long captivity in England, and Elizabeth's patience with her taller and more glamorous rival had at last run out. Philip hailed Mary as a great Catholic martyr and swore to avenge her death. However, numerous delays kept his grand fleet from sailing. Those delays allowed Sir Francis Drake the opportunity to singe the beard of the king of Spain by attacking part of the Spanish fleet at Cadiz harbor in April 1587 and damaging or capturing some thirty vessels, plus valuable war materials, such as wood for the casks which would hold some of the Armada's supplies of fresh water and food.

In February 1588, the Armada's experienced commander, Santa Cruz, died before the fleet was ready to sail. Philip then appointed a very reluctant duke of Medina Sidonia (1549–1592) to take Santa Cruz's place. Although lacking in naval experience, the duke was a fine administrator and by May 1588 he set sail from Lisbon with a fleet of 130 vessels, 20,000 soldiers, 10,000 sailors, and 2,000 guns. They sailed "in the confident hope of a miracle."[13] The English in the meantime had put together a fleet of 190 ships, which rode lower in the water and had more long-range firepower than the Spanish fleet.

The Spanish fleet, somewhat damaged by storms, reached the English Channel at the beginning of August and hoped to be able to gain temporary control of the seas and transport the army of the duke of Parma from the Netherlands to England. Elizabeth of England met with her assembled homeguard troops at Tilbury. Decked out in full armor, Gloriana promised them that she would herself lead them into battle should the Spanish army land in England. The queen proudly informed her soldiers: "I know I have but the body of a weak and feeble woman; but I have the heart and stomach of a King and of a King of England too."[14] Elizabeth knew how to manipulate the prejudices of her audience to full advantage. Such a brave queen seemed well worth dying for.

Meanwhile the Spanish and English fleets had encountered each other in the Channel, but neither side had suffered great damage. When the Armada reached Calais, Medina Sidonia learned that Parma could not reach the coast with his army. Since the Spanish had a shortage of boats that could navigate the shallow coastal waters off Calais, the chances of a successful rendezvous were somewhat limited. Without the transport needed to carry their troops and weapons across the channel, the Spanish would not be able to invade England. In a real sense, the mission had been defeated with most of the mighty Spanish fleet still intact.

On the night of August 7, the English ignited eight of their ships and sent them into the anchored Spanish fleet. The Spaniards feared the burning ships were filled with gunpowder and would explode like bombs in their midst. Dutch rebels had used exploding "hell burners" against the Spanish with great effect years before. Terrible memories of such fire ships lingered among the Spanish and Medina Sidonia gave the order to cut anchors and scatter for safety. The following day the English attacked the Armada before it could fully regroup and inflicted heavy damage. Rather than sail back into the Channel, the Spanish gambled on sailing northward around Scotland, Ireland, and then back home to Spain. Medina Sidonia heroically kept much of his fleet together, despite foul weather, a lack of charts of the treacherous North Sea, and terrible illnesses from insufficient food and water. Less than half of the Spanish fleet ever sailed again.

The defeat of the 1588 Armada did not end the war between England and Spain. The next year Francis Drake led a counterattack against Spain with a huge fleet of 120 ships. Half of them and their crews were lost. Six years later, the Puritan Drake led another expedition against the Spanish, this time to the West Indies, where he hoped to capture a Spanish treasure fleet and destroy Spanish bases in the Americas. Drake's final raid proved a great disaster and he died before returning to England. In 1596 the English did manage to sack Cadiz, which was bravely defended by Medina Sidonia, who burned the fifty ships that the English had hoped to capture. King Philip sent armadas against England later in 1596 and the following year, but they were driven from the Channel by terrible storms. The long and expensive naval duel between England and Spain proved indecisive, except that England kept its Protestantism and its independence. Philip II died in 1598 wondering

why God had not blessed more of his crusades with success.

The Thirty Years' War, 1618–1648

The Religious Peace of Augsburg of 1555, which had brought to a close the first round of armed conflict in the empire between Catholics and Lutherans, proved to be an uneasy truce. Since the signing of the treaty, the Calvinists had made strong headway in several areas of Germany, including the Palatinate, and they demanded legal recognition. Furthermore, lands of the Catholic church were constantly being secularized in Protestant areas, particularly in the north, in violation of the treaty. At the same time Catholics, led by the dukes of Bavaria and the Jesuits, became increasingly aggressive in their desire to regain what they had earlier lost to the Protestants.

Growing political and religious tensions led a group of Evangelical princes and cities to found a Protestant Union in 1608. In response, the Catholics organized a military league under the energetic Duke Maximilian I of Bavaria (1573–1651). Maximilian had been educated at the Jesuit University of Ingolstadt and was determined to use his power to promote Catholicism. Outside the Holy Roman Empire, antagonisms between France and the Habsburgs threatened to erupt into war at any moment. Only the death of the anti-Habsburg leader, King Henri IV, in France, prevented the outbreak of a general European war over a succession dispute in Cleves-Jülich in 1610. A greater crisis soon developed in Bohemia in 1617 when Archduke Ferdinand of Styria, nephew of Holy Roman Emperor Matthias (r. 1612–1619), was designated as king by the Bohemian estates.

As a militant Catholic crusader, Ferdinand was determined to eliminate Protestantism from his domains. He clashed immediately with Bohemia's largely Protestant nobles, who also resented Ferdinand's efforts to increase his authority at the expense of their local privileges. A gathering of Protestant Czech nobles met in Prague in the spring of 1618 to condemn Habsburg policy. Some of them, as a form of protest, tossed two of the Habsburg officials and a secretary out of an upper window of the royal castle in Prague on May 23, 1618, into a dry moat fifty feet below. Their falls were broken somewhat by castle wastes and manure, and all three survived the humiliating, terrifying, and smelly experience, but their master, Ferdinand, was furious with the Czechs for defying his authority.

Hours after learning that Ferdinand had been elected Holy Roman emperor, the Bohemians deposed him as their king and offered the throne to the young Count Frederick V, the Calvinist elector of the Palatinate. The Bohemian rebels were soon joined by Protestants from neighboring Austria, Moravia, Silesia, and Lusatia. However, Frederick's Protestant father-in-law, King James I of England, refused to back him. The Dutch and the German Protestants also offered no real help to Frederick, in whom they had little real confidence. In fact, the Lutheran duke, Johann Georg of Saxony, sided with the emperor, in part motivated by a desire for territorial gain and a hatred of Calvinism. Commanded by Duke Maximilian of Bavaria and Count Johann von Tilly (1559–1632), the Catholic League's army crushed the Bohemian uprising at the Battle of White Mountain near Prague on November 8, 1620. Hundreds of Bohemian nobles were executed and their estates confiscated.

Frederick fled and eventually found refuge in the Hague in the United Provinces. His homeland, the Palatinate, was overrun by Bavarian and Spanish soldiers. In Sep-

tember 1622, Tilly's troops stormed Heidelberg and the first phase of the war was over. Frederick's electoral title was given to Maximilian of Bavaria, who had long coveted the electoral dignity. Duke Johann Georg of Saxony was rewarded with the province of Lusatia.

DANISH INTERVENTION, 1623–1630

Leadership of the Protestant resistance passed to King Christian IV of Denmark. The ambitious Danish king intervened partly in order to save his coreligionists, but primarily to acquire some Catholic bishoprics in northern Germany. England, France, and the United Provinces all encouraged his intervention, but did not provide any substantial financial or military aid. The imperial forces gained yet another brilliant general in the person of Albrecht von Wallenstein (1583–1634), a soldier of fortune who had successfully married for money. An avid believer in astrology, yet shrewdly calculating, Wallenstein is one of the more complex individuals to emerge from the period. Eager to increase his landholdings, Wallenstein offered Emperor Ferdinand II (r. 1619–1637) an army of 20,000 troops. Under Wallenstein and Tilly, imperial forces won a series of victories over Christian and eventually subjugated all of northern Germany as far as Jutland.

On May 22, 1629, the Danish king renounced his ambitions in Germany but was allowed to retain his hereditary lands. Emperor Ferdinand decided to follow up on his generals' victories and turn the Holy Roman Empire into a centralized Habsburg monarchy. He declared the rights of the dukes of Mecklenburg to be forfeited because they had supported King Christian IV of Denmark. The emperor then gave their duchy to the grasping insomniac Wallenstein, who was not even a prince of the empire. Ferdinand then issued an Edict of Restitution on March 6, 1629. It threatened the very existence of Protestantism by prohibiting Calvinist worship and ordering the restoration to the Catholic church of all church properties that had been secularized since 1552.

Even committed Catholic princes in the empire such as Maximilian of Bavaria became alarmed about the emperor's intentions. They had benefited from the loose, decentralized nature of the Holy Roman Empire, and many were also concerned that Wallenstein's immense army of mercenaries could no longer be controlled. At the Diet of Regensburg in the summer of 1630, Catholic and Protestant princes joined hands to demand that the emperor dismiss Wallenstein and force him to disband his army. Powers outside the empire, including France and Sweden, were also concerned about Ferdinand's ambitions.

SWEDISH INTERVENTION, 1630–1635

A staunch and determined Lutheran, Gustavus II Adolphus (1594–1632) regarded Ferdinand's growing might in northern Germany as a threat to Lutheranism generally and to his own empire more specifically. Although not populous, Sweden had an efficient government and valuable deposits of iron and copper, resources in great demand by the militarists of the age. Handsome, well educated, fluent in seven languages, and fond of music and poetry, the king of Sweden was the model of a Renaissance prince. One of the ablest military leaders and tacticians of his day, the so-called "Lion of the North" landed in Pomerania in July 1630 with a well-equipped, experienced army. With gold from France and allies among the German Protestants, Gustavus Adolphus won an overwhelming victory over Tilly at Breitenfeld near Leipzig on September 17, 1631. In the spring of 1632, the victorious

Protestants marched into the Rhineland, then south into the heart of Bavaria, deliberately devastating the countryside in the spring of 1632.

With the Catholic position deteriorating rapidly, Ferdinand II recalled the intense Wallenstein and made him supreme commander. Early in September 1532 the imperial forces held their own in a clash with Gustavus Adolphus outside of Nuremberg. Wallenstein then moved to Saxony, where he planned to spend the winter. The Swedish king followed him and the two armies met in a furious battle at Lützen (near Leipzig) on November 16, 1632. Gustavus Adolphus was mortally wounded in the battle, but his enraged soldiers forced the Imperials to withdraw into Bohemia. The king's able chancellor, Axel Oxenstierna, continued the

Anonymous, *Engraved Portrait of Gustavus Adolphus, King of Sweden.* Foto Marburg/Art Resource.

war. Wallenstein opened negotiations with the Swedes and Saxons, hoping to create an independent state for himself. One of his Irish captains, outraged by Wallenstein's treachery, murdered him on the night of February 25, 1634.

Wallenstein's death helped restore unity among the Imperials, who were now led by the future Ferdinand III, the young heir to the throne. The Habsburgs' position was also strengthened by the refusal of some of the Protestants, such as Duke Johann Georg of Saxony, to cooperate fully with the Swedes. A war between Russia and Poland also drew off some of the Swedish forces. On September 6, 1634, an imperial army, reinforced by Spanish troops, crushed the Swedish army outside of the town of Nördlingen. Almost all of southern Germany now fell back into the hands of the imperialists. Johann Georg of Saxony signed a peace treaty at Prague with Emperor Ferdinand II, which suspended the Edict of Restitution, but prohibited military alliances among the princes and with foreigners.

THE FRANCO-SWEDISH PHASE, 1635–1648, AND AFTERMATH

Following the Swedish defeat at Nördlingen, France, under its brilliant Machiavellian first minister, Cardinal de Richelieu (d. 1642), felt compelled to intervene with troops. France had been sending money to the Protestant anti-imperialists since the early phases of the war because it feared encirclement by the Habsburgs of Spain in conjunction with their cousins in Vienna. Even Pope Urban VIII (r. 1623–1644) gave his blessing to French intervention because he too feared the rise of Habsburg power, which might be used against the papal interests in Italy. Reasons of state had come to supplant religious considerations, at least in the international arena.

Although the coming of French forces did not immediately turn the tide of the war, it did eventually make the imperial defeat inevitable. Spain, with its communications in Germany disrupted, was soon further weakened by an uprising in Catalonia in Spain and the rebellion of proud Portugal in 1640. On May 19, 1643, the French won a stunning victory over the Spanish at Rocroi on the border of the Spanish Netherlands. The recently crowned Emperor Ferdinand III (r. 1637–1657) now found himself increasingly isolated in the empire as Frederick Wilhelm, the young elector of Prussia, made a separate peace with Sweden in 1640. Other Protestant leaders also defected from their alliances with the emperor.

At Christmas of 1641, Ferdinand III agreed to begin peace negotiations with the French at Münster and with the Swedes at Osnabrück. Separate discussions were held between Protestants and Catholics. These cumbersome arrangements made the peace process drag on for years. A final settlement of the German phase of the conflict was not reached until 1648 at the Peace of Westphalia, as all sides jockeyed for more favorable conditions. The western phase of the conflict between France and Spain was not ended until the Peace of the Pyrenees of 1659. Other ongoing regional conflicts were also winding down. Peace agreements between Sweden and Denmark were finally reached in 1660, the same year that Sweden settled a conflict with Poland. Russia and Poland made peace in 1667.

France emerged from the wars as the dominant European power. It had gained the fortress towns of Metz, Toul, Verdun, Philippsburg, and most of Alsace in 1648. In 1659 France received Artois, Cambrai, Roussillon, and a claim to the Spanish throne through the marriage of Louis XIV of France to Philip IV's daughter, Maria Teresa. The 1648 agreements at Westphalia also recognized the independence of the Dutch Netherlands from Spain, as we have seen. The Swedes gained the southern end of the Swedish peninsula, western Pomerania, the bishoprics of Bremen and Verden, and Wismar, plus cash. Sweden was now officially recognized as the leading power in the Baltic.

Inside the devastated Holy Roman Empire, the Religious Peace of Augsburg of 1555 was reaffirmed and extended to Calvinists. The territorial independence and sovereignty of each of the empire's roughly 300 states was recognized. German princes could now once again legally conclude alliances with foreign powers. From the peak of power in 1629, the Habsburg emperor had been reduced to a figurehead in the Holy Roman Empire. His cousin in Spain had also lost a great deal. The Spanish kingdom had fallen a long way from the proud days of Philip II. What had begun as a religious conflict wound up as a chapter in Europe's continuing dynastic power struggles. Political violence was only one of the many legacies of the Reformation Era.

Chronology

1531	Formation of the Schmalkaldic League.	**1566**	Beginning of the Revolt in the Low Countries.
1532	Religious Truce at Nuremberg; Ottomans defeated east of Vienna.	**1571**	Battle of Lepanto; naval defeat of the Ottomans.
1535	Fall of Tunis to Charles V; renewed Habsburg-Valois conflict.	**1572**	Saint Bartholomew's Massacres in France.
		1574–1589	Reign of Henri III in France.
1542–1544	Fourth Habsburg-Valois War.	**1579**	Union of Arras; division of the Low Countries.
1546	Death of Luther; beginning of Schmalkaldic War.	**c. 1581–1666**	Life of Frans Hals.
1547	Charles V victorious at Mühlberg.	**1582**	Murder of William of Orange.
1548	Augsburg and Leipzig Interims.	**1585**	Fall of Brussels and Antwerp to Spanish.
1552	Moritz of Saxony and Henri II of France attack Charles V.	**1587–1589**	War of the Three Henries.
		1588	Spanish Armada attacks England and is defeated.
1555	Religious Peace of Augsburg.	**1598**	Peace between France and Spain; Edict of Nantes.
1556	Abdications of Charles V.	**1606–1669**	Life of Rembrandt.
1558	Death of Charles V.		
1559	Peace of Cateau-Cambrésis; death of Henri II in France; Huguenots in Convention in Paris.	**1609**	Truce between Dutch rebels and Spain; birth of Judith Leyster.
		1610	Death of Henri IV of France.
1560–1572	Dominance of Catherine de' Medici.	**1618**	Beginning of the Thirty Years' War
1561–1562	Colloquies at Poissy and St. Germain-en-Laye.	**1629**	Defeat of Christian IV of Denmark; Edict of Restitution.

1630	Gustavus II Adolphus of Sweden enters the Thirty Years' War.
1632	Death of Gustavus Adolphus.
1634	Death of Wallenstein.
1635	France commits troops to the Thirty Years' War.
1648	Treaties of Westphalia; recognition of the independence of the United Provinces.
1659	Peace of the Pyrenees between France and Spain.
1660	Peace between Denmark and Sweden; peace between Sweden and Poland.
1667	Peace between Poland and Russia.

Further Reading

GENERAL STUDIES OF WARFARE

Frederic Baumgartner, *From Spear to Flintlock: A History of War in Europe and the Middle East to the French Revolution* (1991).

Jeremy Black, *A Military Revolution?* (1991). Important discussion of a major historiographical issue.

David Eltis, *The Military Revolution of the Sixteenth Century* (1995).

Jack Goldstone, *Revolution and Rebellion in the Early Modern World* (1993).

John Guilmartin, *Gunpowder and Galleys: Changing Technology and Mediterranean Warfare at Sea in the Sixteenth Century* (1974).

John Hale, *War and Society in Renaissance Europe* (1985).

Michael Mallet, *Mercenaries and Their Masters: Warfare in Renaissance Italy* (1984).

Geoffrey Parker, *The Military Revolution* (1988).

Kenneth Setton, *Western Hostility to Islam and Prophecies of Turkish Doom* (1992).

Frank Tallett, *War and Society in Early Modern Europe, 1495–1715* (1992). Argues against the notion of a military revolution.

Janice Thomson, *Mercenaries, Pirates, and Sovereigns: State-Building and Extraterritorial Violence in Early Modern Europe* (1994).

GERMANY AND THE SCHMALKALDIC LEAGUE AND WAR

Thomas Brady, Jr., *Protestant Politics, Jacob Sturm (1498–1553) and the German Reformation* (1995). A full-length study of a pivotal figure and the rise of the Schmalkaldic League.

Carl Christensen, *Princes and Propaganda: Electoral Saxon Art of the Reformation* (1992).

Christopher Friedrichs, *Urban Society in an Age of War: Nördlingen* (1979).

Hajo Holborn, *A History of Modern Germany: The Reformation* (1961).

Robert Kolb, *Nikolaus von Amsdorf (1483–1565): Popular Piety in Preserving Luther's Legacy* (1977).

H. C. Erik Midelfort, *Mad Princes of Renaissance Germany* (1994).

Luther Peterson, "Melanchthon on Resisting the Emperor," in Jerome Friedman, ed., *Regnum, Religio et Ratio* (1987).

M. J. Rodriguez-Salgado, *The Changing Face of Empire: Charles V, Philip II, and Habsburg Authority, 1551–59* (1988).

Steven Rowan, *Ulrich Zasius: A Jurist in the German Renaissance, 1461–1531* (1987).

Kristin Zapalac, *"In his Image and Likeness": Political Iconography and Religious Change in Regensburg, 1500–1600* (1991).

FRANCE AND THE RELIGIOUS WARS

Frederic Baumgartner, *Henri II, King of France, 1547–1559* (1988).

Philip Benedict, *Rouen during the Wars of Religion* (1981).

David Buisseret, *Henry IV* (1984).

Natalie Davis, *Society and Culture in Early Modern France* (1965).

————, *The Return of Martin Guerre* (1983). Fascinating account of an imposter.

Jonathan Dewald, *The Formation of a Provincial Nobility* (1980).

Barbara Diefendorf, *Beneath the Cross: Catholics and Huguenots in Sixteenth-Century Paris* (1991).

Julian Franklin, *Jean Bodin and the Rise of Absolutistic Theory* (1973).

Janine Garrison, *A History of Sixteenth-Century France, 1483–1598: Renaissance, Reformation, and Rebellion* (1995).

Mark Greengrass, *France in the Age of Henri IV* (1984).

Malcom Greenshields, *An Economy of Violence in Early Modern France* (1994).

Mack Holt, *The Duke of Anjou and the Politique Struggle during the Wars of Religion* (1986).

De Lamar Jensen, *Diplomacy and Dogmatism: Bernardino de Mendoza and the French Catholic League* (1964).

Donald Kelley, *The Beginnings of Ideology* (1981).

Robert Kingdon, *Myths about the St. Bartholomew's Day Massacres* (1988).

Emmanuel Le Roy Ladurie, *Carnival in Romans* (1980). Intriguing study of popular violence.

J. Russell Major, *Representative Government in Early Modern France* (1980).

Raymond Mentzer, Jr., *Blood and Belief: Family Survival and Confessional Identity among Provincial Huguenot Nobility* (1994).

Robert Muchembled, *Popular Culture and Elite Culture in France*, tr. by Lydia Cochcrane (1985).

Donald Nugent, *Ecumenism in the Age of Reformation: The Colloquy of Poissy* (1974).

Nancy Roelker, *Queen of Navarre: Jeanne d'Albret* (1968).

J. H. Salmon, *Society in Crisis: France in the Sixteenth Century* (1975). A valuable synthesis.

N. M. Sutherland, *The Huguenot Struggle for Recognition* (1980).

Michael Wolfe, *The Conversion of Henri IV: Politics, Power, and Religious Belief in Early Modern France* (1993).

PHILIP II'S SPAIN

Fernand Braudel, *The Mediterranean and the Mediterranean World in the Age of Philip II*, 2 vols. (1972). A modern classic.

William Christian, *Local Religion in Sixteenth-Century Spain* (1981).

Carlos Eire, *From Madrid to Purgatory: The Art and Craft of Dying in Sixteenth-Century Spain* (1994).

J. H. Elliot, *Imperial Spain* (1963).

Maureen Flynn, *Sacred Charities: Confraternities and Social Welfare in Spain* (1989).

Alastair Hamilton, *Heresy and Mysticism in Sixteenth-Century Spain: The Alumbrados* (1993).

Henry Kamen, *Spain 1469–1714*, 2nd ed. (1991).

Marvin Lunenfeld, *The Council of the Santa Hermandad* (1970).

John Lynch, *Spain 1516–1598* (1991).

————, *The Hispanic World in Crisis and Change, 1598–1700* (1992).

William Maltby, *Alba* (1983). A fascinating portrait of the soldier-statesman.

Helen Nader, *Liberty in Absolutist Spain: The Habsburg Sale of Towns* (1991).

Sara Nalle, *God in La Mancha* (1993).

Peter Pierson, *Philip II* (1989).

Ruth Pike, *Aristocrats and Traders: Sevillian Society in the Sixteenth Century* (1972).

I. A. A. Thompson, *War and Government in Habsburg Spain, 1560–1720* (1976).

Michael Weisser, *The Peasants of the Montes* (1976).

THE DUTCH REVOLT
AND ITS AFTERMATH

Alastair Duke, *Reformation and Revolt in the Low Countries* (1990).

Jonathan Israel, *Dutch Primacy in World Trade, 1585–1715* (1989).

————, *The Dutch Republic: Its Rise, Greatness, and Fall 1477–1806* (1995).

Guido Marnef, *Antwerp in the Age of Reformation: Undergrown Protestantism in a Commercial Metropolis, 1550–1577* (1995).

Sherrin Marshall, *The Dutch Gentry, 1500–1650* (1987).

Geoffrey Parker, *Spain and the Netherlands* (1979).

Simon Schama, *The Embarrassment of Riches: An Interpretation of Dutch Culture in the Golden Age* (1987). Magisterial synthesis.

Marjolein 't Hart, *The Making of a Bourgeois State: War, Politics, and Finance during the Dutch Revolution* (1993).

James Tracy, *Holland under Habsburg Rule* (1990).

Martin van Gelderen, ed., *The Dutch Revolt* (1993). A useful collection of documents.

THE SPANISH ARMADA

Felipe Fernandez-Armestro, *The Spanish Armada* (1988).

Wallace MacCaffrey, *Elizabeth I: War and Politics 1588–1603* (1992).

Colin Martin and Geoffrey Parker, *The Spanish Armada* (1988).

Garrett Mattingly, *The Armada*, 2nd ed. (1988). Beautifully written classic.

Peter Pierson, *Commander of the Armada: The Seventh Duke of Medinia Sidonia* (1989).

THE THIRTY YEARS' WAR

Gerhard Benecke, ed., *Germany in the Thirty Years War* (1979). A valuable collection of excerpts from primary sources.

Bodo Nischan, "The Thirty Years War," in J. W. Zophy, ed., *The Holy Roman Empire: A Dictionary Handbook* (1980).

Geoffrey Parker, *The Thirty Years' War* (1984).

J. V. Polisenky, *The Thirty Years' War* (1971).

Michael Roberts, *Gustavus Adolphus*, 2nd ed. (1992).

John Theibault, *German Villages in Crisis: Rural Life in Hesse-Kassel and the Thirty Years' War, 1580–1720* (1995).

Notes

1. Cited in Mark Edwards, Jr., *Luther's Last Battles: Politics and Polemics, 1531–46* (Ithaca, N.Y.: Cornell University Press, 1983), pp. 182–183.
2. Cited in Lewis Spitz, *The Protestant Reformation* (Englewood Cliffs, N.J.: Prentice Hall, 1966), p. 72.
3. Cited in Jonathan Zophy, *Patriarchal Politics and Christoph Kress (1484–1535) of Nuremberg* (Lewiston, N.Y.: Edwin Mellen, 1992), p. 14.
4. Cited in William J. Wright, "Philip of Hesse's Vision of Protestant Unity and the Marburg Colloquy," in Kyle Sessions and Philip Bebb, eds., *Pietas et Societas: New Trends in Reformation Social History* (Kirksville, Mo.: Sixteenth Century Journal Publishers, 1985), pp. 165–166.
5. Cited in Zophy, *Patriarchal Politics*, p. 183.
6. Cited in Roland Bainton, *Women of the Reformation in Germany and Italy* (Minneapolis, Minn.: Augsburg, 1971), p. 42.
7. Cited in Barbara Diefendorf, *Beneath the Cross: Catholics and Huguenots in Sixteenth-century Paris* (New York: Oxford University Press, 1991), p. 99.

8. Cited in Bonnie Anderson and Judith Zinsser, *A History of Their Own: Women in History from Prehistory to the Present*, 2 vols. (New York: Harper and Row, 1988), vol. 1, p. 233.
9. Cited in G. R. Elton, ed., *Renaissance and Reformation 1300–1648*, 3rd ed. (New York: Macmillan, 1976), p. 145.
10. Cited in De Lamar Jensen, *Reformation Europe: Age of Reform and Revolution*, 2nd ed. (Lexington, Mass.: D. C. Heath, 1992), p. 255.
11. Cited in H. G. Koenigsberger, "The Politics of Philip II," in Malcolm Thorp and Arthur Slavin, eds., *Politics, Religion, and Diplomacy in Early Modern Europe: Essays in Honor of De Lamar Jensen* (Kirksville, Mo.: Sixteenth Century Journal Publishers, 1994), pp. 180–181.
12. Cited in Jensen, *Reformation*, p. 290.
13. Cited in Garrett Mattingly, *The Armada* (Boston: Houghton Mifflin, 1959), p. 217.
14. Cited in Lacey Baldwin Smith, *Elizabeth Tudor: Portrait of a Queen* (Boston: Little Brown, 1975), p. 69.

13

THE LEGACY

History is, among many other things, a dialogue between the past and the present. Therefore, it seems appropriate to end this book by discussing some of the ways in which the Renaissance and Reformation movements influenced our world. What changed as a result of these movements? What ideas and institutions grew out of this period of time? Although the Renaissance and Reformation era introduced an abundance of changes in European society, ranging from the introduction of double entry bookkeeping to the use of forks in dining, this concluding chapter will focus on only some of the major developments which emerged from this era.

Religious Life

Clearly the world of 1648 was quite different in many respects from the one we encountered in 1500. At that time almost all of the peoples living in western Europe were nominally Roman Catholics, with just a small number of Jews and Muslims. By 1648 the religious unity of what was called Christendom was gone forever. Large numbers of western Europeans no longer looked to Rome exclusively for spiritual guidance. Clergy in Protestant areas had a different status than Catholic clergy. Many of them

were now free to marry and forced to take on the obligations of citizens, including the paying of taxes. They still performed the remaining sacraments, preached, and comforted the sick and dying, but they were not a part of such a privileged estate. The Reformation changed many aspects of life not just for the clergy, but for the laity as well.

THEOLOGICAL DIVISIONS AND SOCIAL DISCIPLINE

The second half of the sixteenth century continued to witness theological disputes and efforts to create a more "godly" and disciplined society. After the death of Martin Luther in 1546, Lutheranism had broken into two major camps, as we have seen. The followers of Luther's close friend Philip Melanchthon (Philippists) argued with the followers of Flacius Illyricus and Nicholas von Amsdorf (Gnesiolutherans) over such issues as the nature of the Eucharist or whether Lutheran churches should use a version of the old Catholic episcopal system. Disputes among Lutherans also broke out over whether adherence to divine law was necessary for salvation (Antinomianism) and whether humans could do anything toward earning salvation (Synergistic Controversy). The Gnesiolutherans held firmly to their belief in salvation by grace alone, completely denying that good works contributed anything toward salvation. Philippists believed that piety and learning contribute to regeneration. Some of the heat went out of the disputes with the successive deaths of some of the major protagonists (Melanchthon in 1560, Amsdorf in 1565, and Flacius in 1575).

Lutheran princes who hoped to use Lutheranism to enforce social discipline were increasingly disturbed by the failure of the theologians to come to common ground on doctrine. If they could not discipline themselves, how could they discipline their flocks? That is why many, such as Duke Christoph of Württemberg (1515–1568), eagerly supported the efforts of Jacob Andreae (1528–1590) and others to achieve doctrinal unity. The son of an itinerant Bavarian blacksmith, Andreae rose to earn a doctorate in theology and become a Lutheran pastor in Stuttgart. Later Andreae was named a counselor to Duke Christoph and in 1561 chancellor of his alma mater, the University of Tübingen.

A prolific writer, he wrote a "Formula of Concord" in 1577 that helped to unify many of the various Lutheran factions. It was included in *The Book of the Concord* of June 1580, along with Melanchthon's Augsburg Confession, the Apology (Defense) of the Augsburg Confession, the Schmalkaldic Articles, and Luther's Large and Small Catechisms. *The Book of the Concord* was eventually supported by eighty-six princes and town governments and between eight and nine thousand theologians. The princes were led by Elector Augustus of Saxony (1553–1586), who was determined to put a stop to theological divisions among Lutherans. All of the major questions raised in the various doctrinal controversies were discussed and refuted. Lutheranism had finally achieved a great deal of doctrinal cohesion.

The period also saw increased efforts to create state churches that enforced social discipline upon their subject populations. Major confessional statements such as the Calvinist *Second Helvetic Confession* of 1566, the Calvinist *Heidelberg Cathechism* of 1563, and the Lutheran *Book of the Concord* of 1580 were used to attempt to impose discipline and order on society. In his preface to the *Heidelberg Catechism*, Elector Frederick III of the Palatinate explained some of his motives for adopting it. He wrote:

> We have finally recognized and undertaken to fulfill Our divinely ordained office, vocation, and governance, not only to keep peace and order, but also to maintain a disciplined, upright, and virtuous life and behavior among Our subjects, furthermore and especially, to instruct them and bring them step by step to the righteous knowledge and fear of the Almighty and His sanctifying Word as the basis of all virtues and obedience.[1]

Thus Frederick and other princes sought to use the Reformation as a means of consolidating their power and imposing social control upon their subjects. Church ordinances and regulations could be used to make more "godly" cities and territories while strengthening the hand of patriarchal secular authorities. In many areas, this took the form of closing brothels, regulating relief for the poor, and indoctrinating the young. As enforcers of morality under the authority of a prince or city council, Protestant clergy in the Holy Roman Empire became servants of the state. Teams of clergy and civic officials attempted to enforce discipline through periodic visitations, which examined the conduct of parish pastors and their congregations.

How successful they were in instilling piety and morality is a matter of spirited debate. The quest to establish "godly" communities did not seem to succeed. Traditional modes of belief and dissolute behavior persisted despite the exhortations of the preachers and their secular colleagues. Excessive drinking, gambling, illicit sex, and public violence continued to be staples of male bonding and common features of European town and village life. Dancing could not be eliminated in Calvinistic Geneva or elsewhere. Even some of the married Protestant clergy were found in violation of the new discipline ordinances.

Apparently much more successful were the efforts to improve individuals and society through expanded educational opportunities for males and females. Building on the work of Renaissance humanism, many Protestant leaders were interested in increasing biblical literacy to make better Christians and persons. They founded new primary schools for both boys and girls, established Latin schools at the secondary level, and developed academies and colleges for the training of pastors and male church workers. Educational growth also occurred in Roman Catholic areas through the efforts of the Society of Jesus and other groups that stressed the importance of education. Although these efforts made only a slight dent in Europe's massive illiteracy, there is no question that the improvement of education was one of the most important heritages of the Renaissance and Reformation, along with the efforts to improve social welfare systems.

MARRIAGE IN PROTESTANT EUROPE

One of the areas of daily life most profoundly affected by the Reformation was the institution of marriage. No longer a sacrament among Protestants, marriage still occupied a place of great importance. Protestants championed marriage as spiritually preferable to celibacy. While there was variance among various groups in their regulation of marriage, most Protestants stressed

the importance of parental consent and allowed the possibility of divorce with remarriage for adultery or impotence. In some areas, divorce was also permitted for refusal to have sexual relations, abandonment, deadly abuse, or affliction with an incurable disease. While Protestants permitted divorce under certain circumstances, their leaders attempted to discourage the breakup of families. Marriage courts tried to settle marital disputes before permitting divorce. Overall, divorce was still a rarity in the pre-twentieth-century world.

Many of the reformers argued that marriage was the "natural" vocation for women and urged husbands to treat their wives and children in a kindly manner. The Reformation affirmed patriarchy time and

Albrecht Dürer, *The Moor Katherine* (1521). Uffizi, Florence, Italy. Foto Marburg/Art Resource.

time again as wives were continually admonished to be obedient to their husbands. Protestant marriage courts did punish both male and female adulterers. They also attempted to make sure divorced husbands paid child support. Premarital sex, a common practice, was also discouraged in most Protestant areas as was infanticide. The stability of the patriarchal family was considered an important foundation of the patriarchal state.

MARGARET FELL (1614–1702) AND WOMEN AS PREACHERS

Protestant women lost a great deal with the closing of most convents and the strengthening of patriarchy, yet some were able to gain access to newly founded grammar schools. Reformers such as Martin Luther stressed "biblical literacy" and he helped establish schools for girls. Although Lutheran girls were not in school as long as boys, so as not to interfere with their domestic chores, the schools did open some windows of learning for those outside of the cloistered world. Since there were not enough male schoolteachers available, some schools were forced to hire some literate women as teachers, which opened yet another profession to women.

The ministry, however, remained forbidden to women in Protestant as well as Catholic territories. Although some Anabaptist women were allowed to administer baptism and preach, the larger Protestant groups were adamantly opposed to the practice, except in baptismal emergencies. As the magisterial reformer John Calvin put it, "The custom of the church, before St. Augustine was born, may be elicited first of all from Tertullian [church father, c. 160–230], who held that no woman in church is allowed to speak, teach, baptize, or make offerings; this in order that she may not usurp the functions of men."[2]

Not until the rise of the Society of Friends (Quakers) in the seventeenth century in England were women such as Margaret Fell given the opportunity to preach in public. An offshoot of the Puritan movement, the early Quakers based their religion on the exposition of the biblical revelation by ministerial authority. They favored plain living and speaking, exacting conscience, and a complete avoidance of sensuous and formal liturgy.

As a young woman Margaret Fell had been converted to "enlightenment" by George Fox (1624–1691), one of the principal leaders of the Quakers in 1652. After the death of her first husband, Margaret married Fox in 1669 even though she was prosperous. With her second husband and other Quaker missionaries constantly traveling and sometimes being imprisoned, Margaret Fell, who usually remained at the Society's headquarters at Swarthmoor Hall, became known as the "nursing mother of the church." She also did missionary work as well as preaching, writing tracts, and trying to persuade King Charles II that the Friends, those "rude" disciples, were no threat to law and order and should be released from prison and not persecuted.

Her pleas failed and Margaret Fell found herself imprisoned as a religious dissenter from 1664 to 1668 and again from 1670 to 1671. During her first stint in prison, she wrote and published a tract called *Women's Speaking Justified*. In it, Fell argued that "the Lord God in creation, when he made man in his own image, he made them *male* and *female*."[3] Her words seemed to echo those of the early feminist writer Christine de Pizan (1365–c. 1429) centuries earlier. Fell also asserted that as God's creatures, women had the obligation to speak in church and elsewhere when the Holy Spirit moved them. She cited chapter and verse of the Old and New Testament, naming every woman who was recorded as having prophesied, spoken, or argued. Other Quaker women followed in the bold steps of Margaret Fell. Not until the twentieth century were women admitted to the ministry in some of the other Protestant denominations. Most fundamentalist groups of Protestants still have an all-male clergy, as do the Roman Catholics and the Eastern Orthodox.

ROMAN CATHOLICISM REVIVED

In Catholic areas, old institutions and worship practices survived and many in the church felt reinvigorated. The Catholic church had not only survived the Protestant defections, but had emerged with new energy after the reform Council of Trent. Able leaders had emerged and new organizations such as the Society of Jesus and the Ursulines had further strengthened the church. Doctrines had been clarified and reaffirmed and there was now little question about what good Catholics were to believe and practice. Corruption in church practices had been greatly reduced. The Catholic church, while still dominated by aristocrats, was no longer as nepotistic or simoniacal as it had been prior to the Reformation. By and large the education of the clergy had been substantially improved. Even scholasticism had been reinvigorated. The post-Tridentine church not only enforced greater discipline upon the clergy, it also attempted to impose social discipline upon society as well.

In the late sixteenth and continuing into the seventeenth centuries, the Catholic church was able to make some spectacular conversions. For example, Protestantism had made deep inroads into Poland during the first half of the sixteenth century. By the beginning of the seventeenth century, Poland was a Roman Catholic bulwark led by active reformers such as the Jesuit theologian and court preacher Peter Skarga (1536–1618) and others. Jesuits may have played a key role in the decision of Sweden's free thinking Queen Christina to abdicate in 1654 and to turn away from Lutheranism. In the Holy Roman Empire, where the ranks of the Catholic clergy had been thoroughly depleted in the first decades of the Reformation and where even the archdiocese of Cologne threatened to turn Protestant in 1547 and again in 1583, reformed Catholicism slowly began to make a comeback.

In the seventeenth century, reformed Catholicism made a spectacular series of princely conversions, ranging from Duke Wolfgang Wilhelm of Palatine-Neuberg to Elector Frederick August of Saxony. Even important intellectuals such as Angelus Silensius (1624–1677) made surprising conversions to Catholicism. Following his conversion, Silensius gave up his position as personal physician to the Protestant duke of Württemberg and eventually found new employment as physician to Emperor Ferdinand III. Ordained a priest in 1661, he became a leading propagandist for the Catholic Reformation and one of the era's leading lyrical poets. Catholicism also made a comeback in a number of south German imperial cities such as Augsburg, Dinkelsbühl, and Ulm. Those biconfessional towns showed that a community could have adherents of different denominations living in relative harmony with each other. This too was an important lesson of the era.

Witchcraft and Its Suppression

Although there were pockets of toleration in some parts of Europe, not many Catholic or Protestant communities were willing to allow witchcraft by the end of the sixteenth century. European witchcraft was considered to be a dangerous mixture of heresy (treason against God) and sorcery (the magical power to do evil deeds through formulas and rituals). Witches were believed to have made a pact to deny God and serve the devil. Satan then gave the witch the power to cause illness and sometimes even death in humans and animals, bring on bad weather, and destroy fertility in humans or plants. Territorial states also felt threatened by witchcraft as a form of local power that denied the authority of the divinely sanctioned hierarchy.

Such beliefs were well grounded in the popular culture of the time. Many people believed they lived in a world where supernatural forces abounded; some worked for good, some for evil. If God could act in human history, so could Satan and his minions. Alarmed by reports of diabolic activities, the recently elected Pope Innocent VIII (r. 1484–1492) commissioned two Dominicans—Jacob Sprenger and Heinrich Kramer—to draw up the first comprehensive handbook on witchcraft and demonology. Their handbook on witchcraft and demonology was entitled the *Malleus Maleficarum* (The Hammer of Witches) and came out in 1486. It would be used to help witch hunters and courts that handled witchcraft cases identify the signs of witchcraft.

Laced with misogyny, the *Malleus Maleficarum* sums up much of the worst in Western thought about women. For example, Sprenger and Kramer wrote:

> Woman is more carnal than man. . . . She always deceives. . . . What else is woman but a foe to friendship, an inescapable punishment, a necessary evil, a natural temptation, a desirable calamity, a domestic danger, a delectable detriment, an evil of nature, painted with fair colors. . . . To conclude, all witchcraft comes from carnal lust, which in women is insatiable.[4]

With such a mindset helping guide those males charged with identifying, trying, and sentencing suspect witches, it is hardly surprising that the overwhelming majority of the between 50,000 and 75,000 persons executed for witchcraft during the sixteenth and seventeenth centuries were women. Yet witch persecutions were not just manifestations of animosity between men and women; they could also involve tensions between women, such as between a new mother and her midwife or between a conflicted mother and her maid. The witch craze tapped into all sorts of cultural, political, social, and psychological forces present in early modern Europe.

Despite the fact that the revised Imperial Law Code of 1532 made witchcraft a capital offense punishable by death, the witch trials did not involve large numbers of people until the end of the sixteenth century. For decades, Catholics and Protestants were too busy fighting each other to bother with witches. However, as Europe continued to be troubled with periodic famines, inflation, and social tensions, the temptation to use accused witches as scapegoats proved impossible to resist in both Catholic and Protestant territories. The majority of the witch prosecutions took place inside the Holy Roman Empire, with France a close second. Bohemia, Poland, and Switzerland were also active in witch hunting. Fewer prosecutions took place in the British Isles, the Low Countries, and Scandinavia. Catholic Spain and Italy had very few witch trials and very few of their prosecutions resulted in executions. Those areas had long experience in dealing with heretics and many of those accused of witchcraft failed to qualify as such when scrutinized by experienced inquisitors.

Because of the widespread belief in the powers of witches, magic, and the frequent use of torture in judicial proceedings, once started the witch-hunts were hard to stop. When tortured, accused witches confessed to all sorts of diabolical activities. As one convicted witch in Bamberg wrote his daughter in 1628, "I confessed in order to escape the great anguish and bitter torture, which it was impossible for me to bear longer."[5]

Leading authorities such as the political theorist Jean Bodin were convinced that witch-hunts were an absolute necessity. Those who argued that pacts with the devil were frauds and that witches were really harmless and confused old women, such as the German physician Johann Weyer (1550–1578), were themselves accused of being witches. Why would one defend a witch unless one were a witch? In 1623 Pope Gregory XV commanded that anyone who made a pact with the devil or who practiced black magic that resulted in death should be turned over to the secular courts and put to death.

CRITICS OF THE WITCH CRAZE

Among those who dared to criticize the belief in witches were Michel de Montaigne and the seventeenth-century essayist-swashbuckler Cyrano de Bergerac. In a famous letter against witches of 1654 Bergerac wrote: "No, I do not believe in witches, even though several important people do not agree with me; and I defer to no man's authority, unless it is accompanied by reason and comes from God."[6] He found that most of the so-called witches were "crackbrained" shepherds and "ignorant" peasants. Given his renowned skill with a sword, few were willing to challenge Bergerac or accuse him of being a witch to his face.

In fact, the attitude of skepticism about the alleged powers of witches came to be more and more prevalent. Educated people increasingly began to seek natural explanations for things that had previously been attributed to supernatural forces. Courts began demanding more conclusive evidence about evil deeds and the pact with the devil and putting greater limitations upon the use of torture. The same legal authorities who had once vigorously prosecuted witches now began to doubt that some of the people brought before them actually were witches. Some wondered why secular courts were wasting their time on a matter that belonged to the church.

Executions for witchcraft fell off rapidly, especially as economic conditions improved in many parts of Europe toward the end of the seventeenth century. King Louis XIV issued an edict in 1682 which successfully curtailed witchcraft trials in France, the same year in which the last accused witch was legally executed in England. Accused witches were still occasionally executed legally in the Holy Roman Empire until 1775 and in Glarus, Switzerland, until 1782. The belief in the powers of the devil and witches persisted in the minds of Europeans, especially those in the working classes, but at least those in power no longer were so eager to prosecute suspected witches.

The Rise of Science

ASTROLOGY, ALCHEMY, AND MAGIC

The rise of science played a role in the declining belief in witchcraft and is one of the most important legacies of the Renaissance and Reformation period. However, an understanding of the workings of nature and the universe free from such time-honored traditions as astrology, magic, and theological considerations took a long time to achieve. Most Renaissance intellectuals continued to believe, as had most ancient Greek thinkers, that matter was made up of four basic elements: air, earth, fire, and water. Each of those elements in turn possessed characteristics drawn from four basic qualities: heat, cold, dryness, and moistness. Those qualities were related to the four medical humors that determined health: choleric, melancholic, phlegmatic, and sanguine. Even the planets, as they slid past each other in concentric spheres pulled by angels, partook of these same qualities. Thus Saturn was believed to be cold and dry, whereas Mars was hot.

Furthermore, the movement of the planets and stars was believed to have an impact on life on earth. As the planets moved in relationship with each other and the still earth, their movements caused changes in the lives of humans, animals, and crops. By calculating the correct movement of the planets, astrologers could forecast when plagues or famines would occur and determine when was the best time to conceive a child, plant a crop, or go to war. Thus astrologers such as Nostradamus (1503–1566) or John Dee (1527–1608) were in great demand by governments as well as by private citizens. Nostradamus found employment with Queen Catherine de' Medici and fooled her and many others by predicting events *after* they had occurred. John Dee, an outstanding alchemist and mathematician, served both Queen Elizabeth of England and Holy Roman Emperor Rudolf II (r. 1576–1612). The mentally unbalanced Rudolf was particularly fascinated by astrology and kept a large stable of astrologers on hand, including the astronomers Tycho Brahe and Johann Kepler.

A few bold skeptics such as the humanist-philosopher Giovanni Pico della Mirandola noticed in the 1480s that the accuracy of astrological weather predictions was low. He once kept a weather diary and found that the astrologers were correct for only seven out of one hundred days. He dared to write a "Treatise Against Astrology" in which he noted that "Plato and Aristotle, the leaders of the [philosophy] profession, considered astrology unworthy of discussion."[7] He recommended that physi-

cians be trusted more than astrologers on matters of health when they contradicted each other. Yet Pico's reservations about astrology were a minority opinion even among learned humanists. Astrology seemed a useful and time-tested science. Its teachings had been supported by many revered sages and Christian theologians. It was taught in the universities along with astronomy. Almanacs filled with astrological lore and predictions continued to be in great demand throughout the Renaissance and beyond.

Next to astrology and physics, alchemy continued to be a leading science of the day. It had long been observed that many substances in nature change over time. For example, flowers bloom and wilt and change colors. Even basic substances can be altered by heating or cooling. Many alchemists became intrigued with the idea of transforming base metals such as lead into gold. In attempting to do so, however, they learned a great deal about the properties of various substances and developed much of the equipment used by later chemists. The first general discussion of how to produce compounds, solutions, distillates, crystallizations and fusions was the 1597 *Alchemy* of the German physician-poet-historian Andreas Libavius (1540–1616). Although critical of the "magical superstitions" of the influential physician-theorist Paracelsus, Libavius maintained his belief in such traditional alchemical lore as the philosopher's stone, which was thought to be able to change base metal into gold. Science still had not freed itself from magic. The universe still seemed best explained by the astrologers and the mystics.

NICHOLAS COPERNICUS (1473–1543)

All this slowly began to change during the Renaissance with the work of scientists and scholars such as Nicholas Copernicus, Andreas Vesalius, and those who followed them. At the heart of the worldview of the astrologers was the earth-centered view of the universe fostered by a host of scholars in the wake of the Hellenistic astronomer Claudius Ptolemy (second century A.D.). Ptolemy's system placed the earth at the center of the universe. This seemed to satisfy the senses, appeal to human egoism, and agree with certain sentences in the Bible. After all, Joshua had ordered the sun, not the earth, to stand still (Joshua 10:12). Before Ptolemy, Aristotle had postulated that the planets move in circular and uniform orbits in crystalline spheres.

Copernicus, a Polish mathematician, came to the conclusion that while Aristotle was essentially correct, Ptolemy had erred in placing the earth at the center of the solar system. The son of a merchant, Nicholas Copernicus had been educated in theology and law at the University of Cracow. For ten years after that he studied astronomy, mathematics, canon law, Greek, and medicine at various universities in Italy. Returning to Poland, Copernicus spent the last thirty years of his life as a canon of Frauenberg Cathedral and physician to his uncle, the bishop of Ermeland. In his spare time, he continued to observe the stars and make mathematical calculations, despite his poor eyesight. His calculations led him to the startling conclusion that the venerated Ptolemy was wrong about the location of earth and its lack of rotation.

His great book, *On the Revolution of the Celestial Spheres*, was completed in 1530, but circulated in manuscript form only until the year of his death, 1543. Copernicus was quite concerned that even his mild revision of Ptolemy might not sit well with the Catholic church. He humbly dedicated his book to Pope Paul III with the hope that it would not be considered too upsetting to church dogma. However, some Catholics did find

his views disturbing, as did most Protestants who became aware of them. Although it was the Lutheran pastor and astronomer Andreas Osiander who first published Copernicus's major work, he did so with a disclaimer. Martin Luther, who was supportive of the new work done in botany, exclaimed, "That fool [Copernicus] will upset the whole science of astronomy."[8] In the short-run, Luther was wrong, for even most advanced scholars found Copernicus's mathematical proofs to be inadequate and his theory as problematic as Ptolemy's.

BRAHE AND KEPLER

While a few bold thinkers such as the controversial Italian philosopher Giordano Bruno (c. 1548–1600) embraced Copernicus's theory of a sun-centered solar system, most advanced thinkers remained unconvinced. Even the great Danish nobleman and astronomer Tycho Brahe (1546–1601) found a great deal in Copernicus that was unsatisfactory. Brahe, who had lost his nose in a duel as a young man, made his astronomical career in 1572 by providing the most accurate description of the appearance of a nova, a star that seems to suddenly appear because of a rapid increase in light output and then fades away after several months. His book, *On the New Star*, came to the attention of King Frederick II, who rewarded Brahe with the lordship of the island of Hveen and a generous stipend. There Brahe built the laboratory palace of Uraniborg, with multiple observatories, a giant quadrant, a great brass-plated globe for the mapping of observations, equipment for alchemy experiments, and rooms for visiting students and colleagues.

Although Brahe did not think the earth could rotate as Copernicus had argued, he still believed that the earth was near the center of the universe. He also rejected the old Aristotelian notion of crystalline spheres. Instead the keen-eyed Brahe concluded that while the other planets revolve around the sun, the sun and the other planets revolve around the earth.

Brahe's greatest student was a German, Johann Kepler (1571–1630). Kepler, the son of a soldier and an encouraging mother, studied mathematics and theology at the University of Tübingen. There he was very much influenced by Michael Maestlin, the most celebrated astronomer in the empire and an advocate of the Copernican system. In 1594, after taking his M.A., Kepler became a teacher of mathematics at a school in Graz, Austria. There he amazed the locals with his knowledge of astrology and mathematics. His calendars seemed to predict events with uncanny accuracy. Kepler became fascinated with the mystery of planetary motions and published his pro-Copernican *Mysteries of the Cosmos* in 1597, which was based heavily on Brahe's work.

He sent copies of his book to many of the leading mathematicians, scientists, and princes in Europe. Impressed by his mathematics, Tycho Brahe invited him to become his assistant in Denmark. A few years later, Kepler joined Brahe at the court of Emperor Rudolf II in Prague, a ruler obsessed with astrology. Kepler worked with the Dane for less than a year before Brahe's death and succeeded him as imperial astronomer and mathematician, a post with a generous salary. Kepler continued the compilation of Brahe's planetary tables, to which he added some of his own data, which he published in 1627.

Kepler's most famous work was his *The New Astronomy* of 1609, which contained his famous discovery that planetary orbits are ellipses, not circles as Copernicus and most ancients taught. He also demonstrated that the speed of a planet is greater when it is closer to the sun and slower when it is far-

ther away. Not everything was new in his astronomy, for he continued to believe in astrology and in the ancient Pythagorean notion of the harmony of the spheres. After the forced abdication of the increasingly unstable Emperor Rudolf in 1612, Kepler continued as imperial astronomer and mathematician, but moved to Linz as a professor of mathematics. He stayed in Linz for the next fourteen years despite periodic persecutions because of his Lutheranism.

Devoted to his mother, Kepler made several trips to his native Swabia in 1620 and 1621 in order to defend her from accusations of witchcraft. Because he often found his imperial pay in arrears, Kepler went to work in 1628 as an astrologer for Albrecht von Wallenstein, the famous imperial general. After Wallenstein's dismissal from imperial service, Kepler moved to Regensburg, where he died still seeking some of his imperial back pay. By the time of Kepler's death in 1630, he had laid the basis for a clearer understanding of the nature of the solar system and the mathematical relationship of its various parts.

GALILEO GALILEI (1564–1642)

The nearsighted Kepler had not been able to support his theories fully by observation. That honor went to Galileo Galilei, who made great use of the Dutch invention of the telescope. Galileo was the son of a minor Florentine noble turned cloth merchant. Excelling in school, he became a brilliant mathematician, an accomplished musician, and a talented artist and author. After abandoning the study of medicine at Pisa, Galileo took a post in 1592 as a professor of mathematics at the University of Padua, where he remained for the next eighteen years. In 1593 he invented an open-air thermometer. While at Padua, Galileo also discovered the law of the pendulum and used it to measure time.

In 1609 he devised a telescope from a Dutch lens grinder's model. Galileo used his telescope to identify shadows on the moon's surface as mountains, valleys, and plains. As he wrote in his famous book of 1610, *The Starry Messenger*, "The surface of the moon is not perfectly smooth, free from inequalities, and exactly spherical, as a large group of philosophers considered."[9] Galileo also discovered that four satellites swung around the planet Jupiter, just as the moon circles the earth, and that the stars are more numerous and farther from the earth than had previously been assumed. The curious Florentine was also the first to see sunspots with a telescope.

Although some ridiculed Galileo's new discoveries, others applauded him for his challenges to previous understandings of the workings of the solar system. His

Justus Susterman, *Portrait of Galileo*. Tarre del Galla, Villa Galetti, Florence, Italy. Foto Marburg/Art Resource.

growing reputation and talent for flattery won him a new position as philosopher and mathematician to Grand Duke Cosimo II of Florence. He had proposed earlier that the newly discovered satellites of Jupiter be named "the Medicean stars." In 1611 Galileo traveled to Rome to explain his discoveries to church leaders. Many were impressed with Galileo and his pro-Copernican theories, including the head mathematician of the Jesuits as well as Cardinal Maffeo Barberini, the future Pope Urban VIII (r. 1623–1644).

There were also men in high places, however, who found Galileo's barbed criticisms of the ideas of revered authorities such as Aristotle and Ptolemy to be dangerous and his personality to be combative. Many theologians were still wedded to the use of Aristotelian forms of logic to support church doctrine. Denounced by the Inquisition in 1616, Galileo was told to abandon and cease to defend and teach as fact the Copernican notion that the sun is the center of the universe and that the earth moves around it. Galileo refused to do this and in 1623 he published a treatise entitled *The Assayer*, which argued that knowledge of nature is acquired by observation and mathematics, not by merely reading ancient authorities.

The work was dedicated to Galileo's friend Maffeo Barberini, who had just become Pope Urban VIII. Calling Galileo a "great man whose fame shines in the heavens and goes far and wide on earth,"[10] the pope presented the astronomer with costly gifts and a pension for the support of his illegitimate son. Urban refused to lift the censorship of the Inquisition, however, and advised Galileo to avoid theological arguments and treat Copernicanism as a theory. Galileo then returned to Florence and completed his *Dialogue Concerning the Two Chief World Systems, Ptolemaic and Copernican*.

Failing to get permission to publish in Rome, Galileo arranged to have the book published in Florence in 1632. This act of defiance enraged the pope and others in Rome, who summoned the aging scientist to appear before the Inquisition in Rome. There he was interrogated and forced to deny his support for Copernicus. Galileo was ordered to retire to his home in Florence and to avoid saying or writing anything that might cause "suspicion."

Although forced to give up on astronomy, the aging scientist resumed his important work in mechanics, which he had first begun in his youth. His last book, *Dialogues Concerning Two New Sciences*, published in 1638, dealt strictly with mechanics and physics. One of his most important discoveries was the law of inertia, which demonstrated that a moving body will continue in motion in a straight line at a uniform speed unless it is acted upon by another force to alter its direction or speed. This discovery contradicted Aristotle's notion that the "natural" state of a body is rest and anticipated the work of Isaac Newton (1642–1727).

The wonderful story that Galileo dropped unequal weights from the leaning tower of Pisa to demonstrate that bodies fall at a uniform rate is apparently the stuff of legend. It is true, however, that Galileo kept experimenting to the end of his life, even though he had become totally blind.

MEDICINE AND ANDREAS VESALIUS (1514–1564)

If Copernicus started a process that eventually led to more people such as Galileo looking to the stars with greater objectivity and

Tito Lessi, *Galileo Telling His Son of the New Science.* Osservatorio, Italy. Alinari/Art Resource.

precision, so Andreas Vesalius helped to advance medicine. The Renaissance had inherited a wealth of medical knowledge from the ancient Greeks and medieval Muslims. The development of the printing press meant that the works of thinkers such as Hippocrates and Galen were now available to a larger audience than ever before. Some of it was useful, such as the notion that diseases had natural causes and could be treated by rational means and improvements in diet. Some of it was harmful, such as the notion that the human body contained four basic fluids: blood, phlegm, red or yellow bile, and black bile. The proper balance of these four humors was believed necessary for maintaining proper health, as shown in the complexion. Thus bloodletting was commonly used to correct the problem of imbalance among the humors.

The balance of the humors and life cycles was also believed to be linked to the movements of the heavenly bodies. Therefore, Renaissance doctors commonly used astrology to determine the best time for treatment and the type of treatment. Further problems arose from the very training most Renaissance physicians received. Medical schools still used the writings of the prolific second century A.D. Greek physician Galen as their guide to anatomy. Galen had made a number of astute judgments about human anatomy, but his work was fundamentally flawed by his belief that the human organs were similar to those of animals. Galen also incorrectly concluded that women were men turned outside in. The ovaries were "smaller, less perfect testes" and females were less "perfect than men."[11]

Out of deference to the classical and Christian belief in the sanctity of the human body, most dissections prior to the fourteenth century had been limited to dogs, pigs, and, when available, apes from North Africa. Only the anatomical treatise of 1316 by the Italian Mondine di Luzzi was based on the dissection of humans.

Given the limitations of the ancient and medieval knowledge of anatomy, it is easy to see why the work of Leonardo da Vinci (1452–1519) and Andreas Vesalius was so revolutionary. Leonardo, the artist-scientist, had to study human anatomy and other natural things in order to portray them accurately. As he wrote in his *Treatise on Painting*, "We rightly call painting the grandchild of nature and related to God."[12] For him, painting was a branch of science which sought to communicate with precision the miracles of nature.

Andreas Vesalius was born in Flanders and studied at universities in Louvain, Paris, and then Padua in Italy. Only Italian universities were using human cadavers and conducting autopsies. Vesalius, a superior medical student, was invited to join the faculty at Padua at age twenty-three. Instead of reading Galen's description of the organs to his students while a barber-surgeon located each one, Vesalius used the scalpel himself and reverently pointed out errors in Galen. News of his dissections spread, and they became public events.

Then in 1543 he published his *On the Fabric of the Human Body*, which carefully described in words and detailed drawings the parts, organs, and functions of the human body. Regrettably, Vesalius repeated some of Galen's errors, most notably his description of the circulation of the blood. He accepted wholesale Galen's notion of the "septum" as a wall dividing the heart, which he considered porous, and thus facilitating the passage of the blood from the veins to the arteries. The Spanish heretic Michael Servetus actually had a better understanding of the circulatory system, whose workings were not fully explained until the work of the English physician William Harvey (1578–1657), who also studied at Padua.

Edouard Jeana Conrad, *Andre Vesalius Teaching at Padua*. Musee des Beaux-Arts, Marseille, France. Giraudon/Art Resource.

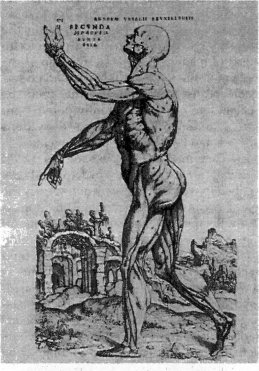

Andreas Vesalius, *Musculature Structure of a Man*. Sixteenth-century print. Collection of Fratelli Fabbri, Milan, Italy. Bridgeman/Art Resource.

Despite its flaws, Vesalius's book had the most accurate anatomical drawings of the time and his understanding of human anatomy represented a considerable advancement. Although the book was criticized by some clerics, it soon became an invaluable guide to physicians and surgeons all over Europe. Shortly after the publication of his masterwork, he left Padua to spend the last twenty years of his life as a court physician to Emperor Charles V and his son, Philip II of Spain. Andreas Vesalius continued his medical research and made several more valuable contributions to the art of surgery. He also published several new editions of the the still admired work of Galen.

THE SCIENTIFIC METHOD
AND FRANCIS BACON (1561–1626)

Galileo's and Vesalius's interests in experimentation were eventually echoed throughout Europe, particularly after Francis Bacon helped to popularize the scientific method. Bacon was the son of Lady Anne and Sir

Nicholas Bacon, lord keeper of the Great Seal under Queen Elizabeth I. A child prodigy, he became a favorite of the queen and the court with his prematurely wise and witty conversation. At age twelve, Francis entered Trinity College, Cambridge, where he studied classical philosophy and developed his distaste for Aristotelianism. According to Bacon, Aristotelianism did not do enough to improve the human condition.

Francis Bacon continued his studies of philosophy, but also had a successful career as a lawyer and member of Parliament. Although never able to win favor with Queen Elizabeth as an adult, he advanced rapidly under the reign of her successor, James I, becoming Lord Chancellor in 1616. Then came an equally dramatic fall as Bacon was charged with bribery, imprisoned, and later banished from the court. Although he was subsequently pardoned, his political career was over. Despite the failure of his political career, Bacon made many significant contributions to philosophy and the rise of science. He sought to organize all existing scientific knowledge and use it to better the human condition.

As part of this ambitious scheme, Bacon published his *Novum Organum* (The New Method) in 1620. He argued for a new method of reasoning based on induction from data. Urging his readers to disregard most of the traditional scientific lore, Bacon stressed the importance of careful observation of nature and arriving at conclusions based on evidence. He had high hopes for an "alliance, so far unconcluded, between the experimental and the rational methods."[13] Although Bacon seldom experimented himself, placed little emphasis on the mathematical dimension of physics, and discovered no new scientific laws, his work as a philosopher of science in popularizing the scientific method was of fundamental importance.

Bacon's call for greater use of experimentation and reason echoed a similar call made centuries earlier by the Oxford Franciscan Roger Bacon (d. 1292 and not related to Francis Bacon). The major difference was that by the seventeenth century the Western world was more ready to listen. Religious objections began to lessen when church officials came to recognize that scientists were not interested in undermining belief in God, but only in discovering more precisely how God's creation worked. Almost all of the major scientists of the first phases of the so-called Scientific Revolution were devout Christians and skilled secular theologians. As the eighteenth-century poet Alexander Pope later expressed it, "The state of Nature was the reign of God."[14]

Part of the reason for that change in attitude was that the new science was quickly shown to have practical applications. The telescope, for example, could be used by generals and admirals to see the movements of their enemies. Merchants could get advance word on what merchant ships were going to arrive safely in harbor from their long-distance journeys. Such foreknowledge could then be used to make profits or avoid losses in the commodities market.

Given the technological advances made possible by the new science, especially for business and warfare, it is hardly surprising that governments became interested in fostering scientific development. A Royal Society for the advancement of science was chartered in England by King Charles II in 1662. An Academy of Sciences was founded by Louis XIV's astute finance minister, Jean-Baptiste Colbert, four years later. Similar organizations followed throughout Europe and the rest of the world. These organizations and others patterned after them furnished laboratories, granted subsidies, brought scientists together to exchange ideas, published their findings, and encouraged scientific achievement generally.

WOMEN SCIENTISTS

Unfortunately scientific development was not fostered among women. Even those enlightened parents who encouraged their daughters to read and write often considered science to be an "inappropriate, inelegant, and unfeminine subject" for girls and women.[15] Women were still not admitted to the universities or the newly created scientific academies, except on rare occasions. Those who made contributions to the rise of science seldom had their work acknowledged. For example, Anne Finch, the viscountess Conway (1631–1679), has only recently had her contributions to the ideas of the philosopher Gottfried Wilhelm Leibniz (1646–1716) recognized. Leibniz is best known as the coinventor with Isaac Newton of differential calculus. Newton in turn became known to French audiences largely through the translation of the talented mathematician Emilia du Chatelet (1706–1749), perhaps the leading woman scientist of her century. Yet she is still best known as the mistress of Voltaire.

Margaret Cavendish, duchess of Newcastle (1617–1673), was the most prolific female scientific author of the seventeenth century. She produced fourteen books on everything from natural history to atomic physics. Because of their special privileges, noblewomen like Cavendish and Chatelet could sometimes get around some of the restrictions placed on their sex. A few of the early female scientists rose from more humble stations. Maria Sibylla Merian (1647–1717) came from an artistic family and worked as a housewife before leaving her husband to join a religious sect. A lifelong collector of insects and plants, Merian published six collections of engravings of European flowers and insects, which were far more scientifically accurate than their rivals. Toward the end of her life she journeyed from Amsterdam to Suriname and to the interior of South America to study plant and insect life for two years. The resulting book of sixty sketches with commentaries cemented her reputation as a leading naturalist. Her *Metamorphosis of the Insects of Suriname* came out in Dutch and Latin to critical acclaim.

RENÉ DESCARTES (1595–1650)

The advancement of science by men and women was clearly one of the greatest legacies of the Renaissance and Reformation. The rise of science also contributed directly to the intellectual revolution known as the Enlightenment. The Frenchman René Descartes was a key figure in both the rise of science and the pre-Enlightenment. Born into the French nobility, Descartes was educated in a Jesuit college. Young René showed great talents in mathematics, philosophy, and theology. At age fifteen, he invented an adding machine. Later Descartes would devise analytical geometry, a method of combining and interchanging algebra and geometry. Determined to educate himself "from the great book of the world," Descartes traveled to Paris and then to the Low Countries, where he enlisted for a time in the army of Maurice of Nassau. After a lengthy period of wandering about northern Europe, the accomplished Frenchman retired to Holland where he could think and write in peace.

One of the finest fruits of his reflections was his famous *Discourse on Method* of 1637. There he made an eloquent defense of the value of abstract reasoning. Descartes argued that it was necessary to question all authority, no matter how venerable and revered. The only thing he could not ultimately doubt was that he doubted (*cogito ergo sum*—I think, therefore I am). Where could this ability to doubt come from? For Descartes, it must come from God, the supreme substance. "I myself am a substance. I should not, however, have the idea of an infinite substance, seeing as I am a finite being unless it were given me by some substance in reality infinite."[16]

Using reason "to the best of my power," Descartes became certain of the existence of God, himself, and the external world. Since reason is identical to all people, whereas the senses vary, it is the best guide to universal truth. From a few simple self-evident truths, Descartes believed he could come to understand much of the whole of God's creation: "Give me extension and motion and I will create the universe."[17] Although other scientists such as Galileo and Isaac Newton demonstrated many of the weaknesses of Cartesian physics, including the belief that the planets were held up by celestial fluids, there is no question that Descartes's emphasis on the use of deductive reasoning made a major contribution to the world of the Enlightenment and the continued advance of science.

Political Changes

If reason could be used to guide humans in understanding the world of nature, could it also have its uses in the world of politics? Here the answers seemed less clear. The Renaissance and Reformation era had produced a rich diversity of political thought and practice. Some political theorists such as François Hotman in France (1524–1590) had argued against absolutism; others such as Jean Bodin and King James I of England (r. 1603–1625) had argued strongly for the divine right of kings to rule. During the period the feudalized monarchies of Europe had seen their sovereigns extend their authority and build their bureaucracies, legal systems, and militaries. The rise of territorial states and divine-right absolutist monarchies was a major trend of the period. Yet republican oligarchies continued in parts of Italy and in the Dutch United Provinces.

THE CONSTITUTIONAL STRUGGLE IN ENGLAND, 1642–1688

In England, the divine-right pretensions of James I's son, Charles I (r. 1625–1649), would be challenged by the rise of Parliament and those who believed in placing limitations upon the authority of the crown. As early as 1565, Sir Thomas Smith, a professor of Roman law at Cambridge, had argued that "the most high and absolute power of the realm of England consists in the Parliament."[18] Common law theorists such as Sir Edward Coke (1552–1634) repeatedly stressed the limits to royal power and the need for the king to be subject to the laws made by Parliament. Adding to the atmosphere of crisis, a fierce Irish revolt broke out in 1641. In 1642 a civil war broke out in England between those loyal to the crown and those who sided with Parliament. Parliament found strong leadership in the person of Oliver Cromwell (1598–1658), a Puritan gentleman farmer and a former member of Parliament.

As a Puritan, Oliver Cromwell was a descendant of those who wished to "purify" the English church of what they saw as vestiges of "popery." King Charles Stuart and his Catholic queen, Henrietta Maria, were far too "high church" for the likes of Cromwell, who favored independent congregations and simple services. The king's archbishop, William Laud (1573–1645), emphasized the "visibility and catholicity" of the church of England.[19] He sought to elevate worship over preaching and drive the Puritans from the established church. All

Sir Peter Lely, *Portrait of Oliver Cromwell*.
Galleria Palatina, Palazzo Pitti, Florence.
Alinari/Art Resource.

this was resisted with great determination by men such as Oliver Cromwell. Cromwell believed himself to be doing the Lord's work in fighting against the king and his supporters. He raised a well-disciplined army of men who "had the fear of God before them."[20] Cromwell led them to victory after victory until Charles's forces were totally defeated. Guided by Cromwell, a High Court of Justice found King Charles guilty of treason and the king was beheaded on January 30, 1649.

The House of Lords and the monarchy were abolished and England was ruled by a small minority in the House of Commons backed by the victorious parliamentary army. They faced opposition from radicals such as the Levellers, who believed in free-

dom of speech, toleration, democracy, and a reduction in social and economic distinctions. Cromwell moved to crush the Leveller movement as it spread into the army. He also invaded Ireland in August of 1649 when Irish rebels proclaimed Charles II, son of Charles I, as their king. His forces attacked the rebel strongholds of Drogheda and Wexford, massacring their garrisons. In the following year, Cromwell's forces devastated Catholic Ireland, where about a third of the population was killed outright or died of starvation. For Cromwell, the Catholic Irish who opposed "his godly authority" were servants of Satan. Resistance to Cromwell's authority in Ireland ended, but at a high price in a legacy of hatred, much of it along religious lines.

The Irish campaign was followed by one against the Presbyterian Scots, who had also proclaimed Charles II as their king. Scottish defiance was completely ended by September of 1651. Cromwell then turned to London, where a growing rift had developed between Parliament and the army. As commander in chief of the army, he dismissed Parliament in 1653 and instituted the so-called Protectorate, with himself as Lord Protector. Although several new parliaments came and went, the incorruptible Cromwell ruled England with an iron hand until his death in 1658.

A year and a half after the Lord Protector's death, the monarchy was restored in the personage of Charles II (r. 1660–1685). Relations between the high church king and Parliament soon deteriorated and finally in 1688 Charles's openly Catholic brother, James II, was bloodlessly overthrown, and a Protestant king and queen, William III of the Dutch Netherlands and Mary II (James's daughter), assumed the throne. A new coronation oath was devised for William and Mary that required that they swear to abide by the decisions of Parliament as well as by the ancient laws of England. This was followed by a Declaration of Rights of 1689, which spelled out, among other things, Parliament's authority to depose a monarch and choose a new one. The so-called "Glorious Revolution" of 1688 thus marked the complete ascendancy of representative government in England and the complete establishment of a Protestant state church.

THE RISE OF ABSOLUTISM

In vivid contrast with England, the Continental states of Austria, Brandenburg-Prussia, France, Russia, and Spain developed autocratic monarchies with expanding bureaucracies in the seventeenth and eighteenth centuries, as did Sweden in Scandinavia. Monarchs such as Charles XII of Sweden (r. 1689–1718) and Frederick II, the Great, of Prussia (r. 1740–1786) used their abilities as successful generals not only to increase the size of their realms, but also to gain control over governmental institutions by keeping their states in an almost constant state of military readiness. In Russia, Czar Ivan IV, the Terrible (1533–1584), destroyed the remaining power of the Tartars in southeastern Russia and annexed most of their territory. He also began the conquest of Siberia and cowed for a while the turbulent Russian nobility. Ivan's oriental-style despotism was not overly influenced by Western models.

It was not until the reign of Peter I, the Great (r. 1689–1725), that Russia turned fully to the West. The giant (six foot, nine inches) czar restored order to Russia after a time of weak rulers. He adopted Western-style bureaucratic systems in both central and local government. Western customs such as shaving, drinking wine, smoking tobacco, and wearing low-cut dresses were forced upon the Russian nobility. The czar personally barbered the members of his court. When the patriarch of the Russian Orthodox church opposed the czar's authority and adoption of Western customs, Peter abolished the office of patriarch. He placed a Holy Synod at the head of the church, composed of a committee of bishops and presided over by a lay procurator-general. The church therefore became an instrument of the state, as advocated by Marsilius of Padua in the thirteenth century and Thomas Erastus (d. 1583), a professor of medicine at Heidelberg, in the sixteenth.

FRENCH-STYLE ABSOLUTISM

In France, Cardinals Richelieu and Mazarin exercised authority in the name of King Louis XIII (r. 1610–1643), who preferred hunting to governing. Richelieu (1585–1642) was determined to make royal power supreme in France. As first minister, he sent the king's soldiers to destroy the castles of nobles who defied the authority of the crown, disbanded their private armies, and hanged a number of the most recalcitrant. He also waged war against the French Protestants and stripped them of some of their military and political rights.

To make the power of the monarchy felt in all corners of France, Richelieu divided the kingdom into thirty administrative districts, called *generalities*, and placed each one of them under the control of an agent of the crown, called an *intendant*. The intendants could override the authority of local governing bodies and often did so. So absolute was the power of the intendants over provincial affairs, even of the most petty nature, that they came to be called the "thirty tyrants of France." They were chosen for the most part from the ranks of the upper middle class and were shifted around frequently lest they become too "sympathetic" with the people over whom they ruled in the name of the king.

Richelieu's policies were continued by his successor as first minister, Cardinal Jules Mazarin (d. 1661). Working closely with the regent queen, Anne of Austria, Mazarin tutored young Louis XIV in the craft of kingship. He advised the young king to be his own first minister and to avoid sharing power with anyone. As king, Louis followed the policy of "one king, one law, and one God."[21] This translated into a brutal campaign of repression and, in 1685, the revoking of the Edict of Nantes, which had been issued by his grandfather, Henri IV. Calvinism was now illegal in France. French Huguenots were ordered to convert to Catholicism and forbidden to emigrate. Thousands managed to do so anyway, and many ended up in Brandenburg-Prussia, whose ambitious Hohenzollern ruler, Elector Frederick Wilhelm, eagerly welcomed them and their skills.

Believing himself to be a divine-right monarch, Louis XIV never once met his national Estates-General in the seventy-two years of his reign. Neither did his great grandson and successor, Louis XV, in the fifty-nine years of his reign. Representative government in France would have no national forum until bankruptcy forced the monarch to summon an Estates General in the spring of 1789 that touched off the far-reaching explosion known as the French Revolution.

Although absolutism was attempted all over Europe, it is important to remember that even the strongest of monarchs in preindustrial Europe had limitations placed on their authority. Spanish monarchs, for example, found opposition not only in the national parliament (Cortes), but also at the local levels. Even the "sun-king" of France, Louis XIV, could not always force independent sea captains to follow his orders. Problems with communications and transportation were compounded by traditions of local authority. It was often far easier for a local magistrate to get a bridge repaired than for an official of the central government to do it. The importance of limiting the power of the state and protecting human rights was one of the great consequences of the period.

As a cautionary tale, the Reformation has also taught us the importance of toleration and the need to live in communities of love despite our differences. As Martin Luther King, Jr., a twentieth-century stepchild of the Reformation, once said: "We must all learn to live together as brothers and sisters or we shall perish together as fools."[22] The need to learn to live together in community is also a part of the enormous legacy of the Reformation.

Chronology

1473–1543	Life of Nicholas Copernicus.
1486	Publication of the *Malleus Maleficarum* (Hammer of Witches).
1514–1564	Life of Andreas Vesalius.
1532	Imperial Law Code makes witchcraft a capital offense in the Holy Roman Empire.
1533–1584	Life of Czar Ivan IV, the Terrible.
1543	Publication of Copernicus's *On the Revolution of Celestial Spheres* and Vesalius's *On the Fabric of the Human Body*.
1563	*Heidelberg Catechism*.
1577	Jacob Andreae's "Formula of Concord."
1580	*The Book of the Concord*.
1583	Near conversion of Cologne to Protestantism.
1610	Publication of Galileo's *The Starry Messenger*.

1614–1702	Life of Margaret Fell.	1643	Beginning of the reign of Louis XIV in France.
1617–1673	Margaret Cavendish.		
1620	Publication of Francis Bacon's *Novum Organum* (New Method).	1647–1717	Life of Maria Sibylla Merian.
		1649	Trial and execution of King Charles I in England; Cromwell's Irish campaign.
1624–1642	Cardinal Richelieu in power in France.		
1624–1691	Life of George Fox.	1658	Death of Oliver Cromwell.
1637	Publication of Descartes's *Discourse on Method*.	1660	Restoration of the monarchy in England.
1641	Irish revolt.	1685	Revocation of the Edict of Nantes by Louis XIV.
1642	Beginning of the English Civil War.	1688	Bloodless Revolution brings William and Mary to power.

Further Reading

RELIGION AND SOCIETY

Robin Barnes, *Prophecy and Gnosis: Apocalypticism in the Wake of the Lutheran Reformation* (1988).

Lawrence Duggan, *Bishop and Chapter: The Governance of the Bishopric of Speyer to 1532* (1978).

Carlos Eire, *War Against Idols: The Reformation of Worship from Erasmus to Calvin* (1986).

G. R. Evans, *Problems of Authority in the Reformation Debates* (1992).

Bruce Gordon, *Clerical Discipline and the Rural Reformation: The Synod of Zürich, 1532–1580* (1992).

R. Po-chia Hsia, *Social Discipline in the Reformation: Central Europe 1550–1750* (1989).

———, *Society and Religion in Münster, 1535–1618* (1984).

H. Larry Ingle, *First Among Friends: George Fox and the Creation of Quakerism* (1994).

Robert Jütte, *Poverty and Deviance in Early Modern Europe* (1994).

Robert Kolb, *Confessing the Faith: Reformers Define the Church 1530–1580* (1991).

Bonnelyn Young Kunze, *Margaret Fell and the Rise of Quakerism* (1993).

Richard Muller, *Post-Reformation Reformed Dogmatics*, 2 vols. (1987, 1993).

Heiko Oberman, *The Impact of the Reformation* (1994).

Steven Ozment, *Protestants: The Birth of a Revolution* (1992).

Jill Raitt, ed., *Shapers of Religious Traditions in Germany, Switzerland, and Poland, 1560–1600* (1981). Fine essays by diverse contributors.

———, *The Colloquy of Montbéliard: Religion and Politics in the Sixteenth Century* (1993).

William Russell, *Luther's Theological Testament: The Schmalkald Articles* (1994).

Gerald Strauss, *Luther's House of Learning: Indoctrination and the Young in the German Reformation* (1978).

Bruce Tolley, *Pastors and Parishioners in Württemberg During the Late Reformation, 1581–1621* (1994).

MARRIAGE AND FAMILY LIFE

Beatrice Gottlieb, *The Family in the Western World from the Black Death to the Industrial Age* (1993).

Joel Harrington, *Reordering Marriage and Society in Reformation Germany* (1994).

Steven Ozment, *When Fathers Ruled: Family Life in Reformation Europe* (1983).

Lyndal Roper, *The Holy Household: Women and Morals in Reformation Augsburg* (1989).

Thomas Max Safley, *Let No Man Put Asunder: The Control of Marriage in the German Southwest* (1984).

Lawrence Stone, *The Family, Sex and Marriage in England 1500–1800* (1977).

Jeffrey Watt, *The Making of Modern Marriage: Matrimonial Control and the Rise of Sentiment in Neuchâtel, 1550–1800* (1992).

WOMEN AND GENDER

Susan Amussen, *An Ordered Society: Gender and Class in Early Modern England* (1988).

Judith Brown, *Immodest Acts: The Life of a Lesbian Nun in Renaissance Italy* (1986).

Patricia Crawford, *Women in Religion in England 1500–1720* (1993).

Natalie Davis, *Women on the Margins: Three Seventeenth-Century Lives* (1995). Fascinating comparisons of a Jewish merchant, a nun, and a botanist.

James Farr, *Authority and Sexuality in Early Modern Burgundy, 1550–1730* (1994).

Craig Harline, *The Burdens of Sister Margaret* (1994).

Anne Laurence, *Women in England, 1500–1760: A Social History* (1994).

Carole Levin and Patricia Sullivan, eds., *Political Rhetoric, Power, and Renaissance Women* (1995). A multidisciplinary collection of essays by various authors.

Phyllis Mack, *Visionary Women and Ecstatic Prophecy in Seventeenth-Century England* (1993).

Joy Wiltenberg, *Disorderly Women and Female Power in the Street Literature of Early Modern England and Germany* (1992).

WITCHCRAFT AND MAGIC

Carlo Ginzburg, *Ecstasies. Deciphering the Witches' Sabbath* (1990).

————, *The Night Battles: Witchcraft and Agrarian Cults in the Sixteenth and Seventeenth Centuries* (1983).

Joseph Klaits, *Servants of Satan: The Age of Witch Hunts* (1985).

Alan Kors and Edward Peters, eds., *Witchcraft in Europe 1100–1700: A Documentary History* (1972). Valuable sources.

Christina Larner, *Enemies of God: the Witch-hunt in Scotland* (1981).

Brian Levack, *The Witch-Hunt in Early Modern Europe* (1987).

H. C. Erik Midelfort, *Witchhunting in Southwestern Germany* (1972).

E. William Monter, *Witchcraft in France and Switzerland* (1976).

Lyndal Roper, *Oedipus and the Devil: Witchcraft, Religion and Sexuality in Early Modern Europe* (1994).

Keith Thomas, *Religion and the Decline of Magic* (1971).

THE RISE OF SCIENCE

Mario Biagioli, *Galileo, Courtier: The Practice of Science in the Culture of Absolutism* (1994).

H. Floris Cohen, *The Scientific Revolution: A Historiographical Inquiry* (1994).

Stillman Drake, *Galileo: Pioneer Scientist* (1990).

Amos Funkenstein, *Theology and the Scientific Imagination* (1989).

Marjorie Grene, *Descartes* (1985).

David Lindberg and Robert Westman, *Reappraisals of the Scientific Revolution* (1990).

Robert Mandrou, *From Humanism to Science, 1480–1700* (1978).

Harold Nebelsick, *The Renaissance, the Reformation, and the Rise of Science* (1992).

Patricia Phillips, *The Scientific Lady: A Social History of Women's Scientific Interests, 1520–1918* (1990).

James Reston, Jr., *Galileo: A Life* (1995).

Edward Rosen, *Three Imperial Mathematicians* (1986).

David Ruderman, *Jewish Thought and Scientific Discovery in Early Modern Europe* (1995).

John Russell, *Francis Bacon* (1979).

Londa Scheibinger, *The Mind Has No Sex? Women in the Origins of Modern Science* (1989).

Michael Sharratt, *Galileo: Decisive Innovator* (1994).

Pamela Smith, *The Business of Alchemy: Science and Culture in the Holy Roman Empire* (1994).

Bruce Stephenson, *Kepler's Physical Astronomy* (1990).

POLITICS

Randolph Head, *Early Modern Democracy in the Grisons* (1995).

Quentin Skinner, *The Foundations of Modern Political Thought.* 2 vols. (1978).

Malcolm Thorp and Arthur Slavin, eds., *Politics, Religion, and Diplomacy in Early Modern Europe* (1994). A fine collection of essays dedicated to De Lamar Jensen.

William Wright, *Capitalism, the State, and the Lutheran Reformation: Sixteenth-Century Hesse* (1988).

THE CONSTITUTIONAL STRUGGLE IN ENGLAND

Julian Davies, *The Caroline Captivity of the Church: Charles I and the Remoulding of Anglicanism* (1992).

Jerome Friedman, *Blasphemy, Immorality and Anarchy: The Ranters and the English Revolution* (1987).

——, *The Battle of the Frogs and Fairfield's Flies: Miracles and the Pulp Press during the English Revolution* (1993).

Pauline Gregg, *King Charles I* (1984).

Christopher Hill, *God's Englishman: Oliver Cromwell and the English Revolution* (1970).

William MacDonald, *The Making of an English Revolutionary: The Early Parliamentary Career of John Pym* (1982).

Conrad Russell, *The Causes of the English Civil War* (1990).

Kevin Sharpe, *The Personal Rule of Charles I* (1992).

David Underdown, *Pride's Purge: Politics and the Puritan Revolution* (1985).

Dewey Wallace, *Puritans and Predestination* (1982).

Austin Woolrych, *Commonwealth to Protectorate* (1982).

ABSOLUTISM

Evgenii Anisimov, *The Reforms of Peter the Great: Progress through Coercion in Russia* (1993).

William Beik, *Absolutism and Society in Seventeenth-Century France* (1985).

Joseph Bergin, *The Rise of Richelieu* (1991).

James Collins, *The State in Early Modern France* (1995).

Jonathan Dewald, *Aristocratic Experience and the Origins of Modern Culture: France 1570–1715* (1993).

J. H. Elliot, *Richelieu and Olivares* (1984).

Richard Golden, *The Godly Rebellion* (1981).

J. Russell Major, *From Renaissance Monarchy to Absolute Monarchy* (1994).

——, *Representative Government in Early Modern France* (1990).

David Parker, *The Making of French Absolutism* (1983).

OTHER TOPICS

John Bossy, *Giordano Bruno and the Embassy Affair* (1991). Was the philosopher also a spy? A fascinating detective story.

Peter Burke, *Popular Culture in Early Modern Europe* (1972).

——, *The Art of Conversation* (1994).

Frank Dobbins, *Music in Renaissance Lyons* (1992).

Ronald Hutton, *The Rise and Fall of Merry England: The Ritual Year 1400–1700* (1994). A study of the rituals which marked the passage of the year.

Joyce Irwin, *Neither Voice nor Heart Alone: German Lutheran Theology of Music in the Age of the Baroque* (1993).

Carter Lindberg, *Beyond Charity: Reformation Initiatives for the Poor* (1993).

Michael Macdonald and Terence Murphy, *Sleepless Souls: Suicide in Early Modern England* (1991).

Ian Maclean, *Interpretation and Meaning in the Renaissance: The Case of Law* (1992).

Roger Manning, *Hunters and Poachers: A Social and Cultural History of Unlawful Hunting in England 1485–1640* (1993).

Carol Menning, *Charity and the State in Late Renaissance Italy: The Monte di Pieta of Florence* (1994).

Sergiusz Michalski, *The Reformation and the Visual Art: The Protestant Image Question in Western and Eastern Europe* (1993).

Ruth Pike, *Penal Servitude in Early Modern Spain* (1983).

Peter Wallace, *Communities in Conflict in Early Modern Colmar* (1995).

Notes

1. Cited in R. Po-chia Hsia, *Social Discipline in the Reformation: Central Europe 1550–1750* (New York: Routledge, 1989), p. 35.
2. Cited in Julia O'Faolain and Lauro Martines, eds., *Not in God's Image: Women in History from the Greeks to the Victorians* (New York: Harper and Row, 1973), p. 202.
3. Cited in Gerda Lerner, *The Creation of Feminist Consciousness: From the Middle Ages to Eighteen-Seventy* (New York: Oxford University Press, 1993), p. 101.
4. *Malleus Maleficarum,* ed. and tr. by Montagu Summers (London: Hogarth Press, 1928), pp. 41–42.
5. Cited in William Monter, ed., *European Witchcraft* (New York: John Wiley, 1969), p. 87.
6. Ibid., p. 114.
7. Cited in G. R. Elton, ed., *The Renaissance and Reformation 1300–1648,* 3rd ed. (New York: Macmillan, 1976), p. 63.
8. Cited in De Lamar Jensen, *Reformation Europe: Age of Reform and Reconciliation,* 2nd ed. (Lexington, Mass.: D. C. Heath, 1992), p. 382.
9. Cited in John Hale, *The Civilization of Europe in the Renaissance* (New York: Atheneum, 1993), p. 352.
10. Cited in Jensen, *Reformation,* p. 382.
11. Cited in Bonnie Anderson and Judith Zinsser, *A History of Their Own: Women in Europe from Prehistory to the Present,* 2 vols. (New York: Harper and Row, 1988), vol. 2, p. 29.
12. Cited in Elton, *Renaissance and Reformation,* p. 67.
13. Ibid., p. 356.
14. Alexander Pope, "An Essay on Man: Epistle III," line 148.
15. Cited in Anderson and Zinsser, *A History of Their Own,* vol. 2, p. 87.
16. Cited in Jensen, *Reformation,* pp. 387–388.
17. See Ernst Cassirer, *The Philosophy of the Enlightenment,* tr. by Fritz Koelin and James Pettegrove (Princeton, N.J.: Princeton University Press, 1951), pp. 51–52.
18. Cited in Elton, *Renaissance and Reformation,* p. 143.
19. See Julian Davies, *The Caroline Captivity of the Church: Charles I and the Remoulding of Anglicanism* (New York: Oxford University Press, 1992).
20. Cited in Jensen, *Reformation,* p. 438.
21. Cited in John Wolf, *Louis XIV* (New York: W. W. Norton, 1968), p. 383.
22. Quoted in a speech at Michigan State University, April, 1966.

INDEX

Absolutism, 207, 209–10
Ad fontes, 56, 71
Adrian VI, pope, 32, 78, 100, 153
Africa, 15, 17–19
  north, 168, 203
  west, 18, 178
Africans, 15
Agriculture, 2, 7–11, 80–81, 177
Alba, duke of, 180
Albania, 17
Alberti, Leon Battista, 13
Albert the Great, 56
Albrecht, archbishop of Mainz, 16, 64, 122
Albret, Jeanne d', queen of Navarre, 174–75
Alcalá, university of, 152, 155
Alchemy, 2, 197–98
Aleander, Girolamo, 72
Alexander VI (Borgia), pope, 34, 36, 48–50, 159
Alexander, Sydney, 2
Alfonso the Magnanimous, 52
Algeria, 168
Algiers, 168, 178
Alsace, 19, 81, 186
Alumbrados, 155
Amboise, conspiracy of, 172
Americas, 8, 18, 183
Amsdorf, Nicholas von, 169–70, 191–92
Amsterdam, 12, 15, 106
Anabaptism, 82, 90, 97, 103–8
Anabaptists, 2, 100–8, 115, 118, 194
Anatomy, 203–5
Andreae, Jacob, 192
Anguissola, Sofonisba, 178
Annates, act of, 131
Anna of Hungary, 31
Anne of Austria, queen of France, 210
Anne of Bohemia, 45

Anne of Cleves, queen of England, 132
Anticlericalism, 44, 72, 130, 144
Antinomianism, 103, 191
Anti-Semitism, 18–19, 56–57, 91–92, 157
Antwerp, 12, 15
Apocalypticism, 48, 82, 91–92, 106
Apprentices, 11
Aquinas, Thomas, saint, 15, 52, 56, 66
Aragon, 18, 42, 178
Archimedes, 9,
Aretino, Pietro, 161
Aristotle, 202
Armada,
  English, 183
  Spanish, 142, 181–83
Arras, union of, 180
Art, 87, 100, 102, 163, 178–79, 181
Arthur, prince of Wales, 27, 126
Artisans, 11, 82, 84
Ascham, Roger, 140
Asia, 15, 155, 157
Asti, Bernardino d', 154
Astrology, 81, 197–98
Astronomy, 198–202
Athens, 17
Augsburg, 12, 31, 66, 88, 195
  diet of 1530, 88–89, 167
  diet of 1547–1548, 169
  diet of 1555, 170
  peace of, 170–71
Augsburg Confession, 89, 192
Augsburg Interim, 169, 171
Augustine of Hippo, saint, 113, 158
Augustinian Hermits, 62, 65
Augustinians, 23, 54
Augustus of Saxony, 192
Austria, 31, 34, 84, 167, 184, 200, 209

Auto de fé, 2, 19
Avignon, 40–42
Avila, 12, 157–58

Babington, Anthony, 148
Babylonian captivity of the church, 40–42
Bacon, Anne, 204
Bacon, Francis, 204–5
Bacon, Nicholas, 205
Bacon, Roger, 205
Balkans, 15, 17
Bamberg, 20, 80, 196
Bankers, 12, 15
Baptism, 22, 103–5, 117, 141, 144
Barcelona, 154
Bascio, Matteo da, 153
Basel, 53, 97–98, 112, 114
    council of, 47
    reform in, 86, 97, 100, 102–3
    university of, 53, 97, 102, 169
Bavaria, 183, 185
    war of succession in, 20, 31
Beaton, David, cardinal, 144
Beijing, 15
Belgrade, 17
Bellarmine, Robert, cardinal, 157
Bergerac, Cyrano de, 197
Bern, 113–14
    reform in, 86, 100, 102
Berlichingen, Götz von, 20
Berlin, 122
Bernini, Gian Lorenzo, 163
Beza, Theodore, 118, 172
Bible, 45, 55, 80, 97, 101, 103, 107–8, 129, 162
    King James, 148
    New Testament, 53–54, 73, 105, 108, 134, 195
    Old Testament, 55, 71, 134, 195
    Polyglot, 152
    translation of, 46, 55–56, 73, 90
    Tyndale, 134, 144
    Vulgate, 52, 56
Black Death, 11, 174
Black Forest, 81–82
Blaurock, George, 103, 108
Boccaccio, Giovanni, 23, 72, 161
Bodenstein von Karlstadt, Andreas, 68, 73–74
Bodin, Jean, 175, 197, 207
Bohemia, 31, 33, 45–47, 123, 183–85, 196
    king of, 30, 105
Boleyn, Anne, queen of England, 128–30, 132–33, 140
Bologna, 36, 160–61
    university of, 102
Boniface VIII, pope, 40–41, 43
Bordeaux, parlement of, 175

Book of the Concord, 192
Borgia, Cesare, 36, 50–51
Borgia, Juan, 50
Borgia, Lucretia, 50
Borromeo, Carlo, cardinal, 163
Bosnia, 17
Bothwell, James, earl of, 146–47
Botticelli, Sandro, 49
Bourbon, Antoine de, 174
Bourbon, Charlotte de, 180
Bourbon, house of, 171, 174
Brahe, Tycho, 198–200
Brandenburg, mark of, 120–22
Brandenburg-Ansbach, 80, 83, 90, 167
    margrave of, 20, 30, 80
Brandenburg-Prussia, 209–10. *See also* Prussia
Braun, Johann, 61
Brenz, Johann, 65, 100
Brothers and Sisters of the Common Life, 54, 56
Bruno, Giordano, 199
Brussels, 134
Bucer, Martin, 65, 91, 100, 102, 112, 114–15, 160, 168
Budé, Guillaume, 27, 111
Bugenhagen, Johann, 92–93
Bullinger, Heinrich, 97, 101–2, 118
    Second Helvetic Confession, 101, 120, 192
Burchardus, Johannes, 51
Burgundy, 32
Business, 15–16, 205
Byzantium, 17, 33

Cabala, 56
Calais, 136–37, 182
Calvin, Gerard, 111
Calvin, Idellete de Bure, 115
Calvin, Jeanne, 111
Calvin, John, 2, 53–54, 90, 102, 111–20, 123, 145, 155, 161, 171, 194
    Institutes of the Christian Religion, 112–13, 116, 118
    theology of, 112–13
    views on women, 118, 194
Calvin, Judith, 118
Calvinism, 33, 111, 120–23, 171–72, 174, 180, 183, 187, 200
Cambridge University, 129, 134, 140
Canisius, Peter, 157
Capitalism, 14–16
Capito, Wolfgang, 100, 102, 112, 114
Capuchins, 153–54, 160
Carmelites, 158
    Discalced, 158
Casimir, margrave of Brandenburg, 83
Castellio, Sebastian, 116, 166
    Whether Heretics Should be Persecuted, 116

Castiglione, Baldassare, 20, 161
  The Book of the Courtier, 20, 161
Castile, 18, 29–30, 42, 152, 157, 178
Cateau-Cambrésis, peace of, 172
Catherine of Aragon, queen of England, 27, 126–27, 129–30
Catholic League (French), 174, 176
Catholic League (Imperial), 122, 184
Cavendish, Margaret, duchess of Newcastle, 206
Cecil, Robert, 140, 143
Cecil, William, 140–41
Celtis, Conrad, 97
Charlemagne, Holy Roman emperor, 17
Charles V, Holy Roman emperor and king of Spain, 16, 19–20, 30–32, 66–67, 70–71, 75, 78, 86–87, 90–91, 100, 122, 128, 132, 136, 156, 159–60, 166–71, 177, 179, 204
Charles I, king of England, 207–08
Charles II, king of England, 194, 205, 208
Charles VIII, king of France, 48–49
Charles IX, king of France, 172–73
Charles XII, king of Sweden, 209
Charles University (Prague), 44–46
Chatelet, Émilia du, 206
Chaucer, Geoffrey, 23, 90
  Canterbury Tales, 23
Chester, 12
Children, 7, 9–10, 13, 193
China, 15
Christian II, king of Denmark, 32, 92, 122
Christian IV, king of Denmark, 184–85
Christianity, 18, 29
Christendom, 2, 16, 55, 57, 178, 191
Christina, queen of Sweden, 195
Christina of Hesse, 91
Christoph, duke of Württemberg, 192
Cistercians, 23
Clement V, pope, 41
Clement VII (Medici), pope, 78, 87, 100, 128, 153, 160
Clement VIII, pope, 176
Clergy, Catholic, 22–23, 40, 46, 53, 72, 81, 144, 191, 195
  celibacy of, 22, 53, 72, 98, 161
  marriage of, 22, 85, 102, 169
Clergy, Protestant, 102, 191–93
Clericos laicos, 40
Cleves-Jülich, 185
Coburg Castle, 88
Coke, Edward, 207
Colbert, Jean-Baptiste, 180, 205
Coligny, Gaspard de, admiral of France, 173
College of Cardinals, 49, 78, 128, 159
Cologne, 11
  archbishop of, 30

crisis of 1547, 168, 195
crisis of 1583, 195
Colonna, Vittoria, 152, 154
Columbus, Christopher, 8, 29
Community of Goods, 108. *See also* Hutterites
Conciliar Movement, 43, 47–48, 163
Confessionalism, 89, 192
Constance, 46
  council of, 33, 42, 44–47, 160
Constantinople, 12, 17, 34, 48
Contarini, Gasparo, cardinal, 115, 122, 152, 155, 159–60, 163, 166
Cop, Nicholas, 112, 155
Copenhagen, university of, 92
Copernicus, Nicholas, 198–99, 201–2
  On the Revolution of the Celestial Spheres, 199
Cortés, Hernan, 12
Coutras, battle of, 175
Coverdale, Miles, 134
Cracow, university of, 199
Cranmer, Thomas, archbishop of Canterbury, 129, 133–36, 141
  Book of Common Prayer, 134, 141
  "Forty-two Articles," 134, 141
Crépy, peace of, 168
Crime, 12–13, 197
Cromwell, Oliver, 207–8
Cromwell, Thomas, 129–34
Cuius regio, eius religio (he who rules, his religion), 86, 170–71

Daily life, 9–10, 12–13
Dancing, 10, 114, 193
Dante, 64, 161
Darnely, Charles, lord, 146–47
Decet Romanum Pontificem, 70
Declaration of Rights of 1689, 209
Dee, John, 198
Denmark, 32, 92–93, 186, 200
Descartes, René, 206–7
Deventer, 54
Devereux, Robert, earl of Essex, 143
Dinkelsbühl, 84, 195
Discipline, church, 162
  social, 102, 114–15, 117, 152, 192–93
Dissolution of the Monasteries, act of, 131
Divorce, 128, 193
Dominicans, 56–57, 155
Dominic, saint, 155
Donatism, 46
Don Carlos, 146
Don Juan, 178
Drake, Francis, 182–83
Dublin, 126

Dudley, Guilford, 135
Dudley, John, duke of Northumberland, 134–36, 142
Dudley, Robert, earl of Leicester, 142–43, 146, 180
Dürer, Albrecht, 1, 18, 79

Eastern Europe, 33–34, 48
Eastern Orthodox church, 2, 16, 22, 34, 196, 209
Eck, Johann, 12, 67, 86, 89, 105, 160
Edinburgh, 145–46
    treaty of, 146
Education, 120, 140, 157, 162, 192–93
Edward I, king of England, 40–41
Edward III, king of England, 44
Edward VI, king of England, 132–34
Einsiedeln, 98–99
Eisleben, 92
Eisenach, 61
Elizabeth, electress of Brandenburg, 121–22
Elizabeth I, queen of England, 1, 118, 133, 136, 140–56,
    173, 181–83, 198, 205
    character of, 140–41
    religious settlement of, 141–42
Elizabeth of Valois, 172
Emden, 123,
England, 10, 27, 29, 42, 54–55, 102, 123, 130, 134,
    136–37, 142, 144–45, 153, 178, 181–84, 196, 208–9
Enlightenment, 206
Erasmus, 1, 52, 54–55, 72, 97–98, 102, 151, 161
Erastus, Thomas, 209
Ercole I, duke of Ferrara, 113
Erfurt University, 62, 66
Estates-General, French, 210
Este, Alfonso d', duke of Ferrara, 50
Este, Beatrice d', duchess of Milan, 34
Eucharist, 21, 44, 100, 113, 117, 141
Excommunication, 40, 46
Exsurge Domine, 68–69
Evangelicals, 86–88, 100, 167

Faber, Johann, 99
Farel, Guillaume, 54, 113–16, 118
Farnese, Alexander, duke of Parma, 176, 180
Felix V, pope, 52
Fell (Fox), Margaret, 194–95
    Women's Speaking Justified, 195
Feltre, Vittorino de, 52
Ferdinand I, Holy Roman emperor, 31–32, 78, 82, 86,
    105, 167, 170
Ferdinand II, Holy Roman emperor, 182–85
Ferdinand III, Holy Roman emperor, 186, 195
Ferdinand, king of Aragon, 27, 29, 31, 34–35, 67, 126,
    154
Ferrara, 113
Fieschi, Catherine (St. Catherine of Genoa), 152
Finch, Anne, viscountess of Conway, 206

Fish, Simon, 130
    "Supplication of Beggars," 130
Fitzjames, Richard, bishop of London, 130
Flacius Illyricus, 169–70, 191–92
Flanders, 10, 42, 136, 179, 203
Florence, 12, 15, 23, 34, 37, 48–50, 148, 201–2
Formula of Concord, 192
Fox, George, 195
France, 7, 29, 34, 42, 82, 112, 114, 120, 134, 141, 144,
    168, 171, 178, 182–84, 186, 196, 209–10
    civil and religious wars in, 171–77
Franche-Comté, 178
Franciscans, 51, 154
Francis of Assisi, saint, 154
Franco, Veronica, 161
François I, king of France, 26, 28, 31, 54, 66–67, 74, 112,
    168
François II, king of France, 145, 172
Franconia, 75
Frankenhausen, battle of, 83
Frankfurt am Main, 30, 115, 145
Frederick III, elector of the Palatinate, 120, 192
Frederick V, elector of the Palatinate, 184
Frederick III, the Wise, elector of Saxony, 62–63,
    65–67, 70, 73, 87
Frederick I, king of Denmark, 33, 92
Frederick II, king of Denmark, 199
Frederick II, king of Prussia, 199
Frederick Wilhelm, elector of Prussia, 210
Freiburg im Breisgau, 104
French Revolution of 1789, 210
Fugger, house of, 12, 64–65, 67
Fugger, Barbara, 15
Fugger, Jacob, the Rich, 15–16
Fuggerei, 16

Gaismair, Michael, 84
Galen, 203–4
Galileo, Gallilei, 200–2, 204, 207
Gardiner, Stephen, 136
Geiler von Kayserberg, Johann, 52–53
Gender, 3, 10, 20–21
Geneva, 102, 111, 113–17, 119–20, 123, 145, 154, 171, 193
    academy of, 119–20
    reform in, 113–20
Genghis Khan, 15, 33
Genoa, 15, 18, 152
Gentileschi, Artemisia, 2, 163
George, duke of Saxony, 83, 90
George, the Pious, margrave of Brandenburg-
    Ansbach, 83, 90
George III, prince of Anhalt, 122
Germany. *See* Holy Roman Empire
Ghent, 12, 197
Glarus, 97, 197

Glorius Revolution of 1688, 208–9
Golden Bull of 1356, 30
Gospel, 79, 82, 84, 92, 103
Granada, 16, 29, 178
Grebel, Conrad, 97, 103–4, 107
Greece, 17, 179
   classical thought of, 2, 55–56, 197, 203
   language and literature of, 22, 27, 52, 55–56, 73,
     111–12, 119
Gregory VII, pope, 40–41
Gregory XI, pope, 41–42, 44
Gregory XV, pope, 197
Grey, Lady Jane (Dudley), 135–36
Grotius, Hugo, 181
Grumbach, Argula von, 86
Guicciardini, Francesco, 161
Guilds, 13
Guise, Charles de, archbishop of Reims, 171
Guise, Henri, duke de, 173–75
Guise, house of, 144, 172
Gustavus I, Vasa, king of Sweden, 33, 92–93
Gustavus II Adolphus, king of Sweden, 93, 185–86
Gutenberg, Johann, 51

Habsburg, house of, 16, 27, 30, 67, 79, 87, 167, 171, 183,
   186
Habsburg-Valois wars, 27, 74, 82, 113, 167, 171
Hagenau, religious colloquy in, 115, 168
Hals, Franz, 181
Hamilton, Patrick, 144
Hampton Court, 127–28
Hanseatic League, 32
Hans of Küstrin, 122
Harvey, William, 116, 203
Hawkins, John, 182
Hebrew language, 56, 71, 73, 97, 112
Hedio, Caspar, 115
Heidelberg, 65
   academy of, 120
   Cathechism, 120, 192
   university of, 88, 102, 120–21, 209
Henri II, king of France, 19, 161, 170–71
Henri III, king of France, 173–75
Henri IV, king of France, 8, 172–77, 183, 210
Henrietta Maria, queen of England, 207
Henry I, king of England, 126
Henry II, king of England, 44
Henry VII, king of England, 27, 126, 146
Henry VIII, king of England, 27, 29, 54, 66, 126–35,
   140, 144, 148, 153, 168, 176
Heraclitus, 2
Heresy, 43–47, 68, 70, 116, 144, 154, 157, 166, 195
Hesse, 75, 87–89, 100, 106, 167–69
Hitler, Adolf, 91
Hohenzollern, house of, 64, 122

Holbein, Hans, 132
Holocaust, European, 91
Holy Roman Empire, 10, 15, 19, 30–32, 42, 53, 55–56,
   64–65, 71–73, 79, 86–92, 103, 105, 108, 113, 120,
   144, 157, 168, 171, 183-87, 192, 195–97
Horb, 104
Hotman, François, 120, 207
Howard, Catherine, queen of England, 133
Howard, Thomas, duke of Norfolk, 147–48
Hubmaier, Balthasar, 82, 105, 107
   Concerning the Christian Baptism of Believers, 105
Huguenots, 171–73, 182, 209
Humanism, 1, 27, 52, 56, 72, 79, 144, 193
Hundred Years' War, 42, 137
Hunne, Richard, 130
Hungary, 16–17, 31, 33, 86, 108, 123, 166, 168
Hus, Jan, 33, 43, 45–47, 68
Hussite Revolt, 33, 47, 68
Hut, Hans, 104
Hutten, Ulrich von, 57, 69, 74–75
Hutter, Jacob, 108
Hutterites, 108
Hymns, 87, 123

Iconoclasm, 100, 102, 179
Ignatius of Loyola, 1–2, 152, 154–57
   Spiritual Exercises, 155–57
Imperial Council of Regency, 79
Imperial Supreme Court, 79, 90, 167
Index of Forbidden Books, 53, 161
India, 156
Indulgences, 16, 46, 55, 57, 63, 98, 161
   controversy of 1517, 1, 16, 63
Ingolstadt, university of, 86, 105, 183
Innocent III, pope, 40, 128, 153
Innocent VIII, pope, 196
Innsbruck, 16, 170
Inquisition, 116
   Roman, 160, 201
   Spanish, 2, 19, 29, 152, 155
Ireland, 42, 208
   revolt of 1598, 142–43
   revolt of 1641, 208
Isabella, queen of Castile, 16, 27, 29, 31, 34, 67, 126, 152
Islam, 17, 29, 178
Italy, 1, 8, 18–19, 26–27, 31, 34–35, 41–42, 48–50, 56, 82,
   113, 116, 128, 156
Ivan III, czar of Russia, 33–34
Ivan IV, czar of Russia, 34, 209

James I, king of England and Scotland, 142, 147–48,
   182, 184, 205, 207
James II, king of England and Scotland, 208–9
James V, king of Scotland, 144

Jan of Leiden, 106–7
Japanese, 157
Jerome, saint, 52–53
Jerusalem, 154–55
Jesuits. *See* Society of Jesus
Jews, 2, 18–19, 29, 92, 105, 152, 157, 191
    expulsions of, 19, 29, 105, 152
Jiménez de Cisneros, Francisco, cardinal, 151–52
Joachim I, elector of Brandenburg, 64, 122
Joachim II, elector of Brandenburg, 121–22
Joao, king of Portugal, 19
Johann, the Constant, elector of Saxony, 82, 87–88, 122, 167
Johann Frederick, elector of Saxony, 92, 168–70
Johann Georg, elector of Saxony, 184, 186
Johann Sigismund, elector of Brandenburg, 120–23
John of Gaunt, 44
John Paul II, pope, 78
Joseph Clemens, archbishop of Cologne, 163
Joseph of Rosheim, 19
Jost, Ursula, 103
Journeymen, 11, 13
Juan, prince of Spain, 31
Juana, the Mad, princess of Spain, 29, 31
Juana of Austria, 156
Juan de la Cruz, saint, 157–58
Judaism, 92
Julius II, pope, 27, 36–37, 64, 126, 152

Kalmar, union of, 92
Kappel, peace of, 101
Kempis, Thomas à, 152, 154
    Imitation of Christ, 152, 154
Kepler, Johann, 198–200
Kett, Robert, 134
Knights' Revolt of 1522–1523, 74–75, 78, 82, 114
Knox, John, 117–18, 144–45, 147, 161
    Against the Monstrous Regiment of Women, 118, 145
Königshaufen, battle of, 83
Koran, 161
Kramer, Heinrich, 196
Kress, Christoph, 70–71, 83, 87
Kublai Khan, 15

Lainez, Diego, 155, 157
Laity, 21–22, 79–80
Languedoc, 168
Latimer, Hugh, bishop, 136
Lateran Council, fifth, 153
    fourth, 152
Latin language and literature, 22, 44–45, 52, 54–55, 61, 97, 140
Laud, William, archbishop of Canterbury, 207
Lausanne, 119

Law, 81, 112, 119, 198
    canon, 21, 44, 167, 198
    civil, 167
    customary, 81
    English common, 207
    imperial, 196
    international, 181
    Roman, 81
Lawyers, 11, 14, 112
Lefèvre d'Etaples, Jacques, 54
Leibniz, Gottfried Wilhelm, 206
Leipzig, 185
    colloquy of, 168
    debate of 1519, 67–69, 89, 170
    Interim, 169
    university of, 46, 67
Leo X (Medici), pope, 32, 37, 57, 64–67, 80, 100, 127, 152, 172
Lepanto, battle of, 178–79
Letters of Obscure Men, 57, 74
Levellers, 208
Lewis IV, Holy Roman emperor, 43
Leyster, Judith, 181
Libavius, Andreas, 198
Lisbon, 12, 182
Lithuania, 33
Liturgy, 1, 86, 93, 114, 121, 151
Lollards, 44, 144
London, 12, 15, 134–36, 208
Louis XII, king of France, 34–35, 113
Louis XIII, king of France, 176, 209
Louis XIV, king of France, 186, 197, 205, 210
Louis XV, king of France, 210
Louis II, king of Hungary, 32, 86
Louise of Savoy, 27
Louvain, university of, 54, 78, 144, 203
Low Countries. *See* Netherlands
Ludolf the Saxon, 152
Lusatia, 33, 184
Luther, Hans, 61–62, 85, 90
Luther, Katherine (von Bora), 84–85, 122, 170
Luther, Magdalena, 85, 91
Luther, Margaret (Lindemann), 61, 90
Luther, Margaret, the younger, 85, 170
Luther, Martin, 1–2, 16, 37, 43, 53, 55, 59, 61–75, 78–92, 98–100, 104, 112–13, 121–22, 127, 151, 160–61, 166–68, 170, 191, 199
    "A Mighty Fortress," 87
    catechisms, 90, 292
    "Ninety-five Theses," 57, 64, 98
    theology of, 63, 69–70, 79, 84, 87
    views on women, 85–86
Lutheranism, 33, 80, 83, 92–93, 111, 120, 122–23, 169–71, 195, 200

Lutherans, 79, 122–23, 168–70, 183, 191–92
  Gnesio, 170, 191–92
  Philippists, 170, 191–92
Lyon, 12

Machiavelli, Niccolò, 35–36, 161
Madrid, 19, 173
Magdeburg, 64, 169–70
Magic, 195–96
Mainz, 16, 20
  archbishop of, 30, 64
Malatesta, Sigismondo, 20
Malleus Maleficarum (Hammer of Witches), 196
Manresa, 154
Mansfeld, 61
Marburg, 87, 100
  colloquy of, 87, 100, 102
Margaret of Austria, 31–32
Margaret of Denmark, queen, 32
Margaret of Parma, 179–80
Marguerite of Navarre, 23, 27, 54, 72, 112, 166, 174
Marguerite of Valois, queen of France, 172–73, 176
Maria Teresa, queen of France, 186
Marignano, battle of, 26, 98
Marlowe, Christopher, 142–43
Marpeck, Pilgram, 107
Marriage, 9, 85, 91, 193–94
  diplomacy, 30, 91, 146, 171–72, 176, 186
Marsilius of Padua, 42–44, 47, 209
  Defender of the Peace, 43
Martin V, pope, 42, 47
Martyrs, 104–9, 137, 142
Mary I (Tudor), queen of England, 3, 126, 135–37, 142, 145, 159, 172, 181
Mary II, queen of England, 208
Mary (Stuart), queen of Scots, 3, 140, 142, 144–48, 182
Mary of Guise, queen of Scotland, 144–45
Mary of Hungary, queen, 32
Mass, Catholic, 21–22, 99–100, 112
  Lutheran, 121
Mathematics, 198, 200, 206
Matilda, queen of England, 126
Matthias, Holy Roman emperor, 183
Matthys, Jan, 106
Maurice of Nassau, 180, 206
Maximilian I, Holy Roman emperor, 15, 19, 27, 30–31, 34–36, 56–57, 66, 74
Maximilian I, duke of Bavaria, 183–84
Mazarin, Jules, cardinal, 210
Meaux, 54
Medici, Catherine de', queen of France, 3, 171–72, 176, 198
Medici, Giuliano, 49
Medici, house of, 12, 37, 49, 64, 78

Medici, Lorenzo (d. 1519), 37, 172
Medici, Lorenzo, the Magnificent, 49, 65
Medici, Marie de', queen of France, 176
Medicine, 199–200, 202–4
Medinia Sidonia, duke of, 182–83
Mehmed II, Ottoman sultan, 17
Melanchthon, Philip, 73–74, 80, 87, 92, 100, 102, 115, 122, 160, 166, 168–70, 191–92
  Loci Communes, 88
Mennonites, 107–8
Merchants, 11, 20, 205
Merian, Maria Sibylla, 206
Merici, Angela, 153
Metz, 186
Mexico, 12
Michelangelo, 2, 64, 163
Middle East, 17, 19, 154–55
Milan, 12, 26, 34, 98, 163, 168
Mirandola, Giovanni Pico della, 56, 198
Missionaries, 120, 154, 156–57, 195
Mohács, battle of, 86
Monasticism, 22, 131, 161
Montaigne, Michel de, 175, 197
Montefeltro, Federigo da, 19–20
Moors, 152
Moravia, 33, 105, 108, 184
Moravian Brethren, 105, 108
More, Thomas, 54, 128–29
  Utopia, 128
Moriscos, 178
Morone, cardinal, 161
Moritz, duke of Saxony, 168–70
Moscow, 33–34
Moses, 56
Mühlberg, battle of, 168–69
Mühlhausen, 82
Müller, Hans, 82
Münster, Anabaptist takeover, 105–7
Müntzer, Thomas, 82–83, 104
Music, 20, 87, 97–99, 118, 121
Muslims, 2, 15–17, 29, 168, 178, 191
Mysticism, Christian, 158
  Jewish, 56

Nantes, edict of, 176–77, 210
Naples, 12, 34–35, 42, 46, 52, 178
Nepotism, 159, 162
Netherlands, 9, 31–32, 67, 78, 105, 107–8, 114, 120, 123, 168, 171, 173, 176–77, 196, 206
  revolt against Spain, 32, 142, 179–82
  United Provinces of, 181–82, 184, 187, 207–8
Newton, Isaac, 202, 206–7
Nice, peace of, 168
Nicholas of Cues, 565

Nikolsburg, 105
Nobility, 19–21, 74–75, 171, 178, 209
Nominalism, 43
Nördlingen, battle of, 186
Norway, 32–33, 92–93
Nostradamus, 198
Noyon, bishop of, 111
Nuremberg, 11–12, 19–20, 66, 69, 71, 78, 82–84, 89–90, 167, 185
    diets of 1522 to 1524, 78–79
    reform in, 79–80, 84

Ochino, Bernardino, 154, 160
Ockham, William of, 43
Oecolampadius, Johann, 97, 100
Oldenbarneveldt, Jan van, 180
O'Neill, Hugh, earl of Tyrone, 143
Orléans, 7
    university of, 111, 119
Oratory of Divine Love, 152–53
Osiander, Andreas, 80, 100, 133, 199
Ottomans, 15, 17–18, 20, 31, 33, 48, 70–71, 86, 90–91, 159, 163, 166–67, 178
Oxenstierna, Axel, 185–86
Oxford University, 43, 45, 127, 134

Pacifism, 103, 106, 108
Padua, university of, 159, 203–4
Palatinate of the Rhine, 121, 183
Palermo, 12
Palestine, 154–55
Palestrina, Giovanni, 163
Pamplona, battle of, 154
Papacy, 41, 47, 49, 52, 55, 74, 91, 127, 129, 132, 151, 160, 174
Papal States, 34, 49
Paracelsus, 198
Paris, 12, 15, 27, 54, 168, 172–73, 176
    university of, 42, 54, 111, 144, 155, 203
Parker, Matthew, archbishop of Canterbury, 141
Parliament, English, 29, 129–30, 136, 141–43, 205, 207–8
    Scottish, 145
    Spanish (Cortes), 30, 210
    Swiss, 100–101
Parr, Catherine, queen of England, 133, 140
Patriarchy, 3, 13–14, 80, 162
Patriciate and Patricians, 11, 80
Paul, apostle, 63, 90
Paul III, pope, 1, 91, 153–56, 159–60, 169, 199
Paul IV (Carafa), pope, 152–53, 157, 159–61
Paul V, pope, 153
Pavia, battle of, 82
Pazzi Plot, 49
Peasantry, 2, 7–11, 20, 79–82, 177, 197

revolts of, 10, 44
Peasants' War of 1524–1526, 10, 20, 75, 79–82, 103, 131, 166
Penance, 22, 63–64
Perrin, Ami, 116–17
Perrin, Francesca, 117
Peru, 8
Persians, 17
Peter I, czar of Russia, 209
Petrarca, Francesco, 40, 161
Petri, Laurence, 93
Petri, Olaf, 93
Pfefferkorn, Johann, 56
Pfeiffer, Heinrich, 82
Pflug, Julius, 169
Philip IV, "the handsome," king of France, 29, 40–41, 43
Philip II, king of Spain, 32, 136–37, 146, 148, 158, 161–62, 166, 170–71, 173, 177–78, 187, 204
Philip IV, king of Spain, 186
Philip of Hesse, landgrave, 75, 87–91, 100, 106, 167–69
Philosophy, 43, 181, 205–7
Pilgrimages, 98, 154
Pilgramage of Grace, 131
Pirckheimer, Charitas, 80
Pirckheimer, Willibald, 69, 79–80
Pisa, 18, 202
    university of, 200
Pius II, pope, 47–49, 56
Pius IV, pope, 161, 163
Pius V, pope, 142, 178
Pizan, Christine de, 194
Plague, 99, 161
Plenitudo potestatis (fullness of power), 50, 128
Pluralism, 41, 65, 127, 162
Poitiers, Diane de, 171–72
Poland, 33, 78, 123, 157, 174, 186–87, 195–96, 199
Pole, Reginald, archbishop of Canterbury, 135–36, 159
Political theory, 175, 207
Politiques, 175
Polo, Marco, 15
Pope, Alexander, 205
Portugal, 12, 19, 42, 156, 178
Poverty, 9–11, 118
Prague, 19, 45–46, 82, 184, 186, 200
    Charles university of, 45–46, 68
Predestination, 52, 72, 113
Presbyterians, 123
Printing, 51–52, 71, 87, 90
Prostitutes, 11, 118
Prostitution, 98, 118, 292
Protestantism, 33, 91, 100, 111, 119, 133, 135, 141–42, 144–45, 151, 155
Protestants, 87, 97, 105, 135, 141, 152, 160, 162–63, 167, 186, 193, 196

Protestant Union, 183
Prussia, 64, 122, 209
Psalms, 87, 100
Ptolemy, Claudius, 199
Purgatory, 64, 161
Puritanism, 141–42, 195, 207–8
Puritans, 123, 141–42, 207
Pyrenees, peace of, 186
   mountains, 154

Quakers. *See* Society of Friends

Rabelais, François, 90, 111–12, 161
Raleigh, Walter, 142
Reformation, 1–2, 7, 61, 72, 75, 78, 92, 161, 166, 187,
   191–93, 196–97, 206, 210
   Anabaptist, 103–8
   Calvinist, 111–23, 179–80
   Catholic, 1, 135, 151–63, 195
   English, 44, 126–35, 141–42
   French, 171–75
   Italian, 152–54
   Lutheran, 74, 92, 122–23, 166
   Scandinavian, 33, 92–93
   Scottish, 144–48
   Second, 120
   Spanish, 151–52
   Swiss, 86, 98
   urban, 79–80, 99–103, 114–15
Refugees, 2, 19
Regensburg, 105, 200
   colloquy of, 115, 12, 160, 168
   diet of, 185
Rembrandt von Rijn, 181
Renaissance, 1–2, 15, 19, 140, 161, 191, 193, 197–98,
   203, 206
Renée, duchess of Ferrara, 113
Rennerin, Margaret, 84
Restitution, edict of, 185–86
Restraint of Appeals, act of, 131
Reuchlin, Johann, 52, 55–57, 74
Reymerswaele, Marinus von, 14
Rhinehardt, Anna, 100
Rhineland, 81, 169, 185
Richard II, king of England, 45
Richelieu, cardinal de, 186, 209–10
Ridolfi, Roberto, 148
Ridolfi Plot, 148
Riedemann, Peter, 108
Right of resistance, 89–90, 167
Rizzio, David, 146
Rohrback, Jäcklin, 83
Roman Catholicism, 1, 40, 74, 93, 122, 132, 135–37, 140,
   142, 144–46, 160, 173, 176–78, 180, 195, 207, 210

Roman Catholics, 97, 101, 105, 122, 142, 160, 167, 170,
   177, 183, 196
Rome, 40–41, 52, 62, 152, 155, 173, 176, 176, 202
   ancient, 11, 34
   sack of, 87, 128, 153
   university of, 155
Rosenblatt, Wibrandis, 102–3
Rostock, Barbara, 103
Rubianus, Crotus, 57
Rudolf II, Holy Roman emperor, 198, 200
Russia, 33–34, 186–87, 209

Saal, Margaret von der, 91
Sachs, Hans, 80
Sacramentarian Controversies, 88, 91, 99–100, 113
Sacraments, 22, 42, 88, 161
Sadoleto, Jacopo, bishop, 152, 155
Saint Andrew's castle, 144
   university of, 144
Saint Bartholomew's Day Massacre, 172–73
Saint Gall, 100
Saint Germaine-en-laye, colloquy of, 172
Salamanca, university of, 155
Salvation by faith alone, 63–64, 69, 79, 192
Salzburg, 84
Samarkand, 15
Samson, Bernardin, 98
Sanchez, Juan, 157
Santa Cruz, admiral, 182
Sardinia, 34, 178
Sattler, Margaret, 104–5
Sattler, Michael, 104–5, 107
Savonarola, Girolamo, 48–51
Savoy, 168
   duke of, 113
Saxony, 30, 33, 37, 61, 122, 168–70, 185
Scandinavia, 32–33, 92–93, 196
Science, 197
Scientific Revolution, 1, 197
Scheurl, Christoph, 14, 80
Schism, great western, 41–42, 44
Schleitheim Statement, 104
Schmalkalden, 167
Schmalkaldic Articles, 192
Schmalkaldic League, 89–90, 122, 167–69
Schmalkaldic War, 122, 166–69
Scotland, 42, 123, 134, 144–48, 208
Scripture, authority of, 44, 162
Selim II, Ottoman sultan, 178
Sennely, 7
Serfdom, 9, 33, 81
Servants, 2, 11, 13, 18, 178
Servetus, Michael, 116, 203
Seville, 12, 159

Sexuality, 85, 91, 98, 118, 196
Seymour, Edward, duke of Somerset, 133–34
Seymour, Jane, queen of England, 132
Seymour, Thomas, admiral, 133
Sforza, Giangaleazzo, 34
Sforza, Ludovico il Moro, 34–35
Shakespeare, William, 1, 18, 128, 142–43
Siberia, 209
Sicily, 12, 34, 42, 178
Sickingen, Franz von, 74–75, 114
Sidney, Mary, 142
Sidney, Philip, 142
Sigismund, Holy Roman emperor, 42, 46–47
Silensius, Angelus, 195
Silesia, 16, 33, 184
Simons, Menno, 107
Simony, 41, 44, 50, 64–65, 159, 162
Six Articles of 1539, 133
Sixtus IV, pope, 49
Skarga, Peter, 195
Slave trade, 15, 18
Slovakia, 108
Slovonic language, 22
Social welfare, 92, 117–18, 142, 192
Society of Friends (Quakers), 3, 194–95
Society of Jesus (Jesuits), 152, 154–56, 160, 176, 183,
    193, 195
Soderini, Piero, 37
Sophia, queen of Bohemia, 45
Sorcery, 195–96
South America, 206
Southampton, earl of, 143
Spain, 8, 16, 19–20, 27, 29–31, 36, 78, 86–87, 141, 148,
    152, 154–56, 171, 174, 176–83, 186–87, 196
Spalatin, George, 65
Spengler, Lazarus, 69, 79
Spenser, Edmund, 142
Speyer, 86–87
    colloquy of, 168
    diet of 1526, 86
    diet of 1529, 87, 122
Spinoza, Baruch, 181
Spiritualists, 115
Sprenger, Jacob, 196
Staupitz, Johann von, 62–63, 170
Stephen of Blois, 126
Stockholm, 92
Storch, Nicholas, 72, 82
Strasbourg, 53, 86, 89, 102–4, 112, 114–15, 119
    reform in, 65, 100, 114–15
Stuart, James, earl of Moray, 146–47
Stübner, Marcus, 72
Sturm, Jacob, 87, 114, 167
Sturm, Johann, 119–20

Suárez, Francesco, 157
Succession, acts of, 131, 135
Süleyman the Magnificent, Ottoman sultan, 17–18, 70,
    86, 90, 167, 178
Sully, duke of, 177
Supremacy, acts of, 129, 131, 141,
Suriname, 206
Swabia, 83
Swabian League, 56, 75, 82
Swarthmoor Hall, 195
Sweden, 32–33, 92–93, 185–87, 209
Swiss Confederation, 31, 86, 100
Switzerland, 1, 87, 97, 101, 114, 196–97
Synergistic Controversy, 191

Taborites, 47
Tartars, 18, 209
Tausen, Hans, 92
Technology, 205
Telescope, 200
Tenochtitlán, 12
Teresa of Avila, saint, 1, 157–59
Tertiaries, 153
Tertullian, 194
Tetzel, Johann, 64
Theatines, 152
Theology, 1, 27, 53, 69–70, 79, 111–13, 198–200, 206
Thiene, Gaetano, 152
Thirty Years' War, 93, 183–87
Thuringia, 82–83
Tilly, Johann von, 184
Tithes, 81
Titian, 178
Toledo, 155
Toleration, 116, 122, 166, 174–77
Torgau, 170
Torture, 196
Toul, 170, 186
Trade, 12, 15
Transubstantiation, 161
Transylvania, 108
Trent, 160
    council of, 91, 100–103, 168, 195
Trier, archbishop of, 30, 75
Tübingen, university of, 56, 88, 102, 169, 192, 200
Tunis, 168
Tyndale, William, 134, 144
Tyrol, 108

Ukraine, 108
Ulm, 89, 195
Ulrich, duke of Württemberg, 20, 91

Unam Sanctam, 41
Uniformity, acts of, 134, 141
Union of Kalmar, 32
Universal priesthood, 46
Urban VI, pope, 42
Urban VIII, pope, 201–2
Ursula, saint, 153
Ursulines, 153, 160, 195
Usury, 15
Utraquists, 47
Utrecht, union of, 180

Valencia, 30
Valla, Lorenzo, 52–53, 55, 161
Valois, house of, 26–27, 34, 67, 174
Vasili III, Russian czar, 34
Västeras, diet of, 93
Venice, 11–13, 15, 18, 34, 36, 84, 159–60, 169, 179
Verdun, 170, 186
Vermeer, Jan, 181
Vermigli, Peter Martyr, 115, 160
Vesalius, Andreas, 202–4
Vienna, 17, 19, 90, 105, 167–68
    university of, 97
Vinci, Leonardo da, 2, 27, 34, 203
Vio, Thomas de, cardinal, 66
Viret, Pierre, 119–20
Virgin Mary, 19, 55, 64, 154
Vladislav, king of Hungary, 31
Voltaire, 206

Waldburg, Georg Truchsess von, 75, 82–83
Waldeck, Franz von, 106
Waldschut, 105
Wallenstein, Albrecht von, 184–86, 200
Walsingham, Francis, 141, 148
Warfare, 2, 19, 34–35, 74–75, 81–84, 98, 166–87,
    175–76, 182–83, 205, 208
Warham, William, archbishop of Canterbury, 129–30
War of the Three Henries, 175–76
Wartburg Castle, 73
Wenceslaus IV, king of Bohemia, 45–46
Westphalia, peace of, 186–87
Weyer, Johann, 197
White Mountain, battle of, 184
Wied, Herman von, archbishop, 168
Wiedemann, Jacob, 108
Wilhelm, duke of Cleves, 132

William of Nassau, 179–80
William III, king of England, 208–9
Wishart, George, 144
Witchcraft, 2, 195–97, 200
Wittelsbach, house of, 31
Wittenberg, 66, 73–74, 144
    university of, 62–63, 169–70
Wolfgang Wilhelm, duke of Palatine-Neuberg, 195
Wolsey, Thomas, cardinal, 29, 127–30
Women, 3, 10, 13–14, 20–22, 29, 57, 86, 118, 156,
    192–95, 203, 206
    as pastors' wives, 85, 102
    education of, 193
    hatred of, 57, 145, 196
    in Bible, 118
    in Peasants' War, 84
    martyrs, 105
    noble, 20–22, 86
    nuns, 22, 80, 85, 172
    preachers, 86, 103, 115, 194–96
    reformers, 103, 115, 152, 195–96
    role in church, 22, 103, 118, 156, 194
    scientists, 205
    teachers, 194
    urban, 11–12
    warriors, 29
    working, 9–10, 13
Worms, colloquy of, 115, 168
    diet of 1521, 31, 70, 74, 159, 170
    edict of, 72, 79
Württemberg, 65, 104
Wyatt, Thomas, Jr., 136
Wycliffe, John, 43–44

Xavier, Francis, 155, 157

York, 12, 127

Zbynek, archbishop, 46
Zasius, Ulrich, 151
Zell, Katherine, 86, 112
Zell, Matthew, 112, 115
Zizka, Jan, 47
Zurich, 97–102, 104–5, 114–15
    reform in, 87, 98–102
Zwickau prophets, 73, 82
Zwingli, Huldrych, 1, 86–88, 97–101, 103, 144, 161
    theology of, 98–100, 113